The Novels of Erich Mari

Studies in German Literature, Linguistics, and Culture

The Novels of
Erich Maria Remarque

Sparks of Life

Brian Murdoch

CAMDEN HOUSE

First published 2006 by Camden House
Reprinted in paperback and transferred to digital printing 2010

Camden House is an imprint of Boydell & Brewer Inc.
668 Mt. Hope Avenue, Rochester, NY 14620, USA
www.camden-house.com
and of Boydell & Brewer Limited
PO Box 9, Woodbridge, Suffolk IP12 3DF, UK
www.boydellandbrewer.com

Paperback ISBN-13: 978-1-57113-476-9
Paperback ISBN-10: 1-57113-476-X
Hardback ISBN-13: 978-1-57113-328-1
Hardback ISBN-10: 1-57113-328-3

Library of Congress Cataloging-in-Publication Data

Murdoch, Brian, 1944–
    The novels of Erich Maria Remarque: sparks of life / Brian Murdoch.
        p. cm. — (Studies in German literature, linguistics, and culture)
    Includes bibliographical references and index.
    ISBN 1–57113–328–3 (hardcover: alk. paper)
        1. Remarque, Erich Maria, 1898–1970 — Criticism and interpretation.
    I. Title. II. Series.
    PT2635.E68Z758 2006
    833'.912—dc22

2006018740

Illustrations of Remarque book covers courtesy of Erich-Maria-
Remarque-Friedenszentrum, Osnabrück University.

A catalogue record for this title is available from the British Library.

This publication is printed on acid-free paper.

Cover image: Remarque's street in his hometown of Osnabrück, showing his
family's house. Courtesy of the Erich-Maria-Remarque-Friedenszentrum,
Osnabrück, © The Fales Library, New York University.

To the memory of Richard and Lydia Riffer

Contents

Preface

ALTHOUGH SINCE 1998, the centenary of his birth, much more of Erich Maria Remarque's work has become available than before, this study is concerned with his principal achievement, his novels, evaluating them on their own terms with regard to theme and style. Two errors have been prevalent in past Remarque studies. The first is that Remarque is a writer of *Trivialliteratur*, a notion encountered especially in German criticism, though things are now beginning to change. Salomo Friedlaender, writing as Mynona in 1929, published an overblown attack criticizing Remarque's style with the arresting title *Hat Erich Maria Remarque wirklich gelebt?* and it has had its successors. This is probably based on a combination of issues: that his style somehow does not match the high seriousness of tone expected of the supposedly great novel; that his works have always been and still are popular; and that most have been filmed. This study presents him as a writer of considerable importance to twentieth-century Germany — and he remains very much a German writer despite his exile years — who treated serious themes in a way that holds the readers' interest. One biography refers to him as a "chronicler of the twentieth century," and most of his novels indeed reflect German problems in that century: two world wars and the successive Weimar and Nazi regimes in Germany, and more particularly their effects on the individual. On the other hand, his themes are also universal, dealing with human relationships. That he is a lastingly popular writer ought also to count in his favor. It is gratifying that in the years since his centenary there has been a marked increase in scholarly studies of his work, as a glance at the current bibliographies in the well-established *Erich Maria Remarque Jahrbuch/Yearbook* makes clear. Admittedly though, scholarly considerations of Remarque have moved fairly rapidly from the dismissive towards the impenetrable. The internationalism of Remarque scholarship is also patent. Earlier studies, too, tended to focus rather too much on Remarque's biography, but we are now able to take a more objective view of the work.

The second error is that he was a one-novel writer. This idea is often encountered, or has clearly had some implicit influence, especially in the Anglo-Saxon world. There are one-work novelists, but Remarque, for all the fame of *Im Westen nichts Neues,* is not one of them, and this study concentrates upon the dozen or so novels he wrote (the precise number is for various reasons unclear). Not all are equally impressive — that would hardly be expected — but all are interesting, and many of them measure up to *Im Westen nichts Neues;* it was by no means his only great novel.

Im Westen nichts Neues — *All Quiet on the Western Front* — does, however, provide an emblematic reason for a study of the novels in English, given that it is so frequently thought of as part of the canon of English literature. When I gave the Remarque memorial lecture in Osnabrück in 1996, I spoke about "Remarque's English Novel, *All Quiet on the Western Front,*" and stressed its deliberate internationalism. Certainly the work often seems to be taught as if it were an English novel, testified to by the astonishingly large number of equally astonishingly banal study notes — pamphlets that pre-digest for the irredeemably hard-of-thinking or chronically indolent what is already a straightforward work. Of his other novels, some actually appeared first in English, translated from typescript during the war and the exile years. Pretty well all of his novels have been translated into a large number of languages, too. Yet Remarque remains a much-read German writer; he is not an outsider as far as Germany is concerned, whatever his personal history, but a German writer who is truly international. There are not many of those.

Various possibilities offer themselves for the arrangement of a study of Remarque's novels, the most obvious perhaps being a simple chronological sequence. I have adopted this, however, only up to a point. I have examined two early, though rather different, novels, *Die Traumbude* and *Gam,* together, but for the major works I separate what might be called the historical-political from *Der Himmel kennt keine Günstlinge,* which is, at least on the surface, about life, death, sickness, and fast cars. This may sound as if one single work is being separated from all the rest, but this is not the case. The 1961 novel is at the end of a series of writings stretching back to the 1920s, in which Remarque developed what is in some respects a non-political theme; but the final stage in that series, *Der Himmel kennt keine Günstlinge,* is not just a culmination of Remarque's writings about fast cars and is by no means entirely non-political. The Second World War plays a considerable part in it, and it brings together a number of the most important themes, voiced also in those novels that have a more obvious historical-political setting, and thus makes for a fitting final chapter, even though this is not its chronological position. Many of the other novels treat the problems of love against the background of historical events. A mere glance at the final paragraph of *Der Himmel kennt keine Günstlinge,* describing Lillian Dunkerque's death from tuberculosis, takes the reader right back to the ending of *Im Westen nichts Neues,* and Paul Bäumer's death near the end of the war.

Given that Remarque is a German chronicler of the twentieth century, it makes sense to group the works as far as possible according to the chronology of the events that they describe, even if this means that the chronology of writing is not followed exactly. Thus *Der schwarze Obelisk,* written in

1956, continues in historical terms from *Der Weg zurück*. So too, the last novel published in his lifetime, *Die Nacht von Lissabon*, and his unfinished final work, *Schatten im Paradies* or *Das gelobte Land* (both versions are now available), may best be grouped with far earlier novels on the theme of emigration. No arrangement will be entirely satisfactory, of course, and other arrangements are always possible.

For assistance in the preparation of this study I should like to express my gratitude — both personal and scholarly — first of all to the colleagues in Osnabrück — Tilman Westphalen, Thomas Schneider, Claudia Glunz, and Beatrice le Coutre-Bick. The work of Tilman Westphalen and Thomas Schneider as editors, and of Thomas Schneider in particular as a critic (and one most generous with copies of his work), is invaluable. His assistance with the illustrations is also gratefully acknowledged. I have been fortunate to have worked with many of the increasing number of other scholars interested in Remarque over the years, and I hope they will forgive me if I do not name them all here; they are in the notes and the bibliography. I should like, however, to record my gratitude to Ian Campbell, great-nephew of Arthur Wheen, the first translator of *Im Westen nichts Neues,* who contacted me from his home in Australia when my own translation appeared, and who has since provided me with much information and copies of his own papers; to Professor Richard Sheppard of Magdalen College, Oxford, for a useful focus; and to my son, Adrian Murdoch, for valuable editorial help. I should also like to thank colleagues and students associated with Stirling University, especially Dr. Heather Valencia, Dr. Maggie Sargeant (now of Heriot-Watt University), and most recently Rikke Christoffersen, discussions of whose doctoral work on the narrative style of the novels have been as valuable to me as I hope they have been to her, and who has shared important insights (and indeed books) with me with great generosity. Stirling University also provided funding for teaching relief to enable me to complete the book. Parts of chapter two were given as lectures in 2004 at Jesus College, Oxford, and in the Stirling University School of Modern Languages. Thanks are due as ever to my wife, Ursula, for her support and for discussions of the novels and this book, and also, again as so often before, to James Walker and the colleagues at Camden House. Errors, of course, remain my own.

B. O. M.
Stirling, 2006

Conventions of Reference

REMARQUE'S NOVELS ARE CITED in principle from the most recent separate edition (paperback where possible, although the five-volume *Das unbekannte Werk,* which contains some of the novels, is available only in hardback) as listed below. All are published by Kiepenheuer and Witsch in Cologne, and most are in the attractively produced and convenient series of KiWi paperbacks issued or reissued at the time of the centenary in 1998. Some had appeared earlier, such as *Im Westen nichts Neues* with a different afterword, and several have been reprinted again since then. *Station am Horizont* has been published both in this series and in *Das unbekannte Werk,* vol. 1, apart from its original serialization. Also in the KiWi series are various collections of smaller pieces and Wilhelm von Sternburg's biography. Details of original publication dates and of the often complicated publication history of the individual works (plus explanations of variant novel titles, like *Geborgtes Leben* or *Bobby Deerfield*) are given in the relevant chapters and in the bibliography, together with details of the films and publications other than novels. Page references are to the editions noted below, but all translations of passages cited are, for the sake of uniformity, my own, even though for most of the texts there are English translations by different hands; the most recent version of *Im Westen nichts Neues* is mine in any case. Published translations are also noted in the chapters and in the bibliography. Any variations are indicated in the notes. The names of countries are those of the period when the novels were written (e.g. Czechoslovakia, Soviet Union).

The Novels

Arc de Triomphe, afterword by Tilman Westphalen (Cologne: Kiepenheuer and Witsch, 1998).

Drei Kameraden, afterword by Tilman Westphalen (Cologne: Kiepenheuer and Witsch, 1998).

Der Funke Leben, afterword by Tilman Westphalen (Cologne: Kiepenheuer and Witsch, 1998).

Gam, in *Das unbekannte Werk,* vol. 1, ed. Thomas F. Schneider and Tilman Westphalen (Cologne: Kiepenheuer and Witsch, 1998), 1, 175–361.

Das gelobte Land, in *Das unbekannte Werk,* vol. 2, ed. Thomas F. Schneider and Tilman Westphalen (Cologne: Kiepenheuer and Witsch, 1998).

Der Himmel kennt keine Günstlinge, afterword by Tilman Westphalen (Cologne: Kiepenheuer and Witsch, 1998).

Im Westen nichts Neues, afterword by Tilman Westphalen (Cologne: Kiepenheuer and Witsch, 1998).

Liebe Deinen Nächsten, afterword by Tilman Westphalen (Cologne: Kiepenheuer and Witsch, 1998).

Die Nacht von Lissabon, afterword by Tilman Westphalen (Cologne: Kiepenheuer and Witsch, 1998).

Schatten im Paradies, afterword by Tilman Westphalen (Cologne: Kiepenheuer and Witsch, 1998).

Der schwarze Obelisk, afterword by Tilman Westphalen (Cologne: Kiepenheuer and Witsch, 1998).

Station am Horizont, ed. Thomas F. Schneider and Tilman Westphalen (Cologne: Kiepenheuer and Witsch, 2000).

Die Traumbude, in *Das unbekannte Werk,* vol. 1, ed. Thomas F. Schneider and Tilman Westphalen (Cologne: Kiepenheuer and Witsch, 1998), 19–173.

Der Weg zurück, afterword by Tilman Westphalen (Cologne: Kiepenheuer and Witsch, 1998).

Zeit zu leben und Zeit zu sterben, afterword by Tilman Westphalen (Cologne: Kiepenheuer and Witsch, 1998).

Abbreviation

Jahrbuch = *Erich Maria Remarque Jahrbuch/Yearbook* (published annually since 1991 by the Remarque-Friedenszentrum, Osnabrück).

1: Erich Paul Remark and Erich Maria Remarque: The Writer and His Works: *Die Traumbude* and *Gam*

IN 1974 A VOLUME APPEARED with the title *100 Great Books: Masterpieces of All Time.* The last part of that title was clearly taken seriously, because the Old Testament was ranked chronologically only ninth. Of course, one can always object to the choices made for collections like this, but it is of interest that only three German-language writers are included in this particular, and rather useful, English compilation, and that only one of them is a novelist; beside Immanuel Kant and Sigmund Freud, the sole German literary figure is Erich Maria Remarque, who had died only a few years earlier.[1] So too, polls are sometimes conducted in the English-speaking world to determine the world's greatest novels. The resultant list, which always contains French and Russian writings, usually includes little German literature. One novel by Remarque, however, is normally present, and he even drew attention to such a list, published by the *New York Times,* in a letter to his publisher in June 1961.

Erich Maria Remarque (1898–1970) was a public figure, a celebrity writer, even something of a playboy in his adult life, and indeed the fairly recent biography of him in English by Hilton Tims pays much attention to his amorous adventures in Hollywood and elsewhere. As a novelist, however, Remarque is a genuinely international figure, while remaining a German writer, interpreting German and European problems for a world audience. Although an exile-writer — he wrote most of his novels outside Germany — he is never an outsider as far as Germany is concerned, but because of his émigré status, a status that lasted for more than half of his life, he is sometimes treated less fully than he might be in literary histories. His status as a popular — the word is sometimes taken pejoratively — writer has doubtless contributed to this as well, perhaps especially in Germany. How Remarque's works are to be integrated into the canon of German literature remains an interesting question.[2]

The terms "exile literature" and "émigré writing" are only of limited use in literary categorization; it is true that a number of major writers shared the experience after 1933 of writing in German and often about Germany, while exiled from Germany itself, but its effects differed in nature and extent depending upon the individual — one need only to think of the proximity in

Hollywood at one stage of Thomas Mann, Brecht, and Remarque.[3] The small world of the émigré writers threw some of them together on occasion, but although there are some indications of the influence of Thomas Mann in more than one of Remarque's novels, they are outweighed by the differences.

It is appropriate to ask, therefore, the basic question that literary critics so often avoid: are Remarque's novels any good? They are morally good in that it is unlikely that they could corrupt anyone — quite the reverse in fact — and they treat invariably serious themes. In terms of literary criticism, however, learned opinion is divided, both within and outside Germany. Sometimes Remarque's novels are still dismissed as *Trivialliteratur,* merely popular writing, not really worthy of analysis, the more so, perhaps, since most of them have even been made into films. On the other hand, learned opinion is not everything, and that simple question frequently means little more than: "does the work suit my taste?"[4] If the pragmatic classical criterion for a good work is applied, namely whether Remarque's work is accepted always, everywhere, and by everyone, then at least one of his novels is unquestionably good, since a great many people have accepted it for a long time. *Im Westen nichts Neues* (*All Quiet on the Western Front,* 1928) is probably the best known and most widely read German novel of the twentieth century, translations of it ranging astonishingly from Aleutian to Zulu. Millions have read it with approval, and it continues to be read.

Even to refer to Remarque as a *German* author begs questions, however. Remarque was born in Germany, and his earliest works appeared under his German birth name of Erich Remark. He wrote in German, and he wrote almost invariably about Germany, even when the novels are set elsewhere. Since we are speaking of the troubled twentieth century, too, and are forced to recall that the Germanness of writers as great as Heine was at one period denied, it may even be necessary to add that he was not Jewish, since he himself raises this as an issue in several of his novels. Could there, then, have been any question of his national designation? And yet, when he died in 1970 he was not, strictly speaking, a German. Since 1947 he had been an American citizen; his German citizenship had been formally taken away, as from so many others, by the Nazi regime in 1938. After the war he lived in Switzerland, and indeed died and is buried there, not even in German-speaking Switzerland, but in the Ticino, at Ronco-Ascona. His gravestone gives his name as Erich Maria Remarque. The author of *Im Westen nichts Neues* had changed the spelling of his name from Remark to the French-looking Remarque — the family was indeed of French, or at least Alsatian origin — but one of the most absurdly tenacious myths about him is that he was really called Kramer. This appeared in at least one official Nazi document and still crops up in otherwise respectable or scholarly works, even though he denied it fairly bluntly in print as late as 1966, and it has been corrected often enough. His birth certificate is in the name of Erich Paul

Remark, born 22 June 1898, and there is even a photograph of it in Thomas Schneider's pictorial biography.[5]

A more serious myth is that Remarque was a one-novel author. He was not. However famous his best-known work may be, even that needs to be read together with its sequel, *Der Weg zurück* (*The Road Back*, 1931). Of course, *Im Westen nichts Neues* has had a remarkable effect, eclipsing many other contemporary and earlier novels and becoming the yardstick against which other war novels were measured for a long time, so that its importance is undeniable. However, Remarque wrote more than a dozen novels, many of them of the highest quality, justifying his designation as a *Chronist des zwanzigsten Jahrhunderts*, a German chronicler of the twentieth century for an international audience. Remarque summarized his own work and his approach in a concise statement: "Mein Thema ist der Mensch dieses Jahrhunderts — die Frage der Humanität. Mein Credo ist das des Individualisten: Unabhängigkeit — Toleranz — Humor" (My theme is man in this [twentieth] century — the question of humanity. My creed is that of the individualist: independence, tolerance, humor).[6] Remarque's chronicling of a war-ridden century embraces the serious themes of life, love, and death, and the basic will to live — the spark of life — in the modern world, but the twentieth century is also the century in which the morality of Germany as a nation was most seriously called into question.

Remarque was not only a novelist; from the beginning of his career he wrote literary and theatrical reviews, and later produced articles associated with or prompted by the issues raised in his novels. Many of these pieces have, since his death, been published in collections such as *Ein militanter Pazifist* (Militant Pacifist, 1994) and *Herbstfahrt eines Phantasten* (Autumn Journey of a Fantasist, 2001). He also published a few unimpressive poems, which are subjected to self-satire in *Der schwarze Obelisk* (*The Black Obelisk*, 1956). His earliest writings appeared under initials, pseudonyms, and the name Erich Remark, as did advertising copy, a comic strip, and articles on a variety of topics, including many on motor racing, and (notoriously) on mixing cocktails, although he himself protested later that he had not, as had been claimed, written a book on the subject. He also pointed out that he wrote this kind of material simply to make a living. Some of this trivia can be of tangential interest, but it remains an open question whether or not the republication of early or expressly non-literary writings enhances or detracts from his reputation. Remarque did also publish a number of short stories, some of which influence the study of his novels. Some of these have survived only in English, having been published in American magazines in the 1930s. One important group — related to his two First World War novels — was retranslated into German after his death and published in 1970 as *Der Feind* (The Enemy), and others have also been translated back into German from published magazines or from typescripts that survive only in English.[7]

Remarque also kept diaries and corresponded with the famous and the less famous on various topics, and some of this material, too, has been published.[8] Such material again varies in the extent to which it can, or should, illuminate his novels. For example, it is intriguing to note that on 22 June 1921 — his twenty-third birthday — Remarque wrote an almost despairing letter to the writer Stefan Zweig passionately soliciting literary encouragement, which, judging by subsequent correspondence, he seems to have been given. Certainly Zweig wrote favorably about *Im Westen nichts Neues.*[9] His correspondence with the actress Marlene Dietrich, with whom he had a close and complex relationship for a lengthy period, has been published separately with the telling subtitle *Zeugnisse einer Leidenschaft* (Documents of a Passion, 2001), although it has to be said that "amorous" does not necessarily equate with "interesting." Remarque's diaries can also be of literary interest, even if we sometimes need to dismiss his own judgments, as he does himself from time to time: in a diary entry for 3 March 1953, he wondered if he was losing his grip and thought that everything he had done was weak. But then he added — and of course he is quite right — that this is a "typische Mittel-Alter-Erscheinung" (a typical phenomenon of middle-age).[10]

After the Second World War Remarque wrote a screenplay for the producer G. W. Pabst (*Der letzte Akt,* about the last days of Hitler, a film eventually screened in English as *The Last Act* or as *The Last Ten Days,* 1955)[11] and several plays of his own. One of these, *Die letzte Station* (The Last Stopping Place), also to do with the last days of the war, was first performed in Berlin in 1956, but was not published at the time, although it was translated from the manuscript into a number of Eastern European languages, where it was successful on stage and television. There was a revival of this play after Remarque's death, titled *Full Circle* and performed in New York in 1973, and both *Die letzte Station* and the film script *Der letzte Akt* were published in 1998 in the five-volume collection of hitherto relatively inaccessible texts called *Das unbekannte Werk* (The Unknown Works).[12] Two further plays, *Die Heimkehr des Enoch J. Jones* (The Return of Enoch J. Jones) and *Brunnenstraße* (Fountain Street) were first performed in Osnabrück in 1988 and 1991 respectively. A Venetian play titled "La Barcarole" on which he was working in 1953 (at the same time as *Die letzte Station* and *Enoch J. Jones*) seems not to have been completed.

Remarque's novels are his central achievement, and even those that Remarque himself did not set much store by — the early novels in particular — can at least throw light on his later development. However, identifying his novels and sometimes their titles can be less straightforward than one might expect, even leaving aside the fact that he almost invariably reworked them, sometimes considerably, and that not all of them were published in his lifetime. The best known of all, *Im Westen nichts Neues,* was published in German and in Germany by Erich Maria Remarque, but in slightly different forms: first as a serial, and then as a book. In fact, Remarque's novels almost always appeared first in serialized form, either in German or in English, with a book version that was not always identical following. Even the many translations of *Im Westen nichts Neues* varied in small respects, and in some cases are slightly closer to Remarque's manuscript than the published German text. In English alone, A. W. Wheen's translation *All Quiet on the Western Front* as published in Great Britain differed from the version published in America, the latter suffering for many years from mild censorship. For the later novels, the production of translations from original manuscripts or typescripts also led to variation, and there were sometimes quite marked differences between the English text, which often appeared first, and the German one, although such anomalies have usually been rectified in the latest editions. All of Remarque's major novels have been translated into English, and — with *Im Westen nichts Neues* an extreme case — usually into a large number of other languages as well, and they have tended to stay in print in German and in other languages for longer periods than do the works of many writers.[13] Few other German novelists, too, have become so much a part of literature in English as well as German.

Im Westen nichts Neues was not Remarque's first novel, however, although he implied occasionally that it was. It was preceded by *Die Traumbude* (Dream Room; Den of Dreams, 1920), published eight years earlier under his original name of Erich Remark. His subsequent dissatisfaction with this novel perhaps contributed to his reasons for changing his name as a writer, although the "new" form is first found as early as 1921. Names are important in his novels, and Remarque clearly liked playing with them and experimented with different versions of his own. The adopted surname is a genuine older form of the family name, and he seems to have started using the familiar version of his name in about 1924, adding the middle name Maria instead of Paul. Anna Maria was his mother's name, but the name of the poet Rainer *Maria* Rilke (1875–1925), an important influence on Remarque, is a far more likely source.[14] A second early novel, which Remarque also referred to as his first, *Gam* (Gam — it is a woman's name — 1923–24) was not published until after his death, although some of it did appear as a short story called "Steppengewitter" (Storm on the Steppes) in the magazine *Jugend* in 1924. A third early novel appeared only in installments in 1927–28, the earliest version of a theme that Remarque would rework later, called *Station am Horizont* (Stopping Point on the Horizon). All three early works have since been republished, or published for the first time, but none have been translated into English.

Remarque left Germany after Hitler came to power and did not return, with the result that the publication history of many of his later works can be confusing, apart from the fact that they were still often printed in serial form before their appearance as books. Several were first published in a language other than German. Thus *Liebe Deinen Nächsten* (literally Love Thy Neighbor) first appeared in English as *Flotsam* in 1939, with a German text later published in Stockholm in 1941. His novel of the Second World War, *Zeit zu leben und Zeit zu sterben* (1954) appeared in the United States in Denver Lindley's translation both in serialized form and as a book in the same year as, but just before the equivalent productions in Germany, and with a slightly but significantly different title: *A Time to Love and a Time to Die.* More importantly, parts of the text were changed somewhat by the publishers when it was first published in Germany, and only recently has the original text been restored.

The bulk of Remarque's novels clearly justify his designation as a chronicler. Both *Im Westen nichts Neues* and *Der Weg zurück,* the only two of his major novels actually to be published before he had to leave Germany, show the reality of life and death during and just after the First World War. *Drei Kameraden* (*Three Comrades,* which first appeared in a Danish translation in 1936), continued the theme of life after the First World War, looking at a group of friends in the politically turbulent period at the end of the Weimar Republic. The next novels in order of writing were also affected by Remarque's own exile and the outbreak of a new war, and take enforced emigration and flight from the Nazi state as their theme. *Liebe Deinen Nächsten,* in 1939, looks at the difficulties of refugees trying to establish themselves in a reluctant host country, while *Arc de Triomphe* (*Arch of Triumph,* 1946) focuses on one single refugee in Paris in the year leading up to the outbreak of the Second World War.

Two further novels of the Nazi period published after the war, but set during its latter stages, try to come to terms with aspects of the way in which Germany was forced to see itself after the Second World War, and both underline Remarque's position as a German despite his continuing exile. *Der Funke Leben* (*Spark of Life,* 1952) takes up an idea voiced in *Im Westen nichts Neues* — the will to live under dreadful circumstances, in this case in a concentration camp at the end of the war. Broader, and a parallel to the famous novel of the First World War, is *Zeit zu leben und Zeit zu sterben,* which was available for a long period in German only in its censored form. While the novel condemns war, the young soldier who is again the central figure has to consider his own responsibility, if not necessarily guilt, as a German in a war that this time could not be seen simply as an outside evil imposed for unclear reasons upon one generation by another. The work is again realistic, and again its hero is killed at the end, so that Remarque's two novels of different wars could well be bracketed together if the theme is taken as war, rather than the specific wars of the twentieth century, especially since the First and Second World Wars look more and more like two acts of the same conflict as historical distance increases. But there are major differences between the novels, both in style and in approach.

With *Der schwarze Obelisk* in 1956 Remarque returned to a deliberate chronicling by showing the early years of the Weimar Republic, the years of inflation in Germany, thus filling the historical gap between *Der Weg zurück* and *Drei Kameraden*. Of the final works, *Der Himmel kennt keine Günstlinge* (*Heaven Has No Favorites*, 1961) is different in that it is ostensibly not historical. To some extent it returns to the theme of car racing that Remarque had used already in *Station am Horizont*, in short stories in the 1920s, and also in *Drei Kameraden*, combining this exciting but dangerous activity with another theme regularly used by Remarque, that of the randomness of death by disease. The novel had another precursor, too, in a film of 1947 based on material by Remarque called *The Other Love*. The first version of the novel itself was written to boost the circulation of a Hamburg magazine, *Kristall*, in which it appeared in condensed form as *Geborgtes Leben: Geschichte einer Liebe* (Borrowed Time: The Story of a Love) in 1959, and it was first published in book form under that title in Russian in 1960. Only in 1961 did it appear in German as *Der Himmel kennt keine Günstlinge*. Remarque seems to have referred to this novel in a letter[15] as his weakest, a point that has been accepted perhaps a little too easily in criticism, so that the novel is often wrongly dismissed; *Der Himmel kennt keine Günstlinge* may equally well be seen as a culmination, bringing together many of the major threads of Remarque's writings in a way that has not fully been acknowledged. A final bibliographical twist, incidentally, was given by the appearance in 1977 of a novel by Remarque ostensibly called *Bobby Deerfield*. This is a simple reprint of the English translation by Richard and Clara Winston of *Der Himmel kennt keine Günstlinge*, published in the wake of the 1977 film of the novel, retitled for one of the main characters for its American distribution. A potential reader who had enjoyed the film would have been baffled to encounter a rather different plot and a character called Clerfayt, while those expecting a new Remarque novel would have purchased one they had already read.

Die Nacht von Lissabon (*The Night in Lisbon*, serialized in 1961, as a book in 1962) takes up again the theme of exile and of refugees escaping from the Nazis in 1942. This is a novel strikingly different in structure from most of the others, although it again looks at the tragedy imposed on people both by other human beings, and by random fate. It is also an exploration of the theme of love against the background of escape from Nazi Germany, and one of his finest works. It was also the last novel published in his lifetime. What is thought of as Remarque's last novel, however, was issued posthumously by his widow, Paulette Goddard, in a form both unrevised and unauthorized by Remarque himself, under the (also unauthorized) title *Schatten im Paradies* (*Shadows in Paradise*, 1971). A later and fragmentary version of what is still the same work was edited in 1998 as *Das gelobte Land* (The Promised Land). The paradise is America, but the theme of the exile reacting to the Nazi regime and of being German still remains. The question marks over the text, however, bring us back in a sense to the earliest novels, *Die Traumbude* and *Gam,* and the question of whether or not Remarque would have welcomed the re-publications of the early works, or the dissemination of an unrevised last work in two separate versions. Remarque's earliest works, and the final one as well, must be treated with due circumspection, but his established body of ten or eleven important novels is quite solid enough for a lasting literary reputation, and if there is some variation in their quality, then this, too, as Sternburg notes in his biography, is hardly surprising. But the implicit notion that Remarque's importance rests principally upon *Im Westen nichts Neues* should be resisted.[16]

Remarque's life outside his writing career has been addressed by a variety of writers, many of them linking aspects of it more or less closely to his works.[17] His home town of Osnabrück, for example, is recognizable as the background for many of the novels, but his having lived there is no more relevant to an understanding of the novels than the fact that the fictional characters in *Der Himmel kennt keine Günstlinge* visit Porto Ronco, where Remarque lived later in his life. All writers draw on their personal experiences, but this does not make their writing autobiographical. It is a salutary warning that much early criticism of *Im Westen nichts Neues* took that work, sometimes firmly, not as a historical novel of the First World War written ten years after the events, but as some kind of autobiographical eyewitness report, even though the first-person narrator is killed at the end of the work. Titles like *Die Wahrheit über Remarque* (The Truth about Remarque) were published around 1930, and even in recent criticism occasionally insufficient distinction is drawn between statements allegedly made by Remarque and those that Remarque, the highly-skilled author, permits his first-person narrator to make. It can also be overlooked that nearly all of Remarque's historical novels require account to be taken of different times: the time in which the work is set; the time in which it was written; and the ever-shifting present of the reader.

Other details of Remarque's personal life can be rehearsed briefly. He was marked out as a member of a specific generation by his date of birth, reaching the age for military service in 1916, the point by which the First World War had established itself as a war of attrition. By this time he was already part of an artistic circle in Osnabrück, some aspects of which are reflected in *Die Traumbude*. Remarque was drafted in November of that year, trained at the Caprivi barracks in Osnabrück, and then at a camp on the Lüneburg Heath. He was sent to the front in June 1917, first to France, then to Flanders at the start of the offensive known as Third Ypres. He was wounded by British forces at Dixmuide at the end of July, and he spent virtually the rest of the war in a military hospital in Duisburg. After the war he resumed the training as a teacher that he had begun in 1916, gained his qualification, and worked as a teacher until late in 1919. He then took a number of other jobs, some musical, and including one with a gravestone manufacturer, reflected in *Der schwarze Obelisk,* although once again the use of a single experience does not make the work autobiographical. He worked from October 1922 as editor and copywriter for the in-house magazine produced by Continental Rubber in Hanover, *Echo Continental.* He had already published essays and reviews, and continued to do so in the early 1920s. After *Die Traumbude* he worked on other writings, including the surviving unpublished novel *Gam,* to which he never referred publicly, and which was only discovered and published after his death. He developed what became a lifelong interest in racing cars: his Lancia, which became a kind of trademark, seems to have been a love of his life comparable with many of his human loves, notably Marlene Dietrich.[18] This is certainly reflected in some of the novels, especially *Drei Kameraden.* From 1924 he edited *Sport im Bild* in Berlin, the magazine in which *Station am Horizont* appeared in installments in 1927–28. After much more work than was admitted in the publicity material or in interviews, he completed and published *Im Westen nichts Neues* in 1928–29; it was issued with considerable hype, and quickly became a bestseller. It set off a literary furor, with reaction and counter-reaction continuing for some time, the whole issue being revitalized when an American film of the work was shown in Germany and famously disrupted by the Nazis by releasing mice in the cinema. With the Nazi accession to power in 1933, his books were publicly burned because of his alleged literary betrayal of the First World War soldier. Nazi literary criticism might not have been very effective (they did not recognize parts of *Im Westen nichts Neues* when they were published in their own press, having been sent in unattributed as "the truth about the war"),[19] but other aspects of their organization were extremely efficient, and Remarque now took up residence as an exile in Porto Ronco on Lake Maggiore in Switzerland, where he had in 1931 bought the beautifully situated Casa Monte Tabor. He had married Ilse Jutta (Jeanne) Zambona in 1925, the couple divorcing in 1930, but remarrying in 1938 to enable Zambona to leave Germany. In July of the same year the Nazi authorities revoked Remarque's own citizenship. Just before the outbreak of the Second World War, Remarque went from Switzerland[20] into even more distant exile via France to America, where he lived a fairly high-profile society life in Hollywood and New York, although he was not always accepted in America by other German literary émigrés, partly because he was a popular writer, but to be fair perhaps also for personal reasons.[21] In 1943, the Nazis guillotined Remarque's sister, Elfriede Scholz, the condemning judge reputedly commenting that if the brother could not be caught, the sister would stand in his place.[22]

Remarque did not return to live in Germany although he traveled there frequently after the war; though invited to reapply for citizenship, he was disinclined to do so because it had been taken from him against his wishes. He did receive a small amount of compensation, which he used to have a terrace built onto his house in Porto Ronco. Having divorced Zambona for the second time in 1957 — they had separated long before, although he continued to support her — in 1958 he married the film actress Paulette Goddard, whom he had first met in 1940, around the time of his final breakup with Marlene Dietrich. He now divided his time between America and his house in Switzerland, and also spent much time in Italy towards the end of his life. The City of Osnabrück awarded the Möser medal to him in 1964 in Porto Ronco, and in 1967 he received the *Grosses Verdienstkreuz* of the Federal Republic of Germany. He died in Locarno on 25 September 1970 and is buried in Porto Ronco.

Wilhelm von Sternburg gives the photographs in his biography captions like "the elegant world-traveler," "the famous writer," "the actor," and latterly "the collector" (of paintings, Greek vases, and oriental carpets, among other things), while in the index to Hilton Tims's biography, the three longest entries under "personality" are "depression," "libido," and "passion for cars." Remarque utilizes all of these aspects somewhere in his writings — even the interest in paintings and carpets. Remarque attracted attention and, in his early days of fame, controversy as well, and other myths than the one about his name attached themselves to him, sometimes with his own connivance. But questions of whether he really had been awarded the Iron Cross or held the title of Freiherr von Buchwald are irrelevant to the evaluation of his work.[23] In her extensive biography of her mother, Marlene Dietrich's daughter has quite a lot to say about Remarque, reporting for example her mother's comments on his sexual behavior, details of which may or may not be true and are hardly relevant, but one comment of hers affords a neat summary embracing his works, his attitude to life, and even his looks:

> I always thought he had the look of a debonair fox, like an illustration out of the Fables of La Fontaine, even the tops of his ears pointed slightly. He had an innate theatricality — an actor in an heroic production standing perpetually in the wings, waiting for the right cue; in the interim he wrote books in which all the male roles represented the powers within him; in life never placed together to form one whole character, just the most intriguing parts of himself, doomed never to meld into one complete man. Not because he didn't know how to, but because he felt himself undeserving of such exemplary completion.[24]

Remarque's liaisons with different Hollywood stars such as Greta Garbo, Dolores del Rio, and especially Marlene Dietrich and Paulette Goddard have, as indicated, been well documented and much speculated upon, and aspects of these and other relationships, particularly with Ruth Albu, Jutta Zambona, and Natasha Paley, seem to be reflected in his different novels.

But Remarque's relationship with the film as such is of greater importance. Most of his own novels were filmed,[25] he wrote an original screenplay, drafted them for some of his own books, and acted as a script consultant, adviser, or adapter — although it is not always clear to what extent — for the German versions of other films (*Das letzte Ufer* — *On the Beach,* 1959; *The Guns of Navarone,* 1961; *The Longest Day,* 1962; and others). Some consideration of the films is, therefore, necessary, since the genre of film, which is notoriously capable of distortion and over-simplification, can by its directness lose or distort the stylistic subtleties of the original, and the existence of the many film versions may well have led to these qualities in the novels being overlooked. On the other hand, some of Remarque's works after *Im Westen nichts Neues* may have been influenced at the writing stage by film techniques, or may have been written with a future film partly in mind. Certainly his episodic style lends itself to filming, and incidentally, to serialization.

As with the book, the film *All Quiet on the Western Front,* made in English in 1930, remains the best known. Most of the novels were filmed in English-language versions. *The Road Back* and *Three Comrades* were both filmed before the Second World War, in 1937 and 1938, and during the war came *So Ends Our Night* (1941, based on *Liebe Deinen Nächsten/Flotsam*). *Arch of Triumph* (1948, with Ingrid Bergman and Charles Boyer) and *A Time to Love and a Time to Die* (1958) appeared after the war, the latter in German and English versions. Since Remarque's death there have also been television films of some of the works. *Die Nacht von Lissabon* (1971) was in production when Remarque died, and there are new English-language versions of *All Quiet on the Western Front* (1979) and of *Arch of Triumph* (1985), plus a German television version of *Der schwarze Obelisk* (1988). The film adaptation in 1977 of *Der Himmel kennt keine Günstlinge,* titled *Bobby Deerfield* in the United States, was distributed as *Heaven has no Favorites* in Australia. Of Remarque's major novels, only *Der Funke Leben* and *Schatten in Paradies* have not been filmed. Some novels have also been filmed in languages other than German or English. One further film, *The Other Love* (1947), is based, according to the opening credits, on a nonexistent short story by Remarque titled "Beyond," but in fact on a sketch or "treatment" surviving in Remarque's papers. In this case the film is in effect a primary text, although Remarque did try to dissociate himself from it; thus it needs to be considered slightly more fully in the context of *Der Himmel kennt keine Günstlinge* to which it is thematically related.

It is significant that Remarque's one film-acting role was as the character of Pohlmann, an older teacher persecuted by the Nazis, in *A Time to Love and a Time to Die,* from which one of his scenes was used to some effect on a poster.[26] The circumstances of the making of that film (which received mixed reviews) in 1958 is almost emblematic of Remarque's life and career:

it was a film about the problems of coping with events in wartime Germany, made in Germany by a distinguished director of German origin, Douglas Sirk (born Detlev Sierck), and also starring a German actress, Lieselotte Pulver, with Remarque himself not only the author of the original book and writer of the first version of the screenplay, but also playing a role. The film was distributed — again underscoring Remarque's internationalism in a film about Germany — in English and in German.

In an interview on the subject of *Im Westen nichts Neues* with Axel Eggebrecht in 1929, Remarque clearly saw his earlier writings as works in which he was struggling to find a style. "Früher hatte ich ganz anders gearbeitet, ich hatte experimentiert, mich ziemlich herumgequält, um einen Stil zu finden, aber es blieb alles matt und farblos . . ." (Earlier I had worked quite differently, I had experimented, tortured myself in all sorts of ways to try and find a style, but everything stayed matt and colorless . . .).[27] The two early novels, *Die Traumbude,* first published in 1920 and virtually forgotten, but now republished, and *Gam,* published in 1998 for the first time, are quite different from each other, but neither of them is without interest, nor entirely devoid of literary merit. Although excessive claims cannot be made for either of them, neither can fairly be described as colorless. Remarque never published *Gam,* and he regretted having published *Die Traumbude.* His negative views on the latter work may be endorsed to an extent, insofar as it is clearly a young writer's novel, with some possible autobiographical elements. *Die Traumbude,* moreover, was published by Erich Remark, and not yet by Erich Maria Remarque, and this sets it off from the rest of his works. As far as *Gam* is concerned, the negative views are less explicit: he simply never mentioned it, and we do not know whether he ever tried to publish it, or even planned to revise it for publication — it could not have been published in the form in which it survives. It seems to have been written in 1923–24, this date being based upon notes and remnants written on the back of galley proofs from the magazine *Echo Continental,* which Remarque was editing at that time, and the short story that overlaps with part of the novel appeared in 1924. Although *Gam* remained unknown, Remarque did in 1942 have the work retyped, so that he clearly did not put it out of his mind. Its modern editors point out that Remarque used many of the character names in later novels (or occasionally as noms-de-plume for himself), and that, as one of the letters shows, Marlene Dietrich at least read the work.[28] It might have appeared under the name Remarque; the author had adopted the form of the name by 1924, and he was well established under that name by the time it was retyped. Moreover, the typescript copy survives in a folder labeled *1. Roman* (First Novel), which may just imply that he wanted to have *Die Traumbude* excluded from his "real" works. On the other hand, Remarque in later years also referred to *Im Westen nichts Neues* as his first novel.[29] In any case, in assessing *Gam,* it has to be borne in mind that the text was not authorized for publication by an author who regularly revised and rewrote his works.

Die Traumbude

Whichever Remarque designated as his first novel, *Die Traumbude* holds that position in plain fact. In a comic but revealing postscript to a letter to his friend Hanns-Gerd Rabe in February 1929 after the success of *Im Westen nichts Neues*, Remarque threatened to box his ears for "die Wiederaufwärmung der Traumbude" (bringing up *Die Traumbude*),[30] and it was by then not a work he was keen on being reminded of. More than with many later works, he drew for it upon elements from his own life, specifically of his membership in a circle of young artists, musicians, and writers grouped around the somewhat older Fritz Hörstemeier (1882–1918) in Osnabrück between 1915 and 1917, while he was undergoing a Catholic teacher training program.[31] This does not mean that an autobiographical interpretation of the novel is called for. Hörstemeier appears in the novel fairly clearly as one of the central figures, Fritz Schramm, and several of the poems he reads to his friends in the work are Hörstemeier's own.[32] Most of the circle of younger friends associated with him can be identified with people Remarque knew. One even wrote to him in 1968 as the character from the novel. Fritz's closest friend, Ernst Winter, is in some respects — but only some — a reflection, or more properly a projection, of the author himself. That is to say, Winter is a pianist and composer (which Remarque had aspirations to be), is much attached to Fritz Schramm (as Remarque was to Hörstemeier), and plays the organ at his friend's cremation (as Remarque did at Hörstemeier's). But to refer to the work as a *roman à clef* or, as Martina Krause does, as *halbbiographisch* (semi-biographical)[33] is not particularly useful; despite the association of most of the characters with actual people — strong in the case of the main character, more tenuous with most of the others — an appreciation of the work gains little from this additional knowledge; this is a point that will be reiterated with many of the novels. The opera singer with whom Ernst Winter has an affair is, for example, supposedly based upon the actress Lotte Preuss, an early passion of Remarque's, but the details of the affair in the novel sound more like adolescent fantasy, and the character in the work owes more to Carmen than to Lotte Preuss.

Where the novel fails is above all in its language, which is, to the modern ear, frequently impossible. Antkowiak, who devotes only a paragraph to the work, significantly does not criticize the content, apart from noting its immaturity, but says bluntly of the style that the book is "in einem unerträglichen Deutsch geschrieben, hier haben sich unklare, schlummrige Gefühle in prosaischen Schnörkeln und Blasen entladen" (in an unbearable German style, vague, halfbaked feelings are poured out in a prosy style embellished with curlicues and soap-bubbles).[34] Nor is it difficult to find examples to bear this out. Here Schramm is in conversation with a young lady visitor, Trix Bergen, who has just praised his free lifestyle, to which Fritz replies:

> "So gut kann es jeder Mensch haben."
> Sie wiegte ein wenig kokett das Köpfchen. "Ja — ein Mann; aber wir kleinen Mädchen —" und sie nahm eine Dattel aus dem Körbchen Obst, das er ihr hinreichte, und knabberte sie mit den weißen Mäusezähnchen ab. (115)

> ["It can be as good as that for everyone."
> She inclined her little head in a slightly coquettish manner. "Yes, for a man; but for us little girls . . ." and she took a date from the little basket of fruit that he offered her, and nibbled away at it with her little white mouse-teeth.]

The passage is not intended to be comical, nor is the girl caricatured — at least, this is not the impression given of her in the rest of the work. The style is characterized by features like the excessive use of diminutives associated with the female characters, overdone attempts to play with sounds and to use them to imitate colors, and perhaps most of all by the equally overdone use of pauses, occasionally with an unconsciously bathetic effect. When first invited to call Schramm "Onkel Fritz," the beautiful young Elisabeth tries it: "'Onkel — Fritz —' sprach Elisabeth andächtig. Er küßte sie auf die Stirn" ("Uncle — Fritz —" intoned Elisabeth reverently. He kissed her on the forehead, 44). When Fritz dies, too, we are told: "Er war — tot" (He was — dead, 158). The significance of a pause at this point can only be guessed at. Perhaps it is the typographical equivalent of a portentous chord on an organ?

Most of Remarque's important works are effectively historical; the two novels of the First World War, for example, look back at the years between 1917 and 1920 from a vantage point of the late 1920s and early 1930s, but their theme was still significant for the world in which they were first published, just as they remain significant now. *Die Traumbude,* on the other hand, is a novel with a completely backward look, certainly for a writer in Germany just after the First World War. The novel focuses on the aestheticism movement associated in particular with the end of the nineteenth and beginning of the twentieth century, and on a world before the First World War, which was now gone and would not return, with ideals and ideas that were no longer relevant. It is in effect an attempt to escape from the war, set in a world where the war never existed. Subtitled *Ein Künstlerroman* (Novel of an Artist), the book appeared in a series called Bücherei der Schönheit (Library of Beauty), and the theme of beauty is the key to the work. It centers upon the painter and poet Fritz Schramm, who is surrounded by a coterie of younger, aesthetically inclined friends, principally the composer and pianist Ernst Winter. That Fritz, at the age of 38, is perceived as being far older than the rest of the group is patently based on the perception of an author in his early twenties, for all that Schramm's attitudes can indeed be patriarchal rather than avuncular. The shifting perceptions that depend upon the age of the reader, combined here with the radical changes in attitudes that the passing years have brought about, both speak against this book. The attitude of most of the female characters towards Fritz Schramm is especially noticeable; from time to time one expects a love relationship to develop, such as that between the forty-year-old Hans Karl Bühl and the far younger Helene Altenwyl in the exactly contemporary play *Der Schwierige* (by the forty-six-year-old Hugo von Hofmannsthal), but it never does. That literary comparison is interesting in a further respect — Hans Karl, in Hofmannsthal's play, has absorbed and been changed by experiences of the First World War, whereas Remarque's Fritz Schramm is a prewar figure.[35] There is nothing in *Die Traumbude* to fix the time at which it is set, but there is no mention of the war. Some of the then liberal, even shockingly bohemian attitudes had long since been overtaken by events so that the effect is not of an avant-garde, but rather of a period love story, written in an overenthusiastic style. The title of an article by Armin Kerker on Remarque's earlier writings, "Zwischen Innigkeit und Nacktkultur" (Between Intensity and Naturism) is significant in this context.

The work is competently structured, however. Fritz Schramm, an established artist but not in good health, is visited by various younger people linked by aesthetic sensibility, in his studio, or more specifically in his *Traumbude,* his dream-room or dream-den, a room dedicated to pure beauty and to the adoration of Beethoven and also of Lu, his now-dead beloved, to whom he remains completely devoted, but with whom his relationship was never fulfilled. She exists in the work only as a picture and portraits play a great part in the work. Fritz meets and becomes close to Elisabeth Heindorf, with whom his closest friend, the pianist and composer Ernst Winter, falls in love. Less well-drawn are Paulchen — a girl — and Fried, whose bohemianism and references to *Nacktkultur* come across as little more than sexually charged adolescent frivolity. Into Fritz's ambit, too, comes Trix Bergen, a young and beautiful girl from provincial Rostock, who has had a series of affairs and has become what the Victorians would have termed a fallen woman. While encouraging her lust for life, Fritz manages to moderate her lust for lust (euphemistically termed *Abenteuerlust,* 119) and eventually mediates a reconciliation with her parents, to whom she returns, though not before she has offered herself to and been refused by Fritz. Fritz instead gives Trix into the charge of the chaste Elisabeth to work as a nurse. Meanwhile, as Elisabeth herself blossoms under Fritz's tuition, Ernst leaves for Leipzig and embarks on a torrid love affair with an opera singer also known to Fritz, Lanna Reiner. There is a studied and somewhat labored contrast between Elisabeth as the devoted and archetypally romantic Mignon — Goethe's poem is quoted in full, sung by Elisabeth while Ernst accompanies her — and Lanna, seen as Carmen. The text of Bizet's *Habañera* is a repeated motif, and Ernst accompanies Lanna, too, as she sings the song that contains in its German version the lines "Liebst du mich nicht, bin ich entflammt — Wenn ich dich lieb, nimm dich in acht" (If you don't love me, then I'm on fire — If I love you, be careful!)[36]

Back in Osnabrück, Fritz comforts Elisabeth with the view that the affair is a kind of passing illness on Ernst's part. Elisabeth understands this, but Ernst himself realizes that the whole thing was a Dionysian intoxication only when he receives news of Fritz's death. Having tried and failed to do so once before, he now breaks abruptly with Lanna, who threatens him briefly with a revolver, apparently switching roles for a moment from Carmen to Don José. Ernst then returns, arranges the funeral, and ultimately suffers a nervous breakdown, from which Elisabeth nurses him back to health. He completes a composition and is given a post as *Kapellmeister,* while Lanna Rainer becomes tidily engaged to a prince. Ernst and Elisabeth are finally reunited — or rather united, as each individual *Ich* merges into a *Du* at the end of the work, brought together by the death of Fritz, whose picture now seems to smile upon them.

The plot is clearly in places overly sentimental as well as overwritten, but the structure holds up, and ideas are presented — as they will be in many of the later novels — through the individual characters. Central to the work is the dialogue between Fritz and Trix in the seventh chapter — the opening of which was cited above as an illustration of the precious style. Fritz interpretation of Trix's wild breakaway from her provincial background is a moral sermon, and a patronizing one at that. He stresses the value of life as such, and of living in a manner that is true to the self; a little later he even cites the tag "know thyself":

> Das Leben ist Gott. Wir sollen uns bemühen, so zu leben, wie es unserer inneren Natur am angemessensten ist. (116)

> [Life is God. We have to make sure we live in the way most appropriate to our inner nature.]

This idea will recur in the mature novels. For a woman, however, the ideal lies:

> im Gang vom Ich zum Du; in der äußerlichen Form — nicht in der tiefinnerlichen Katastrophe des Mannes — in der Hingabe an den geliebten Mann und das Weiterleben im Kinde. (117)

> [in the movement from the "I" towards the "you": in its outward form — not in the catastrophe deep within a man — in submission to the beloved man and in the continuation of life in the child.]

However this might sound in a feminist context, it is really a simple moral precept against love as a commodity and in favor of love as a genuine relationship, and it will reappear in various forms in Remarque's mature novels. Trix realizes that she has been a sexual object, and her first impulse is a melodramatic version of the time-honored German reaction: "ins Wasser!" (I'll drown myself!). But Fritz persuades her that she can rise phoenix-like from the ashes of sin and integrates her into his coterie. He may be a kind of priest-figure, placing the straying sinner back on the straight and narrow, but his assertion of life as a force and his comments on the merging of the self into another are the first indications of what will recur in Remarque's novels as the spark of life that has an independent existence both in war and in the concentration camps, and which demands expression in the face of sickness and death. Fritz has already been working on a painting, we have been told, of the move from the *Ich* to the *Du,* combined with the loss of all egoism into the ultimate *Es,* of life itself. Ernst Winter's private *Rausch,* his affair with Lanna Reiner, is interpreted in Nietzschean terms, returning to Apollonian beauty at the end.[37]

The bohemianism in the work is very much pre-1914, and although Fritz may go through the motions of the aesthetic in his *Traumbude* — the careful placing of roses and candles, for example — his sensibility is not the neurotic passion of the central figure of, say, J.-K. Huysmans's novel *A Rebours* (*Against Nature*), nor is there any pact with the dark forces: Fritz has no portrait in the attic. Indeed, he moves equally well in the bourgeois world, and although he and his friends may joke about some of the figures encountered there, even this is done gently — an overweight and over-poetic society wife is nevertheless *eine gute Seele* (a good soul, 152). There is none of the introspective confusion experienced by Thomas Mann's Tonio Kröger here, and even the merging of love and death, of *eros* and *thanatos,* is anything but Wagnerian. Fritz remains faithful to his dead love in life and perhaps looks forward to joining her; but he never relinquishes the *will* to live. In any case, his death is not a climactic reunion with Lu, but rather the catalyst for that of Ernst with Elisabeth, as if Don José and Micaëla, or maybe Tristan and Isolde were to live happily ever after. Nor, as has been suggested, is there really any hint of homoeroticism in the Fritz-Ernst mentor relationship.[38]

The work has far more to do with *Innerlichkeit* than with *Nacktkultur.* The circle around Fritz Schramm (like, presumably, that around Fritz Hörstemeier) is no Bloomsbury Group, and even in terms of nineteenth-century and especially fin-de-siècle aesthetic writing, to which this is more closely akin, the bohemianism never moves far from German bourgeois norms. Fritz may appear to espouse daring ideas, but he is deeply moral, indeed moralizing, offering guidance to young people who are simply experimenting, and he is more like the Victorian art critic John Ruskin than any of the later decadents.[39] There is at the same time a German provincialism about the work, which Fritz seems to support even overtly and which he underlines in his conversation with Trix. Earlier on, however, he had referred to the German-ness that "jedem echten Deutschen, ich meine keinen verjudeten oder slawischen, im Blute sitzt" (is in the blood of every real German, I don't mean the quasi-Jewish or Slav ones, 35.) Whether or not the historical Hörstemeier is being cited here, giving Fritz that line was nevertheless unfortunate, but as has been pointed out, Remarque's later works make clear that he would hardly have subscribed in any way to the notion of a Jewish-Bolshevik plot against Germany.

In terms of superficial literary style, Remarque was quite right to be embarrassed by the work, and his attempts to disown it are understandable. Once through that barrier, however, the structuring of the work shows some of the promise of the later writer, as does the interplay of relationships. The figure of the lost mentor will recur, for example, in a far more direct manner, in figures like Katczinsky, Steiner, and Pohlmann in *Im Westen nichts Neues, Liebe Deinen Nächsten,* and *Zeit zu leben und Zeit zu sterben* respectively. What Fritz offers his flock is the kind of guidance that Paul Bäumer, in *Im Westen nichts Neues,* clearly missed in the move directly from school to the western front. So, too, the interplay of *Ich* and *Du* and *Es* — the latter as the life force within — will come out again, balanced against the melancholy and the *Sehnsucht* inherent in life in the twentieth century. There are many weak places and this is a young writer's work. But there are signs of what would come later.

Gam

In the notes to the first printed edition of *Gam,* based on the typescript from 1942, is a sketch, also from Remarque's papers, which makes clear that the underlying principle of the work is the more or less schematic confrontation of the central character, a woman named Gam, with different kinds of men and the attitudes to life that they represent.[40] That the protagonist is a woman is relatively unusual in Remarque's work, although he does have other women in primary positions, principally Lillian Dunkerque in *Der Himmel kennt keine Günstlinge* or Joan Madou in *Arc de Triomphe,* but all of them are associated with one central male figure. *Gam* contrasts, too, with *Die Traumbude,* where the female figures — Elisabeth, Lanna, Trix, Paulchen — are themselves sometimes little more than types, representing respectively purity, sexuality, the woman led astray, and the adolescent. In *Gam,* however, the oddly-named[41] central figure remains the point about which the rest of the work revolves. Even though we do not know anything about her background, we are introduced to her abruptly among Bedouins, after which we watch her buy a copy of the *Divan,* the love poetry of the early medieval Arabic poet Abu Nuwâs. Although the novel is a third-person narrative, Gam herself is a focus of consciousness, a technique that Remarque would use frequently in later writings. Thus he allows us to see her thoughts on the possibility of having a child, for example (almost an echo of Fritz's advice to Trix in *Die Traumbude*):

> Ein Wunsch durchströmte sie: Warmes Leben um ihre Knie zu spüren, einen Mund, der unbeholfen erste Worte bildete. — Weiterleben und alle Fragen und Einsamkeiten bannen in einem Kinde.
> Hier lag Erfüllung und Hafen.
> Dennoch wußte Gam, daß sie schmerzlich höher hinaufstoßen mußte, um zu Sich zu kommen. (200)

> [One wish flowed through her, to feel warm life at her knee, a mouth struggling with its first words. To live on, and to lose all questioning and loneliness in a child.
> There lay fulfillment and a haven.
> But Gam knew that she would have to struggle painfully upwards to reach her true self.]

Although Gam, in a profusion of exotic settings, reacts largely passively to things that happen to her (she is actually gambled away at one point), her struggle to find herself is still the underlying theme of the work as she encounters and becomes involved with to varying degrees, a series of different types of men. According to Remarque's plan, Clerfayt (a name that will recur in his writings) represents *gesammelte Energie* (pent-up energy), the *Kreole* (creole) stands for decadence, Ravic (another name that Remarque would use again) is a *kontemplativer Ästhetiker* (a contemplative aesthetic type), while the aptly, if for a German novel slightly oddly, named Fred is a *Durchschnittstyp,* the normal, and by sheer contrast almost the most memorable, everyday sort. Although few women have interactions with Gam, the men who come Gam's way also include a Tibetan Lama and even an executioner, whom she observes beheading a criminal in China. The principal male character is Lavalette, whose name is enigmatically annotated as *Kugelmensch* by Remarque, presumably meaning someone mercurial; certainly he sweeps Gam off her feet and treats life as an adventure. In a memorable scene, with curious pre-echoes of a scene involving survival among more recent graves in *Im Westen nichts Neues,* Lavalette asserts life by making violently expressed love to Gam in an ancient and misty graveyard. With him Gam embarks on what there is in the way of a plot in the work, an adventurous tale involving plans being smuggled from one country to another, a plot that does not actually begin until well into the book. Lavalette's death, shot down at the culmination of a hectic, and in Sternburg's words, positively cinematic car chase, is the end of the novel proper. Fast cars interested Remarque and often served as images of living dangerously, but to the full.

Episodic narrative as such would become a familiar feature of Remarque's style, but here the sole linking theme is Gam herself, as she experiences a sequence of encounters. The novel's setting seems to take in the entire world, sometimes moving so bewilderingly from Africa to South America to India or Cochin China that one might be forgiven for wondering how the protagonist managed to miss any exotic location at all. Once again, however, the time cannot be pinned down, in stark contrast to Remarque's later involvement with novels fixed in time by reference to historical events. *Gam* is a philosophical novel, and Gam herself is permitted to test and therefore to show the reader various responses to life. The overall philosophy is vitalist, and what Gam seeks and finds is the need to experience life for itself and for oneself. The theme of self-knowledge voiced in *Die Traumbude* recurs, and the lesson Gam learns is made clear in an epilogue after the death of Lavalette:

> Die Welt wich zurück zu gläserner Schau. Wertung zerfiel, auch die letzte, schon jenseits der Ethik. Die einfachste aller Wahrheiten brach auf: Es war immer alles gut und recht. Wer sich folgte, ging nicht fehl. Wer sich verlor, fand die Welt. Wer die Welt fand, fand sich. Wer *sich* empfand, war über allem und ging ein zur Ewigkeit. *Immer* empfand man nur sich. (355)

> [The world gave way to a glassy vision. Values disappeared, even the last, away beyond ethics. The simplest of all truths came forward: everything was always right and good. If you followed your self, you did not go astray. If you lost yourself, you found the world. If you found the world, you found yourself. If you found *yourself* you rose above all things and went on into eternity. *Always* you experienced only the self.]

The circularity of this is underlined for Gam by the Tibetan Lama with the image of the prayer-wheel, who points out to her that ends are always beginnings, persuading her to accept life as a series of eternal returns. At the last she is alone, on a retreat, but at peace with herself, back in Europe, unpacking and finding again the copy of Abu Nuwâs's poetry. The self-assertion of life within her has brought her peace, and the final passage has interesting indications of the existential awareness reached by Paul Bäumer at the end of *Im Westen nichts Neues,* who has also lost by then those closest to him, just as she has lost Lavalette. This theme, and indeed the existentialist metaphysics so much associated with twentieth-century European writings in general, persists in many of Remarque's mature novels. Gam thinks: "Solange ich mich empfinde, steht die Welt" (As long as I experience myself, the world will survive, 361), and she walks through a clearly European, even Germanic wood, which contrasts with all the exotic scenery experienced thus far, aware of permanent growth, even where trees have fallen but are overgrown with creeper and fungi:

Gam roch den Duft der Erde — und der Kräuter. Sie brach Rinde und schmeckte sie. Wind kam auf. Ein neues Jahr brach aus der Scholle. Alles war Beginnen. Gam wußte nun alles. Sie neigte das Haupt.—
   Sprach nicht jemand neben ihr: Ich beginne — ich bin bereit — (361)

[Gam smelled the scent of the earth — and of the herbs. She broke off bark and tasted it. A wind came up. A new year was breaking out of the soil. It was all a beginning. Gam now knew everything. She bowed her head. —
   Did a voice near to her not say: I am beginning — I am ready —]

There are indications, then, of what would follow in a few years time in an altogether different context and would persist throughout many of the novels: the theme of *Zufall*, chance, the existential assertion of life as the last indicator of individuality, and especially the seizing of life as an assertion of the true self. In terms of style, this is the first example of a focused third-person narrative. As a novel there are serious defects: the breathless rush from continent to continent, and especially the overt schematization in the way Gam is presented with male type after male type, almost like a chemical substance upon which different reagents are being tried. And yet it remains unfair to treat *Gam* even in the same way as *Die Traumbude,* because it is not a finished work. The most that we can do is to note themes to which Remarque returned and in some cases transformed.

   Whatever priority is given to *Die Traumbude, Gam,* or later *Im Westen nichts Neues,* a fourth claimant to the title of Remarque's first novel appeared before the most famous work, and *Station am Horizont* was certainly the first to be published under the name of Erich Maria Remarque. To be sure, it was serialized in seven installments in a magazine — *Sport im Bild* — starting in 1927,[42] and not published in book form until after Remarque's death, but *Im Westen nichts Neues,* too, was first published in installments and so were most of the later works. Ullstein, which had bought the rights from the magazine owners, a rival company, presumably did not publish *Station am Horizont* in book form simply because it was so different in character from *Im Westen nichts Neues,* which had by then been presented as a first novel; it is concerned, on the surface at least, largely with motor racing, although there are links with the other early novels. The central character, Kai, for example, is involved with three different female character-types in a sexual reversal of the programmatic outline of *Gam,* and the exotic, upper-class and affluent setting is also reminiscent of Gam's world. There are themes and settings in the work to which Remarque would return as late as in *Der Himmel kennt keine Günstlinge,* however, so that it makes sense to consider the work in detail in that context. But one theme that plays no part whatsoever, once again, is the war, although just once a racing car is described as making "ein Heulen wie eine brüllende Granate" (a howling noise like the roar of a shell).[43] *Sport im Bilde* published the final installment of *Station am Horizont* in mid-February 1928. On 10 November 1928 there appeared in the *Vossische Zeitung* the first installment of the magazine version of *Im Westen nichts Neues,* the last and greatest of Remarque's various first novels.

Notes

[1] John Canning, ed., *100 Great Books: Masterpieces of All Time* (1974; reprint, London: Souvenir Press, 1982), 547–51. The discussion by Margaret Goldsmith of *All Quiet on the Western Front* here is cogent and accurate.

[2] Thus Hans Mayer, *Deutsche Literatur 1945–1985* (Berlin: Siedler, 1998), 31. Mayer refers to Remarque only once, and then as an émigré writer. Mayer's work was originally published in 1988–89, and he himself was forced into exile from the Nazis. Hans-Albert Walter, in his *Deutsche Exilliteratur* (Darmstadt: Luchterhand, 1972), 1, 12, talks about the popularity of those exile writers such as Remarque who operate "below or only just over the level of trivial writing." Wilhelm von Sternburg voices the question of Remarque's position in German postwar literary history in his excellent biography of Remarque, *"Als wäre alles das letzte Mal": Erich Maria Remarque: eine Biographie* (Cologne: Kiepenheuer and Witsch, 2000), 380 and elsewhere. Derek van Abbé, *Image of a People* (London: Harrap, 1964), 185. He notes the idea that German intellectuals look down upon Remarque because of a "journalistic delight in . . . melodramatic story-telling," and although he does use the word "vulgarise," he points out the value of writers who pass on to a wide public ideas that might otherwise be self-centered and esoteric.

[3] See the letter to Upton Sinclair dated 15 May 1942 about support for anti-fascist writers, signed among others by Lion Feuchtwanger, Thomas Mann, Franz Werfel, and Remarque: Erich Maria Remarque, *Das unbekannte Werk,* vol. 5, ed. Thomas F. Schneider and Tilman Westphalen (Cologne: Kiepenheuer and Witsch, 1998), 119–21.

[4] Thus Marcel Reich-Ranicki recalls delivering a book from his mother to his teacher as a child: "Es war keines der großen Kunstwerke jener Zeit, wohl aber ein Roman der damals ganz Europa irritierte: Remarque 'Im Westen nichts Neues'" (It wasn't one of the great works of arts of the period, but was probably a novel that was irritating the whole of Europe at the time: Remarque's *Im Westen nichts Neues*). Marcel Reich-Ranicki, *Mein Leben* (Munich: dtv, 2000), 21. This dismissive attitude is far from unique, although Reich-Ranicki, who was exceptionally critical of some of the novels, was still somewhat baffled by Remarque's success in his obituary notice in *Die Zeit,* 2 October 1970, 15. German intellectuals often have difficulty coping with the concept of popularity, and Remarque himself commented on the adverse effects of his own success; see Maggie Sargeant, *Kitsch und Kunst: Presentations of a Lost War* (Bern: Peter Lang, 2005), 71–74. The concept of a literary canon has been much discussed in recent years; see for example Sigrid Löffler's Bithell Memorial Lecture, *Wer sagt uns, was wir lesen sollen? Die Bücherflut, die Kritik und der literarische Kanon* (London: Institute of Germanic Studies, 2002).

[5] Thomas Schneider, *Erich Maria Remarque: Ein Chronist des 20: Jahrhunderts* (Bramsche: Rasch, 1991), 10. The gravestone is on page 140. There are forerunners to this pictorial volume in the catalogue to the exhibition *Der Weg zurück* (Osnabrück: Universität Osnabrück, 1989), and in a rather different volume containing much about Remarque's life and works: Lothar Schwindt and Tilman Westphalen, eds., *Man kann alten Dreck nicht vergraben: Er fängt immer wieder an zu stinken: Materialien zu einen Erich Maria Remarque-Projekt* (Osnabrück: Universität/ Fachbereich SLM, 1984 [typescript]). Remarque signed letters to Marlene Dietrich with names of characters in his books, and the names of his friends crop up in his works from time to time without biographical significance. The Kramer myth was even repudiated by Salomo Friedländer, one of Remarque's early critics, but he also condemned Remarque for adopting what he saw as a pretentiously French form of his name. As recently as ten years after Remarque's death, Ronald Taylor's otherwise useful study, *Literature and Society in Germany 1918–1945* (Brighton: Harvester, 1980), 115, compounds it all by referring to the name as "a 'romanticised' form of Remark, i.e. Kramer, his real name, spelt backwards." Remarque was still defending himself in 1966: "Grosse und kleine Ironien meines Lebens," originally in *Die Welt*, 31 March 1966, and reprinted in: Erich Maria Remarque, *Ein militanter Pazifist: Texte und Interviews, 1929–1966*, ed. Thomas F. Schneider (Cologne: Kiepenheuer and Witsch, 1994), 138–43; *Das unbekannte Werk*, vol. 4, 436–41; and *Herbstfahrt eines Phantasten*, ed. Thomas F. Schneider (Cologne: Kiepenheuer and Witsch, 2001), 254–59.

[6] Cited by Schneider, *Remarque*, 5. The quotation has been used as the title of a paper by Tilman Westphalen.

[7] The stories collected as *Der Feind*, retranslated by Barbara von Bechtolsheim and reprinted in more than one place, appeared first in *Collier's*, as did, for example, the story "On the Road," retranslated by Thomas Schneider as "Unterwegs" in *Das unbekannte Werk*, vol. 4, 378–86 and *Herbstfahrt*, 123–31.

[8] *Das unbekannte Werk* contains a wealth of material. The first of the five-volume set contains the three early novels (*Die Traumbude*, *Gam*, and *Station am Horizont*, the last of which has also now been published separately), and the second volume contains the unpublished version of his last novel, here titled *Das gelobte Land*. The third volume contains the play *Die letzte Station* and the screenplay for *Der letzte Akt*. Volume four contains a varied selection of his stories, essays, reviews, and other prose writings, including pieces about motor racing, and those collected as *Der Feind;* it contains in addition the handful of extant poems, including the verses that accompanied a comic strip about the Contibuben, a pastiche of Wilhelm Busch's *Max und Moritz* advertising Continental tires. Much of this material is also available separately in either or both of the collections *Ein militanter Pazifist* and *Herbstfahrt*. For full publication details (and often facsimiles) of these smaller pieces, see: *Erich Maria Remarque: "Die Traumbude," "Station am Horizont," Die unselbständigen Publikationen, 1916–1998*, ed. Thomas F. Schneider and Donald Weiss (Osnabrück: Rasch, 1995). The fifth volume contains a necessarily limited selection from the letters and diaries (the letter from Remarque to Dr. Witsch referring to the list of great books, dated 15 June 1961, is in vol. 5, 186–87).

[9] For the Zweig letters, see *Das unbekannte Werk,* vol. 5, 49–50 and 80–81, and the editors' notes on page 522 stressing the importance of Stefan Zweig to Remarque's career. See also Sternburg *"Als wäre alles,"* 32 and 114–15 (Arnold Zweig, the Austrian writer's unrelated namesake, was less complimentary about *Im Westen nichts Neues*). Studies of Stefan Zweig have not paid much attention to the connection with Remarque, although one that does so is spectacularly absurd, seeming to think that *All Quiet on the Western Front* is a play that Remarque wanted Zweig to translate: Elizabeth Allday, *Stefan Zweig: A Critical Biography* (London: W. H. Allen, 1972), 95.

[10] For the diary entry, see *Das unbekannte Werk,* vol. 5, 483. The correspondence with Marlene Dietrich is edited by Werner Fuld and Thomas F. Schneider, *"Sag mir, daß du mich liebst"* . . . *Zeugnisse einer Leidenschaft* (Cologne: Kiepenheuer and Witsch, 2001). See also the collection of Remarque materials in the Remarque Archiv in Osnabrück and in the Fales Library, New York University, on which see Thomas F. Schneider, *Erich Maria Remarque: Der Nachlaß in der Fales Library — New York University: Ein Verzeichnis,* 2d ed. (Osnabrück: Universität Osnabrück, 1991) and his volume of *Nachträge* (Osnabrück: Universität Osnabrück, 1991). The Remarque Center in Osnabrück has produced excellent bibliographies for the individual works or groups of works, and their *Erich Maria Remarque Jahrbuch* keeps the current bibliography updated. See also C. R. Owen. *Erich Maria Remarque: A Critical Bio-Bibliography* (Amsterdam: Rodopi, 1984), which is extremely detailed.

[11] The film was based on *Ten Days to Die* by one of the judges at the Nuremberg trials, Michael A. Musmanno (London: Peter Davies, 1951) and was made in Austria; the lead actor Albin Skoda is impressive as Hitler. The writing credits are to Musmanno, Remarque, and also the writer Fritz Habeck. Remarque spoke of having written a "treatment" in a piece originally published in the London *Daily Express* for 30 April 1956 as "Be Vigilant!" and translated by Thomas Schneider in *Ein militanter Pazifist,* 96–101, in *Das unbekannte Werk,* vol. 4, 404–9, and in *Herbstfahrt,* 243–48. On the problems of the film, see Heinrich Placke, "Die politische Diskussion um den Remarque-Film *Der letzte Akt* (Österreich 1955)," *Jahrbuch* 6 (1995): 65–87. A film with the title *Hitler — The Last Ten Days,* made in 1973 with Alec Guiness as Hitler, is unconnected with Remarque.

[12] There are stills from the performance in Schneider, *Remarque,* 111–15. The English text is: *Full Circle,* adapted by Peter Stone (New York: Harcourt, Brace, Jovanovic, 1974).

[13] Remarque has been afforded an accolade granted to works like *Alice in Wonderland* and *Winnie-the-Pooh,* that of *Die Nacht von Lissabon* being translated into Latin: *De nocte Olisiponensi,* trans. Sigrid Albert (Saarbrücken: Societas Latina, 2002); Albert discusses it in the *Jahrbuch* 13 (2003): 93–94.

[14] Sternburg, *"Als wäre alles,"* 117; Hilton Tims, *Erich Maria Remarque: The Last Romantic* (London: Constable, 2003), 35.

[15] To Reinhold Neven Du Mont at Kiepenheuer and Witsch, dated 27 May 1968, *Das unbekannte Werk,* vol. 5, 227. The throwaway statement must at least be relativized.

[16] This idea sometimes seems to underlie works ostensibly concerned with the whole oeuvre: Alfred Antkowiak, *Erich Maria Remarque: Leben und Werke* ([Berlin: Volk und Wissen, 1965]; West Berlin: Das europäische Buch, 1983); Franz Baumer, *E. M. Remarque* (Berlin: Colloquium, 1970; 3d enl. ed., Berlin: Morgenbuch, 1994); Christine Barker and Rex Last, *Erich Maria Remarque* (London: Wolff, 1979) — the dust jacket also glosses Remarque as "Author of *All Quiet on the Western Front*"; Owen, *Bio-Bibliography;* Richard Arthur Firda, *Erich Maria Remarque: A Thematic Analysis of His Novels* (New York: Peter Lang, 1988); Harley U. Taylor, *Erich Maria Remarque: A Literary and Film Biography* (New York: Peter Lang, 1988); Hans Wagener, *Understanding Erich Maria Remarque* (Columbia, SC; U of South Carolina P, 1991. There are of course individual studies devoted to the novel itself. On the other hand, Richard Arthur Firda, *All Quiet on the Western Front: Literary Analysis and Cultural Context* (New York: Twayne, 1993) also examines Remarque's life and his other works, including the early ones.

[17] There is a useful *Kurzbiographie* in *Das unbekannte Werk*, vol. 5, 639–75, and the pictorial biography by Schneider also has a good chronological overview. The best biography, and one that integrates the works well, is Sternburg's *"Als wäre alles."* Tims, *Erich Maria Remarque,* is, as indicated, although a well-written and interesting work, less focused upon the literary work than on Remarque's sequence of frequently difficult and usually intense relationships with a wide range of beautiful ladies. Tims's subtitle, "The Last Romantic," is eye-catching, if not particularly informative: it derives from comments by Marlene Dietrich and Paulette Goddard, neither of whom was using the word in a cultural-historical sense, though it echoes several of his characters. Tims's dustjacket again carries the gloss: "Author of *All Quiet on the Western Front."* See also Julie Goldsmith Gilbert, *Opposite Attraction: The Lives of Erich Maria Remarque and Paulette Goddard* (New York: Pantheon, 1995) — the German translation has the subtitle *Biographie einer Liebe* (Biography of a Love Affair) (Düsseldorf: List, 1997).

[18] See Maria Riva, *Marlene Dietrich* (London: Bloomsbury, 1992), 486 and elsewhere. The Lancia plays quite a part in her tale, and she also refers to its role in *Drei Kameraden.*

[19] See Barker and Last, *Remarque,* 32, for details of the publication of extracts in the Nazi *Völkischer Beobachter* and in *Angriff,* and on the literary reaction to the work in general. Remarque commented on the incident in 1931–32 in a piece not published at the time: "Haben meine Bücher eine Tendenz," in *Ein militanter Pazifist,"* 62–65, and again in a piece that survives in English, translated as "Das Auge ist ein starker Verführer," from 1958, ibid., 102–6. Both are in *Das unbekannte Werk,* vol. 4, 320–23 and 410–14, and *Herbstfahrt,* 222–25 and 249–53. On the book burning, see *10. Mai 1933: Bücherverbrennung in Deutschland und die Folgen,* ed. Ulrich Walberer (Frankfurt am Main: Fischer Taschenbuch Verlag, 1983), 115; on the special problem that Remarque's popularity posed for his detractors, see *Literatur und Dichtung im Dritten Reich,* ed. Joseph Wulf (Reinbek bei Hamburg: Rowohlt, 1966), 54.

[20] See Baumer, *Remarque,* 66, on Remarque's reaction to the discrimination of Jewish refugees by the Swiss authorities after October 1938.

[21] Walter, *Exilliteratur*, 2, 296, points out that Remarque was financially well-off. See also Tims, *Remarque*, 119.

[22] *Elfriede Scholz, geb.: Remark: Im Namen des deutschen Volkes: Dokumente einer justitiellen Ermordung*, ed. Claudia Glunz and Thomas Schneider (Osnabrück: Universitätsverlag Rasch, 1995). See *Das unbekannte Werk*, vol. 5, 232, for a letter dated 31 December 1968 to the City Council of Osnabrück thanking them for the decision to name a street after his sister.

[23] See Sternburg, *"Als wäre alles,"* 431, for comments on the funeral (plus a slightly bemused statement from Marcel Reich-Ranicki). Sternburg's illustrations are between pp. 160 and 161, and 320 and 321. See Tims, *Remarque*, 237. The Iron Cross First Class was indeed awarded in November 1918, just after the Armistice, ratified by the Osnabrück Soldiers' Council. He is supposed to have bought the title by adoption in 1926 from an impoverished and childless title-holder. See Schneider, *Remarque*, 7 and 23. For an interesting series of contradictory truths about Remarque, some of them quite spectacular, see Armin Kerker, "Zwischen Innerlichkeit und Nacktkultur: Der unbekannte Remarque," *Die Horen* 19/Heft 3 (1974), 2–23, see 5–6. Several myths were squashed by Remarque himself, including the Kramer story, in a much-quoted interview with Axel Eggebrecht in 1929, reprinted in *Ein militanter Pazifist*, 43–51.

[24] Riva, *Marlene Dietrich*, 464–65. Tims, *Remarque*, 186, cites other opinions on the impotence question!

[25] There have been many studies of the film of *All Quiet on the Western Front*, and the title of Harley U. Taylor's study, *Erich Maria Remarque: A Literary and Film Biography* is also significant.

[26] Schneider, *Remarque*, 119, and Tims, *Remarque*, facing 113. The English version of the film uses the same title as the translation, which is further away from the echo of Ecclesiastes used by Remarque in his original (the biblical text contrasts a time *to be born* and a time to die). There have been several quite unconnected films called *A Time to Live and a Time to Die*.

[27] *Ein militanter Pazifist*, 48.

[28] *Das unbekannte Werk*, vol. 1, 574–75.

[29] See Schneider and Westphalen's notes, *Das unbekannte Werk*, vol. 1, 574, on the designation of *Gam*. In an interview with Friedrich Luft in 1963, Remarque is equally clear in his references to *Im Westen nichts Neues* as his first novel and *Der Weg zurück* as the second in "Das Profil," in *Ein militanter Pazifist*, 118–33, esp. 120.

[30] *Das unbekannte Werk*, vol. 5, 72. Remarque's later publisher, Ullstein, allegedly bought up all the remaining copies in 1929 and destroyed them. See *Das unbekannte Werk*, vol. 1, 563.

[31] The first edition was published in Dresden in 1920 by the Verlag der Schönheit; it is here cited from the reprint in: *Das unbekannte Werk*, vol. 1, 19–173. See the notes by Petra Oerke, 563–70 on the identification of some of the characters and the autobiographical links, and more extensively in her paper "'Geliebter Fritz': Entstehung und biographischer Hintergrund von Remarques erstem Roman *Die Traumbude*," in *Erich Maria Remarque: Leben, Werk und weltweite Wirkung*, ed. Thomas F. Schneider (Osnabrück: Rasch, 1998), 41–55. For full details of the publication his-

tory, see *Erich Maria Remarque: "Die Traumbude,"* etc., ed. Schneider and Weiss, 21–24. Beside the 1920 edition, that bibliography lists translations into Latvian and Russian (1930), Dutch (1931), and Bulgarian (1991) but not into English. Baumer, *Remarque*, 34, and Last and Barker, *Remarque*, 9, refer to a letter (probably written in the autumn of 1917) to his friend Georg Middendorf in which he speaks of writing a novel. This cannot have been *Die Traumbude*, as they surmise, however, except in a rudimentary form, because everything hinges upon the death of the central figure, and Hörstemeier did not die until the following year.

[32] Wagener, *Understanding*, 4, appears to think that they are Remarque's, although a note at the end of the work indicates that most are by Hörstemeier. Remarque's own poem "Ich und Du," which can be related to Hörstemeier, appeared in the journal *Die Schönheit* in 1918, and there is a facsimile in Kerker, "Innerlichkeit," 13. It is also in *Das unbekannte Werk*, vol. 4, 445.

[33] Martina Krause, "'. . . in den Fluten des radiumhaltigen Kleinstadtwassers': Erich Maria Remarque und Osnabrück," *Jahrbuch* 7 (1997): 27–72, see 31. There are photographs of Hörstemeier in Schneider, *Remarque*, 16–17. See Tims, *Remarque*, 29–30 on Lotte Preuss. One of the few serious analyses of the novel is by Richard Arthur Firda, "Young Remarque's *Traumbude*," *Monatshefte* 71 (1979): 49–55, and see the same author's *All Quiet*, 257.

[34] Antkowiak, *Remarque*, 9. Most surveys of Remarque's work pay scant attention to the work. Wagener has a brief plot summary, Barker and Last, and Tims even less. *Gam* is not mentioned by Tims and was not known to earlier critics.

[35] *Der Schwierige* (*A Difficult Man*) was first published in 1920 in serial form, with a full version in 1921. See the edition by W. E. Yates (Cambridge: CUP, 1966).

[36] See 97, 113, and 127. The relationship between Ernst and Lanna develops in terms of the song. The parallelism of *Carmen* and Remarque's novel would bear further investigation, although Prosper Merimée's story ends tragically. There is an element of the sentiment expressed in the *Habañera* in other women in Remarque's writing, such as the Lillian Dunkerque figure in her incarnations in "*Das Rennen Vanderveldes*" and in *Station am Horizont*, though not in *Der Himmel kennt keine Günstlinge*. Alex Aronson, *Music and the Novel* (Totowa, NJ: Rowman and Littlefield, 1980), 81–82, refers to Thomas Mann's use of the opera in *Der Zauberberg* (*The Magic Mountain*) in 1924.

[37] See for example Erich Heller's essay on "Rilke and Nietzsche" in his *The Disinherited Mind* (Harmondsworth: Penguin, 1961), 107–55, especially 120–21.

[38] Sternburg, *"Als wäre alles,"* 100. Sternburg makes further musical-operatic comparisons. The classic study of the relationship between love and death also appeared in 1920: Sigmund Freud's *Jenseits des Lustprinzips*, translated as *Beyond the Pleasure Principle*, trans. James Strachey (1928; New York: Bantam, 1967).

[39] On the European phenomenon see R. V. Johnson, *Aestheticism* (London: Methuen, 1969), and the useful summary in Gerhart Hoffmeister, *Deutsche und europäische Romantik* (Stuttgart: Metzler, 1978), 188–99. On Ruskin's moral aestheticism, see Jerome Hamilton Buckley, *The Victorian Temper*, rev. ed. (Cambridge, MA: Harvard UP, 1969), 143–60.

[40] *Gam,* in *Das unbekannte Werk,* vol. 1, 175–361. The sketch of the different male types is on 572–73. The sole critique of the novel — which has only recently become available — apart from Thomas Schneider's editorial notes to the edition — appears to be that by Sternburg in *"Als wäre alles,"* 124–30.

[41] Remarque did use the initials G. A. M. to sign articles in the 1920s, but this does not seem to be connected. No one seems to have any idea where this implausible female name came from. Sternburg, *"Als wäre alles,"* 129–30, notes that around this time Remarque met Jutta Ilse Zambona, whom he married in 1925, but a personal connection that might give a clue to the name is unclear. On women figures, see Mariana Parvanova, *". . . das Symbol der Ewigkeit ist der Kreis": Eine Untersuchung der Motive in den Romanen von Erich Maria Remarque* (Berlin: Tenea, 2003).

[42] Printed in double columns, the first installment has the clear heading: *Roman von Erich Maria Remarque* (novel by Erich Maria Remarque). See Schneider, *Remarque,* 39, for a facsimile.

[43] *Station am Horizont,* ed. Thomas F. Schneider and Tilman Westphalen (Cologne: Kiepenheuer and Witsch, 2000), 41. The same idea is used again in *Im Westen nichts Neues* when the central figure returns home on leave. See Schneider's afterword to the edition, 217–19, on the book publication.

ERICH MARIA REMARQUE

Im Westen nichts Neues

Remarques Buch ist das Denkmal
unseres unbekannten Soldaten
Von allen Toten geschrieben

Walter von Molo

German jacket, first edition of
Im Westen nichts Neues

Yiddish translation of
Im Westen nichts Neues

2: From the Frog's Perspective: *Im Westen nichts Neues* and *Der Weg zurück*

THE TITLE OF THIS CHAPTER, which considers Remarque's two novels of the First World War, is a literal translation of the German phrase *aus der Froschperspektive,* which is usually translated as "worm's eye view," although frogs, unlike worms, have harsh voices as well as eyes. Remarque treated the First World War in both novels from this perspective, and although the second of them is set for the most part after the cessation of hostilities, the war informs it so completely that *Der Weg zurück* (*The Road Back*), is not simply a sequel to *Im Westen nichts Neues* (*All Quiet on the Western Front*), but almost a second part of its famous predecessor.[1]

Im Westen nichts Neues made its first appearance in serial form in Germany in 1928, and then, with a great deal of sometimes not entirely truthful publicity (its composition and the revision process had taken longer than was claimed), in a slightly changed and expanded book version in January 1929. It sold a million copies by 1930,[2] was translated into an enormous number of languages,[3] and provoked personal attacks, parodies, and imitations. It remains a bestseller and has been filmed twice, both times in English, and the first version remains one of the classics of early sound cinema. When it was first shown in Berlin in 1930 it was famously disrupted, on the orders of Goebbels, by Nazi activists releasing mice.[4] Remarque was later condemned by the Nazis for "betraying the front-line soldier" and his novel was publicly burned in May 1933.[5]

The popularity of the novel seems sometimes to have baffled the critics. In 1985, for example, Jost Hermand wrote a piece with the revealing title "Versuch, den Erfolg von Erich Maria Remarques *Im Westen nichts Neues* zu verstehen" (An attempt to understand the success of Erich Maria Remarque's *Im Westen nichts Neues*), while a few years earlier, Alan Bance, having noted that "perhaps because of its phenomenal commercial success, it has received relatively little serious discussion," went on to state that "no one would want to claim for the novel a place in the ranks of first-class literature." But there precisely *is* a case for placing the work in the category of first-class literature. There is no critical law defining a great work as one that can be read or understood only by an intellectual elite, and the focus on the work as a commercial phenomenon has often distracted from proper considerations of style, structure, and content.[6]

Some basic misunderstandings were associated with *Im Westen nichts Neues* from the start. Some of the first critics assumed somewhat unreasonably (given the death of the narrator) that Remarque was completely identifiable with Paul Bäumer.[7] Of the literary responses — many of which appeared with covers imitating Remarque's novel — Klietmann's *Im Westen wohl was Neues* (Not Quiet on the Western Front) is the most extreme example of a parodistic attack (carrying the heading *Contra Remarque*), with Nickl's *"Im Westen nichts Neues" und sein wahrer Sinn* (The True Meaning of "All Quiet on the Western Front") the most nationalistic and anti-Semitic in its attack on the publisher, Ullstein. Otto's *Im Osten nichts Neues* (All Quiet on the Eastern Front) is a simple imitation, and *Vor Troja nichts Neues* (All Quiet on the Trojan Front) by "Emil Marius Requark" a not uninventive parody that manages one or two telling blows against the marketing strategy adopted for the work.[8] The influence of Remarque's novel was enormous, not only in German, as is clear even from the novel title *Not so Quiet . . .* by Evadne Price, for example, writing as Helen Zenna Smith in 1930.[9]

In 1931 Remarque published *Der Weg zurück*. The first war novel is set in 1917 and 1918, and its sequel begins with a prologue set immediately after, and referring to, the death of the narrator of *Im Westen nichts Neues* in October 1918. The main part takes place in 1919, immediately following the last month of the war, although an epilogue takes us briefly into 1920. The work is set, then, in the period of the establishment of the Weimar Republic.[10] The new first-person narrator is so similar to that of the first novel in name, background, and attitude that he could be Bäumer brought back to life, but this reinforces the point that the young soldiers of the First World War were both representative *and* individual. *Der Weg zurück* did not meet with the same enthusiasm as the first war novel, although it too was widely translated and also filmed.

Both novels are part of an international body of literature concerned with the war and produced in the late 1920s and early 1930s. The universality of the experience of the trenches was emphasized by the appearance in Germany during the Weimar period not only of many native novels, but of German translations of numbers of war novels from abroad. Most of the contemporary German war novels, even the more obscure ones, were also translated into English, French, and other languages. In Germany the novels included both pacifist anti-war works and novels that took the opposite stance and presented the war as a heroic, and as a testing and strengthening of German virtues in the storm of steel.[11] The emergence of the pacifist *Im Westen nichts Neues* as the leading war novel in an international context is all the more impressive.

Im Westen nichts Neues

That a historical event of the magnitude of the First World War, which cost around ten million lives from most nations of the world, could be encapsulated to any extent in a novel the paperback edition of which has little more than two hundred pages is an achievement in itself.[12] The fact that the body of the novel is a convincingly presented first-person narrative means that it *does* still need to be spelled out that Bäumer is not Remarque, who drew without doubt upon his own experiences in the war and at home in Osnabrück. But *Im Westen nichts Neues* is a work of fiction, and most importantly it has only one character. With two small but significant exceptions, the young soldier Paul Bäumer delivers the work directly to the reader, and therefore everything we see or hear is through him. It testifies to Remarque's skill that Bäumer remains consistent throughout the work, and it is Bäumer's character and background that dictates the style.[13] The choice of a narrator is significant; because Bäumer, drafted in 1916, was still a schoolboy in 1914, he bears no personal responsibility for the war itself, nor indeed does he understand much about it. Equally, Remarque does not permit him any prescience (although of course he speculates) about what happens *after* the war. This has an effect on the way in which other figures are presented to us, and criticism has been leveled at the book for the apparent one-sidedness of some of the characters encountered, or for the limited view of the fighting troops. But since they are all presented through Bäumer, his close friends would clearly be in far sharper focus than an anonymous and unpleasant major, or even an attractive French girl met on one occasion only. Bäumer would in reality have been unlikely to know the names of either of them. Nor would he have had much of a view of the war beyond company level, and his immediate experience with senior or even junior officers would be limited. The most senior officer glimpsed in the work is in fact Kaiser Wilhelm, when he comes to review the troops, but apart from one major and his own second lieutenant, Bäumer mentions no one else above the noncommissioned ranks. *Im Westen nichts Neues,* and to an extent the sequel, seem by this approach to claim the advantages of a diary — that is, its immediacy — with none of the drawbacks of a precise chronology, and Bäumer (and Birkholz in *Der Weg zurück*) present their thoughts, experiences, and reflections directly to the reader.[14]

The individual private soldier Paul Bäumer nevertheless sees himself for most of the novel as part of a group, so that it is the first person plural that predominates much of the work, and the move away from it at the end to Bäumer as an individual gains in significance thereby. Nor, of course, must we forget Remarque as the (concealed) structuring author behind the character, controlling the work as a whole in the variation in chapter lengths, or in the balance of action and periods of inaction, of reported discussion and private reflection. Remarque allows Bäumer to send signals to the reader to consider how single events need to be multiplied by thousands, for example, or indications that a particular train of thought will be able to be taken to a logical conclusion only after the war.

It is also sometimes overlooked that *Im Westen nichts Neues* is not a contemporary account of the First World War. Although both novels contain episodes based upon historical reality,[15] *Im Westen nichts Neues* was not written in 1918, but in 1928, recreating within the Weimar Republic events that had happened ten or more years before, even if those events were part of the experience of many of those living in the new postwar German state. *Im Westen nichts Neues* is historical fiction, and so is *Der Weg zurück,* although by the time of the latter, the sense that history was moving on was more apparent.[16] That Remarque chose to set the two novels during and just after the war itself means that they cannot be historically reflective in themselves, but both raise questions to which the narrator was never in a position to give answers. The burden of finding answers is thus placed upon the reader, whether in 1930 or in the present, and wherever he or she may be responding to the work.[17] In the first instance the target audience was the Weimar Republic itself, because both novels reflect the shared history of those reaching maturity in a postwar Germany that was already beginning to look insecure. But they were addressed, also, to the contemporary world, sending out a specifically pacifist message to Germany's former enemies. Beside these two time levels — that of the action and that of the contemporary reception — stands a third, the time of the present reader. They are addressed also to an international posterity and remain important in their general implications.

There are two places in *Im Westen nichts Neues* in which Bäumer is not in control of the narrative. There is a prefatory statement by the author that was omitted in some translations and appears in others with a significant variation from the text of the first German edition. It may be cited in German from a prepublication version, with the translation by A. W. Wheen, who included it in full in his 1929 translation; the sentence in italics was left out of the first German book edition:[18]

> Dieses Buch soll weder eine Anklage noch ein Bekenntnis, *vor allem aber kein Erlebnis* sein, *denn der Tod ist kein Erlebnis für den, der ihm gegenübersteht.* Es soll nur den Versuch machen, über eine Generation zu berichten, die vom Kriege zerstört wurde; — auch wenn sie seinen Granaten entkam.

> [This book is to be neither an accusation nor a confession, and least of all an adventure, for death is not an adventure to those who stand face to face with it. It will try simply to tell of a generation of men who, even though they may have escaped its shells, were destroyed by the war.]

The statement in its original form was necessary because there were many examples of literature that did present the war in that light. More importantly though, it categorizes the work as a *Bericht*, a report, reminding us that although the fictive narrator would have been dead for ten years when the book appeared, other soldiers had survived. As a parallel with this opening statement, the final half-dozen lines of the novel are spoken by a new third-person narrator within the historical fictionality of the book, commenting on the death of Bäumer.

It was argued early in the criticism of the novel that the presentation of the war by a single individual could not portray a valid picture of the war.[19] There are various responses to this: one is that the first person in the novel is, as indicated, frequently the plural *wir*, so that Bäumer speaks for other soldiers and their experiences. Furthermore, even the notion of "other soldiers" can mean a variety of things, ranging from just Bäumer and Katczinsky (Kat), his mentor, to his immediate groups of school or platoon comrades, to his company, to the German army, or even the Germans as a whole. Refining it again, it might refer to the ordinary German soldier, or indeed to the ordinary soldier as such. Remarque permits Bäumer and his comrades to stress their representative status by pointing out that most of the soldiers of all countries are also ordinary people, and also by introducing overtly what might be seen as a multiplication factor at key points. Thus Bäumer says of the teacher, Kantorek, who had bullied them into signing up: "Es gab ja Tausende von Kantoreks" (18, there were thousands of Kantoreks), and more significantly towards the end of the novel, of the military hospital, which shows the true measure of war: "es gibt Hunderttausende in Deutschland, Hunderttausende in Frankreich, Hunderttausende in Russland . . ." (177, there are hundreds of thousands of them in Germany, hundreds of thousands of them in France, hundreds of thousands of them in Russia).

The *Froschperspektive* need not, then, be as restricted as it might appear.[20] But the narrator is also an individual; wars may be expressed in terms of the often unimaginably large numbers of those who fought or were killed, but such statistics are always made up of individuals. Remarque reduces the *wir* element gradually throughout the work in parallel to what was a war of attrition that ultimately reached the single individual, when at the end Paul Bäumer is not just left alone, but is thrown onto his own inner resources without support from any side. The ultimate expression of Bäumer's existentialist realization of the nature of life in the face of the extreme situation of war links this work with Remarque's oeuvre as a whole.

The fictional time of the novel begins in 1917, well after the outbreak of the war, and the reader is aware of time — more specifically of the seasons — passing until October 1918. Bäumer's own thoughts and conversations with others take the reader back to earlier periods, but in the fictional present the deadly monotony and constant attrition is completely established. The first chapter begins with *wir,* which refers on this occasion to a company of 150 men, just back from what was supposed to be a quiet sector after heavy losses, and with only eighty survivors. The battle has not been an important one, and the reason for the losses is casually put:

> Nun aber gab es gerade am letzten Tage bei uns überraschend viel Langrohr und dicke Brocken, englische Artillerie, die ständig auf unsere Stellung trommelte, so daß wir starke Verluste hatten und nur mit achtzig Männer zurückkamen. (11)

> [But then, on the very last day we were taken by surprise by long-range shelling from the heavy artillery. The English guns kept on pounding our position, so we lost a lot of men, and only eighty of us came back.]

The slang (*Langrohr und dicke Brocken* cannot really be imitated in translation) and the offhand manner of describing the death of nearly half the company is striking, and even more so is the stress on the pure mischance that there just happened to be unexpected heavy shellfire. The impression is one of passivity. The role of Bäumer and the other ordinary soldiers as victims rather than warriors is immediately established.

The first person plural now shifts to two smaller groups: Bäumer and three former classmates, Kropp, Müller, and Leer, who have joined the army straight from high school, then four more friends who were workers — Tjaden, a locksmith; Westhus, a peat-digger; Detering, a farmer; and finally Katczinsky, the father figure of the group, who is already forty and who is presented as someone with enormous capabilities for spotting and avoiding trouble and for finding things that are needed. We have, therefore, a cross section of those fighting at the lowest and largest level, although, for different reasons, none of them understands precisely why they are fighting.

Paul Bäumer is nineteen when the action of *Im Westen nichts Neues* begins, and we learn that he joined up directly from a *Gymnasium* (classical high school). He is educated along traditional lines, is thoughtful, but does not have enough experience to draw full conclusions, especially since he has been thrust into the extreme situation of war. The consistency of the character is made clear in numerous small ways: when wounded and on a hospital train, he is still too embarrassed to ask a nurse when he needs to relieve himself, although he has been under heavy shellfire. On another occasion he describes how Tjaden, his ex-locksmith friend, insults their drill corporal, Himmelstoss, who has been sent to the front: "Tjaden erwidert gelassen und abschliessend, ohne es zu wissen, mit dem bekanntesten Klassikerzitat. Gleichzeitig lüftet er seine Kehrseite" (64, Tjaden gives an unworried and conclusive reply, quoting, though he doesn't know he's doing so, one of Goethe's best-known lines, the one about kissing a specific part of his anatomy. At the same time he sticks his backside up in the air). The quotation is from Goethe's *Götz von Berlichingen,* and it is often truncated in print anyway, though the sense ("you can kiss my ass") is clear and is here even made graphic. The passage is difficult to translate, because the quotation is not known in English, but the real point of Bäumer's report of this small incident is that Tjaden has used the literal expression, but does not know about any literary allusions. Bäumer, on the other hand, uses the literary reference to avoid actually saying what Tjaden has said, and even in describing Tjaden's gesture he uses a euphemism. Bäumer notes several times that everything they learned at school has now become worthless, and this is true; but he cannot escape from his background.[21]

Im Westen nichts Neues presents the war as such being shown with the vivid and deliberately shocking realism associated with the term *neue Sachlichkeit* (new objectivity). The approach here and in many comparable war novels is a quasi-documentary one, but the style is not only one of objective authenticity.[22] The structure is episodic, something that would become a hallmark of Remarque's novels, holding the interest by moving rapidly from one scene to another and alternating the kinds of scenes presented, while picking up themes from one episode to another in twelve chapters that vary in content, emphasis, and length. This enables the work to present a wide range of experiences of the war: we see the soldiers recovering behind the lines, visiting and being treated in a military hospital, on wiring duty, on reconnaissance patrol, under fire in a dugout, going over the top and attacking another trench, going on leave. Further experiences, including a soldiers' brothel, are filled in by *Der Weg zurück*. Movement from the immediate present to the remembered past also enables Bäumer to give us scenes of basic training as well.

The first three chapters are set behind the lines, the work opening with an apparently trivial incident in which Bäumer and his associates receive a double ration of food; we soon discover, however, that it is because they have just sustained the loss of half of the company, and the attrition continues when the reinforcements sent to bring them back to strength are raw recruits, who fall in large numbers. Discussions between the soldiers take us back to the training period under the martinet Himmelstoss as drill corporal, and then in the third chapter the soldiers recollect the satisfactory revenge that they had taken, beating him up when he is drunk, and thus utilizing the pragmatism of violence that he has instilled in them, and in fact is vital for their survival. Revenge on the noncommissioned officer (NCO) is probably part of the fantasy of any soldier, and it certainly has literary antecedents in German.[23] The character of Himmelstoss, however, is developed in the work. Initially frightened when forced to go into battle, he is shamed into gathering his courage, and eventually becomes friendly towards the former recruits. The first two chapters each end, however, with a visit to one of Bäumer's school-friends, Fritz Kemmerich, who is badly wounded in a field hospital in the first, and dead by the end of the second.

Various key themes are voiced in these early chapters. Attention has been paid to a comment by Bäumer describing the feeling of solidarity engendered first by their training, which "im Felde dann zum Besten steigerte, was der Krieg hervorbrachte: zur Kameradschaft" (27–28, grew, on the battlefield, into the best thing that the war produced — comradeship in arms). It is possible to make too much of this comment, and most certainly the development of a close comradeship is not to be taken as a justification for the war; it is just that the war, as an extreme situation, permits it to develop more strongly. The comradeship in *Im Westen nichts Neues* is born of mutual help in battle, and in *Der Weg zurück* Remarque would make clear that while it is a necessity in war, it does not necessarily always survive in peacetime. Equally important is a motif first voiced at the end of the third chapter, in response to someone's reference to them as *eiserne Jugend* (22, iron youth), Bäumer comments that none of them is young, even if they are only nineteen or twenty. Their youth has been taken away from them, and they feel that they are — this is a common literary motif with other writers, too — a betrayed, a lost generation.[24]

The novel now shows the young soldiers in action, first on duty laying barbed wire, and then, after a further period behind the lines, in the field, although we rarely see the soldiers engaged in actual fighting. The episode when they are laying wire shows them being fired upon, rather than firing. Various striking incidents remain in the mind from this section of the work: the young recruit who loses control of his bowels under fire; the slow and grotesque death of a horse (in a scene that once again has literary parallels before and after Remarque), a gas attack, and the fact that the men come under fire in a cemetery and have to take cover against death among the graves and coffins of the fairly recently dead (a sleeve is apparently still intact on one of the bodies). The symbolism of the cemetery scene is clear enough, but it is not gratuitous, nor grotesque sensationalism, as has been suggested.[25] In this incident, too, the young recruit from the earlier scene who soiled himself under fire, is fatally wounded. Kat wants to shoot the horribly wounded soldier, but cannot do so because other soldiers are around. The irony in his being prevented from mercy killing, when they are forced to kill otherwise, is underlined again in the reaction of Detering, the farmer, who wants to shoot the wounded horse, but cannot, because this would draw fire upon them.

The fifth chapter, which contains the arrival of Himmelstoss at the front and Tjaden's insult, is set behind the lines, again a respite from the horrors of the previous chapter. A discussion between the young soldiers focuses upon the realization of the high school recruits that their knowledge has become worthless and they are now unable to think beyond the war. The atmosphere of a more or less flippant conversation gradually gives way to something close to despair in Bäumer's thoughts. He reports one of his friends as saying: "Der Krieg hat uns für alles verdorben" (67, the war has ruined us for everything), and sums up for the reader — in the Weimar Republic and afterwards — their collective state of mind, developing the idea of the loss of youth: "Wir sind keine Jugend mehr. Wir wollen die Welt nicht mehr stürmen. Wir sind Flüchtende.[. . .] . . . wir glauben an den Krieg" (67, We're no longer young men. We've lost any desire to conquer the world. We are refugees . . . we believe in the war). The chapter concludes, however, with a scene in which the ever-resourceful Kat, aided by Bäumer, requisitions — steals — a couple of geese and roasts them. The incident may have adventurous, or even comic elements, but the long process of cooking the geese permits Bäumer to think further, and to comment for the benefit of the reader upon what he has become. He and his older mentor are close, and although Kat, too, will fall before the end of the work, for the moment Bäumer is aware of them both simply as "zwei Menschen, zwei winzige Funken Leben, draußen ist die Nacht und der Kreis des Todes" (72, two human beings, two tiny sparks of life; outside there is just the night, and all around us, death). That spark of life — possibly the most important recurrent theme in Remarque's novels — will survive in Bäumer to the end.

The central sixth chapter is one of the longest in the work, two dozen pages in the standard paperback, as against the final chapter, which is barely two pages long, and although it does show the soldiers fighting, the concept of the soldier as victim as well as aggressor is maintained. The precise nature of the enemy is important, too. The realistically presented fighting makes a deliberate assault on all of the senses, in particular that of hearing. The massive and permanent noise of war is probably the feature that those who experienced it recollected most.

> Plötzlich heult und blitzt es ungeheuer, der Unterstand kracht in allen Fugen unter einem Treffer, glücklicherweise einem leichten, dem die Betonklötze standgehalten haben. Es klirrt metallisch und fürchterlich, die Wände wackeln, Gewehre, Helme, Erde, Dreck und Staub fliegen. Schwefeliger Qualm dringt ein. (81)

> [Suddenly there is a terrible noise and flash of light, and every joint in the dugout creaks under the impact of a direct hit — luckily not a heavy one, and one that the concrete blocks could withstand. There is a fearsome metallic rattling, the walls shake, rifles, steel helmets, earth, mud, and dust fly around. Sulphurous fumes penetrate the walls.]

Cinema audiences in the early 1930s were horrified when films with a realistic soundtrack were first shown. The sound of war in particular, but also sight, feeling, and smell are all invoked in a chapter that makes clear the physical aspects of frontline warfare. The soldiers fight like automata when they go over the top, and they suffer from *Unterstandsangst* otherwise, driven crazy in the confinements of a dugout under heavy shelling. A severely wounded man calls out constantly for some days, but cannot be reached, large numbers of untrained recruits, referred to as *Kinder* (children), are killed, as are some of Bäumer's friends. Tjaden, however, has to be stopped from trying to knock the fuse off a dud shell; a natural survivor, he appears in *Der Weg zurück*, the only member of the group to do so. The novel began with the return of eighty out of 150 men, and this chapter, at the halfway point, ends with the return of only thirty-two. In terms of actual plot, the ironic major achievement in this part of the offensive is the welcome capture of five cans of corned beef.

The physical realism is balanced by Bäumer's thoughts. In an earlier chapter, the front was for Bäumer a whirlpool, sucking him in as a helpless victim, and now it is a cage, again an image of external entrapment, while later on it will be an inescapable fever. Dominating everything is *Zufall* (chance), another key theme throughout the work. An indifferent universe can inflict upon any human being what it will, and in the war a bullet may strike at any time, which leaves the soldier believing in chance and chance alone. The soldiers themselves become not men but dangerous animals, who fight to stay alive, something that also — significantly — distances their actions from those of hatred for any specific human enemy.

> Aus uns sind gefährliche Tiere geworden. Wir kämpfen nicht, wir verteidigen uns vor der Vernichtung. Wir schleudern die Granaten nicht gegen Menschen, was wissen wir im Augenblick davon, dort hetzt mit Händen und Helmen der Tod hinter uns her . . . (83)
>
> [We have turned into dangerous animals. We are not fighting, we are defending ourselves from annihilation. We are not hurling our grenades against human beings — what do we know about all that in the heat of the moment? — the hands and the helmets that are after us belong to Death itself . . .]

The breathless style of the passage is noteworthy, and the length of the chapter also underlines the comments by Bäumer that the horror seems to go and on with no sign of relief. Episodic variation permits us to see periods of waiting, which can be as bad as the fighting, killing rats, and preventing the dugout-crazy recruits from running out into the open. There are calmer moments — at one point two butterflies are seen near their trenches — but the return is always to the fighting, until the few remaining exhausted soldiers return behind the lines.

The next chapter matches this in length; after a brief incident when some of them visit some French girls, Bäumer returns home on leave, and is confronted with his now unimaginably distant earlier life. Here he has to cope with the uncomprehending worries of his dying mother, and with the differently uncomprehending attitudes first of the military — an unpleasant major is critical of Bäumer's *Frontsitten* (front line manners) — and of civilians, as a group of well-meaning middle-aged men at an inn instruct him on what the army ought to do. Neither the major nor the civilians have any idea of the realities of life at the front, which have just been shown so graphically to the reader. Bäumer also has to report to Franz Kemmerich's mother how he died, swearing (ironically) on his own life that Kemmerich died instantly. Bäumer and the others may feel that they are no longer young, but Kemmerich's mother reminds us sharply of the real situation when she asks why "you children" are out there. The conclusion Bäumer draws is that he should never have gone on leave.

A brief interlude in which Bäumer is detailed to guard some Russian prisoners of war reminds us that this was a war on more than one front, and is followed by a return to his unit and the ceremonial visit by the Kaiser, which provides occasion for the soldiers to discuss the nature of the war once again. It is followed, however, by a reconnaissance patrol in which Bäumer kills in terror a French soldier — the only enemy soldier seen closely, and certainly the only one named, Gérard Duval — against whom he is quite literally thrown in a shell hole and whom he stabs. His experience, trapped in no man's land while Duval dies slowly, brings Bäumer close to madness as he realizes that this is a real person, with a name and a family. While trapped with the dying French soldier, Bäumer makes promises to him, declaring that "Es darf nie wieder geschehen" (154, It must never happen again). That last statement is directed at the outside world, of course, from a Weimar Republic concerned to remove the image of Germany as the aggressor. However, when he finds his way back to his own trench, Bäumer is made to watch a sniper at work, and to find a kind of comfort in the circular notion that *Krieg ist Krieg,* war is war. That might during the war itself be enough, but whether it would work afterwards is left open.

The original version of the prefatory statement warned against seeing war as an adventure, and that criticism has been leveled at the incident when Bäumer and his comrades are placed in charge of a food supply dump. They take advantage of this and organize a feast, but Bäumer points out the need for the soldiers to seize any opportunity of light relief, contextualizing this passage as a respite, rather than as an adventure. It is the same reflex action that makes the soldiers use jokey slang evasions for the idea of being killed. The meal, which gives the participants diarrhea, is conducted under heavy shellfire, and immediately afterwards Bäumer and others are wounded and hospitalized, giving him the opportunity to see and to comment upon for the reader another aspect of the war. He enumerates soberly and in detail the various types of wounds — a long list of all the places in which a man can be hit by a bullet — and notes that this is the real indicator of the reality of war: "Erst das Lazarett zeigt, was Krieg ist (177, only a military hospital can really show you what war is).

Bäumer's mood seems to reach complete despair in the two final short chapters. The penultimate chapter is still characterized by the *wir* opening: "Wir zählen die Wochen nicht mehr" (183, we've stopped counting the weeks), but not many of Bäumer's friends are left, and the war seems never-ending. Again some incidents stand out: the farmer Detering's apparent desertion, although he is actually heading homewards towards his farm, rather than trying to escape to the Netherlands; the attempt, also caused by front-line madness, by another soldier to rescue a wounded dog. The horrors of war have been shown in telegrammatic enumeration at earlier points, and here again the style sounds almost like an expressionist poem by, say, August Stramm:[26]

> Granaten, Gasschwaden und Tankflottillen — Zerstampfen, Zerfressen, Tod.
> Ruhr, Gruppe, Typhus — Würgen, Verbrennen, Tod. Graben, Lazarett, Massengrab — mehr Möglichkeiten gibt es nicht. (190)

> [Shells, gas clouds and flotillas of tanks — crushing, devouring, death.
> Dysentery, influenza, typhus — choking, scalding, death.
> Trench, hospital, mass grave — there are no other possibilities.]

A further stylistic variation stressing the apparent endlessness of the war is seen in a sequence of four paragraphs beginning: *Sommer 1918* (Summer 1918), full of the desire not to be killed at this late stage, coupled with the desperate feeling that surely it has to end soon?

Bäumer is still able to voice comments on the nature of the war, castigating the profiteers, for example: "Die Fabrikbesitzer in Deutschland sind reiche Leute geworden — uns zerschrinnt die Ruhr die Därme" (188, the factory owners in Germany have grown rich, while dysentery racks our guts). He also comments on why the war is ending for the German army. It is simply because they are tired and hungry, yet are faced with a well-provisioned and stronger opposition force — America had finally joined the war in 1917, and the allied blockade had affected supplies to Germany itself. But the German army, says Bäumer — and the *wir* voice is highly significant here — has not been defeated in a purely military sense:

> Wir sind nicht geschlagen, denn wir sind als Soldaten besser und erfahrener; wir sind einfach von der vielfachen Übermacht zerdrückt und zurückgeschoben. (192)

> [We haven't been defeated, because as soldiers we are better and more experienced; we have simply been crushed and pushed back by forces many times superior to ours.]

Historically Germany had in any real terms been defeated; but Bäumer's wartime interpretation, while certainly not in line with the famous notion that she had been "stabbed in the back" by left-wing political forces (the *Dolchstosslegende*),[27] may still have struck a chord with the former soldiers in the Weimar Republic who were the first audience for the book. The Nazis, who accused the work of insulting the front-line soldier, presumably overlooked this passage. Remarque himself, however, was specific enough on Germany's actual defeat later, and in a piece written in 1944 he criticized the plethora of books published in the years after the First World War with titles like *Im Felde unbesiegt* (Undefeated in Battle). In *Der Weg zurück* the idea is neatly countered when the new narrator thinks of an essay he wrote at school on the subject of why Germany is bound to win, and considers that the low grade it received was probably about right in the circumstances.[28]

Juxtaposed with the comments and thoughts of Bäumer in the penultimate chapter is a quickening of the final attrition, as the last of his friends are killed. Müller leaves to Bäumer the boots he had inherited from Kemmerich, and which became probably the most commented-upon motif in the work — Tjaden will get them next, and he of course survives.[29] Then Kat is killed by a random piece of shrapnel while Bäumer is carrying him to a dressing station to have another minor wound treated. The loss of the man with whom he had shared the moment of isolation in the battlefield as the spark of life leaves him with an immense feeling of isolation, and means that Bäumer is alone in a final two-page chapter.

Had they returned in 1916, Bäumer thinks that they could have unleashed a revolution — the idea will be developed in other novels — but now he feels that there is weariness without hope. However, this state of mind gives way fairly suddenly to a new attitude: this might, he thinks, just be a transitory melancholy, the trees are green, there is much talk of peace, and he himself becomes very calm: "Ich bin sehr ruhig" (197). Whatever happens, there will be inside him an independent spark of life that will carry him onwards, whether his own individuality wants it or not. Bäumer has used the *wir* voice a great deal, but now he is forced into the first person singular as the last survivor of his group. Beyond this, his thoughts move still further away from the individual that he has become to focus on the independent life force, from the *ich* to the *es*. "Aber so lange es [das Leben] da ist, wird es sich seinen Weg suchen, mag dieses was in mir 'ich' sagt, wollen oder nicht" (197, but as long as life is there it will make it own way, whether my conscious self likes it or not).

But things go further. Bäumer is killed, and now he is completely objectivized as *er*, seen by a third party. His death is as random as Kat's in reality, although in literary terms we recall his promise to Kemmerich's mother that he may not return if he is not telling the truth, and there is also perhaps a sense of expiation for the death of the French soldier. He dies in October 1918, on a day when there is — hence the title — "nichts Neues zu melden" (197, nothing new to report). It is difficult to stress enough the importance of this final section of the novel, in which an objective observer not only reports the death, but speculates on Bäumer's mind at the end: he looked, he tells us, "als wäre er beinahe zufrieden damit, daß es so gekommen war" (197, as if he were almost happy that it had turned out that way). The subjunctive "as if he were" and the qualifier "almost" are both warnings that this is only speculation. The reader has been privy to Bäumer's actual thoughts and experiences, and may well think differently. Of course there will always be an ambiguity: no one can know whether another individual was content to have died at any point. Nor, of course, do we know what happens next: there is no indication of whether Bäumer even believed in an afterlife, let alone whether he now enters one, and the work, like most of Remarque's, is agnostic in that sense.

Im Westen nichts Neues provokes thought about the nature of war in various different ways. The most obvious is the direct presentation of the horrors: parts of bodies hanging in trees, the wounded soldier calling out from no man's land, the slow gurgling death of the French soldier. Sometimes the telegrammatic lists of forms of attack, or weapons, or types of wounds make their point. The reader is, however, also prompted to consider the nature of war by being privy to the inconclusive and often humorous discussions by the young or uneducated soldiers. Thus when the visit of the Kaiser leads to a discussion between the *Gymnasium* pupils and the working-class soldiers of how wars come about, one of the former declares that wars happen when one country insults another. The answer comes that it is impossible for a mountain to insult another mountain; when this is countered by the fact that a nation can be insulted, Tjaden — not one of the high school group — points out that he does not feel insulted and should therefore not be there. The only people to profit from war, the soldiers feel at this point, are those like the Kaiser, who need a famous victory. Of course there is no conclusion. Müller comments that it is better that the war should be fought in France than in Germany, and Tjaden responds that the best of all would be no war at all. Eventually a consensus is reached that the discussion is pointless because it will change nothing. This may be true in the immediate historical context; the message to the Weimar reader, though, is that perhaps things might be changed.

Sometimes Bäumer's comments are addressed directly to the reader. In the second chapter the soldiers visit Franz Kemmerich, who is dying in a field hospital, and Baumer thinks:

> Da liegt er nun, weshalb nur? Man sollte die ganze Welt an diesem Bette vorbeiführen und sagen: Das ist Franz Kemmerich, neunzehneinhalb Jahre alt, er will nicht sterben. Lasst ihn nicht sterben! (29)

> [Now he is lying there — and for what reason? Everybody in the whole world ought to be made to walk past his bed and be told: "This is

Franz Kemmerich, he's nineteen and a half, and he doesn't want to die! Don't let him die!"]

The novel has done precisely what Bäumer has asked: the world has been led past that bed. Later, when he is in a *Lazarett* (military hospital) himself, Bäumer makes a personal statement that gradually develops into a philosophical attitude to the war as a whole:

> Ich bin jung, ich bin zwanzig Jahre alt; aber ich kenne vom Leben nichts anderes als die Verzweiflung, den Tod, die Angst und die Verkettung sinnlosester Oberflächlichkeit mit einem Abgrund des Leidens. Ich sehe, dass Völker gegeneinander getrieben werden und sich schweigend, unwissend, töricht, gehorsam, unschuldig töten. (177)

> [I am young, I am twenty years of age; but I know nothing of life except despair, death, fear, and the combination of completely mindless superficiality with an abyss of suffering. I see people being driven against one another, and silently, uncomprehendingly, foolishly, and obediently and innocently killing one another.]

Most striking is the idea of the victim as killer, the paradoxical *unschuldig töten* (innocently killing). These almost exculpatory words are again clearly directed at the ex-soldiers who survived the war. Bäumer also wonders how the older generation would react if they called them to account. This, too, is what the novel is doing.

Often Bäumer himself is unable to think things through because, since he is actually in the war, those conclusions would lead to madness.[30] For the time being he is forced to cling to the circular statement that "war is war"; sometimes, however, Bäumer decides consciously to store up ideas for later, and thus Remarque permits him to present ideas directly to the later readership. When on guard-duty over the Russian prisoners, for example, he has time to speculate.

> Ein Befehl hat diese stille Gestalten zu unseren Feinden gemacht; ein Befehl könnte sie in unsere Freude verwandeln. An irgendeinem Tisch wird ein Schriftstück von einigen Leuten unterzeichnet, die keiner von uns kennt; und jahrelang ist unser höchstes Ziel das, worauf sonst die Verachtung der Welt und ihre höchste Strafe ruht. (134)

> [An order has turned these silent figures into our enemies; an order could turn them into friends again. On some table, a document is signed by some people that none of us knows, and for years our main aim in life is the one thing that usually draws the condemnation of the whole world and incurs its severest punishment in law.]

Bäumer stops: "Hier darf ich nicht weiterdenken" (I mustn't think along those lines any more), but the importance of this passage for the novel and for Weimar is clear. The distancing from responsibility is as marked as the inclusivity implied by the first person plural, and the questions of guilt and murder will be raised in *Der Weg zurück* and elsewhere. The question of responsibility for war on an individual basis, however, is not addressed until we reach the Second World War and *Zeit zu leben, und Zeit zu sterben*,[31] by which time conditions for Germany were very different.

A war implies an enemy. For Bäumer, however, the principal enemy faced by all soldiers is death itself, and after that the bullying noncommissioned officers of their own army. The declared enemy — the British or French soldiers — are usually invisible, although we are aware of their guns. Bäumer himself meets only the *poilu* Duval and the Russian prisoners of war whom he guards. The absence of a specific enemy was a programmatic policy message for the Weimar Republic. The consistent portrayal of Bäumer as a victim, who was too young to be involved even with the hysteria associated with the outbreak in 1914, and who understands little and can influence even less, is also appropriate to the novel's Weimar context and to the generation that survived the war. The Weimar Republic welcomed the realistic and graphic presentation of the horrors of the war in a way that showed the participants free of responsibility, if not of guilt. Other unresponsible and even guilt-free narrators and protagonists in Weimar anti-war novels of the period include stretcher bearers, women, children, or schoolboys too young to join up, and most extreme of all, but most clearly a participant who is an innocent victim of bestial humanity, Liesl the mare, used as the narrator in Ernst Johannsen's unjustly forgotten *Fronterinnerungen eines Pferdes* (Front Line Memoirs of a Horse).[32] What unites all these involved narrators is the complete lack of awareness of the reasons for war as such, or for this war.

Im Westen nichts Neues needs more than any of Remarque's later works to be located in various contexts, first of all in the genre of the war novel. This itself, however, requires some subdivision: *Im Westen nichts Neues* is a novel about the First World War, but not one written either during that war, like Henri Barbusse's *Le Feu* (*Under Fire*), or just afterwards, such as Ernst Jünger's *In Stahlgewittern* (*Storm of Steel*), nor, on the other hand, at a historical distance so far removed as to be completely divorced from the actual experience (as with recent novels by, for example, Pat Barker). It is a historical novel addressing as its first audience Germans who shared the experiences presented in the work and survived, and it can be contextualized therefore as Weimar literature and hence is a German novel for reasons other than the simply linguistic. As one of the many novels produced at around the same time that took a similarly pacifist and anti-war stance, however, it is both national and international. *Im Westen nichts Neues* is a German novel in that it shows us German soldiers worn down to what amounts to a defeat in 1918. The war in the novel has no beginning, nor do we see the end, because Bäumer dies before the armistice, so that questions of responsibility and indeed of whether or not Germany was ultimately defeated are not raised. It is also worth noting — though the Nazi critics again missed the point — that there is no lack of patriotism in general terms on the part of Remarque's soldiers. All these elements would have elicited a response from those in the Weimar Republic trying to come to terms with the war. At the same time, the intentional internationalism of the novel is clear in the presentation precisely from the viewpoint of the ordinary soldier and member of the lost generation. Equally clear is the expressly pacifist message. In fact, some English-language reviews criticized the novel for offering too mild a presentation of the German soldier. Nevertheless, the work is a clear indictment of all wars. Wars are still fought, even if not in the trenches, and they still give rise to political chaos. They are still fought largely by the young and uncomprehending, who are themselves forced by killing to incur a guilt that they do not necessarily deserve, while the major questions, such as why wars happen at all, often still go unanswered. One criticism of the work was that Remarque did not take a political stand, which means that he did not allow Bäumer to do so. This is partly justified by the consistent character of the narrator, but in fact the work does have a political dimension in various respects. Its pacifist stance and the emphasis on the soldiers as victims of the war are both contributions to the political agenda of Weimar Germany, and in general terms, the attacks on a prewar social system embodied in teachers like Kantorek, and the references to the capitalist profiteering are clear. As an antiwar novel, too, its message could hardly be clearer.

Within Remarque's novels as a whole, the fate of Bäumer may also be taken beyond the confines of the war itself. Remarque shows us a historical event, but also makes clear the way in which it faces an individual with an extreme situation. Bäumer is eventually stripped of all support and left alone, which forces him to the existential realization that the life force will carry him onwards regardless, because it is all that there is. That life force is represented by the spark of life that is with Kat on the battlefield at night in the surrounding sea of destruction. The force is there, too, in nature, which saves Bäumer physically — when he presses himself to the earth, praising it in what is almost an echo of an Homeric hymn[33] — and also spiritually at the end, when his near despair gives way after the promptings of the natural world. He is not content to die, his death is a final reminder of the force of chance, seemingly malignant but actually completely impartial, which is heightened in a war, but is always present in Remarque's novels. The same awareness will come to many of Remarque's later figures. The novel is not just a pacifist work. The human theme of the inextinguishable nature of the spark of life is just as significant.[34]

It is overly tempting to view all of Remarque's other novels in the light of *Im Westen nichts Neues,* but themes first found here do recur and are developed. *Zeit zu leben und Zeit zu sterben* has a number of actual echoes, such as the scenes in the hospital, but picks up and develops the idea of the responsibility of the soldier in a later war where this was far more a German issue. The concentration camp novel *Der Funke Leben* (*The Spark of Life*) — the title harks back to *Im Westen nichts Neues* — uses the narrative technique of shocking realism again, and rather than a soldier in a war, we have an even more extreme situation in which the spark of humanity must struggle even harder to survive. There were, however, aspects of the work that Remarque realized could be misunderstood, and there is indeed some danger in his chosen methodology of placing the burden of discourse upon a later reader. Remarque does indeed allow Bäumer to praise *Kameradschaft* in war, but it is offset by the need to cope with the attrition that takes away all of Bäumer's friends one by one. The closest friendship — with Kat — is fortuitous, and it is brought to an end by and in the war. The ties that bound the men together in war, too, are shown to break down in *Der Weg zurück*, and some of the other important ideas — such as what constitutes murder, or whether war is a justification in itself of the deeds done within it — are also brought back and re-examined in the new novel. Remarque called the second work a necessary one.[35]

Der Weg zurück

The First World War is nominally finished by the time the main part of *Der Weg zurück*[36] begins — there is an *Eingang*, an introductory section set in the last days of the war — but the shooting is not over. Three shots are fired in the course of the new novel, and these are of the greatest importance: the first is at another soldier (although he is a German soldier); the second is at a hated enemy (although he is a German civilian); and the third and final shot is a suicide. In a close parallel to the death of Bäumer, killed by an unseen enemy sniper not long before the armistice in November 1918, the First World War is effectively brought to an end for Remarque's soldiers with the closing scene of *Der Weg zurück* proper, with the death of one of the characters, a former soldier, by his own hand, back on the western front at the end of 1919. He is not the narrator, but he represents at least part of the narrator's attitudes. Following the stylistically distinctive death of Georg Rahe, an *Ausgang*, an epilogue, gives an indication that even if the First World War is over, a new war will come. A phrase like "the Great War of 1914–1918" is in any case open to question. When the war began is clear, but when did it really end? The Allied Victory medal issued to British soldiers after the war was engraved "The Great War for Civilisation 1914–1919," although qualification was based on service from the beginning of the war to the Armistice in 1918. There was no peace treaty until 1919, and given the aftereffects, there is a good argument for claiming that the conflict did not actually end until the death of the First World War corporal, Adolf Hitler, in 1945. *Der*

Weg zurück is, like its predecessor, a work for, and of, the Weimar Republic as well as a historical novel of the First World War, although the possibility of another war was becoming increasingly clear when it was written.

The title of the work is as ambiguous as that of the earlier novel. The narrator, the ex-soldier Ernst Birkholz, discovers in the course of the work that although the troops have physically made their way back to Germany, the road back into life cannot lead them back to their pre-military existence. The only way possible on the road back is forward. Birkholz and Bäumer have similar name elements (*Baum, Birke, Holz:* tree, birch, wood), their backgrounds are identical, and they seem to live in pretty well the same house. Moreover, they have had the same experiences — we learn in the course of the novel that Birkholz had stabbed a French soldier (132), and later on he refers to what sounds like the scene in *Im Westen nichts Neues* in which the soldiers enjoy a feast in a supply dump while under fire.[37] That the recollection comes in a scene in which a presumed war profiteer is holding a formal dinner party indicates that Remarque is drawing a conscious connection between the two novels. At all events, the characters are so similar that one can see Birkholz as living the postwar experiences that Bäumer would have had. In the last analysis, Birkholz is not Bäumer: they are both representative members of the same generation. Bäumer was a fictitious character who did not survive the war, and this novel refers to him and the others, Kat, Haie, and so on, as having been killed.

Although the later novel is also, for the most part, at least, a first-person narrative, the style is not quite the same as in the earlier work. This time two other characters, Ludwig Breyer and Georg Rahe, close friends of the narrator, play a greater part than any of the figures in the earlier novel, and their ideas in particular are foregrounded in a way that does not happen in the earlier work. Remarque again uses discussions by the now former soldiers as a starting point for the reader to consider matters further, but the discussions reported by Birkholz, especially between Breyer and Rahe, are fuller and more serious, as they do have the experience of the war behind them. The work is in that sense more political, but it must be remembered that it remains within its historical context, and the narrator remains consistent. Just as Bäumer probably would have had no clearly formed political views, Birkholz is still learning in 1919, and acts as an intermediary for the Weimar audience, passing on the debates for further consideration. Once again, too, the novel is not entirely a first-person narrative, though the matter is not as clear as with *Im Westen nichts Neues.* The work also operates on several levels. The progress and learning process of the individual, in the person of the narrator, represents one level; but through him not only do we hear of political debates and see the events of 1919 as they happen — the revolutionary conflicts, the food shortages — but we see too the difficulties of coming to terms with the war and the breakdown of some aspects of society in social as well as political terms. Nor is this just a work of the generation robbed of its youth, since older comrades are considered as well. Finally, of course, the work continues the indictment of war, and this is especially clear with some of the motifs that are picked up directly from *Im Westen nichts Neues.*

After the *Eingang,* which is set during in the war and in which people are still being killed, the survivors return to a Germany without firm government and with polarized left- and right-wing forces, and must begin to reconstruct their own lives against this chaos. Just as some survived in the war and others did not, some find it easier to adapt to civilian life than others; even en route back to Germany, one of the soldiers manages to strike a business deal with souvenir-hungry American soldiers, a motif that will recur in *Der Funke Leben.* But although the main part of the novel is set in 1919,[38] the war is kept close through the memories, words, and sometimes the actions of Birkholz and his friends. Birkholz has survived, but he is aware of his own unashamed exultation in still being alive, and comments that "Vielleicht ist nur deshalb immer wieder Krieg, weil der eine nie ganz empfinden kann, was der andere leidet" (33: Maybe that is why there is always a war, because one person can never really feel another person's suffering). This, too, is a key theme in Remarque's work.

The debate in Germany about the war was polarized into those who saw it as a disaster to be avoided in the future, and those who stressed the heroic aspects, and this is already apparent among the soldiers as they return. The *Oberleutnant,* Heel, stresses the heroic side, and the Jewish soldier Max Weil, voices the view that the price was simply too high. Soldiers' and sailors' councils are already established in Germany, and when Birkholz's group returns, Ludwig Breyer, the lieutenant, is attacked by members of such a council, young soldiers and sailors, because he is an officer. One of the others, Willy Homeyer, a large, strong man who plays this somewhat stylized role throughout the work, defends him in a violent confrontation. The attitude of the returning front-line soldiers is scornful towards the sailors, whose role in the war was not great, and to the raw recruits turned revolutionaries, but an older soldier defuses the situation, going so far as to salute them. Birkholz comments that the salute is neither for the uniform, nor for the war, but for the comradeship of the war, which is fast vanishing.

The lack of comprehension by their families of what the soldiers have been through leads to conflicts and sometimes to farce, as when Homeyer "requisitions" a cockerel that belongs to a neighbor. Willy uses soldiers' words — *requiriert, besorgt, gefunden* (requisitioned, acquired, found) — but the return to a civilian moral code now demands the word *gestohlen* (stolen). The soldiers themselves, however, need to achieve a kind of closure, just as Weimar Germany needed to come to terms with the war as such. In one incident, an intensified parallel to the revenge taken upon Himmelstoss, the group of soldiers encounters a former sergeant, Seelig, who had effectively caused the death of the friend of one of the group, Kosole, by refusing him leave. The friend had been killed (the story is one of the extended flashbacks to the war itself), and Kosole seeks revenge. But now Seelig is an innkeeper, and even Kosole feels that this is not the same man. Only when he spots that this innkeeper, who does not even remember the incident, is still wearing his uniform trousers does the military Seelig come back to him, and he is jolted into taking the revenge he needed.[39]

This incident, observed by Birkholz, shows how one character does achieve a personal closure. In parallel to the attrition in the earlier novel, here some of the former soldiers make good, among them Tjaden, who marries a butcher's daughter, while others, who had been good soldiers, fall on hard times. The comradeship of the front vanishes, since it was in any case determined by conditions at the front, and an uncomfortable reunion draws attention to the fact. In a case that merits special attention, we follow the tale of a married soldier, Adolf Bethke, who has returned to his home in the countryside to find that his wife has been unfaithful to him. When Birkholz visits Bethke, who was one of their group, he is at first silent, but then Birkholz tells the reader: "Schließlich höre ich dann alles" (125, then at last I get the whole story), which may then be given as a third person narrative. Despite his wife's genuine contrition, Bethke's initial reaction had been to take revenge on the other man, but this method of closure proves impossible. Later, after a kind of reconciliation, he and his wife are forced by gossip to sell up in the village, and move into the town and to an uncertain and unhappy future. Bethke comments to Birkholz when he sees him at this later stage that he wishes they were still at the front, where things were simpler. The war has destroyed, or at least damaged, a relationship, and this time there are further-reaching social ramifications as well.

More physical results of the war are still visible. Bäumer wished for the world to be paraded past the bed of Kemmerich; Birkholz observes a parade of the war-wounded as a part of a demonstration against rising prices as they move past a newly built dance hall. He also visits one of his comrades in an asylum, to show that minds were broken as well as bodies. For these men the war has not ended at all — they ask for news of it — and Giesecke, whom the others are visiting, is obsessed with a desire to return to Fleury, where he had been buried alive.[40] The idea of returning to gain closure in that way makes an impression upon them.

Ernst Birkholz himself has to make his own way back into the more normal aspects of life. His experiences at home recall strongly Bäumer's home leave and the isolation that he had felt. The situation again becomes farcical when Birkholz dines with a rich uncle, and in the course of a formal meal forgetfully picks up a chop in his hands, to the consternation of the other guests. The devaluation of formal niceties when set against what he has been through is of some interest. Only when he goes off secretly to catch

sticklebacks in a river as he had done as a child and there encounters Georg
Rahe on a similar mission is there any real recapturing of the past, but that
past is too far away. The ex-soldiers had gone into the war as schoolboys,
and they try at first, in vain, to pick up their lives from that point. At a
dance, Birkholz encounters a girl he had known in those days, but is told
that he has become too serious. When the girl leaves him because she has
arranged to meet someone else, he says: "Ich nehme die Mütze ab und
grüsse sie tief, als nähme ich einen grossen Abschied — nicht von ihr — von
allem Früheren" (178, I take off my cap and give her a sweeping bow, as if I
were making a grand farewell — not from her, but from everything that
came before).

Birkholz and the others return to the school itself, determined to take
emergency examinations. Those that have returned — the roll call shows us
how many have not done so — are sometimes wounded, and all of them
have been hardened by their experiences, so that there is a significant confrontation when the head teacher refers to those who "sleep as fallen heroes
beneath the greensward." The ebullient Willy Homeyer will have none of
this cant, and demythologizes it vigorously. Homeyer is speaking from the
immediacy of 1919, of course, but by the time the novel was written the
tendency to romanticize and sanitize the heroic dead was that much more
common, and proportionately more dangerous. The war dead are not sleeping, shouts Homeyer:

> Im Trichterdreck liegen sie, kaputtgeschossen, zerissen, im Sumpf ver-
> sackt. Grüner Rasen! Wir sind nicht doch nicht in der Gesangstunde!
> [. . .] Heldentod! Wie ihr euch das vorstellt! Wollen Sie wissen, wie der
> kleine Hoyer gestorben ist? Den ganzen Tag hat er im Drahtverhau
> gelegen und geschrien, und die Därme hingen ihm wie Makkaroni aus
> dem Bauch. Dann hat ihm ein Sprengstück die Finger weggeris-
> sen.[. . .] Als wir dann herankonnten, nachts, war er durchlöchert wie
> ein Reibeisen. Erzählen Sie doch seiner Mutter, wie er gestorben ist,
> wenn Sie Courage haben!" (114–15)

> [They're lying in filthy shell holes, shot to pieces, ripped apart, sunk in
> the swamp. Greensward! This isn't choir practice! [. . .] A hero's death!
> You've no idea! Would you like to know how little Hoyer died? He was
> lying on the wire all day and screaming, his guts hanging out like maca-
> roni. Then some H. E. took his fingers off [. . .] By nightfall, when we
> could get to him he was as full of holes as a sieve. Go and tell his
> mother how he died, if you're up to it.]

Presented with the realities of the war in the language of *Im Westen nichts
Neues,* and with the pseudo-heroic images debunked, the school authorities
give way and the ex-soldiers are allowed to qualify on their own terms. Willy
Homeyer and Ernst Birkholz becomes teachers in a neighboring village, and

although they are able to surprise the local worthies by drinking them under the table, Ernst himself, who lacks the toughness of his friend, is unable to cope for long with the task of teaching children because he cannot escape from the war, either in his dreams or in the classroom. He has nothing to offer these children, when all that he himself has ever really learned is how to make war.

The difference between the necessarily inconclusive debates in the earlier novel and those between Ludwig Breyer and Georg Rahe (in the reporting presence of Birkholz) is marked in the fourth chapter, near the center of the work.[41] Rahe observes the political chaos. "Sieh dir an, wie sie sich bereits gegenseitig in den Haaren liegen, Sozialdemokraten, Unabhängige, Sparta-kisten, Kommunisten" (195, Look at the way they are already at each other's throats, Social Democrats, Independents, Spartacists, Communists), but Breyer sees the blame in themselves. Echoing Paul Bäumer's comments at the end of the earlier novel, Breyer feels that by 1918 they were simply too beaten down:

> Wir haben mit zu wenig Haß Revolution gemacht, und wir wollten gleich von Anfang an gerecht sein, dadurch ist alles lahm geworden. Eine Revolution muss losrasen wie ein Waldbrand, dann kann man später zu säen beginnen; aber wir wollten nichts zerstören und doch erneuern. Wir hatten nicht einmal mehr die Kraft zum Hass, so müde und ausgebrannt waren wir vom Krieg. (195)

> [Our revolution didn't have enough hate in it, and we wanted to be just from the beginnings, and so it all flopped. A revolution should roar away like a forest fire, and then after that you can start to sow seeds again. Only we didn't want to destroy anything, just renew. We didn't even have the strength to hate, because we were so tired, so burnt out by the war.]

Though evident from an early stage, this was becoming clear by the time the book was written; only an organized and unified revolution could have es-tablished a stable and liberal republic after the war, and that never happened. The two men agree that they still have the war in their bones, but while Breyer feels that they have to — and can — struggle to make sure that it was not all in vain, Rahe thinks they are no longer fit for the task, and in despera-tion sets out to try to rediscover the old comradeship. He sets his road backward and resolves to rejoin the army. Ludwig is equally aware of the damage done to his generation, and although he feels — for the moment — that he has to go on trying, it soon becomes apparent that he, too, is unable to shake off the war.

The underlying political conflict between the right and the left develops to a climax in the later part of the novel, to the point in which the first of the important three shots are fired. Oberleutnant Heel is now part of the new

Reichswehr, whose steel helmets are noted (the *Stahlhelm* was the right-wing veteran's group), and they fire on a workers' group during a demonstration over food prices, in spite of being addressed by the unarmed demonstrators as *Kameraden*. As Birkholz and some of his friends, including Breyer, watch, Max Weil, on the demonstrators' side, is shot and killed at the command of Heel. The comradeship of the front has broken down to the extent that the soldiers are shooting now not at an enemy, but at each other. As they take cover, Birkholz realizes:

> Wir sind wieder Soldaten, es hat uns wieder, krachend und tobend rauscht der Krieg über uns, zwischen uns, in uns — aus ist alles, die Kameradschaft durchlöchert mit Maschinengewehren, Soldaten schiessen auf Soldaten, Kameraden auf Kameraden, zu Ende, zu Ende! (252)

> [We are soldiers again, it's got us again, the war roars over us, loud and raging, between us, in us — it's all over, comradeship has been drilled full of holes by machine-gun fire, soldiers are shooting at soldiers, comrades at comrades, it's over, it's over.]

Breyer offers Heel ironic congratulations, and Birkholz reiterates a little later that the war has started again, but the comradeship has gone.

If that shot is political, however, the next shot fired is personal. Albert Trosske shoots a man he has found with his girl, and despite the efforts of the others to persuade him to escape, he gives himself up, and at the end of the work is tried for murder. The point that comes out in the trial is that the soldiers have been trained to kill people they do not hate, but now one of them has killed in hatred. He is given a fairly lenient sentence, because it is made clear that less than a year before he was in the trenches, but the reader is left, as in the earlier novel, to draw conclusions about war and what constitutes murder. Shortly before the trial, Birkholz visits another old comrade, Bruno Mückenhaupt, who had been a sniper. Bäumer had been made to watch a sniper just after his return after killing Duval, and he had seized upon the notion of "*Krieg ist Krieg*" as a temporary consolation. Birkholz now finds that Mückenhaupt, a solid family man with a child, is still proud of his "hits," and is unquestioning about these acts of killing, seeing no need for justification beyond the fact that it was war, and he had been obeying orders. Indeed, anyone who thinks otherwise is, says Mückenhaupt, some kind of Bolshevik. Various ways of coping with the past are shown in the work, but this complete rejection of the idea that there might even be cause for guilt, is hardly likely to have been uncommon in reality.

In the event, neither Georg Rahe, who tries to go back to the army, nor Ludwig Breyer, who tries to carry on, is able to survive. Ludwig, we discover, has contracted syphilis in one of the official brothels during the war, a fairly clear image (which he himself points out) of the war still in his blood. Although he can be cured, his despair reaches a point where he can only rid himself of the war by cutting his veins. The passage describing his death is not strictly part of a first-person narrative, and on this occasion we do not even have the distancing devices used for the retelling of Bethke's story. However, Birkholz is summoned, finds Ludwig, and after this falls into a state of shock, so that the paragraph describing Breyer's last moments might be ascribed to the fevered imagination of the narrator.

Breyer's suicide is a removal of the war from his system by a knife rather than a bullet, but one final shot remains. Georg Rahe has attempted to re-join the army and try to reclaim the lost comradeship, but returns and tells Birkholz that the attempt failed. The army, he found, is now a disparate collection of idealists, those afraid to go back into civilian life, adventurers and mercenaries, all presenting a caricature of the comradeship, and making clear that that comradeship was just a product of the war. As soon as he was faced with a fight against supposed communists, actually workers, some of whom had been at the front, he was (unlike Heel) unable to fire. For him there had been a kind of honesty about the war, but now things are different, and he realizes that war as its own justification functions only when there actually is a war: "Krieg war Krieg. Aber diese toten Kameraden in Deutschland — erschossen von früheren Kameraden — aus, Ernst" (283, the war was the war. But these dead comrades in Germany — shot by former comrades — that's enough, Ernst). Georg Rahe feels that he has only survived by mistake, and now picks up the idea voiced in the asylum: the return to Fleury.

The resolution of his story is the last section of the final chapter of the novel proper, and it is stylistically different, told by a third person omniscient narrator who is neither Birkholz nor a speculative reporter as in the final lines of *Im Westen nichts Neues*. Rahe returns to the rusting barbed wire of the battlefields until he finds a cemetery, a row — a regiment — of black crosses. Greeting the dead with the words "Kameraden! Wir sind verraten worden! Wir müssen noch einmal marschieren! Dagegen! — Dagegen — Kameraden" (301, Comrades-in-arms, we were betrayed! We must march again. Against it all — against it — comrades!), he fires the last shot of the novel — and of the First World War? — killing himself, and is able to march with the dark army of the dead.[42] Bäumer did not want to die, but Rahe does. Driven by despair and survivor's guilt, he finds that a return to the battlefields is not enough.

Where Bäumer's death marked the end of the novel, *Der Weg zurück* has a coda, an *Ausgang,* separate from the work proper, but nevertheless still part of it, and it reminds us that the third member of the trio, the narrator Ernst Birkholz, whose difficulties we have also seen, does survive. At the end of the book he, like Bäumer, is alone: his friends have either died or moved away, and he has commented on the difficulty of relationships with women, underlined in the tales of Bethke and Trosske. In this epilogue the few remaining friends — we are told that they now rarely meet — gradually leave.[43] But he, too, is *ruhig und gefasst,* calm and composed, and he now, like Bäumer, sees a way forward — not back — a way that will be difficult and in which for most of it he will be alone, but he will be given strength by nature:

> Ich will weitergehen und nicht umkehren. Vielleicht werde ich nie mehr ganz glücklich sein können, vielleicht hat der Krieg das zerschlagen, und ich werde immer etwas abwesend sein und nirgendwo ganz zu Hause — aber ich werde auch wohl nie ganz unglücklich sein, denn etwas wird immer da sein, um mich zu halten, und wären es auch nur meine Hände oder die atmende Erde. (311)

> [I shall go onwards and not turn back. Perhaps I shall never be able to be completely happy again, perhaps the war has finished that off and I shall always be a little absent, and shall not feel completely at home anywhere — but I shall probably also never be completely unhappy, because there will always be something there to sustain me, even if it is only my own hands or the living earth.]

There is no more external support, and the central figure faces again the existential crisis. But the *ich* voice of Ernst Birkholz, who in this passage sounds virtually identical to Bäumer just before he was shot, is alive. Nature, the life force that is in everything, would have sustained Bäumer, and it is there for Birkholz.

Der Weg zurück is as much about the war as its predecessor. Equally, it is just as much a Weimar novel, although one that is more inward looking, showing to contemporary German society the dangers of political polarization while presenting a variety of ways of overcoming the past, and indeed the failure in some cases to get the war out of the system. Bäumer's final thoughts had been right: some would simply come to terms and get on with things, and some could compartmentalize the war and feel nothing for the killing; others could not cope at all. But the answer is one for the individual to discover alone. The First World War may be over, but the ambiguity of Birkholz's position and the difficulties he will have to face are already indicated in the *Ausgang*. In spring 1920, the small group of ex-soldiers comes across some young *Wandervögel,* members of the prewar youth movement, which was partly taken over by the right-wing *Freikorps,* being drilled as soldiers. When Birkholz and his friends — who are not many years older — object, they are called cowards and traitors. The roots of a new war were becoming much clearer, of course, by the end of the Weimar Republic, but they were there in 1920. "Ja" says one of the ex-soldiers, "so geht es wieder los" (307, Yes, that's the way it starts again).[44] The further development of the right-wing groups in the Weimar years would be portrayed after the end of the Second World War, in Remarque's "delayed" novel, *Der schwarze Obelisk;* by 1923 these semi-politicized *Wandervögel* had become teenage Nazis.

Notes

[1] Texts cited are the 1998 KiWi editions of *Im Westen nichts Neues* and *Der Weg zurück*, both with afterwords by Tilman Westphalen (Cologne: Kiepenheuer and Witsch, 1998). The earlier KiWi edition of the former (1987) has a slightly different afterword (referring to the first Gulf War) and a useful selection of materials on the work from 1929 to 1980. The first edition of *Im Westen nichts Neues* was published in Berlin under Ullstein's Propyläen imprint in January 1929 after a *Vorabdruck* in Ullstein's *Vossische Zeitung* starting just before Armistice Day in 1928, ten years after the end of the war. *Der Weg zurück* appeared under the same imprint in 1931, also after a preprint in the *Vossische Zeitung* at the end of 1930. For a full bibliography of editions, including picture books, and translations into all languages of *Im Westen nichts Neues*, see Thomas F. Schneider, *Erich Maria Remarque: Im Westen nichts neues: Bibliographie der Drucke* (Bramsche: Rasch, 1992).

[2] See Thomas F. Schneider, *Erich Maria Remarque: Im Westen nichts Neues: Text, Edition, Entstehung, Distribution und Rezeption, 1928–1930* (Habilitationsschrift: University of Osnabrück, 2000; now published in Tübingen: Niemeyer, 2004 as a book plus CD), and his booklet *Erich Maria Remarque: Im Westen nichts Neues: Das Manuskript* (Bramsche: Rasch, 1996). Schneider notes on page 12 that Remarque's contract with Ullstein demanded that if the book were not to be a success, Remarque would have to work off the advance paid by working for them as a journalist. Remarque claimed in a 1966 piece for the newspaper *Die Welt* that he worked on the novel for only five weeks: "Grössere und kleinere Ironien meines Lebens," *Ein militanter Pazifist*, 141; *Das unbekannte Werk*, vol. 4, 439; *Herbstfahrt*, 257.

[3] The translation by A. W. Wheen as *All Quiet on the Western Front* (London: G. .P. Putnam's Sons 1929; Boston: Little, Brown, and Company, 1929) was made, as were other translations, from a typescript and is slightly different from the German book version. It was bowdlerized when first published in the United States, and the full version was only readily available in a Fawcett paperback after 1979. The quality of Wheen's translation was attacked on publication, although Remarque seems to have liked it, calling it "eine englische Originalarbeit" (an original English work): see the letter by Herbert Read in *Time and Tide* on 26 April 1929. The reviewer for *Time and Tide*, Cicely Hamilton, pointed out gently that Remarque was perhaps not an authority on English. Richard Church praised the translation in the *Spectator* for 20 April 1929. For more detail, see Claude R. Owen, "*All Quiet on the Western Front*: Sixty Years Later," *Krieg und Literatur/War and Literature* 1 (1989): 41–48, and my papers "Translating the Western Front: A. W. Wheen and E. M. Remarque," *Antiquarian Book Monthly Review* 18 (1991): 452–60 and 102, and "We Germans . . .? Remarques englischer Roman *All Quiet on the Western Front*," *Jahrbuch* 6 (1996): 11–34. On Wheen, see Ian Campbell, "Remarking Remarque: The Arthur Wheen Papers," *National Library of Australia News* 8, no. 7 (April, 1998): 3–7, with illustrations of the drafts, showing the shift from "No News in the West" to "All Quiet in the West," with the familiar title only emerging at galley stage. My own translation (London: Cape, 1993) retains Wheen's by now established title. In spite of its flaws (mostly of register), Wheen's translation played an important part in the establishing of the novel as a masterwork of world literature: see the comments by

General Sir Ian Hamilton in 1929 in: "The End of War?" *Life and Letters* 3 (1929): 399–411, see 403.

[4] Lewis Milestone directed *All Quiet on the Western Front* for Universal in 1930. The script, by George Abbott, Maxwell Anderson, and Dell Andrews, is available in German translation by Jürgen Schebera together with full documentation of its first performance, in *Der Fall Remarque, "Im Westen nichts Neues" — eine Dokumentation,* ed. Bärbel Schräder (Leipzig: Reclam, 1992), 104–73 and 289–409; see 409 on the change from the intended final scene to its famous replacement in which Bäumer is killed reaching out for a butterfly. Much secondary literature has been devoted to the film, including most of issue 3 of the 1993 *Jahrbuch.* See Wagener, *Understanding,* 122, on the United States reissue in 1939 and its showing in Germany in 1952. Examples of secondary studies are: Kevin Brownlow, *The War, the West, and the Wilderness* (London: Secker and Warburg, 1979), 214–19; George J. Mitchell, "Making All Quiet on the Western Front," *American Cinematographer* 66 (1985): 34–43; Andrew Kelly, "*All Quiet on the Western Front:* 'Brutal Cutting, Stupid Censors, and Bigoted Politicos'" *Historical Journal of Film, Radio, and Television* 9 (1989): 135–50 — see also his book *Filming "All Quiet on the Western Front"* (London and New York: I. B. Tauris, 1998); John Whiteclay Chambers, "*All Quiet on the Western Front* (1930): the Anti-war Film and the Image of the First World War," *Historical Journal of Film, Radio, and Television* 14 (1994): 377–411. Milestone's film compares well with the exactly contemporary German Nerofilm *Westfront 1918,* based on a novel by Ernst Johannsen and directed by Georg W. Pabst; see Kathleen Norrie and Malcolm Read, "Pacifism, Politics, and Art: Milestone's *All Quiet on the Western Front* and Pabst's *Westfront 1918*" in *Remarque Against War,* ed. Brian Murdoch, Mark Ward, and Maggie Sargeant (Glasgow: Scottish Papers in Germanic Studies, 1998), 62–84. *All Quiet on the Western Front* was remade for television for Norman Rosemont productions, directed by Delbert Mann.

[5] There is an anecdotal but interesting historical report on the reading in 1944 of this proscribed book by Klaus Gruhn, "'Wehrkraftzersetzend': Schüler des Gymnasium Laurentianum Warendorf lernen 1944 *Im Westen nichts Neues* kennen," *Jahrbuch* 15 (2005): 93–100, and see for the response to exile books in schools after 1945 Hermann Glaser, "Das Exil fand nicht statt," in *10 Mai 1933,* ed. Walberer, 260–84. In a brief resumé of his life and works in 1956, Remarque noted that the book was banned in Italy from 1929–45, in Germany from 1933–45, but that it had subsequently been banned in the Soviet Union in 1947 and at that stage still was: *Das unbekannte Werk,* vol. 5, 167.

[6] Jost Hermand, "Versuch, den Erfolg von Erich Maria Remarques *Im Westen nichts Neues* zu verstehen," in *Weimar am Pazifik: Festschrift für Werner Vordtriede,* ed. Dieter Borchmeyer and Till Heimeran (Tübingen: Niemeyer, 1985), 71–78; A. F. Bance, "*Im Westen nichts Neues:* a Bestseller in Context," *Modern Language Review* 72 (1977): 359–73, cited 359, and see the comments by Firda, *All Quiet,* 12, whose book attempts a full-scale "Literary Analysis and Cultural Context." On the work as a bestseller, see Hubert Rüter, *Erich Maria Remarque: "Im Westen nichts Neues": Ein Bestseller der Kriegsliteratur im Kontext* (Paderborn: Schöningh, 1980). On the style see Brian Rowley, "Journalism into Fiction: *Im Westen Nichts Neues,*" in *The First World War in Fiction,* ed. Holger Klein (London: Macmillan, 1976), 101–11; Brian

Murdoch, "Narrative Strategies in Remarque's *Im Westen nichts Neues*," *New German Studies* 17 (1992–93): 175–202; Howard M. De Leeuw, "Remarque's Use of Simile in *Im Westen nichts Neues*," and Harald Kloiber, "Struktur, Stil, und Motivik in Remarques *Im Westen nichts Neues*," *Jahrbuch* 4 (1994): 45–64 and 5–78 respectively; and Thomas Schneider, "'Es ist ein Buch ohne Tendenz' *Im Westen nichts Neues*: Auto- und Textsystem im Rahmen eines Konstitutions- und Wirkungsmodells für Literatur," *Krieg und Literatur/War and Literature* 1 (1989): 23–40.

[7] Most famously by Peter Kropp, *Endlich Klarheit über Remarque und sein Buch Im Westen nichts Neues* (Hamm: Kropp, 1930), which sold well, as did Wilhelm Müller-Scheld, *"Im Westen nichts Neues eine Täuschung* (Idstein/Taunus: Grandpierre, 1929). See the survey by Barker and Last, *Remarque*, 38–44 as well as Owen, *Bio-Bibliography*, and Schräder, *Der Fall Remarque*. See also Thomas F. Schneider on the critical response, "'Die Meute hinter Remarque': Zur Diskussion um *Im Westen nichts Neues* 1928–1930," *Jahrbuch zur Literatur der Weimarer Republik* 1 (1995): 143–70, and Robert Neumann's orginal "Die Meute hinter Remarque," *Die Literatur* 32 (1929–30): 199–200. I have examined the imitative works in detail in my edition: Erich Maria Remarque, *Im Westen nichts Neues* (London: Methuen, 1984; rev. ed. Routledge, 1988), 4–6 and in my monograph *Remarque: Im Westen nichts Neues* 2d rev. ed. (Glasgow: Glasgow University French and German Publications, 1995), 1–13. See on the work *Hat Erich Maria Remarque wirklich gelebt* by Mynona [Salomo Friedlaender] (Berlin: Steegemann, 1929): Manfred Kuxdorf, "Mynona versus Remarque, Tucholsky, Mann, and Others: Not So Quiet on the Literary Front," in *The First World War in German Narrative Prose: Essays in Honour of George Wallis Field,* ed. Charles N. Genno and Heinz Wetzel (Toronto, Buffalo, and London: U of Toronto P, 1980), 71–91. The dust jacket of Friedlaender's book calls it "eine Denkmalsenthüllung" (uncovering/unmasking a monument).

[8] Franz Arthur Klietmann, *Im Westen wohl was Neues* (Berlin: Nonnemann, 1931); Carl A. G. Otto, *Im Osten nichts Neues* (Zirndorf-Nürnberg: Sanitas, 1929); Emil Marius Requark (M. J. Wolff), *Vor Troja nichts Neues* (Berlin: Brunnen/Winckler, 1930); Gottfried Nickl, *"Im Westen nichts Neues" und sein wahrer Sinn,* published by the journal *Heimgarten* as a *Sonderheft* (Graz and Leipzig: Stocker, 1929), referring to the novel as a *Schandmal* (monument of shame), and subtitled *Antwort auf Remarque* (answer to Remarque). E. Erbelding, *Im Westen doch Neues* (Something New on the Western Front) (Munich: Ebering, 1930), is a pro-war piece that merely uses Remarque's title. Most of these works do not bear reading, but their existence makes its own point. I have examined Wolff's parody in detail in "All Quiet on the Trojan Front: Remarque's Soldiers and Homer's Heroes in a Parody of *Im Westen nichts Neues*," *German Life and Letters* 43 (1989): 49–62. These imitations must be distinguished from literary texts that did, nevertheless, take a positive approach to the military aspects, such as those by Ernst Jünger; see Thomas Nevin, *Ernst Jünger and Germany. Into the Abyss, 1914–1945* (London: Constable, 1997), 143, also on diaries. There is an important comparison by Heinz Ludwig Arnold, "Erich Maria Remarque und Ernst Jünger," in *Jahrbuch* 10 (1999): 5–17. As an aside on modern reception, Günther Grass allows Jünger and Remarque to discuss the First World War in his *Mein Jahrhundert* (Göttingen: Steidl, 1999), and trans. M. H. Heim, *My Century* (New York: Harcourt, 1999).

[9] Brian Murdoch, "'Hinter die Kulissen des Krieges sehen': Evadne Price, Adrienne Thomas — and E. M. Remarque," *Forum for Modern Language Studies* 28 (1992): 56–74.

[10] For a historical overview see such works as Werner Conze, *Die Zeit Wilhelms II und die Weimarer Republik* (Stuttgart: Metzler, 1964); *Die Weimarer Republik,* ed. Friedrich Krummacher and Albert Wucher (Munich: Desch, 1965, illustrated); Hans Herzfeld, *Die Weimarer Republik* (Frankfurt am Main: Ullstein, 1966). In English, see John McKenzie, *Weimar Germany 1918–1933* (London: Blandford, 1971) and J. W. Hiden, *The Weimar Republic* (London: Longman, 1974).

[11] The best survey remains that by Hans-Harald Müller, *Der Krieg und die Schriftsteller: Der Kriegsroman der Weimarer Republik* (Stuttgart: Metzler, 1986). See also, however, the following selective chronological list: J. K. Bostock, *Some Well-known German War Novels 1914–30* (Oxford: Blackwell, 1931); William K. Pfeiler, *War and the German Mind* (1941; reprint, New York: AMS, 1966); Wilhelm J. Schwarz, *War and the Mind of Germany I* (Bern and Frankfurt am Main: Peter Lang, 1975); Michael Gollbach, *Die Wiederkehr des Weltkrieges in der Literatur: Zu den Frontromanen der späten zwanziger Jahre* (Kronberg im Taunus: Athenaeum, 1978); M. P. A. Travers, *German Novels of the First World War* (Stuttgart: Heinz, 1982); Margrit Stickelberger-Eder, *Aufbruch 1914: Kriegsromane der späten Weimarer Republik* (Zurich and Munich: Artemis, 1983); Herbert Bornebusch, *Gegen-Erinnerung: Eine formsemantische Analyse des demokratischen Kriegsromans der Weimarer Republik* (Frankfurt am Main: Peter Lang, 1985); Ulrich Baron and Hans-Harald Müller, "Weltkriege und Kriegsromane," *LiLi: Zeitschrift für Literaturwissenschaft und Linguistik* 19 (1989): 14–38; Ann P. Linder, *Princes of the Trenches: Narrating the German Experience of the First World War* (Columbia, SC: Camden House, 1996); *Von Richthofen bis Remarque: Deutschsprachige Prosa zum I. Weltkrieg,* ed. Thomas F. Schneider and Hans Wagener (Amsterdam and New York: Rodopi, 2003).

[12] There is a large body of secondary literature on the novel (some cited elsewhere in this chapter), and it is usually discussed in studies of war novels as such: George Parfitt's *Fiction of the First World War* (London: Faber, 1988) is a study of English-language novels with reference otherwise only to Remarque, Ernst Jünger, Jules Romains, and Henri Barbusse, and this is true too (minus Romains) of Bernard Bergonzi, *Heroes' Twilight: A Study of the Literature of the Great War* 2d ed. (London: Macmillan, 1980). There are monograph-length studies of *Im Westen nichts Neues* by the present writer, *Remarque: Im Westen nichts Neues,* as well as by Firda, *All Quiet,* and Rüter, *Bestseller.* There are various papers in the *Jahrbuch* 10 (2000), and many studies compare the work with other novels of the war: Helmut Liedloff, "Two War Novels," *Revue de Littérature Comparée* 42 (1968): 390–406 (with Hemingway); Holger M. Klein, "Dazwischen Niemandsland: *Im Westen nichts Neues* and *Her Privates We,* in *Grossbritannien und Deutschland: Festschrift für John W. P. Bourke,* ed. Ortwin Kuhn (Munich: Goldmann, 1974), 488–512 (with Manning); Holger M. Klein, "Grundhaltung und Feindbilder bei Remarque, Céline und Hemingway," *Krieg und Literatur/War and Literature* 1 (1989): 7–22. Some studies are less useful than others: David J. Ulbrich, "A Male-Conscious Critique of Erich Maria Remarque's *All Quiet on the Western Front,*" *Journal of Men's Studies* 3

(1995): 229–40 is not enlightening. Given the clarity of the novel it is intriguing to note the continued production of "study guides" in English, which do little more than provide a detailed plot summary (Cliffs Notes, 1965; Monarch Notes, 1966; Coles Notes, 1984; Sparknotes, 2002). See in German however the rather different introductions by Peter Bekes, *Erich Maria Remarque:, Im Westen nichts Neues* (Munich: Oldenbourg, 1998), and Reiner Poppe, *Erich Maria Remarque: Im Westen nichts Neues* (Hollfeld: Beyer, 1998). An adapted and abridged version of the English text was published for foreign students of the English language (such has it become part of the English canon): *Remarque: All Quiet on the Western Front,* adapted by Colin Swatridge (London: Macmillan, 1987).

[13] As noted by Rowley, "Journalism into Fiction," 108. Rowley also indicates the importance of the chapter division and their varying lengths on 109. Rowley's reference, however, to a "curiously unrealistic cross-section of the fighting-troops" (109) is surely explained by the fact that this, too, is dictated by Bäumer's "frog's eye view," a term Rowley cites, 108.

[14] An early subtitle was "Aus den Tagebüchern des Freiwilligen Georg Bäumers" (From the Diaries of the Volunteer Soldier Georg Bäumer — the name was changed later, too). See Schneider, *Text, Edition, Entstehung,* 463. See my paper "Paul Bäumer's Diary" in Murdoch, Ward, and Sargeant, *Remarque Against War,* 1–23.

[15] The debate about the actual reality of the presentation of the war in the novel has continued in various forms since the first objections by those critics who wanted it to be autobiographical. See Günter Hartung, "Zum Wahrheitsgehalt des Romans *Im Westen nichts Neues,*" *Jahrbuch* 1 (1991): 5–17. See also my "Paul Bäumer's Diary." Paul Fussell, *The Great War and Modern Memory* (London: Oxford UP, 1977), 183, counters the notion that the work is as "real and intimate" as letters from the front.

[16] Hans-Harald Müller makes the point clearly in "Politics and the War Novel," in *German Writers and Politics 1918–39,* ed. Richard Dove and Stephen Lamb (London: Macmillan, 1992), 103–20, esp. 112.

[17] On Remarque's discourse technique, already apparent in these early novels, see Heinrich Placke on the works of the 1950s: *Die Chiffren des Utopischen: Zum literarischen Gehalt der politischen 50er-Jahre-Romane Remarques* (Göttingen: Vandenhoek and Ruprecht, 2004).

[18] The much-reprinted French translation and at least one of the recently reprinted Yiddish versions (by Isaac Bashevis Singer) omit the statement, known as "the Motto," entirely. In other translations it is tucked away on the verso of the title page. The English is from Erich Maria Remarque, *All Quiet on the Western Front,* trans. A. W. Wheen (London: G. P. Putnam's Sons, 1929; also in the American edition, Boston: Little, Brown, and Company, 1929). In these and the German first edition it is prominently displayed on a separate preliminary page. Wheen translated from a typescript; my own translation follows the printed German text (thus omits the italicized parts). For variant versions of the Motto, see Schneider, *Text, Edition, Entstehung,* 465–67 (and I am indebted to Thomas Schneider for guiding me through the complexity of this situation). The translation of *Erlebnis* as "adventure" is not exact, but there were many books that did see the war as an adventure. Gunther Plüschow's *Die Abenteuer des Fliegers von Tsingtau,* another bestseller from Ullstein, originally 1916, but printed in 610,000 copies by 1927, and translated as *My Escape from Don-*

ington Hall (London: Bodley Head, 1929), is adventurous, although a single airman who escapes from a POW camp (hence the English title) is not representative; the publishers added a preface in 1927 claiming that it was being presented *nicht als Kriegsbuch* (not as a war book).

[19] As by Rudolf Huch, for example, in a review discussed by Roger Woods in "The Conservative Revolution and the First World War: Literature as Evidence in Historical Explanation," *Modern Language Review* 85 (1990): 77–91, see 86–87. The conservative literature of the war, which justified and to an extent glorified it, objected that the individual could form no overview of the inner sense of the conflict.

[20] See Woods, "The Conservative Revolution," 87–88, discussing Rudolf Huch's criticism of Remarque and the *Froschperspektive*. See also Travers, *German Novels*, 134.

[21] Various German novels blame teachers: see Caroline Martin, "The Conflict of Education: Soldiers, Civilians, a Child, and a Teacher," in Murdoch, Ward, Sargeant, *Remarque Against War*, 39–61. There is an interesting contrast with the situation in English, where the opposite was (or seemed often to be) the case, soldiers drawing strength from what they had learned at British public (that is, private) schools: see on this Peter Parker, *The Old Lie: The Great War and the Public School Ethos* (London: Constable, 1987), 283–84, with reference to Remarque.

[22] See on the style (with comments on "pseudo-authenticity") especially David Midgley, *Writing Weimar: Critical Realism in Weimar Literature 1918–1933* (Oxford: Oxford UP, 2000), especially 14–56. I have discussed the question with regard to Remarque in "Paul Bäumer's Diary," and see Thomas Schneider, "'Krieg ist Krieg schließlich': Erich Maria Remarque: *Im Westen nichts Neues* (1928)," in Schneider and Wagener, *Von Richthofen bis Remarque*, 217–32. On *Neue Sachlichkeit*, see Helmut Gruber, "'Neue Sachlichkeit' and the World War," *German Life and Letters* 20 (1966–67): 138–49.

[23] See my "Narrative Strategies," 180, referring to [Fritz Oswald] Bilse's *Aus einer kleinen Garnison: Ein militärisches Zeitbild* (Braunschweig: Sattler, 1903) (*Life in a Garrison Town*, London: Bodley Head, 1904), which contains also a discussion of comradeship and a scene where a soldier fails to salute a superior.

[24] See Robert Wohl, *The Generation of 1914* (London: Weidenfeld and Nicolson, 1980) for an international overview of the lost generation. Richard Littlejohns, "'Der Krieg hat uns für alles verdorben': the Real Theme of *Im Westen nichts Neues*," *Modern Languages* 70 (1989): 89–94 takes this as the principal theme of the novel, rather than the war as such.

[25] Fussell, *The Great War*, 196 misrepresents the scene, both misunderstanding the text — it is not a civilian cemetery — and by mischievously using phrases, unlike Remarque, such as "graves torn asunder," "stinking cerements" or "the narrator and his chums." There is no doubt of the potential reality of what is clearly also a symbolic scene and it is certainly not a "Gothic fantasia"; the dead were often not left in peace.

[26] Stramm (1874–1915) was himself killed in the war: see his brief poems in *Lyrik des Expressionistischen Jahrzehnts* (Munich: dtv, 1962), 133–34. There are translations of two in *The Penguin Book of First World War Poetry*, ed. Jon Silkin (Harmondsworth: Penguin, 1979), 227.

[27] Hindenburg, in his memoirs, commented that "unsere ermattete Front" (our exhausted frontline) fell like Siegfried, with Hagen's spear in the back: Generalfeldmarschall [Paul] von Hindenburg, *Aus meinem Leben* (Leipzig: Hirzel, 1920), 403. Hitler himself claimed that "Germany was not defeated by the sanctions but exclusively by the internal process of revolutionizing" — thus the English translation of a letter from Hitler to the press baron Lord Rothermere, dated 20 December 1935, in *Fleet Street, Press Barons, and Politics: The Journals of Collin Brooks,* edited by N. J. Crowson (London: Royal Historical Society, 1998), 286. Both recognize a defeat of some sort.

[28] As late as 1940 a pamphlet appeared in a World Affairs series by Cyril Falls called *Was Germany Defeated in 1918?* (Oxford: Clarendon, 1940). See also the larger historical studies of 1918 by John Terraine, *To Win a War* (London: Sidgwick and Jackson, 1978); John Toland, *No Man's Land* (London: Eyre Methuen, 1980); Gordon Brook-Shepherd, *November 1918* (London: Collins, 1981). Terraine's book carries a quotation on the title page from David Lloyd-George's war memoirs: "the conclusion is inescapable that Germany and her allies were in fact defeated in the field." H. Essame, *The Battle for Europe 1918* (London: Batsford, 1972) has a final chapter titled "The Politicians Take Over," and Niall Ferguson's *The Pity of War* (Harmondsworth: Penguin, 1998) ends with two chapters titled "The Captor's Dilemma" and "How (Not) to Pay for the War." See on the (sometimes avoided) question of the opening of the war the papers in: *Forging the Collective Memory,* ed. Keith Wilson (Providence, RI and Oxford: Berghahn, 1996). On the literary response to the concept of defeat in the Weimar republic, see Linder, *Princes of the Trenches,* 151–78. Remarque's 1944 comments were in an unpublished piece surviving in English, titled "Practical Education Work in Germany after the War," now in German translation by Thomas Schneider in *Ein militanter Pazifist,* 66–83 (see 72) as "Praktische Erziehungsarbeit in Deutschland nach dem Krieg" (also in *Das unbekannte Werk,* vol. 5, 387–403 and *Herbstfahrt,* 226–42).

[29] Even Remarque commented ironically on the boots ("Kemmerichs Stiefel in *All Quiet*") in a diary entry on 1 August 1950: *Das unbekannte Werk,* vol. 5, 427. Of course they are a symbol of death, but the real point, alluded to by Remarque in his diary, is their utilitarian value; only because they are of no use to Kemmerich does Müller take them.

[30] This happens in Edlef Koeppen's *Heeresbericht* (Berlin: Horen 1930 and Reinbek bei Hamburg: Rowohlt, 1986). For example, see my "Documentation and Narrative: Edlef Koeppen's *Heeresbericht* and the Anti-War Novels of the Weimar Republic," *New German Studies* 15 (1988–89): 23–47.

[31] See Hans Wagener, "Erich Maria Remarque, *Im Westen nichts Neues — Zeit zu leben und Zeit zu sterben:* Ein Autor, zwei Weltkriege," *Jahrbuch* 10 (2000): 31–52, see 39.

[32] See Brian Murdoch, "Tierische Menschen und menschliche Tiere: Ernst Johannsen: *Vier von der Infanterie* und *Fronterinnerungen eines Pferdes* (1929)" in Schneider and Wagener, *Von Richthofen bis Remarque,* 249–60. The same collection contains articles on many comparable works and also a useful indication of sales figures, 12–11. The other texts referred to here are Ernst Glaeser, *Jahrgang 1902* (1928; reprint, Frankfurt am Main and Berlin: Ullstein, 1986), translated as *Class of 1902* by Willa

and Edwin Muir (London: Secker, 1929); Alexander Moritz Frey, *Die Pflasterkästen* (1929; reprinted in the *Verboten und verbrannt/Exil* series, Frankfurt am Main: Fischer, 1986), translated as *The Crossbearers,* no translator given (London: G. P. Putnam's Sons, 1931); Adrienne Thomas's *Die Katrin wird Soldat* (1930) is in the same series (Frankfurt am Main: Fischer: 1987), trans. Margaret Goldsmith, *Katrin Becomes a Soldier* (Boston: Little, Brown, and Company, 1931).

[33] Bäumer draws life and strength from the earth in the fourth chapter. The motif is a classical one, which Bäumer, as a product of a classical *Gymnasium* (see his dismissive references to Plato and to classical history) might have absorbed: the Homeric hymn to the earth as a mother is in Karl Preisendanz, *Griechische Lyrik* (Leipzig: Insel [1936]), 5, for example, a collection the first edition of which had appeared in 1914.

[34] Remarque made the point in his "Grössere und kleinere Ironien," *Ein Militanter Pazifist,* 141; *Das unbekannte Werk,* vol. 4, 438; *Herbstfahrt,* 256. See Richard Schumaker, "Remarque's Abyss of Time: *Im Westen nichts Neues," Focus on Robert Graves and his Contemporaries* vol. 1, No. 11 (Winter 1990): 124–35.

[35] Friedrich Luft, "Das Profil: Gespräch mit Erich Maria Remarque" in *Ein militanter Pazifist,* 118–33, cited 120. The point is made in the perceptive analysis (principally of *Im Westen nichts Neues*) by Modris Eksteins, *Rites of Spring: The Great War and the Birth of the Modern Age* (London: Transworld, 1990), 368–97. See more on the two works in Kathleen Devine, "The Way Back: Alun Lewis and Remarque," *Anglia* 103 (1985): 320–35. The new work was not well received: see Antkowiak, *Remarque,* 53; Jost Hermand, "Oedipus Lost," in *Die sogenannten zwanziger Jahre,* ed. Reinhold Grimm and Jost Hermand (Bad Homburg: 1970), 218, and Wagener, *Understanding,* 41. American criticism thought more highly of the work: see Barker and Last, *Remarque,* 69.

[36] Again the English translation of the novel was by A. W. Wheen, *The Road Back* (London: G. P. Putnam's Sons, 1931). The film *The Road Back* was made in 1937, also by Universal but directed by James Whale, with a screenplay by Charles Kenyon and R. C. Sherriff, the writer of what is possibly the best-known drama of the First World War, *Journey's End.* It was not critically acclaimed, possibly because of the inevitable comparisons with Milestone's *All Quiet on the Western Front,* and it came under considerable pressure from the German consul as Hitler's representative in Los Angeles: see Jay Hyams, *War Movies* (New York: Gallery, 1984), 46. The summary there indicates that the film emphasised some of the shots fired in the novel. Apparently no 35 mm negative now exists.

[37] See Antkowiak, *Remarque,* 52, and (referring to Remarque's own comments), Taylor, *Remarque,* 88, and Firda, *Thematic Analysis,* 65. Ludwig Bodmer, the first-person narrator of *Der schwarze Obelisk* might also be taken as a further development of the same character at some years distance of writing, as indeed might Robby Lohkamp in *Drei Kameraden.*

[38] The timing is sometimes confused in criticism, but the indicators are clear in the novel itself. See my paper: "Vorwärts auf dem Weg zurück," *Text+Kritik* 149 (2001): 19–29, esp. 20.

[39] See my "Vorwärts auf dem Weg zurück" for a discussion of the passage in the context of closure, with reference also to Arnold Zweig's 1935 novel *Erziehung vor Ver-*

dun (*Education before Verdun*), which uses the notion of precisely such a revenge as the major plot.

[40] See the two stories originally published in English in *Collier's Magazine* and included in Erich Maria Remarque, *Der Feind*, re-translated by Barbara von Bechtolsheim (Cologne: Kiepenheuer and Witsch, 1993): "Karl Broeger in Fleury" (Where Karl had Fought, 1930), 26–33, and "Josefs Frau" (Josef's Wife, 1931), 34–44. There is a Karl Bröger in *Der Weg zurück* (and one is shot in a putsch in 1920 in *Drei Kameraden*). The title story, "Der Feind" (The Enemy, 1930), 9–17, is reported by a friend as coming from Ludwig Breyer, who is described as having fought at Verdun, the Somme, and in Flanders. All the stories are also in *Das unbekannte Werk*, vol. 4, 324–69.

[41] The centrality is underlined by Mark Ward in his analysis "The Structure of *Der Weg zurück*," ed. Murdoch, Sargeant and Ward, *Remarque Against War*, 85–97, esp. 94f. See John Fotheringham, "Looking Back at the Revolution" in the same collection, 98–118; and Anthony Grenville, *Cockpit of Ideologies* (Bern: Peter Lang, 1995), 80–97. On the revolutions and the effect on the Weimar Republic, see Benjamin Ziemann, "Die Erinnerung an den Ersten Weltkrieg in den Milieukulturen der Weimarer Republik," in *Kriegserlebnis und Legendenbildung*, ed. Thomas F. Schneider (Osnabrück: Rasch, 1998), 1, 249–70. For a general history, see Richard M. Watt, *The Kings Depart: The Tragedy of Germany: Versailles and the German Revolution* (London: Weidenfeld and Nicolson, 1969).

[42] Marching with the dead is a traditional motif, used in the context of the first world war in films like Abel Gance's *J'accuse* and plays like Chlumberg's *Wunder um Verdun* of 1931: see my paper "Memory and Prophecy Amongst the War-Graves: Hans Chlumberg's Drama *Miracle at Verdun*," in *The Commemorative Century*, ed. William Kidd and Brian Murdoch (Aldershot: Ashgate 2004), 92–104; Malcolm Humble: "The Unknown Soldier and the Return of the Fallen," *Modern Language Review* 93 (1998): 1034–45; and Linder (with reference to Rahe's suicide) *Princes of the Trenches*, 102. In *Der Weg zurück* and several other works, the dead from *Im Westen nichts Neues* are invoked as a means of linking the novels.

[43] Barker and Last, *Remarque*, 77, stress this, and Antkowiak, *Remarque*, 55, sees the work as a novel of the collapse of comradeship; neither study links this with existential isolation.

[44] Prewar youth groups were taken over from 1919 onwards by parties from the different right- and left-wing political extremes. By 1926 the Hitler Youth was already in being, but became prominent in 1933. See Peter D. Stachura, *The German Youth Movement 1900–1945* (London: Macmillan, 1981), 40–45. For interesting comments on the *Wandervögel* before the war, see Wohl, *Generation of 1914*, 203–9. On the political situation after the First World War and the links — or lack of them — between Versailles and the Second World War, see Zara Steiner, *The Lights that Failed: European International History* 1919–1933 (Oxford: Oxford UP, 2005).

German edition of
Der schwarze Obelisk

Norwegian edition of
Drei Kameraden

3: Rootless in Weimar: *Der schwarze Obelisk* and *Drei Kameraden*

WHERE *DER WEG ZURÜCK* IS SET around the birth of the Weimar Republic, two of Remarque's novels are set entirely within the period of the republic itself, although neither was written during its existence. *Drei Kameraden* (*Three Comrades*) appeared first in 1936 in a Danish translation, then in English in 1937, and was finally published in German in the Netherlands in 1938.[1] It is possible to see it as the third part of a trilogy consisting of *Im Westen nichts Neues* and *Der Weg zurück,* and Remarque himself indicated as much in a preface attached to the earliest, unpublished version of his text in 1932–33. However, whereas the two earlier novels are closely focused on the war and its aftermath, *Drei Kameraden,* in the published version, is set nearly ten years later, in 1928. Although there are references to the war, and even brief allusions to characters in the other two novels, including a mention of the deaths of Kemmerich and Katczinsky, *Drei Kameraden* is in other respects removed in time and place from the two earlier novels.[2] The earliest version seems to have been started in 1932, when Remarque was already living in Porto Ronco, and completed in January 1933. This version had the title *Pat,* and it did begin with a link to the lost generation and *Der Weg zurück,* but it was abandoned, and the text eventually published was written after the fall of the Weimar Republic and Remarque's own final move from Germany.[3] Where the two earlier novels have the war as their theme, that of *Drei Kameraden* is the Weimar Republic itself, and specifically the beginning of its collapse.

In terms of historical setting, *Drei Kameraden* may be set side by side with a later novel concerned with politics and life in the Weimar Republic. Published in 1956, *Der schwarze Obelisk* (*The Black Obelisk*), significantly subtitled *Geschichte einer verspäteten Jugend* (Story of a Delayed Youth)[4] is a more distanced historical novel, demanding different assumptions especially when treated outside the sequence of Remarque's writings, and there are emphases that would probably not have been present had it actually been written before the fall of Hitler. *Der schwarze Obelisk* opens in April 1923, however, in the middle of the hyperinflation, the Weimar Republic's first real crisis, and ends late in the same year, when the crisis is over, while *Drei Kameraden* is set in the approach to the republic's final crisis in 1928 and the beginning of 1929.

Der Schwarze Obelisk has a prefatory statement that stresses its chronological placing (even though it also refers to the world after the Second
World War and even to nuclear weapons), and a brief final chapter looks at
the subsequent fates of some of the characters down to the time of writing,
1955. This structure is a little like that of *Im Westen nichts Neues,* which also
has a prefatory statement, albeit not from the main narrator's voice, indicating that the novel offers a historical report, and an ending, again from a different voice, which is separate from the substance of the work. The milieu of
small-town Germany in *Der schwarze Obelisk* provides a further link with the
two novels of the First World War; the work is again clearly set in Osnabrück, here named Werdenbrück, and there are many reflections of the
places, events, and people of Remarque's own life after the First World War,
most notably his link with the Osnabrück asylum and his job selling gravestones. There are even parallels for the prostitute known as the "iron horse,"
for the public lavatory beside which a battle with Nazi thugs takes place, and
perhaps for the black obelisk itself, although as ever the value of knowing
these connections is limited.[5] In his picture of the Weimar Republic in 1923
Remarque seems, moreover, deliberately to have clarified or helped to explain some of the events in *Drei Kameraden,* and the parallels between the
two works also strengthen the rationale for considering them together.

The first-person narrators of *Der schwarze Obelisk* and of *Drei Kameraden*
are at once involved in the experiences of the story, and report and comment
on their times; both are young ex-soldiers, both have been schoolteachers,
and they continue the direct line from Paul Bäumer and Ernst Birkholz. But
the narrators are not the same in all respects, so that while in *Der schwarze
Obelisk* the development of the narrator's personality is still central, his role
as an objective, and frequently comic-ironic, observer is more prominent.
This does not mean that the new narrator, Ludwig Bodmer applies hindsight in the bulk of the novel; he is entirely believable as a twenty-five-year-
old living through a delayed youth, but he is politically more aware than
his predecessors.[6]

Remarque notes in his prefatory statement that the world of the 1950s
is one of destruction again, of death and of tears, and of maintaining peace
by inventing weapons that could destroy everyone. He proposes, however,
to return to "den sagenhaften Jahren, als die Hoffnung noch wie eine Flagge
über uns wehte und wir an so verdächtige Dinge glaubten wie Menschlichkeit, Gerechtigkeit, Toleranz — und auch daran, dass *ein* Weltkrieg genug
Belehrung sein müsse für eine Generation. —" (9, to the fabulous years,
when hope still fluttered like a flag above us all, and we believed in such
suspicious-sounding things as humanity, justice, and tolerance — and also
in the notion that *one* world war might surely be a sufficient lesson for a
generation. —). This sums up much of Remarque's philosophy, with the
added irony that those times have now become *sagenhaft,* "fabulous," "leg-

endary." And because both of the novels that portray the Weimar Republic are in fact retrospective, that fluttering hope was known to have been illusory when both were written.

The Weimar Republic opened its National Assembly in February 1919 and had to accept the harsh economic penalties imposed upon Germany by the Treaty of Versailles. The first years of the republic, characterized by the politically polarized violence that Remarque had already portrayed in *Der Weg zurück,* remained turbulent for several years after the end of the war, with extreme right-wing and extreme left-wing groups, *Freikorps* on the right, Spartacists on the left, which developed later into the equally polarized opposition between the fascist Nazis and the communist Red Front. Throughout the period it seems to have been the case, however, that right-wing insurgents were treated more leniently in the courts. The Kaiser may have been displaced, but a conservative civil service and army administration remained. Other factors also affected the new republic. From January 1922 the rate of inflation in Germany began to rise, largely at the expense of the working and middle classes, whose wages and savings rapidly became worthless; speculators, on the other hand, were able to buy capital goods on property-backed credit and repay with massively devalued paper. In January 1923, French and Belgian forces entered the Ruhr area, ostensibly to protect the coal supplies that were part of the reparations Germany had been made to pay. Shortly afterwards the German economy collapsed, leading to a period of inflation that had been growing since the war, becoming rapidly worse throughout 1922, and reaching ludicrous proportions, with rates changing twice daily or even more frequently against the dollar, rendering savings, wages, and prices meaningless within hours. The massive numbers of banknotes were literally not worth the paper they were printed on; some had the red overprint *Eine Milliarde,* a billion marks, and that was not the end. All this was brought under control only in the later part of 1923, when Gustav Stresemann's government introduced a mortgage-based currency, the *Rentenmark (Roggenmark)* in October of that year, and whatever the realities of this economic strategy, which has also been seen as a kind of illusion, confidence in it stabilized the situation rapidly. In November of that year, too, Hitler, already styling himself *Führer,* attempted to emulate Mussolini, whose fascists had come to power in Italy in 1922. Hitler staged his "beer-hall putsch" in Munich in an attempt to take over what he saw as a collapsing government. It was suppressed, and in 1924 Hitler was jailed, but only for a short time; the events of 1922 and 1923 marked his debut on the political stage.

A period of relative stability followed from 1925 to 1929. The French left the Rhineland and the Ruhr, and there was an upsurge of cultural activity. This was the period characterized, too, as the roaring twenties of clubs and cabarets. The stabilization was only brief, however, and unemployment, which had already begun to grow significantly by 1928, increased enormously after the Wall Street crash and the Great Depression in 1929. Once again, frequent clashes and open street fighting between different political factions, the increasingly powerful Nazi party and various components of the Red Front, characterized a highly politicized state of affairs for the last years of the republic, until Hitler, whose power base had grown increasingly with financial backing from industry after 1929, became chancellor in January 1933.[7]

Germany had thus recovered painfully from the war, enjoyed a short period of apparent stability between two major economic collapses, and then suffered massive unemployment — six million people by the early 1930s — and political unrest, the whole giving way in the end to the triumph of the Nazis; this is the world the two novels reflect. *Der schwarze Obelisk* begins with the inflation; *Drei Kameraden* ends with the unemployment and renewed street fighting. The Weimar Republic survived the inflation, but the possibility that it would succumb eventually to the extreme right was always there, and indeed it is indicated already in the epilogue to *Der Weg zurück*.

Der schwarze Obelisk

Remarque's retrospective novel begins in April 1923 and ends in December of that year, and has as its most constant theme that of the disastrous hyperinflation. There are regular references throughout the work to the eversinking value of the mark against the dollar, with the rates changing in the later part of the novel by the hour, and this influences much of the action. The novel is narrated by Ludwig Bodmer, a young former soldier, who is employed by the firm of Heinrich Kroll, monument masons providing gravestones and war memorials, and having in their stock the large black obelisk of the title, which the firm has held since before the war and has been unable to sell. It has come to symbolize even for them the old order, a huge stone anchoring them to the period before the First World War. Other symbolic meanings are pointed out in the work by the narrator, however, who takes it to represent a particularly rigid mindset, or by others, and sometimes its function is ironic. Thus it provides a nocturnal urinal for the drunken former sergeant Knopf, one of a colorful group of neighbors; and when it is finally sold and removed it becomes the phallic memorial, as it is accepted by the madam for the grave of a prostitute who had died while plying her trade as dominatrix. It is paid for, what is more, out of her immoral earnings in hard currency, the Dutch guilder, but which now has a non-inflated mark equivalent.

The action of the work is divided between the professional and private activities of Bodmer and his acquaintances on the one hand, and on the other his relationship with a girl with whom he falls in love. Bodmer plays the organ on Sundays in the local psychiatric hospital, and it is there, in a milieu that is deliberately cut off from the real world, that he meets a girl whose real name is Geneviève Terboven, but who is being treated for schizophrenia and calls herself Isabelle. It is the illusory Isabelle with whom he falls in love, or from whom he at least learns that it is possible to fall in love, and in whom he finds a contrast to the women he encounters in the supposedly sane world. On his visits to the asylum, too, Bodmer meets regularly and talks with the priest, Bodendiek, and the doctor, Wernicke, against whose equally firm but opposing sets of opinions he tests his own.[8] In the outside world, most of the action centers either around Bodmer's workplace — the memorial repository, with the inhabitants of the neighboring houses across the old and narrow street — or in the clubs, bars, restaurants, and the town brothel. Only once is there an excursion into a local village to sell a war memorial. Set-piece scenes or sequences of events are often humorous and sometimes farcical or grotesque, and the characters encountered on a day-to-day basis by the narrator are frequently memorable in their eccentricity.

At the beginning of the work we see Bodmer lighting a cigar with a ten mark note and his employer and friend, Georg Kroll, has brought in a suitcase full of cash, with some new but already overtaken 100,000 mark notes. Kroll looks back with ironic nostalgia to the time not long ago when inflation was only three hundred percent, and we are regularly made aware of the dollar rate. Towards the end of the novel, before the *Rentenmark* deflation, we reach billions (million millions) in a scene in which Bodmer gives money to some beggars, of whom there are many, who rush off immediately: "der Preis für die Suppe kann in einer Stunde schon um einige Millionen Mark gestiegen sein" (325, the cost of the soup might have risen by a few million marks within the hour). The economics of the period depend upon the holding of capital assets, speculation, and the use of credit that can be paid back at a later rate. The gravestones and memorials are themselves a capital asset, but can easily be rendered worthless if payment is not made on time. There is also a running joke in the work involving a number of meal tokens good for use at a local restaurant run by Eduard Knobloch. Bodmer and Georg Kroll had bought up a large number of these before the real inflation started, and insist on their legal right to use them for meals that should now cost much more. In the course of the work, too, we are given occasional glimpses of hard currency: a prewar gold coin, a check drawn in Swiss francs, and a sum in Dutch guilders, all of which throw the paper artificiality into relief. The reality of the inflation is apparent, however, in its effects; as the dollar rate rises into the millions, the narrator watches a protest procession of disabled veterans and comments that these are hit hardest, since their pensions have become worthless and they have lost so much that their children are no longer adequately fed. We hear of frequent suicides by the poorest, simply unable to cope any longer. The general human effect of the inflation is made clear in Bodmer's comments at the opening of chapter 15, roughly at the center of the novel and summarizing the crisis of the Weimar Republic. We have reached the sultry late summer of 1923:

> . . . der Dollar ist um weitere zweihunderttausend Mark gestiegen, der Hunger hat sich gemehrt, die Preise haben sich erhöht, und das Ganze ist sehr einfach: Die Preise steigen schneller als die Löhne — also versinkt der Teil des Volkes, der von Löhnen, Gehältern, Einkommen, Renten lebt, mehr und mehr in hoffnungsloser Armut, und der andere erstickt in ungewissem Reichtum. Die Regierung sieht zu. Sie wird durch die Inflation ihre Schulden los; dass sie gleichzeitig das Volk verliert, sieht niemand. (219)

> [the dollar has gone up by another 200,000 marks, hunger has increased, prices have gone up, and the whole thing is simple. Prices are rising faster than wages, so that the part of the population that depends on wages, salaries, income, pensions is sinking more and more into hopeless poverty, and the other part is suffocating in uncertain riches. The government just watches. It is getting rid of its debts because of the inflation. Nobody notices that it is losing the people at the same time.]

In *Der Weg zurück* the point was made that the post-1918 revolution in Germany had been halfhearted. Bodmer confirms this and notes further developments:

> Die Revolutionäre waren von sich so erschreckt, dass sie sofort die Bonzen und Generäle der alten Regierung zu Hilfe riefen, um sie vor ihrem eigenen Mutanfall zu schützen. Die taten es auch grossmütig . . . die deutsche Revolution versank in rotem Plüsch, Gemütlichkeit, Stammtisch und Sehnsucht nach Uniformen und Kommandos. (29)

> [The revolutionaries were so shocked by their own actions that they immediately called on the big boys and the generals of the old regime to help protect them from their own outburst of courage. They were happy to oblige . . . the German revolution was submerged in red plush, *Gemütlichkeit,* going to the pub and a longing for uniforms and orders.]

The memorial business, which still anchors Bodmer to the notion of death and to the war, furnishes the novel with a range of characters, such as Heinrich Kroll, Georg's brother, who combines right-wing patriotic-nationalist attitudes with a general failure to grasp aspects of selling in an inflationary time; Wilke the coffin maker, whose trade usually makes it difficult for him to attract women and who is haunted by ghosts at midnight; Kurt Bach, the monument mason who dreams of being Michaelangelo, but carves patriotic lions and mourning angels; and "Tränen-Oskar," who can, usefully, weep at will. The one scene set outside Werdenbrück and involving most of these characters is an important one in political terms. A local village has bought from them a war memorial, which is to be dedicated at a ceremony organized by the anti-Semitic former Major Wolkenstein, now an enthusiastic supporter of the right, for whom the war, "der Massenmord ist zum Abenteuer geworden" (118, the mass murder has become an adventure). He appears in full imperial uniform, which is in fact illegal, though he knows this will be ignored. He has suppressed all real memory of the war and turned everything into the nationalistic pride that actually starts wars:

> Wer nicht nationalistisch ist, beschmutzt das Andenken der gefallenen Helden — dieser armen, missbrauchten, gefallenen Helden, die alle gern noch gelebt hätten. Wie sie Wolkenstein von seinem Podium herunterfegen würden, auf dem er gerade noch seine Rede hält, wenn sie es nur noch könnten! Aber sie sind wehrlos und sind das Eigentum von Tausenden von Wolkensteins geworden . . . (118)

> [Anyone who isn't a nationalist is sullying the memory of the fallen heroes — those poor, abused, fallen heroes who would all rather still have been alive. How they would have swept Wolkenstein off the podium where he is just now giving his address, if they only could! But they are defenseless and have become the property of thousands of Wolkensteins . . .]

That potential multiplication of nationalists like Wolkenstein is a technique from *Im Westen nichts Neues,* and indeed, although the novel was written in the 1950s, the abuse of the dead, made to march for either political wing, was already a well-established literary theme in the Weimar period.[9]

The memorial itself had caused controversy when Wolkenstein objected to the addition of the names of two Jewish brothers killed at the front; they are added down at the bottom "wo die Hunde es wahrscheinlich anpissen werden" (117, where the dogs will probably piss on it), and only then so that someone else's reservist son, who died of flu without ever leaving the town, could also be added. At the dedication, Wolkenstein's nationalistic speech invokes the myth of how the undefeated German army had been stabbed in the back and calls for revenge. However, one man in the village displays the black, red, and gold flag of the Weimar Republic rather than the old imperial black, white, and red flag. He is set upon by a mob, urged on but not joined by Wolkenstein, and for displaying what is the official flag of the state the man is beaten up and dies. Although Bodmer and Georg Kroll manage to exploit the incident to pressure the local community into paying for the memorial (something they were trying to avoid), the overall effect is pessimistic. No one will be found responsible for the deed, and Bodmer sums up the position again. "Politischer Mord, wenn er von rechts begangen wird, ist ehrenwert und hat alle mildernden Umstände. Wir haben eine Republik; aber wir haben die Richter, die Beamten und die Offiziere der alten Zeit intakt übernommen" (128, Political murder perpetrated by the right is honorable and always has mitigating circumstances. We've got a republic, but we've kept the judges, the officials and the officers of the old regime).

Characters like Heinrich Kroll and the horse butcher Watzek, an early adherent of Hitler, demonstrate the rise of the right. Watzek's lively, if over-sexed wife, Lisa, is much desired by Riesenfeld, who supplies the firm with granite for the memorials, but she has an affair, in fact, with Georg Kroll. At one point the suspicious Watzek waits for the errant Lisa armed with a cleaver, but Bodmer manages to distract the cuckolded horse butcher from his murderous intent by getting him to talk about a speech Watzek has just heard by Hitler on the radio. In 1922 and 1923 Hitler had begun to move into public life, largely in Bavaria, and by 1922 the title *Führer* was already being used in the party newspaper. The hero-worship of Hitler voiced by Watzek is more or less plausible even in northern Germany in 1923, but a speech in 1923 by any politician on the radio is not, and this detail is no-ticeably anachronistic. Remarque ought perhaps have let him read the speech in a newspaper.[10] Be that as it may, Watzek claims that Hitler will change everything, and Bodmer comments that that slogan: "Alles muss anders werden!" (everything must change) is the rallying cry of every demagogue.

The political attitudes of the work are clearer than in most of Remarque's novels. The extremism of Heinrich Kroll, for example, is set up as a target for counterargument. When Georg Kroll produces an imperial *Goldmark,* a prewar gold coin, and he and Bodmer comment that it is now worth eight months pension for someone severely wounded in the war, Heinrich sees it as a reminder of a time when there was employment, a thriving economy, and respect for Germany, drawing the conclusion: "Dass wir wieder einen Kaiser und eine anständige nationale Regierung haben müssen" (298, That we need a Kaiser and a decent nationalist government again). Bodmer indi-cates that he has forgotten the single word *weil,* "because":

> Wir haben heute fünf Millionen Arbeitslose, eine Inflation und wir sind besiegt worden *weil* wir vorher Ihre geliebte nationale Regierung hat-ten! *Weil* diese Regierung in ihrem Grössenwahn Krieg gemacht hat! *Weil* sie diesen Krieg verloren hat! Deshalb sitzen wir heute in der Scheisse. (298)

> [We've got five million unemployed, inflation, and we were defeated *because* we had your beloved nationalist government! *Because* that gov-ernment was megalomaniac enough to start a war! *Because* they lost that war! That's why we're in the shit now!]

While the crazy inflation may cause human tragedy, it is also seen as making the whole period into a time of carnival absurdity. The "time of folly" is still part of the German carnival tradition before Lent, and here the idea is reinforced by the frequent comic incidents, some of them pure farce. Towards the end of the novel, for example, ex-sergeant Knopf is brought back home drunk, but apparently dying. The extended scene centers physically upon the celebrated obelisk, on which Knopf as usual urinates, involves noisy farting, a confrontation with the local busybody, Witwe Konemann, a comically tragic chorus from Knopf's wife and daughters, the appearance of Heinrich Kroll in imperially striped pajamas, of Lisa Watzek in an evening dress back from a nightclub, and the rapid departure of a couple who have been using the darker corners of the display of gravestones for their own purpose. It is a minor running motif in the novel that the display purpose gravestones are more sinned against than sinning, and as such are often concerned with future life as much as with future death, presided over by the phallic obelisk. Knopf, too, has been the butt of a number of jokes in the work, as when Bodmer, speaking through a discarded piece of piping, masquerades as the voice of God to frighten him away from the obelisk by threatening to strip him of his rank, something he finds impossible to cope with. The announcement of his imminent death by the doctor proves wrong, however, and there is again much comic negotiation about whether or not he should retain or resell the gravestone that his family has already purchased. Having decided to keep it as a capital asset, the deflation suddenly renders his negotiations nugatory. Although a farcical figure, Knopf is also sinister in his very indestructibility as the smalltime representative of the old regime, and eventually, we are told, he is killed not by alcohol but by a car.

Bodmer observes a range of further interestingly odd, almost carnivalesque, characters that include a lady whose specialty is pulling nails out of a wall with her buttocks and winning bets by doing so, and Renée de la Tour — her real name is Lotte — who can sing both soprano and bass and who is the girlfriend of a far more significant figure, Bodmer's friend and former comrade Willy. Willy is a thriving speculator in the first part of the work, but his innate adaptability enables him to take in his stride the collapse of his enterprises when the mark is deflated; he is an embodiment of positivism and we have met him before. Remarque, who sometimes uses the same name for different characters — there are several Nazis called Steinbrenner — often links his novels by indicating that his characters have shared acquaintances in the past, and there are references to the dead of *Im Westen nichts Neues,* for example, in several of the novels, providing regular reminders not just of the war, but of the war as Remarque himself had portrayed it. Bodmer's ever-capable friend Willy has the same physical appearance and forceful personality as Willy Homeyer in *Der Weg zurück,* and in a scene with their unpleasant former headmaster, which again echoes *Der Weg zurück,* we learn that he is indeed called Willy Ho(h)meyer.[11]

The novel also traces Bodmer's personal development, and as an honest narrator he shows himself in negative situations. Bodmer is rootless emotionally and intellectually, but his problem is that he is trying too hard. A girlfriend, the forceful and uncomplicated Gerda sums up his problem in a phrase that is as German as it is difficult to translate: "Aber ich fürchte, du kannst nicht einmal pissen ohne Weltanschauung" (235, but my worry is that you can't even piss without a philosophical standpoint). When Bodmer asks Wernicke, the doctor at the psychiatric hospital where he plays the organ in the church, whether the fact that he feels responsible for everything in the world betokens some kind of mental abnormality, the doctor replies: "Sie sind völlig uninteressant. Ein ganz normaler Durchschnittsadoleszent" (247, you are completely uninteresting. A perfectly normal, average adolescent). His late adolescence is borne out in his relationships with various women, first the flighty Erna, to whose rejection he reacts with childish jealousy. He is jealous, too, when a new lover, Gerda, an acrobatic dancer, seemingly responds to the blandishments of Eduard Knobloch, who in fact simply gives her a job. That Bodmer's emotional development regarding relationships with women is a product of the war becomes clear in the course of another ultimately farcical incident, in which the poetic club of which Bodmer is a member arranges a kind of excursion to the local brothel, so that one of their number can lose his virginity. Bodmer tells us in this context how, when he was still at school, he and some friends went by mistake into the apparently respectable café that fronts the brothel, and got to know the prostitutes, who treated them as their children and helped them with their homework, later rejecting them (when they returned as soldiers) as sexual partners because it would not seem proper. This contact with the brothel leads in the end to Bodmer supplying the obelisk as a gravestone after the demise *in medias res* of the dominatrix known as "the iron horse" (*das eiserne Pferd,* also *Ross*), a generic nickname used for different prostitutes in *Drei Kameraden* and in *Arc de Triomphe.*

Bodmer's most significant lessons in life come not in the supposedly normal world, which is normal neither in the political nor in the economic sense, but in the confines of the psychiatric hospital, in his relationship with Bodendiek, the priest, Wernicke, the doctor, and especially with Geneviève Terboven, who calls herself Isabelle while she calls him Rudolf or Ralph. Her naïve but relentless questions force him to think in a new direction, and he and Isabelle come close to one another in a kind of love affair that cannot ever be real. She questions, for example, the laws of physics (where does the picture in a mirror go, or what appears in a mirror at night?) and does not understand the outside world, but all this helps Bodmer to simplify his own questions as to the meaning of life. In his growing affection for her, Bodmer discovers an awareness of life for its own sake. He declares his love in a moment that he knows as he experiences it cannot last, and there is a nice irony in his process of learning from a woman who is herself the illusory projection of a disturbed mind. Bodmer realizes:

Du süsses und geliebtes Leben, ich glaube ich habe endlich gefühlt, was Liebe ist! Es ist Leben, nichts als Leben, der höchste Griff der Welle nach dem Abendhimmel, nach den verblassenden Sternen und nach sich selbst — der Griff, der immer wieder vergeblich ist . . . aber manchmal kommt der Himmel der Welle entgegen und sie begegnen sich für einen Augenblick. (305)

[You sweet and lovely life, I think I have felt at last what love is! It is life, nothing more than life, the furthest reaching up of the wave towards the evening sky, towards the fading stars and towards itself — the reaching up that is always in vain . . . but sometimes the sky comes down towards the wave and they touch for a moment.]

But only for a moment, because Bodmer has already learned in the war that "[j]eder hat seinen eignen Tod und muss ihn allein sterben, und niemand kann ihm dabei helfen" (89, everyone has his own death and has to go through it alone, and no one can help), and that "das bisschen Beieinand-ersein" is no more than "ein sanfter Betrug" (88, the little bit of together-ness is just a gentle deception). But it will do, since that is all there is. In the end, everyone is isolated.

In fact Isabelle has begun to be cured of her schizophrenia, and Dr. Wernicke was using Bodmer to help. It transpires that Geneviève's mother had married a man called Rudolf or Ralph, upon whom the daughter was also fixated, causing her to create for herself an imaginary personality whose affections are projected upon Bodmer. The mother has divorced the man, who has now died, and thus the object of conflict has been removed. Isabelle can again become the well-brought-up and wealthy young Geneviève Ter-boven, who remembers little of her unreal relationship with Bodmer. But Bodmer, though feeling a sense of loss, has realized that the nature of life is the seizing of what moments one can without any ruminatory *Weltan-schuung,* and that life and love are interchangeable.

The two older men, the analytical scientist-doctor on the one hand and the priest on the other both contribute to Bodmer's learning process.[12] Some of the discussions he has with them are again set-piece arguments, but both characters are acceptable and individual, and neither can be dismissed. Bodmer might reject the doctor's insistence upon the exclusive importance of science, but the doctor also tells him, after he has shown Bodmer the psychiatric wards for those damaged by the war, to abandon his excursions into the subconscious and praise life simply because he is alive. Interestingly, Wernicke even rejects Bodmer's experiences of the war. Human sympathy — the genuine ability to share in another's suffering — is a problem beyond Bodmer and even beyond the church. Nor does Bodmer return to orthodox religion, but the priest Bodendiek comments to Wernicke (who reports it) that he feels Bodmer may be on the way back to the church. The intolerance sometimes shown by the church is brought out at various points, but Bodmer, who as the organist is physically on the fringe of the church, has a significant debate with Bodendiek when he discusses the death of his own mother, although he tries to conceal from the priest whom he is talking about. She had died in agony and, according to the rules of the Catholic church, in a state of mortal sin, so that by those rules she will burn in hell for all eternity. Bodendiek gives way, and comments: "Die Kirche hat Regeln. Sie hat Regeln um zu verhüten und zu erziehen. Gott hat keine. Gott ist die Liebe" (93, the church has rules. The rules are to protect and to educate. God doesn't have any rules. God is love). Bodmer rejects the notion of a love that can appear sadistic, but Bodendiek encourages his doubts: "Zweifel ist die Kehrseite des Glaubens" (93, doubt is the other side of belief). Bodmer feels disgruntled that Bodendiek always has an answer, but of course, that is an answer, and he himself uses elements of it in talking to a woman whose husband has committed suicide and cannot be buried in consecrated ground. Remarque's characters tend to concentrate upon life, rather than upon the metaphysical, which can wait, but the door is often left open. The position is summed up by Ravic in *Arc de Triomphe* in the phrase: "Aber ich bin auch kein Atheist. Ich bin nur ein Schwergläubiger" (81, but I'm not an atheist. I'm just a reluctant believer).

The Isabelle episode helps Bodmer towards a philosophy of life, but there are two other conclusions to the novel, a political one and a personal one. The political conclusion may be expressed in historical terms as the currency deflation and the temporary defeat of the right, just as Hitler, who plays a considerable part in this work, did seem to have been stopped after 1923 when the government of the republic apparently gained a grip on the economic situation. An early scene in the novel places Bodmer with Georg Kroll and the redoubtable Willy in the Café Central, where a group of young right-wingers make the café band play the relatively new national anthem, *Deutschland über alles,* and demand that everyone should stand up — a technique of deliberate provocation.[13] Bodmer and the others react angrily, and these young nationalists once again refer to Bodmer and the others as Bolsheviks and cowards. Willy drives them off — by literally farting in the face of one of them — but more of them gather. Bodo Ledderhose, another former soldier-comrade, however, who is there with a local choir, offers his help, and when the trio leave and are surrounded by these proto-Nazis, he and his friends help to dispatch them. That they fought in the trenches for these people is a basic irony found here and in much of Remarque's writing. This battle is picked up again, however, at the end of the work, when once again Bodmer and his associates, including Willy, who is easily recognizable by his red hair, dubbed ambiguously *den roten Hund* (369, the red dog), are attacked. The nationalist thugs are now specifically Nazis, characterized by their *scheissfarbene Uniformen* (373, shit-colored uniforms) and jackboots, so that the battle is between the new right-wing nationalism, which would lead Germany into a new war, and those who served in the war itself and knew that one war was enough. Bodmer links the intolerant mindset of the nationalists to the famous black obelisk.[14] The battle is a violent one, fought ironically up against the public lavatory (*Pissbude* — the piss-house, 371). Georg commands them back to it in military fashion, so that their rear is covered, and the word *verschanzen*, to dig in, is also used (372). The war is still being fought. A decisive moment in comes, however, when one of the ex-soldiers, who lost an arm in the war and is called, appropriately in this context, Götz von Berlichingen, after the ironhanded hero of Goethe's play, removes his metal prosthesis and swings it like a medieval battle-club until the Nazis are driven off.

Bodmer decides to leave the town, partly because of an ongoing problem with Watzek, who realizes that his wife, Lisa, is having an affair with someone and thinks that it may be Bodmer. His expedient departure is approved by Georg Kroll, who is having the affair, and by Riesenfeld, who would like to, and who finds Bodmer a newspaper job in Berlin. His last triumph is the sale of the black obelisk, and he leaves after a farewell session of the poets' club, serenaded by Ledderhose's choir until the police take them away. Bodmer has refused, however, even to be made an honorary member of the poets' club. He is going away just to be himself, to go out into the world "[a]ls kleiner Funke Leben, der versuchen wird, nicht zu erlöschen" (379, as a small spark of life that is going to try not to be extinguished).

The 1923 narrative, the bulk of the work, ends with some hope for the future, although the novel has plenty of ambiguities: Isabelle is not real; the apparent restoration of financial order is based on a kind of illusion that none of the characters really understand; the threat of the incipient Nazi movement has not gone away entirely. But Bodmer has learned at least to seize life, and just for the moment the Nazis have been beaten off, the crazy inflation has been curbed, and he can — in a real sense — move on. Of course the hope did not last. A final and quite separate, brief twenty-sixth chapter takes us beyond the novel to 1955, and thus leapfrogs beyond the time of *Drei Kameraden* to sum up thirty years in a couple of pages and show the sometimes predictable fates of the characters. Some had joined the Nazis and prospered, even after the war; others, including Georg Kroll and the sculptor Kurt Bach, suffered under the regime. Bodmer's two mentors, Wernicke and Bodendiek, hid Jews in their hospital, but Bodendiek is sent to a remote village after criticizing a bishop who worked with the Nazis, and Wernicke, after refusing to carry out fatal injections on the mentally ill, is sent to the front in the Second World War, where he — like Willy and various others — is killed. Geneviève is never heard of again, but in any case, her importance lay in her role as Isabelle, who never really existed.

Der schwarze Obelisk operates on several levels. It is a *Bildungsroman* in which the education of the central figure takes place mostly inside the boundaries of a psychiatric hospital and involves an illusory love affair with a woman who does not exist, and which contrasts with his physical affair with the acrobat, Gerda. He learns, in fact, a similar lesson from both of these, and also from Wernicke and Bodendiek: to stop asking questions that do not have an answer, and to take life as life, so that when his one-year emotional apprenticeship is over, he is left only with the spark of life that cannot be extinguished. As a picture of the Weimar Republic, the novel offers a snapshot of a crisis period that was both a *scheusslicher Karneval,* a dreadful carnival (the adjective is interesting), and a *mächtige Seifenblase,* a huge soap bubble (375). And now the carnival is over. The final chapter not only tells us about the characters in the novel, but something about the town. Bombs destroyed much of Werdenbrück, we are told, but the psychiatric hospital and the maternity hospitals were relatively unscathed. Indeed, they soon filled up again and have even been extended. The narrator explains, rationally enough, that they escaped because they were outside the town. But they are also outside time, be it novelistic or historical. Life will go on and the maternity hospital will need to be extended. But so will the asylum.

Drei Kameraden

The dates between which *Drei Kameraden* is set are clear from the novel: from mid-1928 to the start of 1929. What is less specific is its location. It is presumably set in Berlin, although Berlin is not named; references are to *die Stadt* (the city), the distinctive dialect is not used, and there are no clearly identifiable locations beyond occasional references to, say, the Nikolaistrasse or to the canal (perhaps the Landwehrkanal) to provide establishing shots, as in comparable novels like Erich Kästner's *Fabian* of 1931.[15] Instead we have a generalized city background: cafés and bars open all hours, prostitutes, suburbs and working-class districts. The street violence in 1929 at the end of the novel is another indicator of Berlin, but again nothing is specific. Sometimes, in fact, the overall feel is precisely not of that city; the characters go "to the station" rather than to a particular Berlin terminal, and the principal character visits a cloistered garden attached to a Catholic cathedral in an *Altstadt,* which sounds more like Osnabrück than Berlin. This is not, then, a Berlin novel, but a novel of the later years of the Weimar Republic. The political picture is again interrelated with a love story, the relationship between the first-person narrator and Pat(rice Hollmann), whose name was to have been the title of the work. Pat suffers from tuberculosis, and although there is hope of a sort throughout the relationship, the sickness triumphs in the end, so that Pat, and thus the relationship, dies. The symbolic parallel is with the Weimar Republic itself: brought about by the war and still suffering its effects, sustained by the hope that Remarque referred to retrospectively in his preface to *Der schwarze Obelisk,* and sometimes looking as if it had recovered, it, too, was always doomed. The notion of comradeship as a valuable but fragile thing is dealt with here once more, too, but the conclusion reached at the end is that spelled out in *Der schwarze Obelisk,* namely that comrades and lovers still have to die alone. The narrator is left alone at the end of the work: Pat is dead, one of his close friends has been murdered, and even a car, which has a name and which has been a bond between the group of three friends at the start and through much of the work, has been sold.

At the end of *Der schwarze Obelisk,* the narrator, Ludwig Bodmer, set off for a job in Berlin in a spirit of confidence at the end of 1923, the currency had stabilized, and a group of Nazi thugs had been beaten off. *Drei Kameraden* may be seen — if read after the 1956 novel — as a continuation with a similar narrator, who might well have come from Werden-(Osna-)brück to the city, although he is not working for a newspaper. But although Bodmer in *Der schwarze Obelisk* had acquired some measure of emotional stability, the rootlessness of the lost generation still remains. So too, where the Weimar Republic had survived the crisis of inflation, it would not survive the next crisis; *Drei Kameraden* has unemployment as a running theme, but it is never defeated, and at the end the Nazi thugs kill one of the narrator's friends.

The date is established at the start when the new first-person narrator, Robert (Robby) Lohkamp is celebrating his thirtieth birthday and uses the occasion to review his life thus far. He was eighteen in 1916, has been a soldier, and has been wounded (almost a two-paragraph reprise of *Im Westen nichts Neues*), and in 1919 he experienced former comrades fighting against each other (the plot of *Der Weg züruck*). Then came the political turmoil of 1920, in which we hear that Otto Köster and Gottfried Lenz — the two friends with whom he now works and who make up the three comrades of the title — have been involved in political activity and arrested. It is not yet clear on which side of the political divide they are, although it is likely to be on the left. Lohkamp himself seems throughout the work less politically inclined than the others, but he is, of course, as a first-person narrator, also a mediator and observer. He goes on to recall the inflation year 1923, the theme of *Der schwarze Obelisk,* and after that stops itemizing the years. After the war Lohkamp has had a series of random jobs (we hear that he, too, was once intending to be a schoolteacher), and even now, in the apparently stable period of the Weimar Republic, he has in the past year moved from working as a pianist in the Café International[16] to working with Köster and Lenz in a garage and auto-repair workshop. The three men were fellow soldiers and indeed school friends, and Köster, who owns the concern, was their company commander in the war. Lenz, we are told, had spent time in South America before joining Köster, and he categorizes himself as "the last romantic," though the description might also be applied to Lohkamp.[17] All three share the rootlessness of the generation destroyed by the war. Their drinking, especially Lohkamp's, as a response is another running theme in the novel.

Lohkamp's lodgings are a microcosm of the Weimar Republic: the area around Frau Zalewski's *pension* boasts the Café International, the *Gewerkschaftshaus* (trade union center), and the Salvation Army building, with a cemetery that is no longer used, and next to that a fairground. The motif of the dead in *Der schwarze Obelisk* was similarly ambiguous, because the gravestones belonging to the Krolls were not attached to graves. Of course, war memorials are also often cenotaphs (literally "empty tombs"). Trivial enjoyment in the funfair is here juxtaposed with the forgotten dead, though not war dead, and also with café society, the workers, and the poor. The lodgers in the *pension* are equally representative: the rootless Lohkamp, a struggling student, an accountant in his forties, a Russian émigré, a retired civil servant, a nurse who has lost her husband in the war and her children through malnutrition in 1918, a secretary who is sleeping with her boss.

The auto repair work is making some money, although things are not exactly flourishing. The three friends spend much time on their own car — it is given the name Karl — which looks like an old wreck, but which has a souped-up engine. After an impromptu race with the bemused driver of a large Buick, the comrades meet the driver's attractive companion, Patrice (Pat: the allegedly English spelling of the forename is presumably a phonetic form of Patricia) Hollmann. She gradually becomes the object of Lohkamp's growing love, though his problem with the acknowledgement of this love matches the emotional immaturity of Ludwig Bodmer; alongside this comes the gradual revelation of her serious, but not immediately apparent illness, tuberculosis, which we discover was brought on from malnutrition during the war. The experiences of Lohkamp and those associated with him as they try to survive in the declining Weimar Republic is integrated with the development of the love relationship in real and in symbolic terms. The picture of the healthy looking but sick society and its decline, because of the ongoing damage caused by the war, is as much the substance of the novel as the love story.

Motorcars play as considerable a role in the work as gravestones do in *Der schwarze Obelisk*. The three friends buy a showy Cadillac, for example, which is then sold and resold, and which aids Lohkamp in his courtship of Pat. They also buy an antiquated taxicab, which they use to supplement the failing income of the workshop until it, too, has to be sold. Eventually a would-be lucrative repair job proves their downfall when the payments for it cannot be covered. Their own racing car, Karl, plays a slightly differently symbolic role: it has more inner force, more life than it seems to have from external view, and it is victorious in unofficial races and also at an official racing meet.[18] However, the actual theme of motor racing is not overly prominent here, and the car is also the symbol of friendship between the comrades. At two points in the story it is instrumental in trying to save the life of Pat: first — successfully — in getting a doctor to her in record time around the significant midpoint of the novel; and secondly when it is sold to buy her more time in a sanatorium at the end of the novel, this time fruitlessly.

Like Bodmer, Lohkamp encounters and observes a range of people representative of the Weimar years. He has been playing the piano in a café bar where he now spends a great deal of his time, usually drinking excessively, and which is a base also for Valentin Hauser, who was in the same company with them in the war,[19] and who is drinking his way through a small inheritance on the grounds that — although he knows the war was a long time ago — the fact of having survived it can never be celebrated enough. He is alive, but cannot move on to anything. He recalls every moment and detail of the war, and functions as a kind of memory of the war that cannot even be wiped out by drink. The café is the base, too, for the prostitutes, both female and male; Lohkamp has had a relationship with one of the girls in the past.

The war is still the reason for the permanent insecurity of the major figures, even if they are less extreme than Valentin. The point is made in small matters; Köster asks Lenz to turn off the headlights of a car on one occasion because it reminds him of the searchlights — he had a been a pilot — and Lenz does well at a fairground hoopla because he was the best grenade thrower in his company, but it is also made clear in more expansive passages. Lohkamp himself draws a clear bridge back to *Der Weg zurück* and the debate between Ludwig Breyer and Georg Rahe when he thinks

> daran, wie wir damals zurückgekommen waren aus dem Krieg, jung, ohne Glauben, wie Bergleute aus einem eingestürzten Schacht. Wir hatten marschieren wollen gegen die Lüge, die Ichsucht, die Gier, die Trägheit des Herzens, die all das verschuldet hatten, was hinter uns lag; — wir waren hart gewesen, ohne anderes Vertrauen als das zu dem Kameraden neben uns und das eine andere, das nie getrogen hatte: zu den Dingen, — zu Himmel, Tabak, Baum und Brot und Erde; — aber was war daraus geworden? Alles war zusammengebrochen, verfälscht und vergessen. Und wer nicht vergessen konnte, dem blieb nur die Ohnmacht, die Verzweiflung, die Gleichgültigkeit und der Schnaps. Die Zeit der grossen Menschen- und Männerträume war vorbei. Die Betriebsamen triumphierten. Die Korruption. Das Elend. (49)

> [about how we had come back from the war, young, without any belief, like miners from a collapsed shaft. We had wanted to march against all the lies, the selfishness, the greed, the lethargy for which all that lay behind us was to blame; we had become hard, trusting nothing except the comrade standing beside us and with one other unfailing trust — in things like the sky, tobacco, trees, and bread and the earth; — but what

happened? Everything was smashed, faked, or forgotten. And if you couldn't forget, all you had left was impotence, despair, indifference, and liquor. The time of man's — or mankind's — great dreams was past. What triumphed was pettiness. Corruption. Misery.]

The passage is important not least in its use of tenses. The narrator has not actually given way to the drunken despair indicated, but he could still do so, as others do in the work. For the narrator the love element, with some prompting from his comrades, will offer him hope, the hope referred to retrospectively in a political context in the preface to *Der schwarze Obelisk*. However, even the hope of love proves in the event unsustained, and the isolation of the individual is what will remain. In the political context, too, there is an awareness on the part of some of the characters, reported by the narrator, of the state of the republic. Interestingly, when it first begins to be apparent that Robby Lohkamp is in love, his slightly older friends are cynically but affectionately amused. These friends include Ferdinand Grau, an artist who makes a living by painting portraits from photographs of the recently deceased. Lenz notes that all of them are living only on illusion and credit now — another comment on the economic state of the Weimar Republic — but Grau develops this idea into a philosophy. Yes, he comments, they are all living on illusions about the past and credit against the future, and only the simple and non-skeptical — like Robby Lohkamp — can in these circumstances experience "die Liebe, den Glauben an die Zukunft, die Träume vom Glück" (60–61, love, belief in the future, dreams of happiness). Lohkamp is presented with these ideas when he is thinking already of Pat, and Lenz reminds him of them later, when Lohkamp is sitting in the empty café playing soldiers' songs from the war that sound like ghosts from the past. Later still, Grau returns to the theme and applies it to Lohkamp's entire generation, even if they are not much younger than he is. In doing so he links the political theme of the novel with that of the love story: "Was wisst ihr Burschen denn vom Dasein! Ihr fürchtet euch ja vor euren eigenen Gefühlen. . . . ihr seid vernünftig in der Liebe und unvernünftig in der Politik, — ein erbärmliches Geschlecht! (102, What do you guys know about life? You're afraid of your own feelings . . . you're careful in love and careless in politics — a wretched generation!). One critic has referred to the three friends as "emotional anarchists who believe in nothing"[20] but Lohkamp is led out of this and into his love for Pat.

The various misfortunes of other characters observed by Lohkamp are not always to do with the war, at least not directly so. The major theme of unemployment as an indicator of economic collapse is developed in parallel to the indications of Pat's illness, which is a product of the war, and it too becomes more serious as the novel progresses. The friends buy the old taxi, for example, because its previous owner cannot afford to keep it, and the scene of the auction — there are dozens every day — reflects the economic situation as people try and realize a little cash by selling their *armseligen Kram* (pitiful bits and pieces). Two further scenes in particular make the point: on one occasion Lohkamp visits a betting shop with a friend, which turns out to be full — the narrator registers surprise at this — of ordinary workers, clerks, and so on. While he is there a man faints with hunger, having gambled the little money he had for food — apparently a regular occurrence. A prostitute gives the unemployed and desperate man a bread roll she takes from someone else, and also a few coins. Later, Lohkamp and Pat visit a museum on a Sunday and are surprised to see it full. They are told that this is not an unexpected surge in historical interest, but that these are mostly the unemployed. Entrance is free on some days, and they have nothing to do, and in winter it is even fuller because the museum is warm.

There is a gradual attrition in the fellow residents of the *pension* where Lohkamp lives. The student is forced to give up his idea of studying; the nurse has to move into the equivalent of the poorhouse when the children's home in which she works collapses for lack of funds — the pastor running it has lost the money on the stock market; the Russian is still searching in vain for a job. Hasse, the accountant, who was always in terror of losing his job and consequently worked all hours, loses his wife instead, and when she leaves him, his depression causes him to hang himself. In a small but significant scene, when Orlow, the Russian, tries to keep the others away from the unpleasant sight, the retired civil servant insists that he should be present, and will not, as a German, be pushed aside by a foreigner he calls "an Asiatic." The ground was always fertile for Nazi racial policy. When a doctor and two police officials arrive to deal with the dead man, one of them comments that this is the twelfth suicide this week, although Hasse is unusual in that he was not out of work. The others nearly all took their own lives "wegen Arbeitslosigkeit. Zwei Familien, eine mit drei Kindern. Mit Gas natürlich. Familien nehmen fast immer Gas" (276, on account of unemployment. Two families, one of them with three children. Gas, of course. Families almost always gas themselves). The same point is found in *Der schwarze Obelisk* for slightly different reasons. Here we are told of a pensioner who has gassed himself and is found with overprinted and worthless inflation banknotes in his hand.

Drei Kameraden is a difficult novel to analyze in linear progression because it is multilayered. The two major themes — the spread of unemployment and the love story of Robby and Pat — both depend, however, to an extent on attitudes and states of mind that themselves go back to the war. Robby's friends are overtly cynical, drinking to life, but to a life that is rootless: "Weil wir leben! Weil wir atmen! Weil wir das Leben so stark empfinden, dass wir nichts mehr damit anzufangen wissen!" (299, Because we are alive! Because we're breathing! Because our zest for life is so strong that we no longer have any idea what to do with it!). This emotional bankruptcy matches the mortgaged and rapidly crumbling economy of the republic.

Lohkamp's courtship of Pat is not an easy one. Because he, like Bodmer, is unsure of himself in personal relationships, he reacts with a positively childish jealousy after he has taken Pat to the theatre, and they have met other friends of hers at nightclubs, unaware of how much she loves him.[21] Once they do come together, however, Robby becomes gradually aware of Pat's illness, which she has tried to conceal from him. The image, which Remarque uses again in *Die Nacht von Lissabon* and *Der Himmel kennt keine Günstlinge,* of an illness that can allow the patient to appear blooming when the reality is quite different, is important. In its most general sense it can imply a simple *memento mori,* a reminder that in the midst of life death is always present, but here it also mirrors the apparently energetic and fun-loving, but in fact mortally sick Weimar Republic.

Pat's illness reaches a crisis roughly at the midpoint of the novel. The pair take holiday by the sea, during which Pat suffers a major hemorrhage and nearly dies. Faced with Pat's serious illness, Lohkamp realizes that she is now as much a *Kamerad* as those he served with, and that he and his friends must get her through this, and what will develop as a normal love between a man and a woman is couched in terms of the war: just as *Kameradschaft,* comradeship, meant during the war standing by your comrade in any life and death situation, Robby is in this crisis Pat's comrade. She depends upon him: "Pat konnte nicht sterben. Sie konnte nur sterben, wenn ich den Mut verlor" (200, Pat couldn't die. She could only die if I lost my nerve). His references of endearment to her later as *alter Bursche,* old buddy, are more than just grammatically masculine.[22] The close comradeship between the three men, and indeed their car, is brought into play when Otto Köster brings the somewhat surprised doctor, Professor Felix Jaffé, from his hospital to the coast in record time.[23] Part of his surprise is the speed, but also that the object of this wild ride is not in fact Köster's own girlfriend, but someone else's. Otto did not tell him in advance where they were going in case he refused to come, and the doctor comments that his opinion of doctors was not high if he thought that; the sympathetic figure of Jaffé pays, as it were, for the negative images of doctors in the two First World War novels.

Pat survives on this occasion, but Robby now has a clear idea of how seriously ill Pat is, and at the same time he becomes aware that the feelings they have for each other have to be accepted. This emotional shift on Lohkamp's part is underlined at the end of this central chapter when Pat announces simply: "ich bin ja glücklich" (203, I am happy). Thus far, Lohkamp had thought that the only person one can rely on is oneself, but now that single word brings home to him that he can mean so much to another person that she is happy simply if he is there. This train of thought — he sees it as a definition of love, and of a love that is multilayered — is developed to a climax: "Es ist Liebe und doch etwas anderes. Etwas, wofür man leben kann" (204, It is love, but something else. Something you can live for). With nice literary irony he also thinks that these thoughts can never be expressed by a generation unable to put its feelings into words, although as narrator that is exactly what he is doing.

Professor Jaffé — who observes and understands this crucial scene — is developed as a character of some importance in the work, especially after their return to the city. Even on this first major encounter with him, however, his comments on life are of interest, when he contrasts the fears of unemployment with the obsession with work, which can exclude other aspects of living. However, although he is a man of science, who ought perhaps there-fore to deal in certainties, his real role in the novel is to provide hope, and he does this when Lohkamp, who has visited him to establish the details of Pat's illness, has learned that she will have to return to a sanatorium. At Lohkamp's despairing question of why Pat should be sick when others are healthy, he insists that Lohkamp accompany him on his hospital rounds. This is a variation on a recurrent scene in Remarque's novels. Bäumer's general view of the military hospital in *Im Westen nichts Neues,* which would be matched by a similar scene in *Zeit zu leben und Zeit zu sterben,* served to show that war did not just kill. Here the effect, ironically, is the reverse, offering hope rather than increasing despair, although many of the people shown are seriously ill:

> Sie haben jetzt gesehen, dass viele dieser Menschen schlimmer krank sind als Pat Hollmann. Manche von ihnen haben nichts mehr als ihre Hoffnung. Aber die meisten kommen durch. Werden wieder gesund. Das wollte ich Ihnen zeigen (236).

> [Now you've seen that a lot of these people are much more seriously ill than Pat Hollman. Many of them haven't got much more left than hope. But most of them pull through. Get better. That's what I wanted to show you.]

He also explains that his own wife had died suddenly in the European influenza pandemic at the end of the war. The double lesson, then, is that disease is random, but that there is always hope. Showing him the hospital is the equivalent for Lohkamp of the shock technique used on the reader in other novels, though with a different message. It has a more exact parallel in *Der schwarze Obelisk* when Dr. Wernicke takes Bodmer around his mental hospital, showing him his worst cases precisely so that he will learn to be grateful and also to trust his feelings rather than constantly trying to analyze life. Lohkamp learns that he has to be there for Pat. The message of not giving up hope — in life, in the state, in God — recalls the medieval sin of *desperatio,* the irredeemable state of despair that meant that the soul was lost. In medieval works, like Wolfram's *Parzival,* a character who approaches this state of mind is often helped out of it by an older and wiser mentor, and this is the case here between Lohkamp and Jaffé.

Jaffé is a secular figure, but the religious counterpart, though less prominent than in *Der schwarze Obelisk,* is present later in the novel in a scene in which Lohkamp visits the cathedral to steal some roses from the cloister garden, but he is interrupted by a priest. He pretends to be praying, but is at the last station of the cross, so that the priest engages him in conversation. Lohkamp cannot say what he is praying for, so that the priest says that he will "um Hilfe in der Not für einen Unbekannten beten" (259, pray for help in need for an unknown person). The reference to Pat is clear, though Lohkamp's prayers were not genuine. The priest leaves, assuring him of God's help even if this is not always comprehensible. Lohkamp cannot accept this and thinks of all those comrades whom God failed to help, and concludes: "Verdammt, es war etwas zu viel Blut geflossen in der Welt für diese Art von Glauben an den himmlischen Vater!" (259, Damn it, too much blood had been spilt in the world for that kind of belief in a heavenly father). Jaffé, the man of science, has offered a hope, which is by definition uncertain, in probability or possibility, rather than anything sure and certain. Lohkamp's reaction to the priest's words looks like a final rejection of what seems to be cradle Catholicism on his part. However, it is the inclusion of this encounter in the novel at all that is important: a reminder of other possibilities.

When Jaffé tells Lohkamp that Pat has to go back to the sanatorium over the winter, however, Lohkamp precisely does demand some kind of certainty. He wants to be assured that Pat will come back, and if such an assurance is impossible, then he wants her to stay with him. When Jaffé indicates that to stay will certainly mean that Pat will die, Lohkamp's response is that it means that she will not die alone. Bodmer commented, and Lohkamp will learn that the individual always has to die alone. Jaffé points out that the younger man's attitude is a kind of despair, and that he would try everything "und wenn ich genau wüsste, dass es zwecklos wäre" (280, even if I knew for sure that it was of no use). He underscores again the absolute necessity for hope, and when Lohkamp asks what hope actually means, Jaffé replies:

> Alles . . . Immer alles. Ich kann Ihnen jetzt nicht mehr sagen. Das andere sind Möglichkeiten . . . Aber ich hoffe bestimmt, dass sie im Frühjahr zurückkommen kann. (280)

> [It's everything . . . it always is. I can't say any more definite to you now anything else is a possibility . . . But I certainly hope that she will be able to come back in the spring.]

Lohkamp agrees to take her to the sanatorium. On his return, however, things are not well economically. In an earlier scene the three friends had physically fought off a rival group to retrieve a damaged car for repair. Now its owner has gone bankrupt and is not insured and the business continues to decline. By November 1928 they are forced to sell more of their assets, and Lohkamp returns to piano playing in the evenings. Parallel with this, too, is an increasing unease in the political situation, and one evening Köster comes to find Lohkamp to help him look for the third comrade, Lenz. There have been several fights in political assemblies already, and Lenz has gone to one that may turn violent. In the attempt to find Lenz, who is red-haired and thus conspicuous, much like Willy in *Der schwarze Obelisk,* they arrive first at what is clearly a right-wing assembly, a Nazi group with young men in uniforms, a band with flags, and a speaker who sounds like Hitler, whose captivating words reach a crescendo with the phrase "Das muss anders werden!" (Things will have to change). This is also the phrase attributed to Hitler in *Der schwarze Obelisk.* Remarque does not permit his narrator to spell out in *Drei Kameraden* which side is which, something that has occasioned critical comment, although it is not hard to work out. The point is made in other novels, of course, perhaps most clearly in *Der Funke Leben,* that one totalitarian regime is like another. Here, interestingly, Köster and Lohkamp both function as outside observers, looking at the reaction of the audiences as they have all their problems solved, have someone else think for them, have faith. "Es war gut, zu glauben" (318, It was good to believe). They move on to a second meeting, with different uniforms and flags (red ones this time, one must assume), with a less effective speaker who uses numbers rather than the catch phrases of the demagogue. Lenz is at neither. Still searching, they come (and it makes for a nice juxtaposition) to a fortune telling booth that is also doing a good trade, and this provokes a summary:

> "Otto," sagte ich zu Köster, der vor mir herging, "jetzt weiss ich, was die Leute wollen. Sie wollen gar keine Politik. Sie wollen Religionsersatz."
>
> Er sah sich um. "Natürlich. Sie wollen an irgend etwas glauben. An was ist ganz egal. Deshalb sind sie auch so fanatisch." (319)
>
> ["Otto," I said to Koster, who was just ahead of me, "now I know what people want. They don't want politics. They want a substitute for religion."
>
> He looked round. "Of course. They want to believe in something. It doesn't matter what. That's why they are so fanatical."]

They find yet another hall in which a meeting is taking place, and when a fight breaks out, they spot Lenz and drag him away from the mêlée, apparently successfully. Coming away he has a horoscope from the fortune teller who assures he will live until he is eighty, and then they see a black cat — taken as unlucky — but do not turn around, as superstition demands. These two incidents simply show that there is no way of predicting the future: suddenly they are faced with four young men in what are patently Nazi uniforms, who apparently recognize Lenz and shoot and kill him. A doctor who inspects the body comments on the war wounds in his arms, and the others observe that the young men who killed him were children when the war ended, another familiar theme. While there is no real doubt that the assassins are fascists,[24] what is unclear is why they kill Lenz — an error of identity, or his recognizability as an opponent after he had been dragged away from the fight at the meeting. To place the two novels *Drei Kameraden* and *Der schwarze Obelisk* for a moment in their order of writing, it is possible that the latter novel was intended not just to precede, but to some extent to clarify the earlier one. In *Der schwarze Obelisk,* Willy Hohmeyer had brushed with the Nazis already and is recognized by his red hair when another Nazi group attacks them later. The assassins in *Drei Kameraden* are wearing military-style boots, and at the end of *Der schwarze Obelisk,* Remarque even has his narrator comment on the trademark jackboots of the Nazi mob that attacks them.

Köster claims falsely to the police that he would be unable to identify the assassins, because he wishes to take his own revenge, a motif that is varied in several of the novels. There is a considerable amount of violence on the part of the characters in the war novels that is not associated with the war — the beating up of Himmelstoss in *Im Westen nichts Neues,* or of Seelig in *Der Weg zurück,* and in this work, too, Lohkamp has had to prove his worth by fighting a competitor cabby (who later becomes his friend), and also a cheating hotel doorman. Violence is part of them, and the blurring of the idea of murder is another ongoing theme. That it is still an echo of the war is clear — they associate Lenz's death with the fall of a comrade in arms, and soldiers' songs are in their mind when he is buried. Köster comments that he once killed a young English pilot in the war and could keep his mind quiet with the phrase *Krieg ist Krieg,* war is war, but this is a murder that has to be avenged. This is an interesting variation on the theme explored already in the two war novels: this actually is murder, and Köster wishes to punish it appropriately, but without recourse to the law as such. The rationale is that the killers will count on a lenient sentence if apprehended by the police, and indeed there is evidence that right-wing criminals were almost invariably better treated by a highly conservative judiciary.[25] In the event, the matter is settled for them by another friend, Alfons, who shoots the killer in self-defense.

The unity of the three comrades has been destroyed by the political chaos in Germany, and the end of the novel returns to the parallel story of the love between Robby and Pat, parallel because there, too, the hope that has sustained them proves to be a forlorn one, since Pat cannot be saved. The final chapters of the work are set in January 1929 in the sanatorium. Although Karl the car and the fellowship could assist in saving Pat at the midpoint of the novel, this time even the sale of the much-loved car (it is even referred to it as *ein Kamerad,* 361) to buy Pat more time in the sanatorium is not enough. The act of selling the car is one of pure friendship on Otto Köster's part,[26] but the comradeship that went back to the war had already ended when Lenz was killed, and this is another blow. The final blow is the existential one for Lohkamp: that Pat, too, must die. She has learned to play poker (a regularly used image of Remarque's) in the sanatorium, but the gamble of life defeats her. At the end, increasingly weak and bothered by the loudness of the ticking of the clock, she tries to make Robby leave. Death is an individual matter after all: "Ich werde schon allein damit fertig" (382, I'll manage it on my own). Robby, too, is left alone at the end with Pat's body:

> Ich habe gesehen, wie ihr Gesicht anders wurde. Ich konnte nichts tun als leer dasitzen und sie ansehen. Dann kam der Morgen, und sie war es nicht mehr. (383)

> [I watched her face change and become different. I could do nothing but sit there, empty, and watch her. Then the morning came, and it wasn't her any more.]

One of the earlier stages of the novel had it ending not with Pat's death, but with Köster and Lohkamp continuing — literally soldiering on — more or less resolutely as "Soldaten in der grossen Armee des Lebens" (soldiers in the great army of life).[27] The love between Robby and Pat has been intense, and Robby has learned the value of feelings, but the final awareness of isolation is a human lesson. Pat at least has been happy, but unhappiness is summed up in *Der schwarze Obelisk* in terms of existential isolation: "Unglück ist, dass man sich immerfort verlassen muss . . . Immer stirbt einer zuerst. Immer bleibt einer zurück" (181, Unhappiness means that you always have to leave someone . . . One of them always dies first. One of them is always left behind).

The hope implied in the Weimar Republic was a forlorn one. Ludwig Bodmer recovered from the war, but with no expressed aim beyond keeping the tiny spark of life from being extinguished. He was given an idea of love that was based on an illusion, although it taught him that love is a possibility. *Drei Kameraden* is a genuine love story, but at the same time a picture of the dying Weimar Republic. Bodmer and his friends survived the Nazi attack, but the death of Lenz at the hands of the Nazis is the beginning of the end; the narrator's comrade in arms and his comrade in love have both died, and the future is bleak. But just as the love story was always doomed in view of Pat's initially far from obvious illness, so too the Weimar Republic was doomed, even if this was not always apparent. The recovery from crisis in 1924 was, like Pat's, only a temporary one. Love, parting, and death are principal themes, too, in the next two novels in historical chronology, and also in the order of writing. But they are not set in Germany.

Notes

[1] The Danish edition, *Kammerater,* was translated by Sonja Heise (Copenhagen: Gyldendal, 1936), but from what Remarque described in a letter of 11 June 1937 as a "falsche, vorletzte, wesentlich weitschweifigere, schlechtere Fassung" (wrong, penultimate, considerably more rambling, worse version): *Das unbekannte Werk,* vol. 5, 278. The English text is by A. W. Wheen (Boston: Little, Brown, and Company, 1937), and it was serialized in the US magazine *Good Housekeeping.* See Tims, *Remarque,* 89, on the publishing history. The German text appeared in 1938 (Amsterdam: Querido), and is here cited from the KiWi edition of 1998 with an afterword by Tilman Westphalen. It was dedicated to J. R. Z. (that is, Jutta or Jeanne Remarque Zambona, from whom he was already divorced, but upon whom the figure of Pat was supposedly based in physical terms), and the work has again a number of incidental echoes of Remarque's personal life, even down to the dog, Billy. The work was filmed in 1938 as *Three Comrades,* directed by Frank Borzage and with a screenplay by F. Scott Fitzgerald. On the conflicts between Fitzgerald, Joseph Mankiewicz, and Louis B. Mayer of MGM, and the question of censorship or adaptation to make the film less anti-Nazi, see Tims, *Remarque,* 90–92. See also Taylor, *Remarque,* 105–14, on the film, which was relatively well-received by the critics. A Russian film, *Tsveti ot pobeditelei* (Flowers from the Victors, 1999), directed by Aleksandr Surin, is also based on the novel.

[2] Remarque's original preface is in Schneider, *Remarque,* 70. It is of course possible to link the three early novels; Antkowiak, *Remarque,* 72, refers to *Drei Kameraden* as the last of a series, and Wagener, *Understanding,* 45, takes it as the last part of a trilogy, while noting that Remarque himself did not do so. Rikke Christoffersen, "Three Comrades — One Perspective: Conceptualising Remarque's *Drei Kameraden* with the Two Early War Novels," *Jahrbuch* 15 (2005): 36–62, makes the connection on stylistic and other grounds. Firda, *Thematic Analysis,* takes *Der Weg zurück* and *Drei Kameraden* together, and Barker and Last, *Remarque,* treat *Der Weg zurück, Drei Kameraden,* and *Der schwarze Obelisk* as a group.

[3] See Thomas F. Schneider, "Von *Pat* zu *Drei Kameraden:* Zur Entstehung des ersten Romans der Exil-Zeit Remarques," *Jahrbuch* 2 (1992): 67–78. Schneider gives an earlier synopsis, and also an outline of the *Pat* version. He also notes a great variety of alternative titles, 68 and 76 n. 8. The change of title is also discussed by Reiner Jeglin and Irmgard Pickerodt, "'Weiche Kerle in harter Schale': Zu *Drei Kameraden,*" in Schneider, *Erich Maria Remarque: Leben, Werk und weltweite Wirkung,* 216–34, as well as Tilman Westphalen's afterword to the KiWi edition. By the time of the last version, Remarque was assisting other writers to escape from Germany.

[4] The first edition was published in 1956 in Cologne by Kiepenheuer and Witsch; cited here from their 1998 paperback, with afterword by Tilman Westphalen. *The Black Obelisk* was translated by Denver Lindley (New York: Harcourt, Brace, 1957). The work was filmed for German television in 1988, directed by Peter Deutsch. On the earlier dramatization see Frank Woesthoff, "Zur Verfilmung der Isabelle-Szenen für die Inszenierung der Probebühne *Der schwarze Obelisk,*" in Schwindt and Westphalen, *Man kann alten Dreck nicht vergraben,* 26–32. See Peter Junk, *Isabelle: Szenen nach Erich Maria Remarques Der schwarze Obelisk* (Osnabrück: Universität Osnabrück, 1994).

[5] Schneider, *Remarque*, 28, provides a photograph of stones, including a black obelisk, from the firm of Vogt in Osnabrück, for whom Remarque worked and upon whom the Firma Kroll is based. For the numerous other parallels see the *Textcollage* on *Der schwarze Obelisk* in Schwindt and Westphalen, *Man kann alten Dreck nicht vergraben*, especially the two editors' "Werdenbrück- und Osnabrück-Register," 199–226. In this alphabetic list we can find, for example, reference to Eduard Petersilie (who published nationalist poems under the name Peter Silie), who ran the Germania hotel in Osnabrück (see *Zeit zu leben und Zeit zu sterben*), and who can be linked to Eduard Knobloch, who runs the Walhalla (still an agreeable hotel in the center of Osnabrück). See also Tims, *Remarque*, 34–35 on Biedendieck, the model for Bodendiek. See Tilman Westphalen's afterword to the KiWi edition. Sternburg, *"Als wäre alles,"* 400, sees this as the most biographical of all Remarque's novels.

[6] Bernhard Nienaber, *Vom anachronistischen Helden zum larmoyanten Untertan* (Würzburg: Königshausen and Neumann, 1997), 182, characterizes Birkholz, Bodmer, and Lohkamp by their melancholy, their extraordinary ability to hold their liquor, and also by their complete political innocence. The first two features are correct, but the unpolitical aspect is more difficult to accept. All of these first-person narrators are necessarily mediators; they select political scenes, and either comment themselves or report comments on them and on the broader political situation by others. All three seem to some extent innocent in that respect, but all three are hardly impervious to politics and Bodmer is particularly aware. *Der schwarze Obelisk* and *Drei Kameraden*, while both love stories as well, are very much political novels. Bodmer's anti-fascist views are especially clear. Antkowiak, *Remarque*, 119–27, has some interesting comments on the differences with Bodmer, although he is surely not a completely static figure.

[7] See the summary by William Carr, *Hitler: A Study in Personality and Politics* (London: Arnold, 1978), 12. On the Weimar Republic, a first-class visual picture of the period is provided by Torsten Palmer and Heinrich Neubauer, *The Weimar Republic Through the Lens of the Press (Die Weimarer Zeit in Pressefotos und Fotoreportagen)*, trans. Peter Barton, Mark Cole, and Jackie Cox, German and English editions (Cologne: Könemann, 2000). For views of activities of the left in the conflicts in 1923 and also in the later period of the Weimar Republic, see issues 5/1 and 5/2 (1993–34) of the left-wing journal *Revolutionary History*, with details, for example, of the bias shown towards right-wing criminal acts by the judiciary in Al Richardson's introduction to 5/1, 1–8. On the liveliness of the period see Anton Gill, *A Dance Between Flames: Berlin Between the Wars* (London: John Murray, 1993) and Peter Gay, *Weimar Culture* (London: Secker and Warburg, 1969). For a clear picture of the inflation, see Walter Tormin, "Die Entstehung und Entwicklung der Weimar Republik bis zu Eberts Tod," in his edited volume *Die Weimarer Republik*, rev. ed. (Hanover: Literatur und Zeitgeschehen, 1968), 82–136, esp. 123–31. At the end, after the issue of the *Rentenmark*, the old paper mark was set at 4.2 *Billion* to the Dollar (the German *Billion* means one million million; *Milliarde* is a thousand million).

[8] Both Wagener, *Understanding*, 88–89, and Sternburg, *"Als wäre alles,"* 399, rightly link the pair with Naphta and Settembrini and their influence on Hans Castorp in Thomas Mann's *Zauberberg* (*The Magic Mountain*), a work that (perhaps unsurprisingly, given its status in twentieth-century literature) also influenced Remarque in *Der Himmel kennt keine Günstlinge*.

[9] As in Hans Chlumberg's play *Wunder um Verdun* (*Miracle at Verdun*) in 1930, which focuses upon war memorials, and where the dead actually come back and — albeit fruitlessly — complain about such abuse of their memory. See my "Memory and Prophecy," 92–104, with other contemporary examples of the motif.

[10] On the use of the Führer title in analogy to Mussolini's of "il Duce," see Ian Kershaw, *The "Hitler Myth": Image and Reality in the Third Reich* (Oxford: Oxford UP, 1987), 22. On the development later of the "Führer principle," see Helga Grebing, *Der Nationalsozialismus: Ursprung und Wesen,* 17th ed. (1959; Munich and Vienna: Olzog, 1964), 94–95. Hitler's first radio broadcast was on 31 January 1933, and the type of radio mentioned and also an allusion to IG-Farben are rather less noticeable anachronisms. See finally Tilman Westphalen's afterword to the KiWi edition of *Schatten im Paradies,* 500. Although they have been seen as a deliberate strategy (Placke, *Die Chiffren des Utopischen,* 82), one wonders how much these points would have been or are now noticed. Hitler's radio broadcast is out by ten years, but the others are close enough to be blurred. It has also been noted, of course, that Shakespeare allows a clock to chime in *Julius Caesar.*

[11] Barker and Last, *Remarque,* 85, cite Hanns-Gerd Rabe, Remarque's friend, who reports that there actually was a prostitute with the "iron horse" nickname in Osnabrück, and they claim that she "figures more prominently" in *Der schwarze Obelisk,* although they can hardly be the same person, since one dies in 1923; but they see the two characters named Willy only as "similar," 106.

[12] Antkowiak, *Remarque,* 129, sees the two men as representatives of *erstarrte Welten,* rigid worlds; this is only true to an extent, and neither is simply a representative figure. Antkowiak recognizes, too, that Bodmer is less rigid towards religion than to science. See 132, finally, on the function of Isabelle.

[13] The *Deutschlandlied,* "Deutschland, Deutschland über alles," with words by Heinrich Hoffmann von Fallersleben (referring in 1841 to the pre-eminent need to unify Germany and sometimes misunderstood as an assertion of superiority), set to the familiar melody of Haydn's 1797 Austria hymn, was adopted as the national anthem of the Weimar Republic in August 1922 and became a nationalist-political weapon: see Otto Biba, *Gott erhalte! Joseph Haydns Kaiserhymne* (Vienna: Doblinger, 1982), 17. Bodmer and the others are uncomfortable about it in the scene in which the war memorial is dedicated and prefer a neutral song about comrades.

[14] The polyvalence of the symbolism has been noted. Tilman Westphalen points out in his afterword, 400–401, the implicit irony in its designation as being made of S.S.-Granit (*schwarz, schwedisch,* black Swedish). That it has been around for a long time makes it backward looking, but those initials point forwards, since the initials SS have a later and more sinister meaning; the Nazis also brooked no contradiction, and the obelisk symbolizes their "potenzstrotzende Männlichkeitswahn" — their phallocentric machismo. Westphalen points out too that it is indeed also a phallic symbol, fit for the memorial of a sadomasochistic prostitute.

[15] Erich Kästner's *Fabian* (1931; Frankfurt am Main: Ullstein, 1984) also deals with themes like unemployment and economic instability, hunger and political violence. It was translated into English as *Fabian* in 1932 and republished in an unexpurgated version in 1990 (London: Libris). See also Klaus Neukrantz's left-wing documentary novel *Barrikaden am Wedding* (Barricades in the District of Wedding), first pub-

lished by the Internationaler Arbeiter-Verlag in 1931, about the street fighting in the Kös(s)linerstrasse in Berlin in May 1929; it was republished with a historical appendix (Berlin: Oberbaum, 1970).

[16] On Berlin and café society, see Gill, *Dance Between Flames,* 190–91. Remarque's own particular haunt seems to have been the Eden Hotel Bar. Gill points out that the innumerable cafés catered to all levels of society.

[17] The subtitle of Hilton Tims's life of Remarque, "The Last Romantic" is supported by two prefatory quotations claiming this title for Remarque himself, by Marlene Dietrich and Paulette Goddard Remarque, respectively. Dietrich, interestingly, justifies this by noting how he had the capacity to understand the emotions of others. The idea of being the last of anything is a Romantic notion of itself, of course.

[18] See Christoffersen, "Three Comrades," 47–48, on the presentation of the (sometimes almost sentient) car.

[19] The character is not unlike Valentin Laher in *Der Weg zurück.* See Barker and Last, *Remarque,* 90–91, on his role here. At one point, the narrator remembers a group of soldiers in 1917 including Breyer, and if this is Ludwig Breyer in *Der Weg zurück,* Lohkamp would (since Kemmerich and Katczinsky have also been mentioned) have been in the same company as the narrators of the two First World War novels, and, given the linking presence of Willy Ho(h)meyer in both *Der Weg zurück* and *Der schwarze Obelisk,* probably Bodmer as well.

[20] Harry T. Moore, *Twentieth Century German Literature* (London: Heinemann, 1971), 82. He also sees the work as "another 'road back' story," which is perhaps more questionable in 1928, at least as an overarching judgment. Ferdinand Grau might almost be an extension into the postwar world of Fritz Schramm in *Die Traumbude.*

[21] See Haim Gordon, *Heroism and Friendship in the Novels of Erich Maria Remarque* (New York: Peter Lang, 2003), 87–88.

[22] Christoffersen, "Three Comrades," 52, comments on Pat's boyish physique.

[23] The chapter in which this happens is in fact roughly the same plot as a piece called "Josefs Moment" (Josef's Moment), which Remarque had published in *Sport im Bild* 33 (1927): 1366–68: also in *Das unbekannte Werk,* vol. 4, 291–95 and 522 nn, and *Herbstfahrt,* 64–68.

[24] Antkowiak, *Remarque,* 63, cites Ilja Fradkin as seeing in the work an illusionary neutrality, demonstrating a utopian dream of comradeship; he demands that one must take sides. He also seems to think that the murderer is not of the right, although surely the military uniform and general background give this away, as Barker and Last, *Remarque,* 87, point out. They also rightly draw attention to Remarque's permanent difficulty in convincing critics that he was not politically aligned. Sternburg, *"Als wäre alles,"* 255, is equally clear that the assassins are Nazis.

[25] In his brief comments on the novel, Moore, *Twentieth Century German Literature,* 82, is implicitly critical of their act, seeing it as part of their emotional anarchy, and noting that they are using the illegal methods that they profess to despise.

[26] See Gordon, *Heroism and Friendship,* 99.

[27] See Schneider, "Von *Pat* zu *Drei Kameraden,*" 71. The sentence is in capitals in the outline. The synopsis of *Pat* ends with the arrival of Köster, Schneider, 75, and

note 19. Christoffersen, "Three Comrades," 56, notes the point and makes important observations on the style of the final paragraphs of the published novel, 55. It invites comparison (undertaken by Christoffersen) with the ending of *Im Westen nichts Neues* as an observed death.

Dutch edition of
Liebe Deinen Nächsten

English edition of
Arc de Triomphe

4: The First Europeans: *Liebe Deinen Nächsten* and *Arc de Triomphe*

Two of Remarque's novels, both first published in America, are concerned with the precarious lives of refugees from the Nazis in Europe during the period from Hitler's coming to power to the outbreak of the Second World War. The emotional rootlessness of the Weimar novels has become real in these works. The first of them carried the motto, in the English version: "To live without roots takes a stout heart." Long omitted from German editions, it has now been restored, albeit with a singular noun: "Man braucht ein starkes Herz, um ohne Wurzel zu leben —." *Liebe Deinen Nächsten* (*Flotsam*) was written in 1938–39, when Remarque lived first in Vienna, then Paris, and Porto Ronco, after which he emigrated to the United States in August 1939. Although the English title is a good one, it loses the highly significant biblical reference to the second of the two commandments in Matthew 22:37–40 and Mark 12:29–31, the injunction to "love thy neighbor as thyself."[1] The novel is set in 1936 and early 1937: one of the central characters is employed before and after the turn of the year on the building of the *Exposition Internationale,* the Paris World's Fair, held from May to November 1937.[2] The second, *Arc de Triomphe* (*Arch of Triumph*), was written over a long period, from 1940 to 1945, when it was finally published. Its action begins in November 1938, the twentieth anniversary of the armistice that ended the First World War, and concludes with the outbreak of a new war at the start of September 1939.[3]

The historical events are closer in these novels than in any of Remarque's other works. Whereas *Arc de Triomphe* is set in Paris, the earlier work, which ends in Paris, is a novel of borders and border crossings — Germany, Czechoslovakia, Austria, Switzerland, and France. The refugee, running from one regime and not admitted by other countries for lack of a visa and hence always on the move, is "ein Pionier des Weltbürgertums . . . einer der ersten Europäer (156–57, a pioneer of world citizenship . . . one of the first Europeans); the same phrase is applied at the end of *Arc de Triomphe* to a group of refugees at the start of the war. Although both novels end in Paris, in *Liebe Deinen Nächsten* the central characters are at the conclusion preparing to move even further on to Mexico; at the end of *Arc de Triomphe* the principal character is about to be taken away to a French internment camp, to an uncertain future.[4] Both are third-person narratives, but both take us frequently into the thoughts and minds of the principal characters. In the later novel, for example, a central chapter taking the reader into the dreams and thoughts of the central figure is about as close to a first-person narrative as it is possible to go. Both novels were filmed.[5]

A further novel, *Die Nacht von Lissabon* (*The Night in Lisbon*) has been grouped with these two works to make a trilogy of émigré novels, although it was written some considerable time later. Remarque himself referred in a letter in July 1964 to the works as a trilogy, which had, however, come about *ohne meinen Willen,* by accident, and he claimed that with *Die Nacht von Lissabon,* he had drawn a line under the theme of emigration.[6] It is in some respects close to the two earlier novels in that it presents events that took place during the war in 1942, and it looks even further back to 1939. The novel may be treated in a separate chapter, however, since Remarque was not, as it happens, done with the theme of emigration. On grounds of style, too, we may place *Die Nacht von Lissabon* beside the posthumously published *Schatten im Paradies* (*Shadows in Paradise*) and the related fragmentary version of the same text, *Das gelobte Land* (The Promised Land).

The usual caveat applies as regards the supposedly autobiographical elements in these novels, in which Remarque again uses places, perhaps incidents, and occasionally names from his own past. Ravic's age in *Arc de Triomphe* is the same as Remarque's and Paris is Paris, but this whole line of criticism may be summed up once and for all by the fact that someone is referred to in *Arc de Triomphe* as part of a comic anecdote whose stage name is Gustav Schmidt, but whose real name is Alexander Marie Graf von Zambona (54); that Zambona was Remarque's first wife's name is at best an inside joke. To be fair, Remarque did comment in a diary entry for 30 May 1941: "Gestern Abend ungefähre Grundidee zum: *Arc de Triomphe* gefunden. Ähnelt verzweifelt einer Autobiographie der letzten Jahre, — emotionell" (Yesterday evening got the rough basic idea for *Arc de Triomphe.* Despairingly like an autobiography of the last few years — emotional). But it was not completed until much later, even if some of the fictional narrative of Ravic and the singer and actress Joan Madou might reflect isolated aspects of Remarque's own relationship with Marlene Dietrich, in letters to whom he sometimes signed himself "Ravic." It is not the real name of the literary figure either.[7]

Both *Liebe Deinen Nächsten* and *Arc de Triomphe* have the same political-historical theme, and Remarque uses his central characters as mouthpieces to comment on the events and underline an overall plea for tolerance and humanity. There are, however, personal and individual stories in both works, a complex relationship dominating *Arc de Triomphe,* and two separate love stories in *Liebe Deinen Nächsten.* Both novels make clear the insistence on maintaining the spark of life under difficult circumstances, and *Arc de Triomphe* explores the notion in some depth in psychological terms.

Liebe Deinen Nächsten

The two central characters in this novel are Josef Steiner, a veteran of the First World War and hence around forty years old in 1936. He is a political refugee from Germany who has had to abandon his beloved wife, Marie, and flee after he has been tortured by the Nazis; and Ludwig Kern, who is twenty-one, a medical student, and who has fled Germany because he is half Jewish. In the course of the novel Kern meets and falls in love with Ruth Holland, whose name recurs in *Der Funke Leben*. Steiner becomes Kern's friend and mentor, almost a father figure, and even refers to him occasionally as "baby." Remarque noted in his diary in 1941 that some reviews of the English version of the novel claimed that he had made a mistake in making Kern rather than Steiner the main character. The point is debatable, although there is a greater concentration on Kern's experiences in the later part of the novel. At all events, Remarque commented: "Typisch, — weil ich Kern kannte. Reine Erfindung immer wahrhafter. Kern lebte in Porto Ronco vor mir, — das verschob das klare Bild der Erfindung" (Typical — because I knew Kern. Pure inventions always more plausible. Kern lived in Porto Ronco right in front of me — that distorted the clarity of invention). On the characterization in general he noted apropos of another questionable review a week later:

> Findet die Minor-Charaktere viel interessanter als die Hauptch. Stimmt. ich wollte das auch. Wollte Kern u. Ruth als Dutzendmenschen durchgehen lassen. Darin liegt wohl der Fehler des Scriptes. Hätte andere Typen nehmen müssen. Bestimmt! Das ist die Schwäche. Als "Hotel International" wäre es viel besser gewesen. Lernen.

> [[The review] finds the minor characters much more interesting than the major ones. It's true. I wanted that, too. Wanted Kern & Ruth to go though just as ordinary people. That's the mistake of the text. Should have taken other types. Certainly! That's the weakness. It would have been a lot better as "Hotel International." Learn.][8]

Remarque seems to have taken on board the two criticisms of *Liebe Deinen Nächsten* in writing *Arc de Triomphe*, which, although centered on a single character and the significant events associated with him, also shows us a range of different refugees in and around the Hotel International, the equivalent of the Hotel Verdun in the last part of *Liebe Deinen Nächsten*. In *Arc de Triomphe* the balance between the refugee milieu and the foregrounded plot is more carefully done, and although there are no direct links except Paris, *Arc de Triomphe* may be seen as a loose sequel, beginning less than two years after the earlier novel ends.

In fact *Liebe Deinen Nächsten* does also present a wide range of refugees, and the problem with the novel, as Remarque himself realized, is not whether Ludwig Kern and Ruth Holland on the one hand or Steiner on the other should be taken as central, but whether the focus upon either detracts too much from the work's general presentation of the experiences of these enforced first Europeans. It is only in the final few chapters, seventeen to twenty, in the Hotel Verdun that the reader is shown other refugees as individuals rather than encountering them only in connection with Kern or Steiner, so that those chapters, while bringing several of the plot lines to a conclusion, have a separate feel about them. A single example of this is provided by the stylistically distinctive section in the final chapter showing the death and entry into heaven of the elderly Jewish refugee Moritz Rosenthal. He has appeared in the work at intervals, and, as *Vater Moritz* (Father Moritz), is a senior representative for all the refugees. The sudden move at the end of the work, however, from the portrayal of the real world to that of another in which a welcoming angel greets the old man is almost like a short story, although the provision of a literal glimpse of heaven is itself interesting.

Kern and Steiner first meet when the place they are staying (without passports) in Vienna is raided and they are jailed, with a number of other refugees, for a short time before being deported to Czechoslovakia. The casual brutality of the police sets the tone for the work as a whole: the sole "crime" these people have committed is that they have had to flee their own country (Germany in the case of Steiner and Kern, Poland, Italy and Russia in others) for political reasons or because they are Jewish. Even when the police take them away, ordinary people shout abuse after them, and one even calls out *Heil Hitler*! From the interrogation by the police we learn that Kern, a medical student, is half Jewish, and is stateless at the age of twenty-one because the Germans had thrown him out as an alternative to a prison camp: "Und wenn wir eingesperrt werden mussten, wollten wir es lieber in einem anderen Lande als in Deutschland" (15, and if we were going to be jailed, then we would rather be jailed in a country other than Germany). He is the son of a perfume manufacturer, and his Jewish father has also been driven out and his factory confiscated; his mother has escaped to relatives in Hungary. An identity card got him temporary residence in Czechoslovakia, and thereafter he has crossed the border to Austria where he has been working illegally selling soap and perfume. The refugees have been betrayed on this occasion out of petty malice — this, too, is a dominant theme — and the presiding officer even comments sarcastically of this heterogeneous group: "Sieht nicht nach kommunistischem Komplott aus, was?" (16, Doesn't look much like a communist plot, does it?).

In the cells Steiner befriends Kern and begins what is a kind of education, first by simple encouragement and then by teaching him to play poker. The cells also contain another inmate who looks down upon the refugees because he has a legitimate passport and is "ein anständiger Taschendieb und Falschspieler" (19, an honest pickpocket and cardsharp). He does, however, give Steiner some useful lessons. The other refugees include a man who had just bought a cooked chicken that he will now be unable to eat; this becomes a recurrent, if weak, comic motif. After two weeks Kern is released and expelled from Austria — he thinks of himself as "das winzige, flackernde Fünkchen Leben Ludwig Kern" (23, the tiny, flickering little spark of life, Ludwig Kern) — and with Steiner crosses the border back to Czechoslovakia. During this incident, Kern and the reader learn that Steiner is not a Jew, and that his wife, Marie, is still in Germany, and he does not know what has happened to her. In a narrative section addressed to the reader and not to Kern, further details are given of how Steiner had escaped from a concentration camp and had managed to make brief and dangerous contact with his wife. He had urged her to divorce him so that she would be left alone, and she reluctantly agreed so that he would escape. After he had done so, crossing the border at night, his first act had been to turn back and say his wife's name. The story of Steiner and Marie will not be picked up again until the end of the work.

Resuming direct conversation with Kern, Steiner tells how he had fought in Flanders in the First World War, and describes how, after his closest friend had been wounded, he himself had eaten a meal with great relish while his friend was dying. The enhancement of the urge to live in the face of death is a theme in several of the novels, and Steiner draws once again the existential conclusion that also appears elsewhere in the novels: "dass neben dir jemand verrecken kann — und du nichts davon spürst. Mitleid, gut — aber die Schmerzen spürst du trotzdem nicht" (32, that someone can kick the bucket right beside you — and you can't feel any of it. Pity, yes, OK — but you still can't feel his pain). The point of *Liebe Deinen Nächsten* is that many people do not even try to do so, indeed, do not even get as far as the pity. Steiner then takes his leave of Kern — he will return to Austria, and Kern will head for Prague — with a final word of advice derived from his lessons in poker playing, one of Remarque's favorite symbols for life: "Mehr bluffen" (33, bluff more often).

Prague simply offers another temporary stay for refugees on a short-term permit, and Kern comes into contact with several others: the professor and expert in cancer research now reduced to the status of an unsuccessful peddler; the man who screams in the night; Marill, a former *Reichstag* delegate. Many of these refugees turn up with some regularity throughout the work. Kern also encounters Ruth Holland, by the accident of blundering into her room at night, and she will play a large part in the rest of his experiences. Later, by dint of purchasing some *eau de toilette* that he can sell, which turns out to be that made in what was once his father's factory, he finds out that his father is in Prague, and he eventually contacts him, now a pathetic figure, guilt-ridden because his Jewishness has caused so many problems for his wife and son. To his father's comment that his son still has hope, the young Kern is skeptical, but he does still have hope, and it is reinforced when he begins a relationship with Ruth Holland, who has also had to escape from Germany, a Jewish girl rejected with scorn by her Aryan lover. Her mother is dead, and her father had fallen fighting for Germany in the First World War, but his name has been scratched from the war memorial because he was a Jew.

She and Kern become involved when a woman in the refugee hotel gives birth but then dies. That episode gives rise to comments on the chaos of the militaristic age, and the doctor comments sardonically that it is all "beschissen. Schöne Aufgabe: man flickt sie mit der grössten Kunst zusammen, damit sie mit der grössten Barbarei wieder in Stücke gerissen werden. Warum nicht gleich die Kinder totschlagen! Ist doch viel einfacher" (85, crap. Nice job — you patch people up with the greatest skill so that they can be ripped apart again with the greatest barbarity. Why not kill the children at birth? It would be a lot simpler!). A further comment on the same subject by Marill, a former parliamentary deputy, echoes the theme of murder voiced in the First World War novels: "Kinder töten ist Mord. Erwachsene töten ist eine Angelegenheit nationaler Ehre" (85: Killing children is murder. Killing adults is a matter of national honor). The doctor agrees that something like cholera is positively harmless compared with war.

While in Prague, Kern is cheated by anti-Semitic and/or opportunistic customers, aware that he is no position to report anything to the police. However, Remarque also shows us unexpected goodness, as when an apparently threatening German seen in a restaurant and assumed to be a Gestapo agent helps him and Ruth, explaining that he has realized their situation, and because "Ich war Kompagnieführer im Kriege. Einer meiner besten Leute war ein Jude" (96, I was a company commander in the war. One of my best men was a Jew). Remarque has been criticized for presenting stereotypes in this novel,[9] but he is in fact at pains to deny the stereotypes and to show that there are good and bad members of any group. Not all Jews are friendly and not all Germans are monsters. This deliberately stereotyped German officer, complete with monocle and dueling scars, turns out precisely not to conform to his image, nor is his comment the same as the familiar evasion "some of my best friends are Jews," since he makes a practical gesture of help towards his neighbor. The apparent stereotype is used to show the danger of stereotyping. Shortly after this incident, Ruth (whose passport is still valid) leaves Prague for Vienna, while Kern is deported, crossing the border back into Austria, this time with the old Jew Moritz Rosenthal.

Remarque uses his favorite technique of rapid changes between different episodes, so that the early chapters of the novel continue to parallel the story of Steiner. Back in Vienna, the more experienced refugee manages to buy a false pass in the name of an Austrian, having raised the money by using (sometimes dangerously) the cardsharping tricks he has learned. Historically the discussion of passports in chapter 5 is interesting,[10] and they are a realistic recurrent theme in the émigré novels, since most refugees had none; the point is made at the end of the novel that these pieces of paper are the great weapons of the age, something to live or die by, like the sword in earlier times. Steiner is satisfied with his new identity, and the first thing he does, having also changed his appearance, is to seek out the policeman who was violent when he and Kern were arrested and beats him up in an alleyway, a scene reminiscent once again of the revenge taken on individuals in several of the earlier novels. More violent acts of revenge with a more clearly political dimension taken on specific Nazis will become a new theme.

Circumstances have brought Steiner, Ruth Holland, and Ludwig Kern together in Vienna once again, and there is a now an extended period of calm, taking us to the end of the ninth chapter and the end of the first of the two unequal parts into which the novel is divided. Steiner is working in the fairground in the Prater, the park in Vienna, and persuades the director, Leopold Potzloch, to take on Kern as general assistant, occasional pianist, and audience plant in a memory-man act. Reunited with Ruth, Kern spends with her what is presented as an idyll, an evening in the fairground after the booths have closed, where they can be absolutely alone even if they are aware that this is just a respite, "ein bisschen Zusammengehören in all der Flucht und der Leere" (129, a little bit of togetherness in the middle of all the running away and the emptiness). The scene ends as they shelter from a storm on a carousel, which at one point even starts to turn of its own accord, and which echoes, probably consciously, that in Rilke's famous poem on the theme in his *Neue Gedichte* of 1907. The various animals, going round and round forever, are like "die sanfte, ferne Vision eines verzauberten Paradieses" (130, the gentle, distant vision of an enchanted paradise). But with the next chapter and the second part of the novel, the idyll is over.

Ruth Holland has taken up her university studies again, and Kern, coming one day to meet her, becomes involved in an anti-Semitic demonstration. When he attempts to aid Ruth, he is forced to join the mêlée, fighting alongside a stereotypically blond, Germanic student. The police arrest only the Jews, plus the blond student, who demonstrates yet again an unexpected, if slightly ambiguous attitude, having joined in not to defend the Jews as such, but because of the broader issue of injustice. Never named, and referred to only as *der Blonde,* he bluffs the jailers into providing some creature comforts and teaches Kern how to box, which helps Kern to discourage the unwelcome attentions of a homosexual prisoner when he is sent to jail for two months. Steiner lets him know that Ruth is safe, and Kern continues his education, learning French, and encountering once again the man with the roast chicken. At the end of his sentence he is deported, though he is given some money by one official and is taken to the Czech border by another, who feels that refugees are beneath his dignity when he could be guarding mass murderers and similarly impressive criminals.

Kern has now become an experienced refugee and returns straight away to Austria, where Steiner tells him that Ruth has also been deported and is now in Switzerland. Kern stays for a day or two, but an incident at the shooting gallery in which he fears he may have been recognized prompts him to move on to find Ruth, crossing the Upper Rhine at night near Feldkirch in the far west of Austria (Schwarz does so in the opposite direction in *Die Nacht von Lissabon*), and making his way to Zürich. Here a Jewish refugee organization is unable to help because he is only half Jewish and by religion a Protestant (we are made aware in other novels by Remarque of the special difficulties of being a German refugee who is not Jewish), but he is helped by another refugee, Georg Binder, and it is a regular feature that most help comes from other refugees, this recalling the comradeship of the frontline. It is even described that way, albeit with an ironic twist: "Kameradschaft der Illegalen — fast wie bei Verbrechern" (162, comradeship of illegal immigrants — almost like the fellowship among thieves). Binder provides Kern with advice on staying in Switzerland, and also a list of addresses for begging; he is a pragmatist who, while aware of basic moral precepts, knows too that they can be overridden by necessity. Kern, he says, needs a story:

> Die Wolhtätigkeit ist eine Kuh, die wenig und schwer Milch gibt. Ich kenne Leute, die drei verschiedene Geschichten auf Lager haben, eine sentimentale, eine brutale und eine sachliche; je nachdem, was der Mann, der seine paar Franken Unterstützung 'rausrücken soll, hören will. Sie lügen, gewiss. Aber nur, weil sie müssen. Die Grundgeschichte ist immer dieselbe: Not, Flucht und Hunger. (161)

> [Charity is a cow that doesn't give much milk and what there is is hard to get. I know people who have three different stories ready for use, a sentimental one, one about brutality, and one matter-of-fact one, depending on what the man who is supposed to be coughing up a couple of francs wants to hear. Sure, they are lying. But only because they have to. The basic story is always the same: suffering, being on the run, hunger.]

The passage is important for a number of reasons. The notion of lying — acknowledged by Binder — is itself questionable here, because the refugees telling the different stories genuinely have experienced the basic problems, so that what is at issue is usually not lying, but adaptation or embellishment. However, the passage can also apply self-reflectively to the novel itself, which is designed to provoke a different sense of charity in the mind of the reader by way of stories that do play on sentiment, like some aspects of the love story, or contain brutality, like in Steiner's past, or are matter-of-fact, like the pragmatic acceptance of life in many of the cases. The basic story is always the same, however, and all three presentations of it are viable. Remarque has been criticized, too, for showing excessive brutality and also for sentimentality, though precisely why these are grounds for criticism is less frequently discussed. The advocation of the deliberate use of sentimentality here in an ironic context makes a critical comment on the critics.

Kern and Ruth enjoy an emotional reunion and are able again to spend some time together, although neither expects to stay long in Zürich. "Wir sind ja Staatsfeinde. Gefährliche Staatsfeinde. Sollten uns eigentlich wichtig damit vorkommen, was?" (164, we're enemies of the state. Dangerous enemies of the state. We ought to feel pretty important, eh?). Kern still hopes for a miracle, and minor miracles do seem to happen, but these are really strokes of luck and are offset by the equally unexpectedly negative things that happen (as opposed to the negative things always anticipated by the refugees, such as deportation or imprisonment), but which are therefore not perceived as miracles. Luck is random, and can be good or bad.

Considerable attention is paid to the attempts of Kern and Ruth to survive in Switzerland, although the narrative returns occasionally to Steiner in Vienna. The characters encountered by the pair, however, provide insights into a range of possible reactions to the political situation. Thus Arnold Oppenheim, a rich Jewish businessman is scathing about East European Jews and is even — with huge political naïveté — complimentary about Hitler's Germany, claiming that the individual sometimes has to suffer if the country is to make progress. In contrast, Kern is tricked and robbed by a perfectly genuine ex-inmate of a German concentration camp, who had legitimately been imprisoned on criminal grounds and is cynically unrepentant about stealing from the poor. So too, when Ruth falls ill, Kern tries to beg money from a German, Ammers, who seems friendly, but turns out to be a Nazi who denounces Kern. The police officer who arrests Kern has no sympathy whatever with Ammers and permits Kern to escape. Then, even though a Jewish doctor is found who will treat Ruth and takes her to hospital, Kern is re-arrested and again denounced. In spite of a satisfying verbal attack on Ammers — the medical student Kern offers a convincing diagnosis of cancer of the liver, which Ammers believes — Kern is yet again jailed and then deported, this time to France via Basle, although he has agreed to rendezvous with Ruth in Geneva.

Kern's appearance before the Swiss judge provides opportunity for a broad discussion of the plight of the refugee, as Kern points out that he has no choice but to break the law regarding immigration, and that the League of Nations is still debating what is to happen to them. His position as a German, rather than as a Jew, is of some interest, and Kern makes clear that he no longer exists at all as far as Germany, and elsewhere he is of interest only to the police. The judge states the obvious conclusion: "Sie müssen doch irgendwie existieren dürfen" (209, you must be allowed to exist somehow); officials are often sympathetic in the novel, even if what help they can give is limited. When Kern is asked whether he believes in anything at all any more, however, he gives first of all what seems to be a totally cynical, if understandable answer: "O ja; ich glaube an den heiligen Egoismus! An die Unbarmherzigkeit! An die Lüge! An die Trägheit des Herzens!" (210, oh yes, I believe in holy egoism! In hard-heartedness! In lies! In not being bothered). But this is not the real answer. Kern goes on: "Ich glaube auch an Güte, an Kameradschaft, an Liebe und an Hilfsbereitschaft! Ich habe sie kennengelernt. Mehr vielleicht als mancher, dem es gut geht" (210, I also believe in goodness, in comradeship, in love, and in help. I've met all those things. More, maybe, than a lot of people who are better off).

Having crossed back into Switzerland, Kern falls asleep in a church, and a sympathetic priest, who thinks he has been praying, gives him money, after which he actually does pray. Remarque often brings his principal protagonists into contact with a priest, but this time the encounter is brief and devoid of debate, with Kern interestingly making his own decision to return to pray. But the metaphysical commitment is ironic:

> Er . . . betete nun tatsächlich. Er wusste nicht genau zu wem — er selbst war protestantisch, sein Vater war Jude, und er kniete in einer katholischen Kirche — aber er fand, dass in Zeiten wie diesen wahrscheinlich auch im Himmel ein ziemliches Durcheinander sein musste, und er nahm an, dass ein Gebet schon den richtigen Weg finden würde. (223–24)

> [Now he really did pray. He wasn't exactly sure to whom — he was a Protestant, his father was a Jew, and he was kneeling in a Catholic church — but he reckoned that in times like this there was probably a bit of confusion in heaven, too, and he assumed that a prayer would find its own way.]

In Geneva, Kern is struck by the magnificence of the League of Nations building. The League was established in 1920, but was never particularly effective, and Hitler was contemptuous of it, withdrawing Germany from it in October 1933. In that same month the League appointed a commissioner for refugees, especially from Germany, but as the novel indicates, practical help was slow and patchy, and the League was also ineffectual against German remilitarization and Hitler's invasions. Kern and another refugee, who is trying to be sent to prison where he will at least be warm and fed, are moved on by the doorman of this fine, symbolic building, suspicious of these shabby unknowns, who are in reality part of one of the League's greatest problems.[11] Reunited with Ruth, Kern learns first that the odious Ammers is indeed being treated for liver disease by the Jewish doctor — a small touch of individual revenge provided by fate — and the pair leave for Paris.

The second protagonist, Steiner, is seen less frequently in this middle section of the work. The two strands of the narrative are, however, tied together as Steiner wonders what is happening to *unser Kleiner* (184, our youngster), and eventually he decides that he will himself move out of Austria before the presumed *Anschluss* with Germany, which did not come until March 1938. He spends some time on the Swiss-Austrian border, making money from his card-playing skills, but then heads for the town in which Ruth had been taken ill and Kern had been arrested. His eventual goal is also Paris. As in the Kern-episodes, the reader is introduced through Steiner to other refugees, often just as vignettes, such as Dr. Goldbach, a Jewish lawyer who works briefly with Steiner in the fairground but who tries to make a living selling ties. Abandoned by his far younger wife, he neatly but mechanically cuts up all the ties that he has been trying to sell; he does not, however, commit suicide, and the chapter ends with him merely crouching down "als fröre er und hätte nicht mehr die Kraft, sich wirklich zu wärmen" (205, as if he were freezing and no longer had the strength to warm himself properly). He does not appear in the narrative again, so that what remains in the mind is the broken figure and the futile act of material, but not personal destruction.

The final section of the work — chapters 16 to 19 — bring the refugees all together in Paris, where the Hotel Verdun is truly European, full of different nationalities, and Paris itself is "die letzte Hoffnung und das letzte Schicksal von allen" (243, the last hope and the final fate for them all). The words are those of the erstwhile parliamentary deputy Marill, who is there already. Once more, however, we are shown that the real enemy is bureaucracy, which treats different refugees on a scale ranging from those who can obtain residence or work permits, down to a symbolically isolated group of orthodox east European Jews in caftans who speak only Yiddish and cannot find interpreters to help them. They can do nothing but plead, using the repeated word *mentsh,* "human being," but with further connotations in Yiddish (and in German) of humanity and decency.[12] But whatever the gradations of misery, the political situation in the outside world affects all refugees, who are used as the universal scapegoats. Kern does manage to find work at the end of 1936, helping to build the 1937 exhibition, although he is later arrested again for doing so without a permit, and deported and imprisoned for a while once more. He and Ruth are joined by Steiner, who has, while still in Switzerland, satisfyingly tricked a sum of money out of the egregious Ammers, which he gives to the pair. The final chapters of the novel contain two separate elements, however, apart from the ongoing narrative of Kern and Ruth: the first is the fuller presentation of other individual refugees; the second is the dramatic final narrative of Steiner.

Some of the refugees are familiar — Marill offers regular and pithy comments, for example — but others are new: the man with a Jewish wife who is dying, and who reproaches herself that he has had to leave Germany on her account, or the two friends who argue about the relative merits of expensive cars when they have nothing even to spend on food. Two separate tales are particularly striking. At the beginning of 1937, we hear of an actress, Barbara Klein, twenty-eight and devoid of all hope, who takes an unknown man into her bed almost as an act of charity in its own right, and afterwards slits her wrists, simply tired of going on. The second separate tale is of the death of Father Moritz, the old Moritz Rosenthal, buffeted by the "wind of time," who is first lulled to sleep by another elderly refugee, Edith Rosenfeld, who sings him the familiar Yiddish lullaby "Rozhinkes mit mandlen."[13] In the next and final chapter, just before the end of the work, the apparently dreaming Rosenthal reaches (by ship) what is clearly heaven — another border — and instinctively hides until an angel, in an echo of Genesis 3:9, calls him out of hiding and welcomes the fact that he has no passport and no visa and has been a Jewish refugee. The passage, as noted already, is different, but its position at the end of the work is significant. Death may be a positive answer after all, and there may be a reward in heaven.

There are more deaths to come in the final chapter. Steiner had decided to return to Germany using his fake passport to see his dying wife Marie once more. His return to Germany is described in the penultimate chapter in a long and stylistically different lyrical passage that expresses his emotional return to what is, after all, his homeland. He finds his wife, now dying in hospital, and convinces her that he will be safe. He is, however, recognized by a former tormenter, Steinbrenner, and arrested, although he is allowed to stay with his wife until she dies. When he is being led away afterwards, he hurls himself at Steinbrenner and the pair both fall to their deaths from the fifth-floor window of the hospital. It is a suicide and a gesture of defiance against a single Nazi, and it will be echoed in *Arc de Triomphe* and especially in *Zeit zu leben und Zeit zu sterben*. Steiner is an ordinary man who gives his own life and kills one Nazi, arguably as personal revenge. The message of the novel, however, is entirely anti-fascist, anti-Nazi, and the final act of Steiner's life cannot but be applauded. *Liebe Deinen Nächsten* is a political, historical, and human novel in which we are shown clearly where all sympathies must lie: with the refugees and against those at every level who oppress them and fail to show humanity. It is a historical novel in that it shows the plight of refugees all over western Europe in the later 1930s, and the splendid but unapproachable League of Nations building in Geneva offers a memorable contrast to the many people, the political flotsam who are precisely not loved by their neighbors. In the novel, too, are individual human tales of good and bad, and the two love stories, Ludwig Kern and Ruth Holland, and Steiner and Marie, both making a positive point. These two narratives are joined at the close of the work when Steiner's money comes via Marill to Kern and Ruth so that they can escape from Europe altogether to Mexico and the hope of a genuinely new life.

The last chapter, then, refers to various borders: that between this world and the next, whether there is an afterlife, as with Moritz Rosenthal, or whether we do not know, as with Steiner; the usual European borders; and the unknown border to a new world. At the end, the injunction *Liebe Deinen Nächsten* has triumphed because Steiner's posthumous love for his friends has given them a new chance. There is no grandiosely sentimental ending as the couple sails into the sunset, however; just apprehension for the future, and neither of them knows exactly where Mexico is. As a final irony Ruth comments: "Aber ich weiss auch nicht mehr, wo Deutschland liegt . . ." (319, But I no longer know where Germany is either).

Arc de Triomphe

Liebe Deinen Nächsten has hanging over it the threat of the Second World War, but it is still a little way in the future, even if construction work is being done on an international exhibition at which the Nazi and the Soviet pavilions would vie symbolically in size and dominance. *Arc de Triomphe* is set in an even darker time, beginning just before Armistice Day 1938 and ending (after a sultry summer) at the beginning of September 1939 and the outbreak of the war. The action is mainly in Paris, framed by references to the Arc de Triomphe, the monument to revolutionary and Napoleonic military victories, under which was placed, much later, the Tomb of the Unknown Soldier of the First World War. Already ambiguous — the Unknown Soldier was by 1938 being used as a focus for nationalism more often than as an indictment of war, not just in France — the arch is, as Tilman Westphalen has pointed out, a symbol of human aggressiveness, seen in the novel a little later as "das riesige Tor des Hades" (19, the mighty gateway to hell), as well as a symbol for Paris. We may add to the symbolism the manner in which the monument dwarfs the grave.[14] The arch (and sometimes the grave) reappears throughout the novel. Near the beginning the central figure, Ravic, sees how "fern, schwebend und dunkel, erschien vor dem regnerischen Himmel die Masse des Arc de Triomphe" (11, in the distance, dark and hovering, the great bulk of the Arc de Triomphe rose up against the rainy sky); at the end of the novel, when war has broken out, we are told "Es war so dunkel, dass man auch den Arc de Triomphe nicht mehr sehen konnte" (480, it was so dark that you could no longer see the Arc de Triomphe). There is no cause at the end for triumphalism of any kind, and at the same time the light on the grave — pale enough when it is first encountered — is also invisible, and the message of the First World War has been forgotten. With this much-revised and rewritten new novel, Remarque did indeed take on board to some extent the idea of focusing on a group of refugees in the Hotel International, but with considerable skill he does so in *Arc de Triomphe* while offering us a plot — strictly speaking a double plot — that centers upon a single memorable character.

The novel is once again a third-person narrative that concentrates closely on the single central character, whose present we follow, whose past we are shown in some detail, and into whose dreams we are permitted. This is the surgeon Ravic, who is never given a forename; we know in any case that this is not his real name and that he has had to use several others. We are faced, therefore, with a central figure whose name we and the other characters must use throughout, even if it is not his name in fact, and only at the end do we learn that his real name is Ludwig Fresenburg. That name, full and unmistakably German, will reappear, incidentally, in *Zeit zu Leben und Zeit zu sterben.* He is indeed a German, another escapee from a Nazi concentration camp, who has moved around Europe and ended up in Paris, where he practices medicine illegally. Although a first-rate surgeon, he has no license to work in France, and hence is employed for small sums by a French doctor who is then able to claim his skills as he takes the far larger fees from the patients. He lives, too in the Hotel International, the equivalent of the Hotel Verdun, and through this the reader encounters a range of refugees not unlike those already met in *Liebe Deinen Nächsten.* Two plots, however, center upon Ravic. The first is his problematic love affair with the unstable singer and film actress Joan Madou that begins with her contemplating suicide and ends with her violent death. She does, however, restore a sense of life in Ravic, who has been emotionally deadened by his experiences in Germany. The second plot is his revenge on one of his former Nazi torturers, whom he encounters by chance in Paris. The two plots are interlinked, and Ravic achieves renewal and closure at the same time. That he is a surgeon also offers in the relevant scenes a reminder of the chance nature of life and death in any circumstances, but it also underlines his humanity because he treats the sick even when they are distasteful. For all that, in his revenge on the Nazi torturer, he is able to take life.

Ravic is forty[15] as the work opens, and he encounters Joan Madou for the first time one night when he is wandering the streets by the Seine and finds an unknown woman standing by the Pont de l'Alma apparently contemplating throwing herself into the river. The narrative of this initial chance meeting is one of Remarque's most impressive and sustained openings. Ravic persuades her away from the river, and although he is himself now desperately tired, they go to a café and drink calvados. This becomes a deliberate, if slightly overdone, leitmotif, the calvados itself becoming stronger as their love develops. Since she is reluctant to return to her own lodging — we do not discover why until later — she goes back with Ravic to his room, past the Étoile and the Arc de Triomphe with the lonely grave. The scene is described in terms almost of universal despair, and the pale flame looks in the mist and the night like "das letzte Grab der Menschheit inmitten von Nacht und Verlassenheit" (15, the last grave of mankind, surrounded by night and loneliness). But the significance of the "einsame, bleiche Flamme" (the pale, lonely flame) on the grave is picked up neatly in following paragraph to give us a variation on one of Remarque's most constant images, the spark of life, as the pessimistic image of the "last grave of mankind" is transformed completely. It is still a small, perhaps insignificant-looking flame, but it represents now not universal death, but expressly life, and it betokens companionship, not loneliness. We have a long way to go with the relationship between Ravic and Joan — they do not even know each other's names — but already she is, despite her depression, a spark of life, and she will slowly rekindle the spark in him, which has been lost in a tiredness that is more than physical:

> Er hörte neben sich die tappenden, weichen Schritte der Frau, die ihm schweigend folgte, den Kopf gesenkt, die Hände in die Taschen ihres Mantels vergraben, eine kleine, fremde Flamme Leben — und plötzlich, in der späten Einsamkeit des Platzes, obschon er nichts von ihr wusste, erschien sie ihm einen Augenblick gerade deshalb zugehörig zu ihm. Sie war ihm fremd, so wie er sich selbst überall fremd fühlte, und das schien ihm auf eine sonderbare Weise näher als durch viele Worte und die abschleifende Gewohnheit der Zeit. (15)

> [He heard the pattering of the woman's soft footsteps as she followed him, saying nothing, her head down, her hands plunged deep into her coat pockets, a small, unknown flame of life — and suddenly, in the late-hour loneliness of the place, although he knew nothing about her she seemed for a moment for that very reason to belong to him. She was a stranger to him, just as much as he felt himself to be a stranger, everywhere, and that brought her oddly closer to him than many words and the everyday wearing down of time.][16]

That well-crafted paragraph, indicating with a few sketched physical details her sense of isolation, and then taking us into his state of mind, sets the tone for the relationship that will develop. Its position after the description not just of the Arc de Triomphe, but specifically of the eternal flame places the relationship into a spatial and historical context, but it is positive and almost hopeful, rather than elegiac. She will indeed rekindle in him the flame of life.

In an interesting variation on the stock love story, the woman returns with Ravic, but his French colleague Veber summons him immediately to the private hospital where he attempts, but fails, to save a girl's life after a botched abortion. Returning in the small hours, depressed by his failure, by way of a bar and then the Osiris brothel where he acts as medical inspector and drinks regularly with their overseer, Madame Rolande, he finds the unknown woman still in his room. Preoccupied with the death of the girl, Ravic suddenly feels the contrast with this woman. "Etwas, das atmete. Ein bisschen fremdes Leben — aber Leben. Wärme. Kein erstarrender Körper. Was konnte man sich schon anderes geben als etwas Wärme? Und was mehr?" (31, Something that breathed. A scrap of unknown life — but life.

Warmth. Not a stiffening corpse. What else could one person ever give another apart from a little warmth? And what was more than that?). He takes the woman into his bed.

On the following morning he discovers that she has been unable to return to her own rooms at the Hotel Verdun because her male companion has died. Ravic takes charge of the situation, feeling no particular emotion towards the woman but a simple responsibility and sorts out her affairs for the moment, learning (and at once forgetting) that her name is Joan Madou. When he leaves her — it is now the morning of 11 November 1938 — he runs into the Armistice Day celebrations in the crowded Place de l'Étoile, twenty years after the First World War. The extended opening of the novel ends back by the Arc de Triomphe, with the comments of a stranger: "Waffenstillstand," sagte eine Frau neben Ravic. "Mein Mann ist im letzten Krieg gefallen. Jetzt ist mein Sohn dran. Waffenstillstand. Wer weiss, was noch kommen wird . . ." (48, "Armistice," said a woman next to Ravic. "My husband was killed in the last war. Now it's my son's turn. Armistice. Who knows what might happen next . . ."). The idea will be picked up at the end of the novel.

The chronicling of Ravic's life in Paris shifts episodically from one sphere to another. In the medical context we learn that he had been chief surgeon in a large hospital in Germany, but is now exploited by Professor Durant and treated with contempt by Eugenie, the theater nurse. Another context is that of the Hotel International, where we encounter many other refugees through Ravic, most notably the Russian Boris Morosow, who works as a doorman at the Scheherazade Club. Further contexts are more personal, giving us on the one hand the story of the development of Ravic's complex relationship with Joan Madou, and with another woman, Kate Hegström, who is dying of cancer, and on the other his pursuit of the Nazi Haake, once he establishes his presence in Paris. The various spheres impinge upon each other.

The second occasion on which we see Ravic as a surgeon gives an opportunity for an extended exposition of his past and present with his French colleague and friend Veber and the nurse Eugenie as prompters. Against Eugenie's rigid and intolerant religion, Ravic insists on the sanctity of human life in its simplest form: "Man verehrt den Funken Leben" (50, the spark of life is to be revered), he tells her, whereas organized religions — all of them — usually cause bloodshed. From his conversation with Veber we learn that his position is not unique even for a doctor — he speaks of hundreds of similar cases — but that living illegally in France is better than being in a German concentration camp. Ravic also tells Veber that this is the third name he has had to use to avoid being indicted for a "second offense" when caught without papers, which would have meant a longer spell in jail. He talks about the times when he has been arrested:

"Dreimal. Ebenso wie hundert andern auch. Im Anfang, als ich noch nichts davon wusste und auf die sogenannte Humanität vertraute. Bevor ich nach Spanien ging — wo ich keinen Pass brauchte — und eine zweite Lektion in angewandter Humanität erhielt. Von deutschen und italienischen Fliegern." (52)

[Three times. Just like it has happened to a hundred others. At the start, when I didn't know anything about it all, and trusted in the thing called humanity. Before I went to Spain — where I didn't need a passport — and got another lesson in applied humanity. From German and Italian planes.]

There is no doubt about Ravic's personal political opposition to fascism, but we may note that he went to Spain because he did not need a passport, and we hear details later of his activities there as a doctor, assisting those injured by German and Italian bombs. The political intricacies of the Spanish Civil War[17] play a part later in the work, where it becomes clear that Ravic has no sympathies for Franco, but equally is hardly a communist. Politics as such are by no means as clear-cut as some critics would have liked Remarque, or his characters, to believe.

Ravic's work as a doctor in Paris demonstrates both his own humanity and how this can be exploited by the unscrupulous, although Remarque does not make the matter entirely straightforward. Ravic saves a second girl from the ravages of the same backstreet abortionist, but when he confronts the woman who has performed the abortion, she outfaces him. She, too, is operating illegally, but she is also offering a much-demanded service not available in official medical practice. In other incidents, however, it is clear that Ravic is being abused. He performs operations for the celebrated, but no longer competent surgeon Durant, but when Ravic holds out for more money (to go on a holiday with Joan Madou) and refuses to operate until payment is agreed, Durant does so with ill grace. Later, though, Durant calls upon Ravic in desperation, having botched an operation, and this time pays appropriately. Between these two episodes, Ravic, having stopped to help someone after an accident, is called upon by the police as a witness. His status comes out and he is deported under yet another name, having been examined by an unsympathetic official, Leval, upon whom he had operated in secret not long before, and who invokes, with an irony that Ravic notes, the name of the fraudulent Durant. Durant has apparently told Leval, with breathtaking hypocrisy, of foreigners who claim to have been surgeons but who perform abortions and bungle operations. Ravic is aware that this is Durant's revenge for Ravic's demand for more money, but the hearing with Leval contains various significant exchanges. Leval establishes, for example, that Ravic is German and claims that he does not look like a refugee, by which he means that Ravic does not look Jewish — the unpleasant nurse

Eugenie had earlier made the same assumed link, and in her case a basic anti-Semitism had been extended to cover all refugees. In the interview, Ravic makes clear to the official the whole situation, although it falls upon deaf ears:

> Ich handle in Notwehr — und Sie möchten, dass ich mich wie ein Gauner fühle, der um ein mildes Urteil bittet? Nur, weil ich kein Nazi bin und deshalb keine Papiere habe. Dass wir uns noch immer nicht für Verbrecher halten, obschon wir Gefängnisse, Polizei, Demütigungen jeder Art kennen, nur weil wir am Leben bleiben wollen — das ist das einzige, was uns noch aufrechterhält. (239)

> [I'm acting in self-defense — and you want me to feel like some petty crook trying to get a lighter sentence? Just because I'm not a Nazi and because of that haven't got any papers? The fact that we still don't consider ourselves to be criminals, however familiar we might be with jails, the police, and all sorts of humiliations, simply because we want to stay alive — that's the only thing that keeps us going.]

The shift from the first person singular to the inclusive plural in the middle of the statement is noticeable. When the official suggests crassly that Ravic ought to have remained in Germany and that the situation there has been exaggerated, Ravic thinks of how an only slightly different incision during his operation would have left him unable to talk such nonsense. The reader knows about Ravic's experiences in Germany, but the official's argument is not unusual.

Ravic is deported and returns after a time, following the pattern of *Liebe Deinen Nächsten,* and is involved with other medical cases — such as the boy who loses a leg when he is run over, but who cheerfully exploits the situation to gain compensation. Durant's desperate call upon Ravic later, too, represents a moral revenge of sorts, although Ravic is eventually betrayed to the police by the ever-malicious nurse Eugenie. However, two further instances in the medical context are linked more specifically with his private life, the first when he treats Kate Hegström and establishes that she has cancer, and the last time he is seen in the novel, when he tries in vain to save the life of Joan Madou, a parallel to the first time he appears as surgeon, failing to save a girl who is also in a sense a victim of love and error. One overlap between Ravic's medical and private worlds, finally, is provided by his functioning as the medical inspector for the Osiris brothel. The hierarchy of the private hospital and the brothel indeed complement one another, and there is an ongoing friendship between Ravic and Madame Rolande, who is in charge of the prostitutes though she is not *the* madam, who is an altogether more august personage, and who, in contrast to the pharisaical Eugenie, does not betray him after the death of Haake. The hardheaded world of the Osiris is far more humane than that of the hospital.

Ravic's closest friend at the Hotel International, and his ally in the matters of Haake and Joan, is the Russian Morosow, who has been an officer in the White Russian forces and is now a refugee from the Soviets. Remarque frequently introduces Russian émigrés into his novels, and they usually have valid papers. Their position is put into context in a passage in *Die Nacht von Lissabon,* where one of the narrators comments that they "waren die erste Welle der Emigration . . . Man hatte noch Mitleid mit ihnen. Man gab ihnen Erlaubnis zu arbeiten und Papiere. Nansenpässe. Als wir kamen, was das Mitleid der Welt längst aufgebraucht"[18] (were the first wave of refugees . . . People were still sympathetic towards them. They gave them work permits and papers. Nansen-passports. When we turned up, the world's sympathy had long since run out). Those comments are made in 1942, but the details apply equally well to the time of *Arc de Triomphe.* There is a touch of envy for the Nansen-passports, issued under an agreement by the League of Nations in Geneva in July 1922 by host nations to refugees from the new Soviet state on the instigation of the polar explorer Fridtjof Nansen, who was a League commissioner, after the complex civil war (historians now refer rather to a plurality of civil wars) that went on until 1920. Morosow had fought against Lenin's Bolsheviks although he does not claim Tsarist connections either, and he has been in Paris for many years. His first prominent scene is when he and Ravic are playing chess together in the dining room of the Hotel International, nicknamed "the catacombs," when they become aware of noise from what Ravic dubs the "fascist section" from a group of Spanish refugees. Ravic had also been in Spain, but on the other side and as a doctor, while these are monarchists uncertain about returning because Franco was not good enough for them. Morosow suggests that they are celebrating "das Massaker von Guernica. Oder den Sieg italienischer und deutscher Maschinengewehre über Bergarbeiter und Bauern" (59, the massacre at Guernica. Or the victory of German and Italian machine guns over miners and farm workers). The presentation of this group of so-called refugees is subtle: there are hints that they were simply avoiding the fighting, happy for German and Italian forces to do it for them, and they have the same simplifying view of things that we have seen in the equating of refugees with Jews. They offer Ravic a drink, on the grounds that he has once prescribed medicine (in fact a laxative) for their colonel, but wish him to drink to Franco, since Germany and Falangist Spain are now friends. They do not expect Morosow to drink because Soviet Russia had opposed Franco. Of course, Ravic has fled from the Germany that supports Franco, and Morosow, as a White Russian, had actually been fighting against communism, although this confuses the Spaniards further because it does not occur to them that being against communism does not mean that one is in favor of fascism. Morosow and Ravic are dismissed as decadents and democrats, and only Morosow's physical presence, and a glass of water thrown in the face of one of them, eventually drives them away, permitting Ravic and him to continue their game of chess, a regular symbol of nonviolent politics. Later in the novel, when these Spanish monarchists have left, we are shown their rooms being cleaned, and Ravic discovers the owner exchanging the portraits of King Alfonso and Franco for pictures of Marx, Lenin, and so on, ready for Republican refugees. The pragmatic landlady has a supply of portraits of political figures from all sides and all countries, stored on the principle of what goes around, comes around. There is even, Ravic learns, a portrait of Hitler. When he expresses a wish that the rooms could be full of such pictures, the landlady is baffled only for a moment: Ravic would like the Nazis to be the refugees.

The Hotel International houses all nationalities, and it is pointed out that the catacombs, the basement dining room, was the name of the refuge of the early and persecuted Christians in Rome. Episodes involving different refugees are interpolated, and when they die, their passports live on, swiftly adopted by someone new. Memorable, for example, is Seidenbaum, a fatalist aware that one cannot run away forever; and also Rosenfeld, who has been living by selling some valuable (and unrecognized) paintings that he had managed to smuggle out of Germany. He has always followed another refugee, Meyer, who is nicknamed the *Totenvogel,* the bird who predicts death, because he is always able to tell in advance when it is time to move on, and indeed is currently planning to do so. New Zealand is suggested, and to the comment that it is a long way away comes the answer: "von wo?" (375, from where?). Rosenfeld plans to sell more of his paintings and move with him, although in the event other circumstances — the lack of a valid visa — trap him, and he and Seidenbaum are arrested with Ravic at the end of the novel. As the war draws nearer, rooms become vacant at the Hotel International, and by the end of the work only those unable or unwilling to flee are left behind to be rounded up like the first Christians in the catacombs.

Ravic's own story falls into two parts. The tale of his relationship with Joan Madou is foregrounded, with the episodes involving Kate Hegström as an additional strand; although the resolution of the Haake-narrative — the other part of his story — comes later, it is appropriate to treat it first because it defines Ravic's past, and has conditioned his state of mind at the start of the novel, something that the relationship with Joan changes. The reader learns about Ravic's past in Germany through his memory and thoughts. In the sixth chapter, he recalls being tortured by the Gestapo in 1934,[19] and there is an unelaborated reference to the face of Sybil, found hanged just afterwards. All this is prompted by Ravic's having thought he saw the face of Haake — we have no more details of him yet — who was one of the torturers. The brevity of this reference, but at the same time the clearly vivid nature of the memories, is effective as a literary device, the more so as Ravic himself (and hence the reader) is not sure that he really has seen Haake.

Ravic thinks he spots him again in the twelfth chapter, and this time we are given a far longer insight into his memory, coupled now with the hope of revenge, as Ravic sits outside a café, looking at the moonlight on the Arc de Triomphe. This time we are given the details of the friends whom he had been protecting from the Gestapo, a Jewish writer, and a fellow soldier who had saved his life in the First World War. He has been tortured for information about them, and the Jewish writer is captured in any case and slowly tortured to death by Haake. Haake himself is invariably described as smiling — *lächelnd* — the mark of the willing executioner, this repeated idea ensuring that he can command from the reader neither engagement nor sympathy. Indeed, in *Die Nacht von Lissabon* there is a Gestapo torturer referred to only as *der Lächler,* the smiling one, who is characterized as one who tortures for pleasure, as opposed to the brutal type who does so to force his will on the victim. Sybil, with whom Ravic's relationship was only superficial, is tortured to persuade him to talk, but she resists and is killed. Ravic is sent to a concentration camp and escapes from the camp hospital. The idea of revenge remains in his mind, and all he can recall of Sybil, now simply *jene Frau* (174, that woman) is her tortured face and agonized death.

The third insight into Ravic's mind comes at roughly the midpoint of the work, in the fifteenth of the thirty-three chapters, in a stylistically different passage in which we enter Ravic's nightmares. The chapter is relatively short, but moves from Ravic's dreams and his state of mind to his awareness that his relationship with Joan, who is with him, has changed his attitudes radically. His dream is of being in Germany and suffering the familiar inability to run away from the now *hämisch lächelnd* (206, maliciously smiling) Haake. Half-waking, he recalls the real nightmare of being in Germany, "gehetzt von den Schergen eines blutigen Regimes, das den Mord legalisiert hatte" (206–7, hunted down by the executioners of a bloody regime that has legalized murder). His experiences there, however, had deadened him emotionally. He remained physically alive only by clinging to the notion of revenge and avoiding any other potentially damaging emotion. His meeting and relationship with Joan Madou, however, brings him out of this state and teaches him that life is not something that operates simply on a desire for revenge and the suppression of all else, but is valuable in its own right. He declares his love for Joan, and realizes that "nie war das Leben so kostbar wie heute — wo es so wenig gilt" (214, Life was never as delicious as it is today, when it counts for so little).

The unusual chapter is the pivot point both of the relationship with Joan and of the Haake narrative. When we encounter Haake again, he is real. Ravic speaks to him, is not recognized, and establishes that Haake is only sporadically in Paris. Ravic gains his confidence (again with a false name), and they arrange to meet when Haake returns. A misunderstanding means that they do not initially make contact, but Ravic, who has borrowed a car for the pursuit, finds him by chance at the Osiris, takes him into his car, ostensibly to drive to another brothel, and kills him. The revenge taken on Haake differs from other comparable acts in the novels in its deliberate premeditation. Even after the event Ravic is less exercised about the disposal of the body than that the killing was an execution without a judgment. In the thirtieth chapter we see again into Ravic's mind as he imagines a conversation with Haake that would have made clear to the latter why Ravic was killing him. Ravic's thoughts in this chapter are given additional force by being set in italic type in the printed text, as he gives the reader a precise justification for what is in fact a murder. He runs over in his mind those whom Haake has tortured to death: Max Rosenberg, because he was a democrat, Willmann, who was a Catholic and refused to accept Hitler as the new Messiah, Riesenfeld, who was a pacifist. Only after he has disposed of the body, however, does he think of Sybil again, realizing that he is now able to think of her as she had been in the two years she had lived with him, not as the tortured mask of fear he last saw. He has committed murder, but his understandable revenge has provided a closure for himself. He tells Morosow that in the present climate, with a new war about to break out, there is no reason for being sentimental about the removal of a murderer; Morosow, in fact, still has his own mental list of those for whom he seeks vengeance for the death of his father long before.

Invoking a central idea found in different forms in the First World War novels and also in *Drei Kameraden,* Ravic comments that the twentieth century has effectively redefined murder, and that this has opened the way to the moral justification of the personal, rather than a legal or divine operation of a *lex talionis.* Steiner's killing of Steinbrenner and Ravic's of Haake have been seen both as acts of political resistance and as simple individual revenge rather than generalized expressions of "moral or ethical outrage,"[20] but these views are not incompatible. Ravic's vengeance is not just for himself, but for the other victims, including Sybil; however, Ravic is a fictional character, and the most important moral outrage is that felt by the reader.

Ravic's suppression of all feelings other than revenge had meant that he was almost devoid of emotion when he met Joan Madou, but their awkward love story restores to Ravic a wider view of life. The relationship is not an easy one, and indeed, after the chance meeting by the Seine and their night together, Ravic forgets about her until she contacts him once again. We discover that she is half Romanian, half British, but brought up in Italy, and Ravic enlists the aid of Morosow to get her a singing job at the Scheherazade nightclub in Montmartre. He is reluctant to come close emotionally for some time, and the relationship is largely an exploration of love, summed up in a brief dialogue about the problematic definition of happiness — another of Remarque's recurrent themes — at a fairly early stage:

Ravic erwiderte nichts. Was redete sie da, dachte er. "Du wirst mir
gleich noch sagen, dass du mich liebst," sagte er dann.
"Ich liebe dich."
Er machte eine Bewegung. "Du kennst mich doch kaum."
"Was hat das damit zu tun?"
"Viel. Lieben — das ist jemand, mit dem man alt werden will."
"Davon weiss ich nichts. Es ist jemand, ohne den man nicht leben
kann. Das weiss ich." (154)

[Ravic didn't reply. What was she talking about, he thought. Then he
said: "The next thing is that you'll say you love me."
"I love you."
He gestured. "You hardly know me."
"What's that to do with it?"
"A lot. Love — that's for someone you want to grow old with."
"I don't know anything about that. It's someone you can't live
without. I do know that."]

There is a conflict, which Ravic himself notes a little later, between the spon-
taneity expressed by Joan and the idea of growing old together, the
bourgeois ideal that is expressed to some extent by Kate Hegström as a
contrasting view of love, and found too in later works, notably in *Der Himmel
kennt keine Günstlinge*. Joan is aware that Ravic is resisting her love, while
she is able to fall in love with him completely, as she has done with others.
Ravic continues to be analytical; she insists on the pure feeling of the moment. Significantly, just after the scene in which Ravic sat thinking of revenge on the smiling Haake, he does acknowledge (in a phrase Remarque
uses with variations in more than one context)[21] that a man without love is
like the walking dead ("ein Toter auf Urlaub," 176). The acceptance of this
complete and immediate love — however fleetingly associated with the moment — restores Ravic to life. Ravic learns that love is for the moment. To
Joan's "Wir sterben nicht" (176, We shan't die) he replies: "Nein. Nicht wir.
Nur die Zeit" (No. We shan't. Only time will). What Ravic calls later "eine
hübsche, kleine Bürgerlichkeit" (189, a nice little bourgeois existence) is not
possible in any case on the edge of the abyss in 1939, and the best that they
have is a brief (and even then occasionally stormy) holiday. Ravic is aware
that the love between them is an accident, and also that Joan Madou herself
is not even faithful, but she has given him life again. The familiar motif of
the spark of life returns later in the work as he stands in the rain outside her
window — she might not even be in — and acknowledges her effect upon
him, worshipping her (*anbetend*), both like the Madonna or the victory god-
dess Nike:

weil du den Blitz geworfen hast, der gezündet hat, den Blitz, der in
jedem Schosse ruht, den Funken Leben, das schwarze Feuer; hier stehe

ich, nicht mehr wie ein Toter auf Urlaub mit kleinem Zynismus, Sar-
kasmus und etwas Mut, nicht mehr kalt; lebendig wieder, leidend
meinetwegen, aber offen wieder den Gewittern des Lebens, zurück-
geboren in seine schlichte Gewalt. (326)

[because it was you who cast the lightning that set off the fire, the
lightning that is there in every womb, the spark of life, the black fire;
here I stand, no longer a walking dead man with a little amount of
cynicism, some sarcasm and a bit of courage, no longer cold; alive
again, yes, maybe suffering, but open again to the storms of life, born
again into its simple power.]

At the end of their relationship Ravic understands that a long-term view of
love is never possible, is just "die alte ewige Gaukelei" (381, the old eternal
trick) and that love is necessarily incomplete, because "man wusste, dass
einer zuerst sterben würde" (381, you knew that one of the two has to die
first). This is one of the most prominent of Remarque's recurrent themes.
When Ravic leaves Joan, and she asks the question of what they had, Ravic
answers with the single word: love (384). The notion of Ravic as a kind of
born-again existentialist will take a different turn at the end of the work, but
by then Joan is herself dead, shot by accident by a foolish new lover, and
Ravic fails to save her. As she talks to him — slipping at the last into Italian
— he declares to her not his love, but what she has done for him: "Du hast
mich leben gemacht. Ich war nichts als ein Stein. Du hast gemacht, dass ich
lebe . . ." (470, You made me live. I was nothing more than a stone. You
have made me live . . .). Ravic repeats the declaration several times.[22]

The relationship with Joan is juxtaposed with Ravic's friendship with Kate
Hegström. We assume that she and Ravic have been close, and now she is
dying; Ravic knows that her cancer is inoperable, but this is concealed from
her. The situation again arouses in Ravic the heightened hunger for life motif that is present in several of the novels, from *Im Westen nichts Neues* on-
ward; indeed it makes Ravic think of an incident after the death of a friend in
the First World War involving a soldier called Katczinsky. Kate functions
primarily, however, as a symbol of the randomness of death, only thirty-four
years old, but condemned by disease. When told by another surgeon that
she has little time left, she decides to stay in Paris for what will be her last
summer and which is of course also the last summer of peace for Europe. At
the end she does leave, escaping the war, although death is already inside
her. Ravic waves her goodbye, and almost immediately afterwards, Joan is
shot; Ravic has lost both women.

Examining the various narrative strands separately detracts from the
overall effect of the book, an important part of which is the historical awareness throughout of things coming to an end, that this is the last summer in
the last place that is relatively safe, and the last chance for private revenge.

This awareness is not made obtrusive: a reference at the end of a chapter to a newspaper headline, for example, might refer to German troops on the Czech border, and thus remind the reader of the progress of international events. Ravic and the other refugees, represented best perhaps by the *Totenvogel* Meyer, know that war will come. Only the French seem unaware, and indeed historically the allied nations did cling to the idea that peace was possible: Britain's appeasement or America's isolationism were cases in point. Veber, even to a late stage, assures Ravic that the talk of war is simply meaningless political maneuvering. But the war does come. The comments of a petrol station attendant in the penultimate chapter form a pendant to those made by the woman in the crowd at the Armistice celebration at the start of the novel:

> Mein Vater fiel im letzten Krieg. Mein Grossvater 1871. Ich gehe morgen. Es ist immer dasselbe. Seit ein paar hundert Jahren machen wir das nun schon. Und es nützt nichts, wir müssen wieder gehen. (451–52)

> [My father was killed in the last war. My grandfather in 1871. I'm going tomorrow. It's always the same. We've been doing it for a few hundred years now. And it makes no difference, we have to go again.]

The shift to the all-inclusive first person plural is again significant. Almost the last thing Ravic does in the hospital is to deliver a baby, a boy destined for who knows what future war.

Eugenie had notified the police about an illegal doctor called Ravic, but when the French police come to take away the remaining refugees to a camp outside Paris — Ravic has already packed his belongings in anticipation — the central figure of the novel undergoes another rebirth, which is also a going back. He gives for the first time his full German name, Ludwig Fresenburg, and this is a positive point; Ravic, who had been devoid of emotions, living only for revenge, has been taken back to his earlier state. It is still unclear what will happen — the lights are all out and the Arc de Triomphe is no longer visible, but he is aware that "Der Mensch kann viel aushalten" (480, humans can stand a lot). Ravic appears once again in Remarque's last novel, *Schatten im Paradies,* having apparently made it to America.

The regularly reiterated criticism that Remarque's characters are not sufficiently political almost invariably misses the point that what matters is the impact of the novels as such. The characters, insofar as their experience and sometimes age permits, do make political and moral decisions, but the last judge is the reader. Antkowiak sees, for example, in Steiner's behavior only "antifaschischiche Lichtpünktchen" (flickers of antifascism), but the entire novel is antifascist in the same way as *Im Westen nichts Neues* is antiwar. Politics is in any case a generalization of personal views. The death of a single Nazi in each of these novels (and others) may have a personal importance for the characters, but the value for the reader is different. These two refugee novels also raise specifically the problem of pacifism as a universal moral principle in the face of an evil on the scale of the massive totalitarian regimes of the twentieth century, here particularly of Nazism. The ironic questioning of the definition of murder in the First World War novels, raised again but not tested in *Drei Kameraden,* here reaches its (literary) resolution. Trosske killed a man he hated, but was imprisoned for murder because killing in a war is supposedly different. But the hatred felt by Steiner and Ravic is different, and in any case perhaps one can say that it is part of a war. The political and philosophical complex that lies between the absolutism of "Thou Shalt Not Kill" and an appropriate response to Nazism is a question leveled at the twentieth century itself. Most people are (rightly or wrongly) not directly active in political terms, and that is what these novels reflect; Remarque's novels are rendered more significant by the normality of his protagonists. But politics cannot be avoided, certainly not for much of the twentieth century, and any political system or adherent to such a system ignoring qualities like humanity and tolerance and the rights of other individuals condemns itself by its own actions.

Notes

[1] *Liebe Deinen Nächsten,* afterword by Tilman Westphalen (Cologne: Kiepenheuer and Witsch, 1998). The first publication was the English translation by Denver Lindley as *Flotsam,* in serialized form in *Colliers* between July and September 1939, then in book form (Boston: Little, Brown, and Company, 1941) with a first German edition published by Fischer in Stockholm in 1941. Westphalen comments on the motto (cited here from Denver Lindley's translation) on 321 and 338. The line appears in *Das gelobte Land* with the plural: "Man braucht ein starkes Herz, um ohne Wurzeln zu leben" in *Das unbekannte Werk,* 2, 86. Most other translations keep Remarque's biblical title, and only the French version has the neutral *Les Exilés* (The Exiles). In *Schatten im Paradies* the narrator says that had it not been for one of the characters, they would all be *nichts als Treibgut* (just flotsam), KiWi edition, 272.

[2] See A. J. P. Taylor, *From Sarajevo to Potsdam* (London: Thames and Hudson, 1966), 152–53, for comments on and a photograph of the grandiose German and Soviet pavilions. The Spanish (republican) pavilion exhibited Picasso's painting *Guernica:* see 146–47. The time-establishing reference is important; Taylor points out that the exhibition emphasized not peace but national rivalry, and strikes by French workers meant that some pavilions were never completed, hence the employment of illegal migrant workers. On the time-settings for all the exile novels, see Sternburg, *"Als wäre alles,"* 289.

[3] *Arc de Triomphe,* afterword by Tilman Westphalen (Cologne: Kiepenheuer and Witsch, 1998). Again the first edition was the English text *Arch of Triumph,* preprinted in *Colliers* in September and October 1945, trans. Walter Sorell and Denver Lindley (New York: Appleton-Century-Crofts, 1945). Given that the monument at

l'Étoile is customarily known in English as the Arc de Triomphe, thus distinguishing it from triumphal arches in European cities and from the smaller triumphal arch in the Place du Carrousel, the Anglicization of the title remains inexplicable, unless it is to direct extra attention to the notion of triumph in an ironic sense. The German text was first published in Zürich by Micha, 1946. Remarque's diaries contain frequent references to his rewriting of the "Ravic-Manuskript" going as far back as 1940. See *Das unbekannte Werk*, vol. 5, 335 and 337, entries for 3 and 18 December 1940.

[4] France fell less than a year later, in June 1940 when the German entered Paris. For an independent view of the internment of foreigners, including German nationals, Jewish, and otherwise, living in Paris at the time, and their movements thereafter, see the witty memoirs of the photographer Erwin Blumenfeld, *Durch tausendjährige Zeit* (Berlin: Argon, 1988), chapters 51–65; translated as *Eye to I* by Mike Mitchell and Brian Murdoch (London: Thames and Hudson, 1999). Blumenfeld escaped to America.

[5] *Flotsam* was released in 1941 as *So Ends Our Night*, directed by John Cromwell for United Artists, with Fredric March, Glenn Ford, and Margaret Sullavan playing Steiner, Kern, and Ruth Holland. It was felt to be worthy but unimpressive, not least by Remarque himself: "Nicht schlecht. Etwas lang, auch wohl langweilig" (Not bad. A bit long, probably also boring"). He went on to make other criticisms in the same diary entry on 22 January 1941, *Das unbekannte Werk*, vol. 5, 345–46. The 1921 silent film *Flotsam* listed under Remarque's name on the Internet Movie Database is unconnected, but the 1951 film *Demir Perde* (The Iron Curtain) by the veteran Turkish director Semih Evin is also based on the novel. Lewis Milestone, who had made *All Quiet on the Western Front*, filmed *Arch of Triumph* in 1948 with probably the most distinguished cast of any of the Remarque films, with Ingrid Bergman and Charles Boyer, plus Charles Laughton (Haake) and Louis Calhern (Morosow). Surprisingly, it was a failure commercially, and Remarque noted in his diary on 22 April 1948: "Fürchterliche Kritiken" (dreadful reviews), *Das unbekannte Werk*, vol. 5, 397. The tagline was "The Story of an Outcast and a Killer." Waris Hussein remade it for TV in 1985, again in English and with a first-rate cast (Anthony Hopkins, Lesley-Anne Down, Donald Pleasance). A Polish TV film, *Łuk Triumfalny*, was made in 1993 and broadcast in February 1994. On the films see Taylor, *Remarque*, 147–52 and 171–80.

[6] Letter to Dr. Joseph Caspar Witsch of 15 July 1964 in *Das unbekannte Werk*, vol. 5, 204. He may already have been working on *Das gelobte Land/Schatten im Paradies* at that stage anyway. See Westphalen's afterword to *Die Nacht von Lissabon*.

[7] See Barker and Last, *Remarque*, 111; the diary entry for 30 May 1941 is in *Das unbekannte Werk*, vol. 5, 352. Wagener, *Understanding*, 63, properly notes in this context that these parallels are less than useful in understanding the novels. See Taylor, *Remarque*, and especially Hilton Tims's biography for details of the relationships with Zambona, Dietrich, Natasha Paley, as well as with Garbo and with Ruth Albu (given that there are several Ruths in the novels).

[8] The book appeared on 31 March. See Remarque's diary entries for 22 and 30 April 1941, *Das unbekannte Werk*, vol. 5, 351–52. The first refers to notices in the *New York Times* and the *Herald Tribune;* the second to a review in the *New Yorker*. In fact the reviews the work received, both as *Flotsam* and of the later German text, are

of considerable interest. See Westphalen's afterword, 335–37, citing one in the *Chicago Daily News* that likened it to the Sermon on the Mount. See also Hans Wagener, "Remarque in Amerika — zwischen Erfolg und Exilbewusstsein," *Jahrbuch* 10 (1999): 18–38.

[9] See Wagener, *Understanding,* 58, on the scene; it is not entirely clear what is meant here by stereotypical. One point about clichés and stereotypes, incidentally, is that they have some truth in them.

[10] Taylor, *Remarque,* 148, and Wagener, *Understanding,* 57, rightly stress that the work is (also) "a repository of exile lore" (Taylor's phrase).

[11] There are comments on the ironic treatment of the League in Fabienne Amgwerd, "Form und Funktion des Komischen bei Remarque," *Jahrbuch* 15 (2005): 7–35, especially 25.

[12] Denver Lindley's translation is uncharacteristically shaky in this episode in that he renders *Jiddisch* as "Hebrew."

[13] By Abraham Goldfaden, though taken over into the folksong repertoire. Remarque's version is a kind of hybrid German-Yiddish. I am indebted to Dr. Heather Valencia for details about the song. The scene was sentimentally illustrated in the serialization in *Collier's:* see Schneider, *Remarque,* 82.

[14] See Westphalen's afterword to the edition. The "gates of hell" reference is in fact in the third mention of the Arc de Triomphe, not the second. See my "Memory and Prophecy" on the use and abuse of the Unknown Soldier.

[15] The Sorell-Lindley translation claims that he has "more than forty years" behind him, although the German simply says "vierzig Jahre" (13). He is once again exactly of an age with Remarque and most of his central figures. The English translation, however, has small deviations in a number of places from the German text, which are specific rather than interpretative, and these may be linked with the version from which it was translated.

[16] The passage is a difficult one to translate. Sorell and Lindley render the last clauses as: "in an odd fashion, this seemed to bring her closer to him than many words, and the grinding habit of time." This does not match the German exactly, but does express what seems to be the intended sense.

[17] In Spain in 1936 a group of generals mounted a coup against the narrowly elected composite left-wing government of the Republic, which developed into a protracted civil war. The fascist governments in Germany and Italy joined in against the government, and to a lesser extent the Soviet Union supported the republicans, so that it came to be perceived as a conflict between fascism and communism. The war drew in large numbers of foreigners (into the International Brigade) principally on the republican side. By the end of March 1939, Franco's right-wing (Falangist) forces had taken Madrid and had control of Spain.

[18] The passage cited is on page 38 of the KiWi edition. Barker and Last, *Remarque,* 112, point out Morosow's similarity with Melikow in *Schatten im Paradies* (although Morosow *does* have a Nansen-passport, and Ravic refers to him as a *Nansenpassbesitzer,* 92). Morosow is in other respects a continuation of Orlow in *Drei Kameraden* (doorman, vengeance for his father). At the end of *Die Nacht von Lissabon,* the

framework narrator hands the passport on, ironically, to a new wave of Russians who do not have passports.

[19] The English text refers to a summer evening in 1933 at this point. In chapter 12, we learn (in both versions) that he has been arrested in August 1933. The timing is not absolutely clear, but this may be an error in the German text.

[20] See Antkowiak, *Remarque*, 81, for the first idea, and Wagener, *Understanding*, 59, for the second. Antkowiak is interesting for the views of other Soviet critics on the novel. Tims, *Remarque*, 144, seems to agree with Antkowiak, although Sybil was not Ravic's wife, and he did not leave her behind in Germany in that sense.

[21] See Barker and Last, *Remarque*, 92 and 122.

[22] See Helga Schreckenberger's admirable summary in "'Durchkommen ist alles': Physischer und psychischer Existenzkampf in Erich Maria Remarque's Exil-Romanen," *Text+Kritik* 149 (2001): 30–41, esp. 34–35.

German edition of
Die Nacht von Lissabon

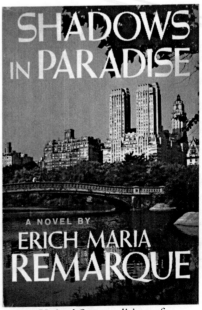

United States edition of
Schatten im Paradies

5: Shadows: *Die Nacht von Lissabon* and *Schatten im Paradies/Das gelobte Land*

R EMARQUE RETURNED TO THE refugee theme in two more novels, only one of which was published in his lifetime. *Die Nacht von Lissabon (The Night in Lisbon)* first appeared in book form, after the customary serialization, in 1962, and was the last novel he saw published. It is also a work of high quality.[1] *Schatten im Paradies (Shadows in Paradise)* appeared in the year after Remarque's death, 1971, in a text published by his widow, Paulette Goddard. Although it existed in a complete manuscript that was edited and to an extent cut by the publisher (Droemer-Knaur in Munich rather than Remarque's by then usual Kiepenheuer and Witsch), Remarque had never arranged a publishing contract and seems therefore not to have intended doing so. There is, moreover, a later, incomplete revision of this work surviving in a mixture of manuscript and typescript. An edited text appeared with the title *Das gelobte Land* (The Promised Land) in 1998.[2] In spite of the publicity claims made when *Schatten im Paradies* was published that several texts existed and this was the version that Remarque had been working on almost to the end of his life, there seem really only to have been two, and that which forms the basis for *Schatten im Paradies* was the earlier of them. *Das gelobte Land* is different from *Schatten im Paradies* in a number of respects, although large portions were retained. What we have of Remarque's incomplete second version has itself undergone revisions, and all we have of its projected ending is a series of notes.

It is ironic that just as there are various claimants to be Remarque's first novel there are various possibilities, too, for his last. *Schatten im Paradies* has established itself, however dubious the text, as the "last complete novel," but in real terms, his last novel was *Die Nacht von Lissabon*. However, both of them follow on in terms of historical content fairly closely from *Liebe Deinen Nächsten* and *Arc de Triomphe*, so that it is appropriate to treat them outside the chronology of writing. *Die Nacht in Lissabon* is set for the most part in 1942, although it is, as we discover in the final pages, being recounted, as with *Der schwarze Obelisk*, from a postwar perspective by a narrator whose experiences match those of Kern, Ravic, and other refugees. He has come to Lisbon after the fall of France and at the end of the main part of the work leaves for America. *Schatten in Paradies* is set in America during the war, and the main narrative ends with the end of the war in 1945, though it is again retrospective, with a narrator who has also escaped from Germany and has also traveled what Remarque in both novels refers to as the Via Dolorosa, ending in Lisbon and the escape by ship to the New World. *Schatten im Paradies* in particular, however, also directs itself at postwar Germany strongly. The later émigré novels also differ from the first two in that they are first-person narratives. The two final novels, however, only seem to differ from each other in that *Die Nacht von Lissabon* is set entirely in Europe (and partly in Germany), but *Schatten im Paradies* has its action in America; the latter novel is in spite of that still primarily concerned with the European world of the refugees, and the war is still present, even though America itself was not physically affected. *Schatten im Paradies* is again a German novel, and not by virtue of language alone.

Die Nacht von Lissabon

The structure of *Die Nacht von Lissabon* is relatively complex. A framework narrator is telling the story of what happened to him in 1942, and although he is doing so from a point well after the war, this does not become clear until the final four paragraphs, and there is no prologue to provide an immediate context. The comments made by the narrator in the course of the work do not betray any knowledge of later events, so that the present of the work may be taken as 1942. A second narrator looks back a few years, however, to the beginning of the events that he is remembering and passing on to the first narrator, and he brings those events down to the present of 1942.

The framework narrative may be conveyed in a few sentences, and it takes up only a single night and some of the following day. The first narrator, who is never named, has been trying to get money and papers together so that he and his wife might escape to America on a ship that is waiting in the harbor. His own papers are — he tells us ironically — only *etwas gefälscht* (7, slightly forged), but he is unable to raise the seemingly impossible fare. He encounters another man, also a refugee, who offers him a miracle — *Wunder* is a key theme in the work — promising and eventually giving him the tickets and all the necessary papers. These were intended originally for himself and his wife, who has just died. In exchange he asks simply to be able to tell the narrator his own story, to fix it in his own memory.

That story forms the bulk of the novel. The second narrator relates, with interpolations and occasional discussions, how, having once been in a German concentration camp and then a refugee, he had returned to Germany (to Osnabrück) from Paris a little before the outbreak of war in 1939 to see his wife and had escaped again with her. They are interned in France, again escape, undergo considerable difficulties, and eventually reach Lisbon,[3] where his wife dies. The nature of her illness become clear in the course of the work. It is already clear that there are some similarities with the Steiner narrative in *Liebe Deinen Nächsten,* and the man's gift of tickets and papers to the first narrator also recalls that of Steiner's money, passed on to Kern and Ruth Holland so that they can escape. There are other similarities in individual motifs with earlier works, such as *Arc de Triomphe*.[4]

Although we never discover the name of the framework narrator, we do learn that his wife's name is Ruth; however, this is immaterial because both of them change their names to go to America, and the concept of names as random tokens or signs, often a theme in Remarque, is here made central. Refugees lose more than property or their country; they may also lose, and have to rethink, their identity. Just as Ravic — the name by which we know the character throughout the novel — is not a "real" name, here the absence or loss of names is an expression of the loss of identity as a theme of the twentieth century.[5] The second narrator has a name, Josef Schwarz, but it is not entirely his own, and this fact is important. This time the reader is regularly made aware that Schwarz is not really the name of the narrator, although we are told that the name Josef is genuine. Where the name Ravic, which is, unlike Schwarz, ostensibly Czech rather than German, is provided for the reader by the third-person narrator of *Arc de Triomphe*, here the character explains in detail that Schwarz is simply the name on his passport, and then — indicating for the first time another theme of the work — he tells us that he acquired that passport by what he calls a private miracle. To the first narrator's comment that there are no longer any, he responds that miracles do still happen, otherwise many of them would simply not survive.

The interventions of the framework narrator when Schwarz is telling his tale are of varying importance; some are simply prompts as to what happened next, or requests for clarification. Schwarz, too, sometimes has to interrupt himself to provide additional pieces of information for the listener and reader — that his wife's Nazi brother had denounced him, for example. While the two men are talking, things are still going on around them, and sometimes their description by the framework narrator can have an ironic effect. At the end of the first chapter, for example, a woman in the bar where they find themselves announces with boredom to a companion that she really doesn't want to go back to America, reminding us how much the framework narrator desperately does and Schwarz once did want to go to America. The passing of the night is marked skillfully, Schwarz continuing his narrative as the pair move from one bar to another; they are taken for homosexuals at one, offered women at another, and eat and drink sporadically until dawn. Remarque is skilled at giving clues to the passing of historical time by reference to known events, but here he does it on a small scale. Often at the openings and endings of the chapters the two refugees discuss both the philosophical and practical aspects of exile, and in the eighteenth and final chapter of the work, Schwarz's narrative is brought down to the 1942 present, and the framework narrator joins in as part of Schwarz's now-ending story, sees him leave the novel, and takes over his name. During the course of the novel the basic miracle — Schwarz's gift of getting to America — is done gradually; the tickets are promised, then handed over, and then the passports, complete with visas.

Schwarz gives as a prelude to his own story the tale of the original — the real — Josef Schwarz, whose forename he shared, and who was an Austrian refugee whom he barely knew in Paris in 1938. This original Schwarz, having had a heart attack, before he died gave the narrator his passport, and also some valuable postage stamps and drawings. The new Schwarz had the passport changed, adapting for example the date of birth, since the first Schwarz was twenty-five years older.[6] Schwarz is therefore really Schwarz II, and at the end of the work he hands the passport on to the unnamed first narrator, who now becomes Josef Schwarz III. Ironically, just as Schwarz II and his wife have different names throughout the main story and cannot therefore live as man and wife, this also causes complications when the passports are handed on to the framework narrator and his wife. When they divorce after reaching America, we are told, they have to marry again first so that the divorce will be official. Documents have far-reaching effects.

In the course of the novel there is one single indirect reference to the new Schwarz's real name. His wife, we hear, has retained his surname to annoy her family, and since she is Helen Baumann, he was presumably Josef Baumann, but the fact that this is mentioned only once indicates a deliberate distancing, and by the end of the work, the framework narrator tells us that he cannot remember it. The original Schwarz, an Austrian who managed to escape just before the *Anschluss,* was presumably Jewish. He is even referred to by the main narrator as *der ewige Jude* (the wandering Jew, 83), a notion used in other novels as a shorthand for "refugee." The precise reason for exile makes little difference, and in this work some of the terminology of the Jewish Diaspora is used as paradigmatic for all refugees.

The German Baumann has become the Austrian Schwarz, then, and his wife's maiden name, Jürgens, is established for the reader not only because her brother plays a direct role, but because the new Schwarz actually comments on its German-ness. When Schwarz tells Helen of his new name, she is at first reluctant to accept it, although he himself questions what a name is: "Ein Zufall oder eine Identifikation" (83, an accident or an identification), going on to say that he has heard "dass es in Indonesien Sitte sei, ab und zu die Namen zu wechseln. Wenn jemand seiner Persönlichkeit müde wird, wechselt er sie, ergreift einen neuen Namen und beginnt ein neues Dasein" (83–84, that they have a custom in Indonesia of changing their names every so often. When someone gets tired of his old personality he changes it, takes a new name and begins a new existence). Schwarz's flippant comment conceals the truth that he is also deliberately seeking a new existence. His exile has necessitated it, but he has accepted it willingly, as must the reader therefore, and he remains Schwarz until the end, when he takes the passport of the other narrator, planning on keeping it only as long as it takes to get him into the French Foreign Legion, a place where, proverbially, all identity can be lost. There are reminders throughout the novel of the fact that Schwarz is the name of a dead man, and there is a contrast with Ravic once again in that while the latter reverts to his real identity at the end of *Arc de Triomphe,* the name Schwarz is passed on, and its most recent bearer becomes someone else. It is interesting, too, that the reader is in fact provided with all the real names, albeit somewhat obliquely.

Die Nacht von Lissabon is the story of a relationship as much as of exile. The change of identity goes hand in hand with a change of attitude on Schwarz's part towards his wife and to their marriage. He tells the framework narrator at the start that — quite apart from the fact that he had had to flee Germany for political reasons — his marriage had already become commonplace and unsatisfactory, *eine mittelmässige Ehe* (22, a mediocre marriage), and he succumbs to the dangerous urge to go back to Germany principally to see if anything can be rescued emotionally. The situation is not the same as that of Steiner and Marie in *Liebe Deinen Nächsten,* which is based on love alone. Schwarz has no real idea of how he will be received, but he, too, is driven by desperation, knowing that a war is about to start in a matter of weeks, rather than months, and that Germany might well win, after which he has no idea of what might happen to him.

Schwarz travels first to Switzerland and then crosses illegally into Austria, wading through the upper Rhine by Feldkirch, a border familiar in *Liebe Deinen Nächsten* and here interpreted by Schwarz as Lethe, the river of forgetting, applying the idea to his own past self. Austria is already part of the Reich, and Schwarz is appalled first at the bloodthirsty arrogance, but also at the persuasive effect, given the absence of any foreign comparators, of the newspapers he sees. He begins to think that his wife may have been swayed by propaganda and fallen in with the wishes of her pro-regime family, or has married again. He reaches Osnabrück, and with the help of an old friend makes contact with his wife. Actual action in this part of his narrative is limited, and the emphasis is on his fear of capture in a sequence of minor events. While killing time by attending a mass in the cathedral, for example, Schwarz thinks first of the tortures the church has perpetrated over the years, and then of the fact that he had been tortured in a concentration camp by being put on a cross, in a deliberate and cynical *imitatio Christi,* during which his wife's brother, his tormentor, had referred to "your church."[7] By the steps leading up to the Town Hall, where the Peace of Westphalia was signed and the Third Reich announced, Schwarz again wonders whether its demise will ever be announced there, too, but at the time, 1939, or indeed in the narrative present, he has little hope.

His relationship with his wife is tentative at the start, although she has not divorced him, nor indeed changed her name, setting her apart from her family. Their reunion progresses, however, and the sensual Helen takes him back into her bed.[8] Her sexuality is an expression of her hold on life, and we gather that it is has not been restricted to Schwarz as she quickly puts away a photograph. Her pragmatic sexuality, which brings Schwarz out of himself again, recalls that of Joan Madou; that she also has parallels with Kate Hegstroem in *Arc de Triomphe*, however, comes out more gradually. During Schwarz's account of his reconciliation with Helen, the framework narrator makes a throwaway comment about how, when things are bad, they could always be worse — one might have cancer. He has named the first disease that came into his head, but Schwarz reacts sharply. The framework narrator and the reader will not find out until later that Helen has cancer, and Schwarz himself does not know at this stage, so that it must be given its proper place in the narrative. It becomes a dominant motif later, with Helen pitting her life against the disease as well as against the politics of the time.

Initially Schwarz is unsure of why he has returned, although it is not for Helen's sake. In fact he has done so out of desperation with his earlier existence, aware that he was unable to build a new life before he has settled matters with the old one: "Gangräne hatte eingesetzt, und ich hatte die Wahl gehabt, im Gestank der Gangräne zu krepieren oder zurückzugehen und zu versuchen, sie zu heilen (75–76, Gangrene had set in, and I had had the choice of rotting in the stench of the gangrene or of going back and trying to cure it).

The startling and drastic disease image makes clear that his return was to achieve closure with Germany, with his marriage, with exile. The intervening years had left him spiritually bankrupt — he uses the term — and his return has been a kind of suicide), but one that gives him the possibility of rebirth. Helen will help him in this, although he can explain none of this to her; she (and he thinks all women) can be persuaded by action rather than explanation. Schwarz's attitude to her has changed. In the past he would have wanted details of her other relationships; now he accepts things as they are. Tension is introduced when Helen's Nazi brother, Georg, visits suddenly, forcing Schwarz to hide. Outside, too, there are constant indicators of the war that is about to begin, but Helen announces suddenly that she, too, wishes to leave Germany. She has a valid passport in her own name, and explains that she has had to acquire it to visit a doctor in Switzerland, and will pretend to do so again, and meet Schwarz in Zürich. She assures her husband that she is not actually ill, although we shall find out later that this is not true. The pair do manage to get out of Germany and rendezvous before going on to France.

Schwarz's progress into and out of Nazi Germany, trying to be as unseen as possible, allows Remarque to show the reader glimpses of what is going on, and one incident requires comment; just before he leaves Münster, Schwarz observes two SS-men beating up a man:

Es war die ewige Szene der Menschheit — die Knechte der Gewalt, der
Opfer, und der ewige Dritte, der Zuschauer, der die Hände nicht hebt
und das Opfer nicht verteidigt und nicht versucht, es zu befreien, weil
er für seine eigene Sicherheit fürchtet und dessen eigene Sicherheit
eben deshalb immer in Gefahr ist. (117)

[It was the eternal scene for mankind: the servants of force, the victim,
and the eternal third party, the observer, who doesn't raise a hand to
defend the victim and doesn't try to rescue him, because he is afraid
for his own safety, and whose own safety is for that reason always in
danger.]

Schwarz knows that it would be useless, even counterproductive to inter-
vene, but he makes himself sit in a waiting room openly as a token risk to try
and regain a little of his self-respect. The notion of the impotent and frus-
trated observer will become a main theme in *Schatten im Paradies,* but as far
as Schwarz is concerned, he will vow at the end of the work to go on living
so that he can strike against the torturers if possible. The passage both underlines the status of the exile writer as an observer and encapsulates the
message of the work for the reader, who is also an observer of these particular servants of force.[9]

While trying to cross unofficially from Austria into Switzerland, Schwarz
runs into difficulty with the police, but when they check his passport they
find a letter (in Helen's hand, in fact) on official stationery of the Osnabrück
Nazi party, ostensibly signed by Helen's brother, purporting to identify
Schwarz as a party member of a secret mission. Schwarz comments to the
framework narrator that she has rescued him by a theatrical trick, a *Deus ex
machina*. In literary terms this is exactly what it is, and the self-reflexive
comment, permitted by the use of the two narrators, legitimizes it. Schwarz
decides to trust to chance and travel to Switzerland by train, where the letter
is read again, but this time there is an irony of a different kind when another
man in the train — clearly another refugee — attacks him verbally, assuming
that Schwarz genuinely is a Nazi. When Schwarz agrees with everything the
man says, his interlocutor assumes that he is being mocked. The refugee
whose real name is not Schwarz, and who is certainly not a Nazi, has been
forced into an even more false position. He even has to act as devil's advo-
cate when, having agreed with the other man that Germany will go to war,
he adds: "Aber wie wird es, wenn Deutschland gewinnt?" (134, What will
happen if Germany wins?). The man can only reply: "Wenn ihr gewinnt,
dann gibt es keinen Gott mehr" (134, if you win, then there really isn't a
God).

The ninth chapter in the work — roughly the halfway point — opens
with a more extended discussion between the two narrators. It is nearly
morning, and Schwarz, on what should have been his happiest night and ac-

tually is the worst, stands between night and day; the town he can see contains both the coffin with his wife, and the ship that is about to set off for America. His debate with himself — here the framework narrator acts as a sounding board only — comes closer to a resolution of the question that is raised with other lovers, that of the death of one partner. Schwarz wonders whether he and Helen are not now, however, merged completely:

> ist sie vielleicht jetzt erst ganz mein, in dieser trostlosen Alchemie, in der sie nun nur noch antwortet, wenn ich will und wie ich will, eingegangen und nur noch da in dem bisschen Phosphoreszieren hier unter meinem Schädel? (138)

> [is she perhaps only now completely mine, has she entered that sad alchemy in which she only answers me when and how I want her to, only there in the tiny phosphorescent flickers inside my head?]

The merging of the *Ich* and *Du* is only possible by means of memory, and this is what his narrative is providing: both an immediate expression of that memory and also a fixing of it as a memorial. It is important that the tale is presented to an audience, the framework narrator and re-teller of the tale, because only this can contextualize the various miracles that happen to Schwarz, and indeed that which he creates for the framework narrator. The real miracle for Schwarz, as he now begins to realize, is his relationship with Helen as such, however, and the miracle for the framework narrator, as the reader discovers at the end, turns out to be an imperfect one. The definition of a miracle is not straightforward.

Schwarz has reached the late summer of 1939. He and Helen have escaped from Germany and hope this time for miracles on the world political stage like the Munich agreement of 1938, which famously promised "peace in our time," but which was merely a temporary stay. Once they manage to enter France, however, Helen argues that they should enjoy life as much as they can. In her case the *carpe diem* response is prompted by the awareness that she has cancer, but so, too, has the world: the crisis will come before long. In Paris the two are visited by Helen's brother Georg, who tries to bully Helen to return just before the imminent war, but she refuses to return and her insistence on seizing the moment is underlined by the purchase of an expensive dress, another image that Remarque uses elsewhere. The war begins. The two narrators recall as shared memories the first days of the war. They remember the blackout in Paris as if darkness had fallen on the world, and both the image and the immediate events recall the conclusion of *Arc de Triomphe,* as Schwarz and Helen are interned together, even with Spanish republican refugees. "Der Eifer, mit dem die Antifaschisten in einem antifaschistischen Lande eingefangen wurden, war nicht ohne Ironie; man hätte glauben können, man wäre in Deutschland" (182, the eagerness with which the anti-fascists in this anti-fascist country were rounded up was not without irony; you could have believed that you were in Germany).[10] The twentieth century, says Schwarz, may even be characterized by such unconscious and malevolent ironies that have nothing to do with wit. He is aware that France had to do something with nationals from fascist countries and that their camps did not involve torture or murder, but he does recall the cold and discomfort. He manages to persuade himself, with great, and again ironic, difficulty, that "Gerechtigkeit war ein Luxus für ruhige Zeiten" (191, justice was a peace-time luxury).

Schwarz and Helen are separated, eventually interned in different camps, and their later story of survival is set against the history of events, beginning with the fall of France in mid-1940, at which point they are in the Vichy sector, unoccupied but under permanent threat of Nazi intervention.[11] Schwarz recalls the despair that this political situation brought with it, and also the way in which hopelessness inculcates a reduction of feelings by the concentration on survival alone. When at this point the framework narrator asks about God, Schwarz replies that God can only be found when one is stripped of everything else, but the fall of France had brought him so low that he can believe in nothing any more, and cannot indeed find God. All he has left is the image of the self in a mirror, or even between mirrors as the eternally repeating self, making clear the *lächerliche Isoliertheit des Menschen* (194, the ridiculous isolation of the human being). The individual becomes subject to chance rather than to reason. In this frame of mind, Schwarz, who has already tried in vain to escape, simply walks out of the internment camp, explaining confidently to the young guards that he has been released. The plausibility of this has been criticized,[12] but the discussion of chance and the necessary existential dependence upon it prepares the reader for it. Schwarz finds his wife's camp, and manages to make contact with her. She has been involved, Schwarz is told, with a camp doctor, but the reasons for this are left ambiguous, and Schwarz does not yet know about her cancer. She manages to leave the camp with him, and together they take what is now referred to as the Via Dolorosa, the path of refuge down to the Pyrenees, to Spain and Portugal. Their departure is matched by a scene in which a Jewish family decide to return to Germany on the erroneous grounds that since they will eventually be forced to do so, they will be better treated if they do so voluntarily. Even the position of the Jews is a paradoxical one, as Schwarz comments: France did not want them, but would not let them escape in time. However, a sympathetic French prefect assists Schwarz and his wife. Her brother is making inquiries about her, but the prefect agrees to say that she has died, a motif that takes on force later. Using terms from the Jewish exodus in parallel with the Christian image of the Via Dolorosa, Schwarz explains that they will cross the Red Sea:

Das ist ein Ausdruck unter Flüchtlingen. Wir leben wie die Juden beim Auszug aus Ägypten. Hinter uns die deutsche Armee und die Gestapo, zu beiden Seiten das Meer der französischen und spanischen Polizei, und vor uns das gelobte Land Portugal mit dem Hafen von Lissabon zum noch gelobteren Lande Amerika. (232)

[It's an expression refugees use. We're living like the Jews during the exodus from Egypt. Behind us is the German army and the Gestapo, on each side the sea of French and Spanish police, before us the promised land, Portugal, with the port of Lisbon, which leads to the even more promised land of America.]

The Via Dolorosa is a road leading to death, of course, where the crossing of the Red Sea was an escape. As far as a visa is concerned, Schwarz explains once more that he has no other choice but to believe in miracles, and in fact he will indeed obtain one by such a miracle, but will pass it to the framework narrator. Schwarz also gives Helen at this point a small portion of poison that he has obtained, for use in case of torture.

Helen bids farewell to the doctor to whom her fellow internees thought she had been rather too close; however, he explains to Schwarz that she is extremely sick. She insists that she is not and stresses that she does not look ill — a motif Remarque is fond of — and she takes with her the expensive dress that they have bought in Paris. They embark on what Schwarz himself calls an odyssey, only the hazards are not Scylla and Charybdis, but the vicious circles (a nice image) of bureaucracy. Meanwhile, references to Helen's illness become more frequent. The pair spends time in various places, including a spell in an abandoned château, where in a brief idyll they find and wear costumes from the *belle époque*. Here and in these costumes Helen notes that they are both technically dead — she has allegedly died in the camp, and he has the passport of Schwarz, who died in Paris. The whole imagery here is complex; high society in pre-revolutionary France, too, was glittering, but the guillotine stood at the end. Helen explains that this is not true for them because they are already dead. When Schwarz continues to look forward to the possibility of escape to America, Helen insists once more on the moment, and picks up a theme (and an adjective) that Schwarz himself had voiced at the start of the novel:

"Was wäre sonst aus uns geworden? Ein mittelmässiges, langweiliges Paar, das in Osnabrück ein mittelmässiges, langweiliges Leben geführt hätte mit mittelmässigen Gefühlen und einer Urlaubsreise im Jahr.— (241)

[What would have become of us otherwise? A mediocre, boring couple who would have led a mediocre, boring life in Osnabrück with mediocre emotions and one holiday a year. —]

This is the high point of their love story in the work. Again with a complex irony, only having had to take flight could the couple celebrate this idyll. But they do so in an artificial, temporary, and borrowed isolation, in a remote place and, because of their eighteenth-century costumes (there is an echo here of a fancy-dress scene in *Arc de Triomphe*), they are outside history as well. The provisionality of all relationships, condemned in any case by the inevitable loss of one partner, is regularly underscored by Remarque when he sets idylls like this in provisional situations — Ruth and Kern in Vienna in *Liebe Deinen Nächsten*, Ernst and Elisabeth in Germany in *Zeit zu leben und Zeit zu sterben*, and Ross and Natascha in New York in *Schatten im Paradies* are all examples of the same motif. At the end of the section, Schwarz and Helen hear planes flying over, rattling the rococo mirrors on the walls.

As they move on to Marseilles the point is approaching where the narrative of Schwarz's travels will reach the present of the framework. Having established that the ship will not leave for another day, which gives the framework narrator time to organize his new papers, Remarque now gives us another time check: it is 7:30 in the morning. Schwarz is aware that they will be coming in an hour to collect his dead wife, and asks the first narrator what kind of story he has been telling. The reply offers an interesting interpretative internalization: "Wie die Geschichte einer Liebe" (254, like the story of a love). Schwarz is relieved, and the point will be reinforced again later. Continuing his narrative, Schwarz tells how he discovers from yet another doctor the true nature of Helen's illness: she has terminal cancer, but chose not to be operated upon and simply to ignore the illness.

Some further incidents on their flight have to be noted. A chance encounter with an American — another miracle, in itself perhaps the least credible of those in the story, although in the event it does not help Schwarz and contains its own ironies yet again — permits the pair to obtain visas for America. There would otherwise be a difficulty with Helen, since immigrants likely to be a burden on the state would not normally be granted a visa. The young American vouches for them, and the visas are granted, but when Schwarz goes to collect them, Georg arrests him. Assisted by another Gestapo man, referred to simply as "the smiling one," echoing Haake in *Arc de Triomphe*, Georg attempts to get from Schwarz the whereabouts of Helen. After a beating, Schwarz agrees to take him to her, and is taken into Georg's car. The plot at this point is at its closest to *Arc de Triomphe*, although Schwarz is, unlike Ravic, not in command of the situation. He does, however, manage to retrieve a razorblade sewn into his clothing and cuts Georg's throat, then buries him in a remote area. The similarity with the death of Haake is not just in the detail; the killing of the isolated Nazi is the same gesture as that made by Ravic (and by Steiner in *Liebe Deinen Nächsten* and Graeber in *Zeit zu leben und Zeit zu sterben*), and again, if this were reality, and if the normal rules of civilized society were applied, it would be

murder. Here it is an act of immediate self-defense as well as a private revenge, and a blow against Nazism in a world where the normal rules are in
abeyance. It differs from Steiner's opportunistic suicide, Graeber's seizure
of the moment, and Ravic's deliberate plan.

Schwarz uses Georg's car and papers for them to travel through Spain
and into Portugal, and almost into the narrative present of the novel. But
Helen is dying, and says to Schwarz that they will not see the promised land
together. The biblical allusion is again one based upon the Jewish exodus,
but this time the image is not a positive one. Moses — who killed the Egyp-
tian overseer, and who also, according to tradition, recorded the whole story
— is not permitted to cross the Jordan into Canaan, though he is within
sight of his goal. Rather, the responsibility is passed to Joshua, the equivalent
here, perhaps, of the framework narrator. Nevertheless, before Helen dies
she responds to the question of what they have become, which echoes the
earlier discussion of the mediocrities that they might have become, by assert-
ing that they have been "Alles, was wir konnten. . . . Und das ist genug"
(300, all that we could be. And that is enough). It is not the disease that kills
her, however. When Schwarz finds her dead, she has broken the mirrors —
the representatives of the self[13] — destroyed the expensive dress, another
symbol of living, and taken the poison to avoid the tortures not of the Nazis,
but of the disease.

Now that the two timelines have merged, the framework narrator is in a
position to evaluate the whole story, to sum up and to comfort Schwarz. He
assures him that Helen had committed suicide because the pain was too
great and that a dying person must be allowed to choose when that point
has come. More importantly, he also assures Schwarz that Helen did not
take her own life to avoid going to America with him. The reality is quite
different: she has clung to life for his sake for as long as she possibly could
and has at least allowed them to get within sight of the promised land. Now
it is up to Schwarz to maintain the memories and to work out what kind of
life he has led. Schwarz suggests that of a cuckold or of a murderer? The
framework narrator tells him: "wenn Sie wollen, auch das eines Liebenden
und, wenn Ihnen etwas daran liegt, das einer Art von Heiligen. Doch was
sollen die Namen? Es war da" (303–4, if you like, also that of a lover or that
of a kind of saint. But what do names matter? It existed).[14]

Schwarz will not commit suicide. Georg is dead, but the smiling torturer, the worse, impersonal one, who simply delighted in the abuse of force
as such, is not, and it would be "ein Verbrechen, ein Leben mit Selbstmord
zu verschwenden, das man gegen Barbaren seinesgleichen einsetzen kann"
(305, a crime to waste by suicide a life that could be used against barbarians
like him). Schwarz takes the first narrator's passport to get into France to
join the Legion, and there is a new Schwarz. The two men see Helen's body
taken away: she is dead, and nothing, not even her husband, is any concern

of hers now. He gives a number of letters that she had kept, and that he had never read, to the framework narrator, who eventually throws them overboard, also unread, en route to America. Only the last few paragraphs gradually reveal that even the 1942 present was reflective. We are told briefly that he and Ruth divorced not long after arriving in America, having had to marry first, because their new papers were in different names. The narrator tells us then that he had become interested in art, something he says is a legacy of the original Schwarz (and which points on to *Schatten im Paradies*), and after the war he returns to Europe, where he — with difficulty — establishes his own identity again (ironically while many former Nazis are trying to lose theirs). There he is able to hand the Schwarz passport on to a Russian, one of the new wave of refugees, this time from communism. He tries to find the narrator Schwarz, but has forgotten his real name, which was indeed only used once in the narrative, and is never able to do so.

The work bears the designation *Roman* (novel), but as has been pointed out, it is more like the novella in many ways, a form early Italian in origin, but developed especially in Germany in the nineteenth century and later. The framework is a feature of this style, as is a concentration of narrative theme. Interestingly, Boccaccio's original *novelle* in the *Decamerone* were told by refugees (from the plague), and a German example, which would have been known to Remarque, Stefan Zweig's *Schachnovelle*, is set on a ship taking refugees from the Nazis to the new world.[15] As such, *Die Nacht von Lissabon* is different from most of Remarque's other novels, which customarily present a wide range of characters and alternative strands of action. Here as in the novella there are virtually no deviations from the main narrative, apart, perhaps from the brief story of the Jewish boy who travels with Schwarz and Helen across Spain to Portugal. The framework narrator prompts Schwarz to recount what has happened to him, but this seems like a kind of afterthought.

There are different facets to the central story. As indicated by the internal comments, it is a love story. Helen demonstrates her love for Schwarz for as long as she can, but then the love continues only in his mind, and the narrative fixes it for him. The most novellistic feature of the work, the "novelty," might be seen as the miracle of the provision to the framework narrator of the means of escape. However, the presentation of miracles in the work is always ambiguous: certainly they need not always be positive, at least not obviously, and not always in the long term. As with other novels, the extent to which it is anti-fascist lies in the conception as a whole, the implicit rejection of all that Nazi Germany stands for: if Germany were to win the war, it would prove that there was no God. The actual blow against Nazism in the killing of Georg links the personal and the political strands of the work, since it removes a man who wished to impose his own power on others and had also tried to separate Schwarz and Helen. Perhaps most importantly, the work is about identity and existence. One is placed on earth for a limited time, and it does not matter whether or not you are really Schwarz or are Jewish or Austrian or German. It is life itself that matters once again, and Helen — whose life span is limited by disease — teaches that to her husband. Even in the worst of circumstances, they both avoid mediocrity while keeping the spark of life going. The last lines of the novel return, significantly, to the concept of identity and to the theme of mediocrity in general. The framework narrator tells us how he thought he had spotted Schwarz in Osnabrück, but the person turned out to be a married post-office official with three children, a mediocre life, therefore, and a name, Jansen, which is given to us in the last line of the work. That name is entirely unimportant and the reader has no reason whatsoever to retain it; the final irony is that we do not know the name of the narrator, but we do know this man's name. However much the events of the twentieth century might have conspired to strip people of their identity, their human essence remains, and how they live their lives and whether or not they waste it (to use Schwarz's final idea) is what is important.

Schatten im Paradies

Die Nacht von Lissabon is a skillful and successful novel, and as such contrasts with *Schatten im Paradies,* which is not really Remarque's novel; even the title is not necessarily the one he would have chosen. In a trenchant afterword to the now standard edition (once again with Kiepenheuer and Witsch), Tilman Westphalen cuts through the hype with which *Schatten im Paradies* was published. Death did not lift the pen from Remarque's hand as he finished writing this book; the text published in 1971 is based on a manuscript completed in 1967 or 1968, but not revised. Remarque's working method always involved a great deal of rewriting, but here the revisions and cuts were made by Droemer-Knaur in Munich, who had outbid other publishers, and it was further cut in the English translation, which appeared in 1972. All changes were authorized by Paulette Goddard.[16] The title appears to have come from a publisher's reader, and other provisional titles included (in English) "New York Story" and "New York Intermezzo," as well as "Meeting of Shadows" and "The Caravan Passes." The chosen title does, to be fair, reflect nicely different aspects of the book: that America is a paradise with shadows, and that the émigré characters, haunted by shadows of the past, are themselves shadows in this paradise. Westphalen notes that the ideas for the novel go back as far as the early 1950s, when Remarque had been involved in an affair with Natasha Paley(-Wilson), a photographic model in New York.[17]

Remarque seems to have begun reworking the material early in 1968, so that we have also a fragmentary form with evidence of much revision and with a different working title, *Das gelobte Land,* under which the fragment has now itself been published. Remarque changed or reassigned a number of the names in the work, added material, and was also apparently planning a different ending. We have, therefore, two closely linked but different texts, one incomplete, and neither published by Remarque. Marc Wilhelm Küster concluded his archival study of the background by referring to *Schatten im Paradies* as "ein Betrug" (a deception), foisting a draft version upon the reader, and damaging the reputation of the author.[18] In the afterword to their 1998 edition of *Das gelobte Land,* on the other hand, Tilman West-phalen and Thomas F. Schneider point out rather more pragmatically that our knowledge of the situation does not affect the fact that *Schatten im Paradies* is considered, like it or not, to be part of the oeuvre and will continue to be read as such. "Die Rezeptionsgeschichte ist nicht nachträglich zu revidieren" (You can't revise the history of a work's reception after the event).[19]

We now have indeed no choice but to take *Schatten im Paradies* as it is, even though its lack of revision is sometimes still visible; the sudden appearance of Ravic, who continues to be called Ravic even though he explains that he has reverted to the name Ludwig Fresenburg, for example, is a case in point. Furthermore, it does conclude the sequence of emigration novels, the narrator explaining in a backward-looking prologue how he had sailed from Lisbon to the United States. As with *Die Nacht von Lissabon,* which does not have such a prologue, the last few paragraphs are also retrospective, although the narrative line presented in the body of the work is consistently immediate. Apart from the prologue and concluding paragraphs, the action is set entirely in America, but it remains nevertheless a German novel, addressing not principally the assimilation of the refugees, but their ongoing feelings about events in Europe. The work documents the inner struggle of many of those concerned to come to terms — the phrase *die Vergangenheit bewält-igen* (19, to come to terms with the past), much used in literary contexts in Germany since 1945, is voiced expressly. This thought process can begin once the simple question of survival is no longer in the forefront. There are, it is true, some characters in the work who do assimilate themselves to America, and the reaction to American mores is sometimes an issue, especially in the Hollywood portion of the work, but the problems of the rootless émigrés, particularly in their relationship to Germany, and in their urge for revenge, predominates. The emphasis is not upon immigrants planning to stay and thus coming to terms with a different but established way of life. The provisional nature of the life of the émigrés in America during the war is underlined by their sometimes limited visas, and a crisis of a kind is provoked for the narrator and others when the end of the war actually comes. The narrator himself does not necessarily want to become an American, just to become something, and thinks of himself as a *Weltbürger,* a citizen of the world (37).

The style is quite different from the tight, novellistic form of *Die Nacht von Lissabon*. We are presented, albeit in a first-person narrative, with a range of different émigré attitudes in an approach that is closer to that of *Liebe Deinen Nächsten* and *Arc de Triomphe*. The narrator of *Schatten im Paradies* uses the name Robert Ross, also that of a character in the play *Die letzte Station*, and he is a German who is not (unlike many of his associates) Jewish, a former journalist expelled from Germany. We learn later that he has been in a concentration camp but was released precisely because he was not a Jew, and also in passing that his father has been killed because he did not escape in time, although full details of Ross's background are not always clear.[20] He has an American visa in a passport he inherited by means of *Wunder,* miracles, the passport itself having come from a dead man who "called himself Ross." We learn that Robert is his real forename, though he claims barely to remember his real surname. All this harks back to the situation of the narrator in *Die Nacht von Lissabon.* Ross finds accommodation in New York in a hotel run by a Russian named Melikow, and we learn that Ross had spent two years hiding from the Germans in a Belgian museum, able to come out only at night, although there he has given himself a thorough grounding in art history. This enables him to get jobs selling works of art, first for the twin brothers Lowy, and then for the dealer Silvers. The former are sympathetic and to a large extent comical figures. One of them comments, for example, on the proposed marriage of the other to a girl who is not Jewish: "Meine arme Mutter, hätte sie das noch erlebt . . . sie würde sich im Grabe umdrehen, wenn sie nicht vor acht Jahren eingeäschert worden wäre" (91, My poor mother, if she were alive to see it, she'd turn in her grave if she hadn't been cremated eight years ago). The cremation point is, incidentally, picked up and developed seriously later on, as various characters die and, although Jewish, are cremated, something that is also linked with the crematoria of the camps. The far sharper operator Silvers, for whom Ross works for much of the novel, uses him to help secure the sales of paintings to rich customers often by ethically unorthodox methods. The involvement of Ross with the business of selling for large sums of money paintings that are frequently, though not always, status symbols rather than appreciated art, is an ongoing comment on the mercantilistic and philistine aspect of American society. There are other asides on American society in the work, among the most memorable being the observation that there are no prostitutes, but people visit psychiatrists instead.

In an interlude in the later part of the novel, in chapters twenty-four to twenty-six out of the thirty-four chapters, Silvers takes Ross with him to Hollywood, hoping for a new and lucrative market, and this gives an opportunity for a satire on west coast society and the film industry, but with an edge relating to perceptions of the war. The real war is still on, but it is literally made unreal by Hollywood, the center of illusion and unreality. With

Ross in Hollywood is Tannenbaum, whom he knows from New York, a Jewish actor who specializes in playing Nazis, presumably having been able to overcome his own personal past to do so. When Ross visits a studio for the first time with Tannenbaum, he is frightened to see a group of SS troops until it dawns on him that they are actors. Eventually he points out that some of the details are wrong, and he is hired as an adviser in view of his firsthand knowledge of the concentration camp.[21] However, when Ross tries to rewrite a script to make the depiction of the camps realistic, the studio rejects it out of hand as so unbelievable that — importantly — it will not recoup the millions of dollars invested in the making:

> "Das, was Sie vorschlagen, Robert, glaubt uns kein Mensch! Ist es wirklich so?"
> "Schlimmer. Viel schlimmer."
> Holt spuckte in das Wasser. "Niemand wird es uns glauben." (372)

> ["What you're suggesting Robert — nobody will believe us! Is it really like that?"
> "It's worse. Much worse."
> Holt spat into the water. "Nobody will believe us."]

The producer insists that they have to stick to the melodramatic patterns of the B-movie Western; Hollywood adheres to what Ross calls the romantic notion that evil deeds arise only from the completely evil. The producer, Holt, is also quite unable to grasp Ross's related point that the horrors of Nazi Germany depend also upon ordinary people.

> Das wirkliche Grauen — der Kleinbürger, pflichtbewusst und schlau und mit gutem Gewissen bei der blutigen Arbeit, nicht anders als beim Holzsägen oder beim Fabrizieren von Kinderspielzeug —, das konnte ich ihm nicht begreiflich machen. (388)

> [The real horror — the ordinary person, aware of his duty and clever and doing the blood-soaked business with a clear conscience, no differently than he might saw logs or make toys — that was what I couldn't get across to him.]

It is part of the postwar strategy of *Bewältigung der Vergangenheit* to draw attention to, rather than suppressing or denying, the role of what were later termed Hitler's willing helpers, and voicing the idea in the context of the clear distinctions demanded by Hollywood is telling. Holt, the producer clings to his preconception that a murderer is by definition evil, and Ross explains repeatedly that the Nazi atrocities were not carried out by some race of aliens who had suddenly dropped into Germany, "sondern von guten Deutschen, die sich ganz bestimmt auch für gute Deutsche hielten" (390, but by good Germans, who certainly considered themselves to be good Germans). Others make the same point on different occasions. Holz is just as insistent that no one would believe this, prompting Ross to recall in exasperation that in 1914 tales of German atrocities in the First World War were widely believed, but were not true, whereas now nobody will believe the atrocities that are true. When Holt confirms this, Ross admits defeat and shortly afterwards returns to New York, commenting that the Nazis are no subject for films. The Hollywood chapters are a clear indictment of attitudes to Nazi Germany by outsiders who ought to be touched by it: America is at war with Germany; both the producer and the director are Jews. They are also aimed at postwar Germany.

The various other characters with whom Ross comes into close contact throughout the work provide further impetus for him to think of his own possible reactions to Germany and the war: simply to be unable to forget the pain of Europe; to feel collective guilt as a German; or to be driven to revenge, like Orestes, who in the plays by Aeschylus avenges the death of his father Agamemnon by killing Clytemnaestra, but is then himself pursued by the Furies until Athena brings an end to the blood feud. Orestes (Ross applies the parallel to himself, 76) is an ambiguous figure, an avenger and a victim, and Ross, too, is ambiguous. He is a refugee, he is a victim of the Nazis, he has been in a concentration camp; but he is still a German, and he is not a Jew — he has great difficulty in persuading a Jewish lawyer to help him because of this. The lawyer offers the stereotyping opinion: "Zumindest steckt ein Stück Nazi in jedem Deutschen" (62, There is at least a little bit of Nazi in every German), and Ross has to counter this by using the generalizations that were used against Jews. Blanket anti-Germanism is the same as blanket anti-Semitism. In general terms he becomes aware early in the novel that even though he may be in the Promised Land, the past has come with him, and he is unable to get the shadows out of his dreams. "Diese aber blieben wie klebriger, nasser Rauch — ich spürte Kälte im Nacken —, wie Rauch, fader, süsslicher Rauch. Rauch aus Krematorien. (77, These stayed with me like sticky, wet smoke — I felt a shiver at the back of my neck — like smoke, dull, sweetish smoke. Smoke from the crematoria).

Ross meets other émigrés in the salon of Betty Stein, *die Mutter der Emigranten* (48, mother to all the émigrés), who is consumed with a nostalgic longing to return to her native Berlin, where she had had a theatrical salon, after the war. She is prevented by cancer from doing so and dies not long before the end of the war, and most of the others know that what she wants to return to has long since disappeared. Moller, the writer, commits suicide, as does the doctor, Gräfenheim, unable to cope with what has happened and convinced that even if Germany is defeated there will still be Nazis. Some émigrés assimilate, most notably the wealthy banking family Vriesländer, who help the poorer refugees, and who reinvent themselves with the name Warwick. One of their children even marries into a family that came with an earlier immigration, on the Mayflower. With those who assimilate may be included Remarque's amusing creation of the astonishingly beautiful, but alas, equally astonishingly stupid (and improbably named) Carmen, who marries in Hollywood, and devotes her limited attention principally to raising chickens.

Two characters are the closest to Ross in the novel. One of these is Natascha Petrowna, a model, with whom he eventually enjoys a sometimes graphically described sexual relationship, although it is one that cannot and does not last. He repeats that he worships her (*anbeten*) but whether or not he ever loves her is highly questionable, and the affair leads nowhere, since neither can really settle. The other is Harry Kahn, who, although still young, has been an almost legendary figure in Europe, assisting escapees and bluffing the regime, sometimes disguised as an SS officer, though he is a Jew (the son of an enlightenment Jew and uncircumcised, which has once saved his life) and thinks of himself as a German. Much of the dialogue between Ross and Kahn underlines the complexity of the refugee psyche. Kahn once comments:

> "Sie wissen, wer die besten Patrioten in Deutschland waren? Die Juden. Sie haben das Land mit einer hündischen, sentimentalen Anhänglichkeit geliebt."
>
> Ich schwieg. Ich dachte, dass die Juden das Land vielleicht deshalb so übermässig geliebt haben, weil man sie nie ganz hatte heimisch werden lassen. (103)
>
> ["You know who the most patriotic lot in Germany were? The Jews. They loved the country with a dog-like, sentimental attachment."
>
> I said nothing. I thought that the Jews perhaps loved the country so excessively because they had never been allowed to feel entirely at home.]

It is in their discussions, too, that Ross wonders whether those who are trying hard to assimilate are right, and that maybe it would be possible "nichts zu vergessen und doch alles zu erneuern, es zu sublimieren, bis es nicht mehr schmerzte, es umzuschmelzen, ohne Verlust, ohne Verrat und ohne Desertion" (141, to forget nothing, but still renew it all, sublimate it until it no longer hurts, transform it without loss, without treachery, and without desertion). The last three concepts — loss, treachery, and desertion — are highly significant: these are the shadows that he has brought to paradise with him and that he and others like him cannot shake off at all. How much have they lost, and was their departure an act of treachery or desertion? Moller's suicide is felt by Ross to touch all of them, and his and other cremations are associated by Ross with the crematoria of the camps.

Kahn and Ross go together in one incident to persuade, more or less by blackmail, one Jewish refugee to repay money that he had effectively stolen from another. The incident is significant because Kahn reveals that he has taken Ross with him as an Aryan outsider, to ensure that it is not an entirely Jewish affair. Ross comments "jetzt wurde ich wie ein Nazi als Schreckmittel verwendet" (258, now I've been used as a Nazi to frighten someone). The thought of being used in this way does not appeal to him, and ties in with other incidents earlier in the novel, once where he has had to suffer being taken to an ultra-German restaurant, and another, when he is used as a kind of gigolo to entice an elderly but rich lady to buy some paintings. Kahn himself would like to be a soldier, but as an enemy alien is not allowed to join up, and he suffers from the enforced lack of action.[22] Unable to form a relationship with the beautiful but stupid Carmen, Kahn also becomes aware that when the war is over he will not be able to settle down to a normal petit-bourgeois existence. His words as the war draws to a close — Remarque provides as ever regular chronological markers, especially towards the end of the work — are striking because they recall very strongly, and in part literally, the thoughts of Paul Bäumer before the end of another war:

> "Wir sind verdorben für ein normales Leben," hatte Kahn gesagt, [...]
> "Wir sind verdorben, viele haben etwas abgekriegt wie die Opfer einer Explosion. Ein Teil ist ohne schwere Verletzungen davongekommen, manche haben sogar profitiert, andere sind Krüppel geworden, und die Verletzten, auf die es am meisten ankommt, werden sich nie mehr zurechtfinden, und schliesslich werden sie untergehen." (437)

> ["We have been spoiled for a normal life," Kahn had said . . . "We have been spoiled, a lot of us have been like the victims of some explosion. Some got away without serious injury, a good few even did well out of it, others were crippled, and those who were wounded, the ones most directly affected, will never manage to get back on their feet, and they will go under."]

Bäumer had said *zugrundegehen* rather than *untergehen,* but the sense is the same. And Kahn, not long after, and a few days before Hitler's suicide and the end of the war, can no longer cope without the hatred of the Nazis to sustain him, and shoots himself in his lonely room. In a kind of parody of Goethe's *Werther,* Ross reports finding a cheap American novel at Kahn's side.

The Natascha episodes provide a personal story. The relationship develops somewhat erratically, although it does become almost violently sexual, but it is always provisional and always ambiguous. Natascha is a model, whose clothes, jewelry, and Rolls-Royce are always borrowed, and who lives permanently in the wrong season of the year, since fashion shots are done well in advance. The pair spend time, too, in an apartment block that had once been a brothel and now is full of homosexuals, one of whom owns the place Natascha is living in. Some of this has a contrived feel, and indeed, the eventually doomed relationship contributes little to the work as a whole beyond underlining the rootlessness and inability to settle that they share. It does, however, sometimes serve as a focus for Ross's thoughts, and in almost their first exchange Natascha, having established Ross's nationality, comments that she hates the Germans, to which Ross replies: "Ich auch" (28, So do I). The dominant theme of the work is that of how to be German in the face of Hitler's war, how to cope as a German with what is described later as the *furor teutonicus,* the Teutonic frenzy. Ross feels himself to be in an impossible double bind, trapped by the lawyer's view that all Germans are to some extent Nazis, and the fact that the Nazis did not simply turn up from Mars and take the German nation hostage. It is the question of personal guilt and responsibility that is raised in full in the Second World War novel *Zeit zu leben und Zeit zu sterben.*

We are given perhaps the fullest insight into Ross's own history through one of his dreams, one of the shadows that he has been unable to leave behind. He dreams in the thirteenth chapter that he has killed someone, and also sees the crematoria in a camp with hooks on which people are hanged. He then sees the face and hears the voice of Egon März, his torturer, and is aware that he must make every effort later to remove this man. The ambiguity of the dream is again striking in that Ross actually casts himself both as victim and killer, and the dream recurs some ten chapter later with new developments and a reference to the torturer as *der Lächler,* the smiling one. Waking up and going down to the hall of the hotel where he lives, Ross sees a man asleep with his mouth open, who reminds him first of those hanged in the camps, but then of his own association with Germany:

> Ich gehöre zu ihnen, dachte ich, ich gehöre zu dieser Horde von Mördern, es war mein Volk, ganz gleich ob sie mich gejagt und verstossen und ausgebürgert hatten, ich war unter ihnen geboren, und es wäre töricht, wenn ich mir vormachn wollte, dass ein treues, ehrliches, unwissendes Volk durch Legionen von Mars überfallen und hypnotisiert worsen sei. Diese Legionen waren unter ihm selbst aufgewachsen, sie hatten sich aus brüllenden Kasernenhofschindern und tobenden Demagogen entwickelt, es war der alte, von Oberlehrern angebetete furor teutonicus gewesen, der zwischen Gehorsamsknechten, Uniformvergötzern und viehischem Atavismus aufgeblüht war. (323)

> [I belong to them, I thought, I belong to this mob of murderers, they were my people, never mind that they had hunted and ejected me and taken away my citizenship, and it would be crazy for me to try and convince myself that a decent, honest, and innocent nation had been overcome and hypnotized by legions from Mars. Those legions grew up among them themselves, they had developed from bellowing parade-ground martinets and raving demagogues, it was the old *furor teutonicus* that the older teachers so adored, and that had flourished among the grovelingly obedient, the uniform worshippers and all the bestial atavism.]

The striking passage continues at some length. It is interesting that, writing in the late 1960s about the Second World War, Remarque could still invoke "parade-ground" martinets (like Himmelstoss of *Im Westen nichts Neues*) and thus draw a connecting line in German history from the period before the First World War on to the Second. He even cites in *Schatten im Paradies* the case of Thomas Mann — that most humane of writers, he says, and the leader of the German émigrés in America — who himself expressed some admiration of the *furor teutonicus* in 1914.[23] Seeing the name "Irwin Wolff" over a delicatessen leads Ross to despair at having no way out at all. It is a German name but equally obviously a Jewish one: "Nicht einmal das hatte ich als Ausrede. Nicht einmal diese künstliche Unterscheidung konnte ich benutzen. Ich konnte nicht sagen, dass ich Jude wäre" (324, I didn't even have that as an excuse. I couldn't even use that artificial difference. I couldn't say that I was Jewish). Ross has made the point before that not all Jews are blameless, but that is not the issue here. The novel is intended to stimulate the German reader to similar self-reflection as part of the process of overcoming the past.

To Natascha, Ross says that the refugees are the victims of world history, condemned to wait and watch, the eternal observers (like Schwarz watching the SS men in *Die Nacht von Lissabon*), who can nothing more than cling always to "dem Funken Leben, der in uns noch zittert" (215, the spark of life still flickering within us). This is made even clearer when Ross says to Gräfenheim: "Wir sind Zuschauer . . . Verdammte Zuschauer, die beneidet werden, weil man sie nicht mitmachen lassen will. Das ist es, was unser Dasein hier schattenhaft and fast obszön macht" (299, We are observers . . . damned observers, who are envied because we are not allowed to join in. That's what makes our existence here so shadowy and almost obscene). Not only have the shadows followed them, they are themselves impotent shadows, enemy aliens, and hence, in a reductive version of one of Remarque's favorite concepts, little more than a "Funke Leben, der nicht erlöschen wollte" (301, a spark of life that didn't want to go out).

The end of the novel is hardly positive. Melikow is arrested and jailed for selling drugs. Ross parts from Natascha and never sees her again. The émigrés have talked of revenge, but it becomes clear that this will never come to anything. After the war Ross returns to Germany, encouraged by Vriesländer, who is convinced of Germany's economic capabilities after the war, but quickly becomes aware of the changes: there is now an emigration of Nazis, and the occupation forces cannot control or check them, since the Germans themselves are unwilling to run the risk of "das eigene Nest . . . zu beschmutzen" (493, of fouling their own nest), a criticism that was regularly leveled at Remarque.[24] Suddenly no one remembers names, some forget or deny that concentration camps even existed. The criticism of the constructive amnesia practiced in Germany and elsewhere after the war and beyond is direct, and once again a main character in a Remarque novel realizes — as after the First World War — that Germany does not have revolutions. This time, however, the people persuade themselves that they are too tired to unleash the necessary revolution. Remarque is quite clear in his overall judgment on post-1945 Germany:

> Die Deutschen waren kein Volk der Revolutionen. Sie waren ein Volk von Befehlsempfängern. Der Befehl ersetzte das Gewissen. Er wurde die beliebteste Ausrede. Wer auf Befehl gehandelt hatte, war nicht mehr verantwortlich. (493)

> [The Germans were not a race given to revolutions. They were a race that took orders. Obeying orders replaces having a conscience. It became the favorite excuse. If you were obeying orders, you weren't responsible.]

It is a huge indictment. The ultimate message is the simple one that it is impossible to go back, to reclaim the past or even to complete the unfinished business of revenge. Ironically, Ross looks onwards toward "ein Abend voller Schwermut" (494, an evening of melancholy). This was the feeling that Paul Bäumer wondered whether he would shake off after the First World War. After another war, it is all that is left.

Das gelobte Land

Since *Das gelobte Land* now exists in a published text it has to be afforded at least the same status as *Gam*, although as a fragment it will command — unfortunately, perhaps — less attention than *Schatten in Paradies*, even if it is somewhat nearer to Remarque's own intentions as far as his last novel was concerned. It is difficult to assess within the context of Remarque's novels not only because it is incomplete, but because it both is and is not a new work. Rightly or wrongly, it remains, so to speak, in the shadow of *Schatten im Paradies*. Remarque changed many of the names — some of them more than once — in his revisions, so that Natascha became first Luciana Coleman and then Maria Fiola, a name echoing earlier works, Harry Kahn became Robert Hirsch, and Ross himself Ludwig Sommer, though once again it is not his real name (the real Ludwig Sommer is described, 147), and he has, we learn, once had a companion called Ruth, who is now dead (92). That story is an amalgam of *Liebe Deinen Nächsten*, in which Ruth is left behind in a Paris hotel when her partner is arrested and deported, and *Die Nacht von Lissabon*, in which Ruth commits suicide by poison. Some of the other name changes were minor: Melikow became Meukoff, though in rapid handwriting these forms might look similar; Moller, representing the writer Ernst Toller, now became Teller. Names used in the earlier version were also shuffled around, which makes it particularly confusing to read the two versions in any proximity. Silvers, the over-sharp art dealer in *Schatten in Para-dies* becomes a more assimilated Reginald Black (né Schwarz, perhaps), but the name Silvers is reapplied to the part played by the Lowy twins. None of this is especially important, except that the change of the name from Nata-scha distances the character even further from Natasha Paley, making a bio-graphical reading of the story more difficult. Her role here is also somewhat diminished, and there are certainly fewer of the scenes in *Schatten im Para-dies* in the El Morocco club.

The fragment contains only twenty-one chapters, whereas *Schatten im Paradies* has thirty-four in all. Some material has, however, been added, as have some characters; there is a section at the start in which Sommer is held on Ellis Island prior to entry into the United States, with an interesting little scene ostensibly concerned with learning English and discussing the difficulty for the German speaker of pronouncing the English *th-* sound. But they practice this phonetic problem on newspaper articles on the war, reduc-ing human misery to a lesson, and reading out "thousand, fifty thousand Tote in Berlin, in Hamburg, bis jemand plötzlich erblasste, sich ver-schluckte, aus der Schülerrolle fiel und erschreckt murmelte: "Hamburg? Da lebt noch meine Mutter!" (31, thousand, fifty thousand dead in Berlin, in Hamburg, until someone suddenly went pale, swallowed, forgot his role as a language-learner and murmured in horror: "Hamburg? My mother is still in Hamburg").

The Hollywood section is absent, although at the end of the fragment another character is just trying to persuade Sommer to go there, and since that section comes late in *Schatten im Paradies,* Remarque might still have intended to include it.[25] The art-dealing satires are largely present, however. Some longer passages are taken over in full, though sometimes with changes. Thus in the scene where Hirsch (Kahn) visits the other Jew to persuade him to give back the misappropriated money, stressing that all Jews are victims, but not all are angels (285) and takes Sommer (Ross) with him as a kind of threat, the reason is more bluntly expressed: "weil du wie ein Nazi aussiehst" (291, because you look like a Nazi). Sommer's reaction, too, is not as per-sonal and upset as Ross's. Sometimes ideas are simply given to other charac-ters: that the Nazis did not drop from the sky and overcome an innocent Germany is given this time to Ravic, for example (110).

Sommer is in some ways an even less involved observer than is Ross, but the revenge motif seems still to have been in Remarque's mind, the idea that has been encountered in all the other émigré novels of justified murder for revenge. We do not know for sure how this novel would have continued or ended, but Remarque did leave various possibilities in note form towards the end of his life, certainly after September 1968, clear from the date stamp on the envelope on which some of the notes are made).[26] The notes are far from clear, but they sketch various endings for Sommer (the Maria Fiola plot seems unresolved). In one he meets the man who murdered his father and shoots but does not kill him, and returns (perhaps) to New York. In others he does kill, or he tries but cannot kill the man, and perhaps kills himself. In any event, the planned ending seems not to have been an optimistic one. It would of course have been a murder in cold blood: the war is over and the Nazi regime finished. It is ironic, but perhaps not too surprising, that we do not actually have that ending.

The theme of emigration and exile is one that is all too familiar in the twentieth century in particular, and there has been much interest in the theory of the exile experience in different contexts. Questions arise usually of the problems of assimilation into a new society while retaining elements of the original culture or the memory of the exile experience as such. But Remarque's émigré novels are set close enough to the experiences themselves for assimilation not to be the real issue. *Liebe Deinen Nächsten*, *Arc de Triomphe*, and *Die Nacht von Lissabon* are all expressions of the immediacy of exile, of the efforts simply to stay alive. *Schatten im Paradies* is a little different, in that it does at least consider the possibility of assimilation, but even here it is as much a novel about Europe and Germany as the others, told from the point of view of a narrator who has in fact already returned to Germany. There are common problems that Remarque addresses in all of the émigré novels: the urge not just to maintain the spark of life, but to make what one can from what one has; revenge; the problems of being a German exile who is not Jewish; to have been driven out of a country as a member of a nation despised by the world, but left still with feelings of treachery or desertion. There are no single answers to the question of how these things are to be coped with, nor indeed need novels provide actual answers. For postwar Germany, voicing the question, bringing it into the open so that it could be considered, is part of the process of *Bewältigung der Vergangenheit,* of overcoming the past with as much intellectual honesty as possible.

Notes

[1] Text cited: *Die Nacht von Lissabon,* afterword by Tilman Westphalen (Cologne: Kiepenheuer and Witsch, 1998); first published in 1962 in Cologne by Kiepenheuer and Witsch, after a preprint in *Welt am Sonntag* in January–May, 1961; it was translated by Ralph Manheim, *The Night in Lisbon* (New York: Harcourt, Brace, 1961). *Die Nacht von Lissabon* was filmed for the German TV station ZDF, produced by Zbynek Brynych and broadcast in April 1971.

[2] Texts cited are: *Schatten im Paradies,* afterword by Tilman Westphalen (Cologne: Kiepenheuer and Witsch, 1998); *Das gelobte Land*, in *Das unbekannte Werk*, vol. 2. *Schatten im Paradies* was originally published in Munich (Droemer-Knaur, 1971) and translated (with some further changes) as *Shadows in Paradise* by Ralph Manheim (New York: Harcourt, Brace, 1972). *Das gelobte Land* is the sole edition and it has not been

translated. See Westphalen's afterword to *Schatten im Paradies* and his and Schneider's notes to the edition in *Das gelobte Land* for details of the history of the Droemer text, acknowledging Marc Wilhelm Küster, "Die Manuskriptlage zu Remarques *Schatten im Paradies,*" *Jahrbuch* 5 (1995), 88–108. Neither version has been filmed.

[3] It has been noted that some details of the escape of Schwarz were based partly upon the experiences of Remarque's friend, the novelist Hans Habe (János Békessy, 1911–1977), who did escape with his wife through France, Spain, and Lisbon, and obtained a visa for the United States, which he reached in 1940. See Tims, *Remarque,* 196–97.

[4] But as Wagener, *Understanding,* 100, rightly points out, this is not a reworking of earlier plots; see also Antkowiak, *Remarque,* 145.

[5] Firda, *Thematic Analysis,* 246–47, points this out and stresses the importance of the listener.

[6] The date now reads 22 June 1898, the year presumably easily enough adapted from 1873, and giving us Remarque's own date of birth, again a private joke, since within the novel it is the actual date of birth of none of the passport holders. It is not (Sternburg, *"Als wäre alles,"* 414) the date of birth of the new Schwarz, though he has to assume it (and learn it), and it is transferred to the first narrator at the end. The photograph presumably also changes several times.

[7] There is a similar discussion of the church's history in *Zeit zu leben und Zeit zu sterben.* Schwarz now seems to have few residual religious beliefs. Osnabrück Cathedral possesses, in fact, a notably large thirteenth-century triumphal crucifix.

[8] That our increased awareness of details of Remarque's life can be positively distracting is underlined when Schwarz refers to Helen somewhat idiosyncratically as a "puma" in one of the sexual scenes in *Die Nacht von Lissabon;* it might in this case have been better not to know that this is the nickname Remarque used for Marlene Dietrich.

[9] See Westphalen's afterword, 323–24, for a good discussion of this important passage.

[10] Spanish (now republican) refugees are a theme in *Arc de Triomphe.* See Antonio Vilanova, *Los Olvidados: los exilados españoles en la segunda guerra mundial* (Paris: Ruedo ibérico, 1969).

[11] In June 1940, after some months of "phoney war," Germany invaded. France capitulated, signing an agreement that put half of the country under German occupation. The First World War Marshall Pétain assumed powers as head of state in July and set up what was effectively a puppet state with the capital at Vichy, in the unoccupied area. Tims, *Remarque,* 196–97, refers to Hans Habe's bestseller about the fall of France: *Ob Tausend Fallen* (London: Hamilton, 1943). It was first published in English as *A Thousand Shall Fall* (New York: Harcourt, Brace, 1941). By November 1942 Germany had effectively taken over all of France. The Vichy government was notoriously ready to hand over Jews to Germany. Spain under Franco and Portugal under Salazar were neutral, but sympathetic to the Nazi regime.

[12] Barker and Last, *Remarque,* 116.

[13] This is a fairly regular image in the novels; one thinks for example of the dying Pat asking for a mirror in *Drei Kameraden,* which Robby Lohkamp deliberately drops. See Parvanova, *". . . das Symbol der Ewigkeit,"* 220–31, on the ramified symbolism.

[14] Wagener, *Understanding*, 102, draws attention to the passage, but it is not, in fact, clear that the saint refers to Helen. He may have misread the text as *das einer Heiligen*.

[15] Stefan Zweig's *Schachnovelle* (*The Royal Game*) was his last work, completed just before his suicide in 1942. See my edition: Stefan Zweig, *Schachnovelle* (London: Methuen, 1986) and my "Game and Imagery in Stefan Zweig's *Schachnovelle*," *New German Studies* 11 (1983), 171–89. Remarque was indebted to Zweig for his encouragement about *Im Westen nichts Neues* and was distressed by his suicide. See Remarque's diary entries for late February and early March 1942, *Das unbekannte Werk*, vol. 5, 360–62 nn, 522. Zweig's suicide is mentioned in *Schatten im Paradies*, 55. Firda, *Thematic Analysis*, 247, talks about the earlier traditions of the framework narrative in German, and Sternburg, *"Als wäre alles,"* 413, points out that the work is in the form of a novella. On the novella as such, see for example Martin Swales, *The German Novelle* (Princeton: Princeton UP, 1977).

[16] See Westphalen's afterword to the KiWi edition, 500–501, where the kinds of changes are noted, which range from the stylistic to the political.

[17] This relationship provided some material for the character of Natascha. On Natasha Paley, see Tims, *Remarque*, 146–47 and elsewhere, and Sterburg, *"Als wäre alles,"* 339–51. The psychoanalyst Karen Horney apparently recommended that Remarque work out the relationship in literary form. See Westphalen's afterword, 499, with the note that Paley comes after Marlene Dietrich and before Paulette Goddard "in Remarques bewegtem Liebesleben" (in Remarque's lively love life). There is a letter from Remarque to her in *Das unbekannte Werk*, vol. 5, 122–23, 514 nn, and 546–47 nn. Wagener, *Understanding*, 107–8, gives a brief survey of other parallels with Remarque's life and identifies the origins of some of the characters, such as Moller, who hangs himself, a thinly disguised version of the German dramatist Ernst Toller. Others, like Betty Stein, based on a Betty Stern, are not familiar. See also Barker and Last, *Remarque*, 147. On Remarque's own experiences in the United States, with comments too on *Schatten im Paradies*, see Hans Wagener, "Remarque in Amerika — zwischen Erfolg und Exilbewusstsein," *Jahrbuch* 9 (1999), 18–38, and on the work, Wagener, "Erich Maria Remarque: Shadows in Paradise," in *Exile: The Writer's Experience*, ed. John M. Spalek and Robert F. Bell (Chapel Hill: U North Carolina P, 1982), 247–57.

[18] Küster, "Manuskriptlage," 104. Küster gives a detailed picture of the situation and sees the publication simply as a moneymaking venture. See also Sternburg, *"Als wäre alles,"* 433, for equally pointed comments on the motives of the publisher and Remarque's *geschäftstüchtige Witwe* (business-minded widow), and inaccuracies in the hype. Sternburg discusses only *Das gelobte Land*, as the version closest to Remarque's own intentions. *Schatten im Paradies* was, however, as usual, widely translated and sold fairly well, though it received uniformly negative reviews. Schneider, *Remarque*, 141, has a photograph of Paulette Goddard and the publisher with the manuscript used.

[19] *Das unbekannte Werk*, vol. 2, 436; and see Westphalen's afterword to *Schatten im Paradies*, 499. Other authors — Kafka, Gerard Manley Hopkins — have not wanted their works published, although the situation here is not comparable, and the matter is complicated by the second revised version and what we know of Remarque's usual publishing habits. His letters and diaries were not intended to be published either, but they are at least not presented as anything but what they are.

[20] Barker and Last, *Remarque,* 144, refer to the problems of chronology in Ross's given background, as was pointed out in reviews.

[21] Remarque himself worked as a film adviser. See Hans Beller, "Schreiben im Schatten des Paradieses: Erich Maria Remarque und der Film: Eine Collage," *Jahrbuch* 9 (1999): 39–61.

[22] Antkowiak, *Remarque,* 146, comments on Ross's passivity, though he is expressly anti-fascist. While not aspiring to be as active as Kahn would like to be, he has, of course, no real choice in the matter. Wagener, *Understanding,* 110, notes this, commenting on the role of the émigrés as enforced onlookers. This is one reason that they are dubbed shadows.

[23] The novel (323) mentions Thomas Mann's "Gedanken im Kriege" (Thoughts in Wartime, *Neue Rundschau,* November, 1914), and "Friedrich und die grosse Koalition" (Frederick and the Grand Coalition, *Die neue Merkur,* January/February, 1915). These are contextualized in studies like that of Walter A. Berendsohn, *Thomas Mann: Künstler und Kämpfer in bewegter Zeit* (Lübeck: Schmidt-Römhild, 1965), 61. Other important writers on all sides made comments in 1914 that did not bear close scrutiny later, however.

[24] See Wilhelm von Sternburg's important comments on Remarque's centenary, "Pazifist und Einzelgänger," in the *Frankfurter Rundschau* on 6 June 1998.

[25] That the character to whom Sommer is speaking, is called Siegfried Lenz (412), is a little odd, not for the 1940s of course, but for someone writing in the late 1960s, when the German author of that name had already established himself.

[26] See Westphalen's and Schneider's notes, 439. The notes for a conclusion are on 415–22. That on 418 relates to Ross's dream of having killed a man in *Schatten im Paradies.*

English edition of
Der Funke Leben

Swedish edition of
Zeit zu leben und Zeit zu sterben

6: Educating Germany: *Der Funke Leben* and *Zeit zu leben und Zeit zu sterben*

IN SPITE OF THE UNDENIABLE causal links between the end of the First World War and the conditions that led eventually to a new war, the Second World War was different from the First, not a barely comprehensible universal bloodletting, but a concentrated war against National Socialism.[1] Remarque himself had written in 1944 (in a piece that survives in a typescript in English) on how Germany was to be educated after the Second World War, pointing out that the full horrors of the Nazi regime would need to be laid open.[2] His comments are in a sense those of an outsider, but of course he was not an outsider, but a German. Coming to terms with the immediate past — *Bewältigung der Vergangenheit* — would be one of the hardest tasks faced by postwar Germany, and the attempt took and still takes many forms, from revisionism or even the denial of historical events to a full confrontation with the associated guilt for a war that this time involved civilians as much as soldiers on a universal front line, and embraced not just military deaths, but the tortures and mass murder of civilians in the concentration and extermination camps.[3] Remarque contributed two novels to a documentation of the war and the camps, and thus to the questioning of the way Nazi policies were accepted. They are German novels, written in German and published in Germany. However, both appeared first in English, one was published in German only with difficulty, and the other was available for some time in German only in a cut and significantly amended version. These two works are just as or perhaps even more significant than *Im Westen nichts Neues*. Once again they are historical in setting, have a particular function for the time in which they were written and for later generations in Germany, and carry for the world at large perhaps even more clearly the message that although events of unbelievable barbarity could and did happen, they must not happen again. *Der Funke Leben* was published in 1952, *Zeit zu leben und Zeit zu sterben* two years later in 1954.[4] The former is set in a concentration camp in Germany just as the war is coming to an end in 1945, the latter slightly earlier, on the Eastern Front and then in Germany in 1944, but they are historically close together, and this time it is appropriate to treat them in the order of writing rather than of strict historical chronology,[5] because this permits us to see a development in the challenge to Germany to confront it with its recent past. Remarque also suffered criticism both for not having experienced the bombing of Germany as an exile in the

United States and for daring to set a novel in a concentration camp, which he had patently not experienced.

Various publishers rejected *Der Funke Leben* before it was eventually accepted.[6] *Zeit zu leben und Zeit zu sterben,* however, had a checkered textual history even after publication; first published in an English translation from the typescript, it appeared in Germany as a serial in the *Münchner Illustrierte,* and then in book form in a version censored by the publishers. The cuts and changes imposed by Kiepenheuer and Witsch were intended to defer to what were felt, at least, to be German sensibilities in the mid-1950s. They included the change of a communist into a social democrat, the complete excision of a soldier who is one-quarter Jewish, and most seriously of all, a truncating of several important passages concerned with the book's central theme, that of the shared guilt in the Nazi past. A full German version matching the English text appeared only in 1989. With the availability now of the original, this aspect of the work's history is less important, although it is of interest as a reflection of its time; but it remains an oddity that for many years the novel was read in most of the world in the original, while a different version circulated in Germany itself (and in the Warsaw Pact countries).[7] Even *Der Funke Leben* contained one minor difference between the German version and the English and other translations: the latter were dedicated to the memory of Elfriede Scholz, Remarque's sister, who was executed by the Nazis for alleged defeatism in December 1943. For unclear reasons, the dedication was omitted from the first German publication, but it has now been restored. There are passing allusions to the judicial murder by the Nazis of those denounced for allegedly making negative comments in both novels, but the fact of his sister's death is important to both works.[8]

Remarque did not fight on the Eastern Front in 1944, nor was he in Germany during the war, and certainly he was not in a concentration camp, and this led to critical hostility from those who had been in those situations. A review of *Der Funke Leben* that appeared in the *Hannover Sonntagsblatt* over the signature "Repgow" in October 1952 had the subtitle "Wer es nicht erlebte, sollte besser darüber schweigen" (Those Who Didn't Experience It Should Better Keep Silent). Even Heinrich Böll was critical of the novel, considering that the theme was too tough for Remarque to handle, although he did admit that it would raise awareness.[9] With increasing historical distance from the events, it has become clear that *Der Funke Leben* is able to give the reader an important impression of the world of the concentration camps and of those who ran them, and to provoke thought about how this could have come about. With both novels Remarque relied on research and report for his material, and as an experienced writer was well able to make them vivid.

Like the two novels of the First World War, these equally historical novels operate on various levels. They document historical evil and show us the perpetrators, they address the question of Germany's responsibilities, and they are again in part an indictment of war. *Zeit zu leben und Zeit zu sterben* addresses the theme of *Mitschuld*, the shared guilt that manifested itself in accepting all or even some aspects of the regime, but the concept of collective or generally shared guilt overlaps with the far broader notion of existential guilt. Finally, both novels stress again (and one even has as its title) the spark of life, the keeping of which is the basic response to the human condition in extreme cases, on the battlefield, or in a concentration camp. They give us once more the irreducible definition of the human being.

Remarque's double position as a German writer and an exile was hard for some critics to accept. Thomas Mann's BBC broadcasts to Germany during the war already began to address that point when, as early as 1942, he cited Goebbels's declaration: "Im Falle einer Niederlage werden wir alle an einem Strick gehenkt" (If we are defeated, we shall all be hanged with the same rope), and considered whether there are any grains of truth in it, taking *alle* to apply to the German people. When the war ended, Mann broadcast on 10 May 1945 a message that made clear that the exile writers were still German:

> Wie bitter ist es, wenn der Jubel der Welt der Niederlage, der tiefsten. Demütigung des eigenen Landes gilt! Wie zeigt sich darin noch einmal schrecklich der Abgrund, der sich zwischen Deutschland, dem Land unserer Väter und Meister, und der gesitteten Welt aufgetan hatte.

and later in the same broadcast:

> Ich sage: es ist trotz allem eine grosse Stunde, die Rückkehr Deutschlands zur Menschlichkeit. Sie ist hart und traurig, weil Deutschland sie nicht aus eigener Kraft herbeiführen konnte. Furchtbarer, schwer zu tilgender Schaden ist dem deutschen Namen zugefügt worden . . .[10]

> [How bitter it is when the jubilation of the world celebrates the defeat, the deepest humiliation of one's own country! How clearly can we see in it yet again the abyss that had opened up between Germany, the land of our fathers and teachers, and the civilized world. [. . .]
>
> I say: it is nevertheless a great moment, the return of Germany to humanity. It is hard and sad, because Germany could not bring it about by its own efforts. Dreadful damage, which is hard to erase, has become attached to the name of Germany . . .]

Remarque's Second World War novels both address the problems of which all the exile writers were all too conscious.

Der Funke Leben

Der Funke Leben is probably Remarque's most difficult novel, and certainly Remarque felt that it was difficult to write. He said in a statement that was for a long time unpublished and survives in English that he had begun the novel in 1946 and worked on it for five years, compelled to complete it because many of his friends and family had fallen victim to the Nazis, and because he wanted to help ensure that it could never happen again.[11] After commenting on his difficulties with finding a publisher for the work and on its negative reception when it did appear, he also claimed that as far as the Nazi period was concerned, Germany had already begun to forget — "not to regret. To forget."

Writing about the period at all, and especially about the camps, was enormously difficult for any postwar German writer, forced to tread a line between an accurate replication of the horrors and what might be taken as sensationalism. Further, as was the case with Remarque, the very right to deal with this material at all could be called into question because the writer was not present, or because the writer was not Jewish (although here the principal victims are German, and Jewish critics praised Remarque's courage in writing *Der Funke Leben*).[12] And writing retrospectively — a necessity in this case — can bring the charge of flawed or selective memory. The broad genre of "holocaust literature" to which *Der Funke Leben* may be assigned, has been defined in various ways, one definition including only writings about the extermination camps and the mass murder of European Jewry. Although there are references to it, this is not Remarque's theme, but the novel is thematically part of the broader picture.[13] Criticisms from those who were in the camps may be understandable, but attitudes change with the passing of time and with the realization of the importance of memorial. Specifically German responses to the holocaust have been of some interest.[14] Remarque's novel was a rarity in its time, but it is now — also after the *Historikerstreit,* the "Historians' Debate," in the late 1980s about guilt and the relativization of the atrocities — ripe for reassessment as a vivid and sympathetic portrayal by a skilled novelist bent upon preserving the memory of the events and bringing them to life for later generations. The historical events were well researched, and Remarque himself stressed in his note on *Der Funke Leben* that every detail could be attested.[15] But he did not want to present just a documentation, but rather a novel that would be a story of human dignity itself and of the unbelievable ability to survive: the title encapsulates the theme. The details of the camp given in the novel can all be matched in works by survivors of the extermination and concentration camps, such as the well-known accounts by Primo Levi, Wieslaw Kielar, or Tadeusz Borowski.[16]

Der Funke Leben is set in a concentration camp (not an extermination camp: there are no gas chambers) near the town of Mellern, which is based as ever on Osnabrück. The camp is modeled to a large extent on the actual concentration camp at Buchenwald, near Weimar.[17] Most of the action occurs in the "Small Camp," which contains the prisoners who are mainly too weak to work and have been placed there to die. It is not a first-person narrative, which would presumably have made the work even less acceptable, although Remarque's narrative technique once again focuses principally upon a single central figure, permitting the reader to see things through his eyes and thoughts. This time Remarque's central character, a political prisoner who has been in the camp for twelve years, does not even have an assumed name. For most of the work he is referred to only as *Skelett* (skeleton) 509 or just 509, though his later revelation of his name, Friedrich Koller, is a key point in the work. The word "skeleton" is used as a descriptor for the prisoners throughout. The time of the work is spring 1945; the end of the war is approaching, and a bombing raid on the local town marks the first sign of hope for the prisoners. By this point 509 has been worn down mentally as well as physically, losing even the capacity to hate, because even hatred and memory could be destructive. Reduced to naked survival, he is by now almost like those referred to as *Muselmänner* in the camp, an archaic word for "Moslem," implying here that they now accept anything that happens to them.

The bombing of the town shows 509 that things can change, that the regime that has been in control for so long is vulnerable after all, and he suddenly has the feeling that he does not want to die. This is the first manifestation of the spark of life, which had all but been extinguished, and from this point his will to live begins to grow. Beside 509, a veteran of barrack block 22 in the Small Camp, we encounter a variety of prisoners, including Karel, a twelve-year-old from Czechoslovakia, "Ahasver," an elderly Jew who has wandered from camp to camp, Berger, a doctor, who has to work in the crematorium, and Leo Lebenthal, who has connections with the camp secret supply system. Another — driven completely insane — thinks he is a dog, and has to be hidden by the other prisoners or he will be killed. Bucher, finally, is twenty-five, imprisoned for seven years because his father edited a social-democratic newspaper. He is friendly with Ruth Holland, whose name had been used in *Liebe Deinen Nächsten,* in the women's camp, and the story of their relationship, not really a love story[18] runs through the work as a further affirmation of the theme of life.

The camp is already a memorial: we hear regularly of the dead, and 509 reads, as the light falls on them, their scratched names, including one of a Jewish prisoner who appended to it his military rank and decorations from the First World War; services for Germany had become a *schäbige Ironie* (33, shabby irony). The camp itself contains political prisoners, Jews, Eastern

Europeans, as well as actual criminals, all with distinguishing marks to indicate the type. It is important that 509 and many of his fellow victims are German. As early as April 1945 the British publisher Victor Gollancz published a pamphlet with the title *What Buchenwald Really Means,* which asks for justice for all of the victims, including the Germans, mentioning a German communist who had been in Buchenwald for ten years, and others incarcerated simply for making anti-Hitler remarks. The small publication carried as a frontispiece a cartoon by David Low from the *London Evening Standard* showing a man reading a newspaper with a headline about the concentration camps, and declaring that "the whole German people should be wiped out for this!" In front of him, a group of skeletal figures reply: "Don't forget some of *us* are Germans, friend."[19]

Existence in the camp is shown in deliberately shocking detail: near-starvation (Lebenthal's additional food supplies are drawn from the garbage cans, and on one occasion include a dog as a major delicacy), beatings, terror, the sadism of the SS guards who often kept prisoners alive as objects of torture for as long as possible, hangings, forced-labor details. Nor is sadistic behavior exclusive to the SS; section heads were drawn from prisoners, and Handke, a criminal, placed in the camp for *Sittlichkeitsverbrechen* (sexual offences) is equally vicious and anti-Semitic. He is not an isolated case. That power corrupts is one of the lessons from the camp. Handke is not a Nazi, but simply finds himself in a position where he has some power and no responsibility.

The twenty-five chapters vary scenes involving the prisoners with scenes showing the SS, in particular Neubauer, the *Obersturmbannführer* (equivalent to a major) and commander of the camp. Where some of the SS are portrayed simply as sadists, a more rounded picture is given of Neubauer as he begins to worry about the possible destruction of his family by the bombing and of the small commercial empire he has managed to build up by acquiring businesses and properties after intimidation and denunciation, usually of Jews. He reassures himself, however, that he has always acted legally in technical terms, and the well-maintained fiction of the legal underpinning of Nazi activities is embodied in Neubauer. His story is a counterpoint to that of 509 and the other prisoners, who come ever closer to believing in liberation as he becomes aware that things are not going his way.[20] Mortally afraid that his wife will be overheard making a defeatist comment, he watches his empire crumble as different parts are destroyed by the war, from a huge store down to his cherished pet rabbits, objects of an ironic sentimentality, contrasting with the way he treats human beings. He takes pleasure in his garden, for example, tended by Russian prisoners and with his asparagus and strawberries fertilized by the ashes of sixty people, among them twelve children. Even when his family leaves him and his faith in the regime is shown to have been misplaced, he clings to his enormous capacity for self-delusion:

"Neubauer hatte nichts geraubt. Er hatte nur billig gekauft. Er war gedeckt. Er hatte Quittungen. Alles war amtlich beglaubigt" (45, Neubauer had stolen nothing. He had just bought cheaply. He was covered. He had the receipts. It was all official).

The humiliation and torture of the prisoners continues: at a protracted roll call they are perceived as so many striped maggots — they are often described as insects — but the spark of life is becoming stronger in 509. He obtains a small amount of bread and forces himself not to eat it, although this is difficult, because it is significant to him. The broken and incoherent nature of 509's thoughts at the end of that fifth chapter, giving the temporary effect of a first-person narrative, makes its own point; if I restrain myself, he says,

> dann bin ich kein Tier. Kein Muselmann. Nicht nur eine Fressmaschine. Ich habe dann, es ist — die Schwäche kam wieder, die Gier —, es ist — ich habe es zu Lebenthal vorhin gesagt, aber da hatte ich kein Brot in der Tasche —, sagen ist leicht — es ist — Widerstand — es ist so wie wieder ein Mensch werden — ein Anfang.— (76)

> [then I'm not an animal. Not a Mussulman. Not just a thing for stuffing food down. Then I've — the weakness returned, the greed —, it is — I told Lebenthal earlier, only then I didn't have a piece of bread in my pocket — talking is easy — it is — resistance — it's like becoming a human being again — a beginning —].

Actual resistance begins in the next chapter. A Nazi doctor is seeking "volunteers" for medical experimentation, and Weber, Neubauer's second-in-command and the SS officer actually in charge of the camp, selects six, among them 509 and Bucher, who refuse to sign a form agreeing that they are volunteers. Largely because Neubauer does not like the doctor, and because there is also antagonism between Neubauer and Weber, they are not killed, barely survive both beatings and confinement, and are brought back to the Small Camp as objects of amazement. It is hard for the prisoners to believe that resistance after such a long time would have been possible. The prisoners also get access, however, to a newspaper dated 11 March 1945 — they are themselves unsure of the present date, but do know that this was some weeks before — with a report that the Rhine bridge at Remagen has been crossed. Although the report contains all kinds of justifications, the basic facts are clear: the Allied army has crossed the Rhine unchecked over an intact bridge, and the western defense, the Siegfried Line, has therefore fallen. Remarque recreates with the slowly increasing possibility of release a correspondingly increasing nervousness on the part of those in charge, and this in turn could lead to added sadism or to the death of the prisoners.

509 has won a small victory but remains cautious, aware that "Sinnloser Mut ist sicherer Selbstmord" (126, senseless courage is certain suicide).

Their small resistance has to be kept hidden within them, and he has no illusion about survival in the long term. It is enough if a few survive: "Ein paar von uns müssen übrigbleiben," he says. "Für später. Dieses alles darf nicht umsonst gewesen sein. Ein paar, die nicht kaputt sind" (126, A few of us have to survive. For later. All this mustn't have been in vain. A few who are not wrecked). 509 looks onwards to the time when the far younger Bucher will live beyond the camp, and his comments about that future underline the message of the book: "Man wird alles ableugnen und vergessen wollen. Uns auch. Und viele von uns werden es auch vergessen wollen" (127, People will deny it all, and will want to forget about it. Us, too. Many of us will want to forget it). The importance of memory, the point of the novel, is affirmed by Bucher, however, who will not forget.

This significant passage is offset immediately by a shift to the ongoing story of Neubauer, which contains a parallel passage in which his thoughts are expressed to his chauffeur. Where 509 is, with all caution, looking to a future, Neubauer is now forced to contemplate his past and his deeds over the past few years. The bombs continue to fall, destroying more and more of his dubiously acquired property, and leaving him aware that the war cannot be won after all. His increasingly hysterical wife now threatens to come and join him in the camp, and this, of course, he resists; the awareness on the part of the civilian population of what went on there has always been a complex issue. When Neubauer's chauffeur, too, reveals that his mother has just been killed in the bombing, Neubauer is too concerned with himself to be particularly sympathetic, and offers only a stock response about the bombers as murderers. To his surprise the chauffeur points out that the Germans bombed Warsaw, Rotterdam, and Coventry. Neubauer declares that to have been strategic necessity as opposed to murder, a theme that will be treated again in *Zeit zu leben und Zeit zu sterben,* and lectures his chauffeur on the power of Germany so firmly that he even begins to believe it himself. In fact it is a stream of self-persuasion and self-justification, some of it familiar indeed: "Befehl ist Befehl, das genügt für unser Gewissen. Reue ist undeutsch. Falsches Denken auch. Der Führer weiss schon, was er tut. Wir folgen ihm, fertig" (135, Orders are orders, that's enough for our consciences. Regret is un-German. So is wrong thinking. The Führer knows what he is doing. We follow him and that's it). A little later he even states his motto: "Immer menschlich, solange es geht. Wenn es natürlich nicht mehr geht, Befehl ist Befehl" (145, Always be humane, as far as you can. And if you can't be, then orders are orders). In early April 1945, Hitler was only a few weeks away from suicide in his bunker in Berlin. Neubauer, though, clings to the idea of placing all the responsibility upon Hitler, something that even his wife knows is a *Freispruch,* an escape clause, that will only work for a certain time. It also excludes the concept of *Mitmachen,* of going along with the regime even in the smallest way. She herself is of course married to an SS *Obersturm-*

bannführer, though it is revealed, slightly unconvincingly, that she might instead have married a Jew who emigrated to the United States in 1928.

Although Mellern is not an extermination camp, those detailed to work in the crematoria here were removed to the gas chambers elsewhere after fairly short intervals to ensure that there were no later witnesses, and the approaching end of the war increases the danger for all the prisoners for the same reason. Neubauer is, once the bombing has started, indeed instructed to get rid of the more important political prisoners, mostly communists, and some of these are killed, in scenes of shocking realism, by slow strangulation. In contrast, the obscene attempts by Neubauer to make cosmetic changes at the last moment, placing a few flowers into the camp, for example, serve to highlight what has gone before.

A large group of prisoners is taken from the main camp into the town on a labor detail, and this group includes two of the prisoners who are organizing an actual resistance in the camp. The communists Werner, an old acquaintance of 509 who eventually has to be hidden in the same barracks, and Lewinsky are collecting parts for a gun. The confrontation of the prisoners with the destruction of the town increases their resolve, however, and then the sight of German refugees fleeing from the bombing gives them new life, a spark rekindled in their blood. The scene in which the column of refugees passes the prisoners gives rise to another key passage in the work, and indeed one that is of significance for much of Remarque's work as a whole. The prisoners do not feel hatred or revenge; they are aware that fate strikes the innocent more often than the guilty, and that plenty of these new refugees hardly deserved their fate. What they have, however, is a new awareness of the workings of an impersonal force. They knew that:

> die Gebote der Menschlichkeit waren umgestossen und fast zertrampelt worden; das Gesetz des Lebens war bespuckt, zerpeitscht und zerschossen worden; Raub war legal, Mord verdienstvoll, Terror gesetz geworden — und jetzt, plötzlich, in diesem atemlosen Augenblick fühlten vier hundert Opfer der Willkür hier dass es genug war, dass eine Stimme gesprochen hatte und dass das Pendel zurückschwang. Sie spürten, dass es nicht nur Länder und Völker waren, die gerettet würden; es waren die Gebote des Lebens selbst. Es war das, wofür es viele Namen gab — und einer der älteste und einfachste war: Gott. Und das hiess: Mensch. (154)

> [human laws had been overthrown and almost crushed; the law of life had been spat upon, thrashed and shot; theft had become legal, murder praiseworthy —, and now, suddenly in this breathless moment four hundred victims of capricious fate felt that now it was enough, that a voice had spoken and that the pendulum was swinging back. They felt that it wasn't only countries and peoples who would be saved, but the

laws of life itself. It was something that had many names, and one of
the oldest and simplest was God. And that meant: humanity.]

The again somewhat breathless passage (matching the significance of that
moment) is not easy to render into English, especially the last idea, which
seems to have restored a belief in God, who is equated with humanity. There
is, as customary in Remarque's writings, no metaphysical questioning, however, and the real emphasis is upon human existence, although some of the
Jewish prisoners pray, and when one dying man demands a priest, another
prisoner who can speak some Latin comes and gives him a kind of absolution, which satisfies him even if it is not real.

The prisoners do manage to return safely with enough material and
ammunition to make a gun. Meanwhile, a transport brings a large number of
prisoners into the camp, force-marched west from a camp in the east as the
Germans gave way to the advance of the Red Army. Several are shot as sport
by the SS guards, and when the rest are forced to strip and pass through a
bath for disinfecting, they are terrified because they do not know if this is an
extermination camp or not. Showers were the pretext for the gas chambers,
so that we are reminded of that all too familiar image, even though the camp
depicted in the novel is not itself an extermination camp. The distortion of
human values is underlined again in the grotesqueness of their delight not
to have reached an extermination camp as they dress themselves in random
clothes that have been sent from Auschwitz and still show the blood of their
former owners. The scene is given further point by the fact that the wife of
the commander now arrives at the camp and is confronted with the sight of
these prisoners: the outsider, albeit one married to one of the perpetrators, is
thus brought face to face for the first time with the reality.

509 comes into conflict with Handke, the criminal prisoner who has
some authority, and is forced to promise him money (that in fact he does
not have). Terrified that Handke will report him to the SS, he experiences a
period of extended fear that is portrayed as vividly as the actual tortures and
beatings. When it eventually becomes apparent that he has not yet been reported, 509 asks one of the others: "Glaubst du, dass wir je die Angst wieder
loswerden können?" (188, Do you think we'll ever be able to shake off the
fear?). 509's recovery soon shifts, however, to actual resistance. The new
force within him is a powerful one, enabling him first of all to continue to
defy Handke, and then to volunteer to hide the revolver that has been pro-
cured. This marks a final turning point for 509, who had been at the start of
the work so close to resignation. At the end of the thirteenth chapter,
around the ever-significant mid-point, he realizes the extent to which he has
changed. Robbed of his human individuality, he had become a number
rather than a human being, but now when he is addressed as 509, he replies
that his name is Friedrich Koller. Later on, however, a trick by another pris-

oner working in the crematorium will be needed to provide new clothes and a new identity (taken from a dead prisoner) for 509 in order to save him from further persecution.

Further atrocities in the camp are described in parallel with further signs of the approaching end. A woman in the town shows humanity to a wounded work-detail prisoner after another bombing attack, for example. Neubauer encounters, in a scene that is again somewhat contrived, Josef Blank, the Jew whom he had legally cheated out of the department store and who was tortured and half blinded in the camp, and tries to persuade him that he owes Neubauer his freedom. However artificial, the encounter permits a glimmer of revenge, as Blank observes with satisfaction — smiling for the first time for years — Neubauer's obvious fears.

The holocaust was of course a Jewish tragedy. Concentration camps like that in the novel also contained political prisoners, homosexuals, Roma and Sinti, eastern Europeans, and so on, and there are even anti-Semitic sentiments among the non-Jewish prisoners, which Remarque shows, but this work does not ignore the horrors of the so-called final solution. A large number of Jewish prisoners are brought to Mellern en route to an extermination camp, diverted because the bombing has affected rail links, and this scene — most of chapter 17 — links the work with the more narrowly defined holocaust novel as such. The deliberately objective narrative, observed awkwardly also by the other prisoners, avoids even a hint of personal involvement; it documents, but makes no claims beyond memorial. The Jews here have been rounded up from all over Europe. Unable to accommodate them after the last influx of additional prisoners, it is decided that they should be placed temporarily in the parade ground of the Small Camp, with the existing prisoners locked in their barracks to separate them, before they can be transported further. The Jewish prisoners try to get into the barracks, but the ordinary prisoners are unable to take in any more. The picture given of these new prisoners and their suffering, reduced to something less than human because their religion is different, is sympathetic and important. They remain, clinging to the earth of the concentration camp because they know that they will be transported to their deaths. An extra edge is given to the scene by a debate among those in charge of the camp, who are reluctant to kill them, but only because it is difficult to get rid of so many bodies, which must not be left for the Americans and their accompanying journalists now that the German armies are in retreat; Neubauer corrects himself quickly to "strategic withdrawal" when this is mentioned. Weber comments that: "Man hätte Aufnahmen machen und behaupten können, die Leute wären unterernährt gewesen" (260, They might even take photographs and claim that the people had been undernourished). The cynicism of the statement is almost unbelievable, but there are various elements in play here. The war is ending and the SS know it and know too they must cover their tracks. Possibly this is a crude attempt at self-deception, but the mild concept of "under-nourished" is shocking in the face of the horrors with which we have been presented in graphic terms; the prisoners are called skeletons.[21] Neubauer manages to get rid of the (naturally incredulous) Jewish prisoners by offering them food, which does succeed in persuading them to leave for the further transports. A few escape into the barracks, but the prisoners are unable to conceal them because they cannot allow the barracks to be searched. They are already concealing prisoners from the larger camp who are part of the resistance within, so that even these Jewish prisoners are removed.

A conversation between Lewinsky, one of the organizers of the underground movement in the camp and 509 is significant. Lewinsky is keen for 509 to join his communist cell, but however useful a former editor, which was Koller's job, might be to them, he will not be drawn, equating communism with the ideology of the Nazis. The linking of the two extreme political standpoints is developed in more detail as 509 comments on the new leader of the underground movement in the camp, whom he had known before the war. 509 reveals that his newspaper had been against both the Nazis and the communists, and when asked what he was actually for, his reply is programmatic for the novel as a whole: "Für Menschlichkeit, Toleranz und das Recht des einzelnen auf eine eigene Meinung. Komisch, was?" (289, for humanity, tolerance, and the right of the individual to have his own views. Funny, eh?). The others do however, discuss the question of revenge, and whether or not the SS can be allowed to get away with things, and once again, Remarque is leaving a conversation open for the reader to decide, albeit loading it towards the views of his principal, 509. Werner claims that in the aftermath only a resolute political group, such as the communists, can take over, but 509 is against any totalitarian party and declares that the group represented by Werner and Lewinsky, if they come to power after the war, would soon find him an enemy. He goes on to say:

> "Ihr könnt die Lager hier dann gleich behalten. Und sie füllen."
> "Das können wir," sagte Werner völlig ernst. "Warum kommst du nicht zu uns?" wiederholte er dann.
> "Genau deshalb nicht. Wenn du draussen an die Macht kämst, würdest du mich liquidieren lassen. Ich dich nicht. Das ist der Unterschied. (303)

> ["You could just keep these camps. And fill them."
> "We could," said Werner with all seriousness. "Why don't you come over to us?" he asked again.
> "That's the reason. If you lot came to power outside, you'd have me liquidated. I wouldn't do it to you. That's the difference."]

509 is given the last word and the reader is left in no doubt about totalitarian distortions of the word *Notwendigkeit* (necessity). The debate within the

novel was highly significant for the early 1950s, when a divided Germany had not long been established and the Iron Curtain was in place.

The manner in which Neubauer now begins to reassure himself that his acts have always been humane — *menschlich* — is subtly done, with a constant contrast with the facts, which are anything but humane. Mellern, he tells himself, is not Buchenwald or Dachau or any of the extermination camps. The novel also explores the reactions of the other SS officers as to what they would do — the matter is still kept firmly hypothetical — in the case of a lost war. Weber's comments are especially relevant for a postwar readership; he would soon come to the top again, he claims, maybe as a communist this time, certainly in some police force. Indeed, many of the Webers did not even need to change their identities after the war.[22] Meanwhile, as Neubauer makes cosmetic efforts in the camp, Weber helps him persuade himself that the dreadful conditions in the Small Camp are necessary to isolate disease, that the men are not made to work (in reality they are too ill and weak to do so), and that they are starved only because of the allied blockade. The rest of the SS make their own plans: to escape to Argentina, or to drum up support from the prisoners. A few still believe in a German victory, while others are prepared to become communists, and several persuade themselves that they were never committed Nazis in the first place. All cling to the comfort that they always acted on orders and therefore bear no responsibility on the personal level. At the end, Neubauer persuades himself that he is a soldier, rather than a Nazi, who will surrender with dignity and be treated with chivalry. He is of course treated with disgust and contempt by the liberating forces.

The final resistance of the prisoners comes just before the liberation. The two most resolute of the SS men, Weber and Steinbrenner attempt to set fire to the camp, and in this final mêlée, 509 shoots Weber with the smuggled revolver, but is killed himself. After the liberation he is buried in a coffin, but takes up so little of it that the comment can be made that he had not for years had so much space to himself. He is buried near where his barracks had stood. There is a moving scene, too, when Rosen, whom 509 had rescued, and who is helping to dig his grave, strikes ineffectually at one of the now-captive SS men, but is too weak to cause much damage; the spade is gently taken from him by a GI with the words: "we'll take care of that later" (364).

Once again the principal character has died before the end of the book, but others survive. Berger, who has been a doctor, discovers, although he had not believed it, that he can operate again. Bucher is able to leave after the liberation of the camp with Ruth Holland, who reveals that she had only survived because she had been used in enforced prostitution by the Nazis. Bucher is able to provide an answer for her to help her live with herself after the war and which is also of programmatic importance for the work: "Man hat uns erniedrigt; aber wir sind nicht die Erniedrigten. Es sind die andern, die es getan haben" (307, We've been humiliated. But we are not the humiliated ones. It's those who did it to us). Ruth and Bucher, in their attempts to envisage a time when they will be free of the camp, had focused on a white house, visible in the distance, which had become a leitmotif in their fragmented relationship, and now provides for a somewhat ambiguous ending to the novel. The pair leave the camp and make for the white house, which turns out to be just a shell. "Sie hatten an eine Illusion geglaubt" (371, They had believed in an illusion). But believing in the illusion had helped them to survive. On investigation, they discover that a small back kitchen is still intact, and here they move in. They are both worn down by the experiences of the camp; Ruth looks into a fragment of mirror at her gray hair and missing teeth, then throws the mirror away. But the couple at last have some space. The final paragraph is almost biblical as Ruth comments that they are like the last people on earth, but Bucher counters: "Nicht die letzten. Die ersten" (373, Not the last people, the first). Whether physically they are Adam and Eve is debatable, but there is hope as the sun sets.[23]

Der Funke Leben is a memorial, written lest the events it depicts be too quickly or indeed deliberately forgotten, to the holocaust and of all the victims of the camps. It presents what were at the time of publication more recent historical events than those of the First World War had been in *Im Westen nichts Neues* and *Der Weg zurück*. This time the German people in particular required a different kind of catharsis. The questions of collective guilt and public awareness are not fully developed in this novel, but it is a German work that confronts a nation with its history, a history that contained not only the Nazi machine but at least some of its victims. It expresses also a broader humanitarianism. The events depicted are historical, and to a lesser degree some aspects could be related to the political situation at the time of writing, most notably in the refusal of 509 to align himself with the communists as another totalitarian regime. But the main theme is the extraordinary ability of the human spirit to survive, to retain the spark of life even when every basic value of humanity is distorted.[24] It is worth reminding ourselves, finally, that this is a novel, albeit a well-documented historical one. In simplest terms, the fate of 509 holds the interest within a necessarily graphic description that is as realistic and effective as possible in the medium. It had been put often enough that the scale of the suffering was too great for the later world to assimilate through statistics, while the focus on an individual (Anne Frank is the best example) permits empathy. The absolute necessity of tolerance for the rights of the individual is what gives the novel a lasting, and now perhaps an increasing importance.

Zeit zu leben und Zeit zu sterben

Zeit zu leben und Zeit zu sterben is set over a period of weeks, at the beginning and again at the end on the rapidly collapsing eastern front, but principally in Germany itself under allied bombing in 1944. It shows the emotional and philosophical development of a single soldier, Ernst Graeber, through his experiences in Russia and during two week's home leave in a third-person narrative with a strong focus upon that central figure. His reflections on the war, guided by an older mentor at the front and a former teacher at home, together with his own private experiences of falling in love, and also observing the actions of Nazis and Nazi sympathizers, all combine to cause a change in his own perception of his role as a German soldier towards the end of the Second World War.[25] The last part of the structurally balanced work (Russia-Germany-Russia) sees him back at the eastern front, from which he does not return. Although we see him on the eastern front, we learn that Graeber has fought elsewhere, in France and in Africa, reminding us of the global nature of the conflict. This is the first of several differences in the presentation of the war from *Im Westen nichts Neues,* with which the work bears comparison, and it is far more of an *Entwicklungsroman,* a novel of personal development.

The opening of the work is arresting and vivid, stressing that war means death as dead soldiers are being dug out of the thawing Russian soil in spring 1944.[26] We encounter not only Graeber but his colleagues, including Immermann, a communist; the partly-Jewish Hirschland, transformed in the censored text into an Aryan Hirschmann; the mentor figure Fresenburg, incidentally the real name of Ravic in *Arc de Triomphe,* whom Graeber trusts and who starts him thinking seriously about the nature of the war; and finally Steinbrenner, from the SS, who is a Gestapo spy. Notably, the name Steinbrenner is used for similar figures in *Der Funke Leben* and in *Liebe Deinen Nächsten.* A key theme throughout is the atmosphere of spying and denunciation, both at the front and in Germany itself. Once the men have dug out the already decomposing bodies, they are then formed as a firing squad to execute some supposed Russian partisans, including a woman. The enthusiasm of the SS soldier for such activities is made clear, and this Steinbrenner is much in line with his namesakes. We do not see Graeber in combat, except in defense and under fire, although he does form part of this firing squad. When, at the end of the novel, he is shown firing another shot, it is at another German, the SS soldier.

Graeber has grown up under the Nazis. In the first part of the novel he reluctantly accepts the familiar excuse when it is presented to him by one of the other soldiers:

"Wir beide haben den Krieg nicht angefangen und sind nicht dafür
verantwortlich. Wir tun nur unsere Pflicht. Und Befehl ist Befehl. Oder
nicht?"

"Ja," erwiderte Graeber müde. (39)

["Neither of us started the war and it isn't our responsibility. We're just
doing our duty. And orders are orders. Aren't they?"

"Yes," said Graeber tiredly.]

In the First World War novels Remarque allowed his soldiers to present
questions of that sort for the reader to consider. In this new war, the question of responsibility and of obeying orders has to be explored openly and
in far more detail, and Graeber is ripe for change. His first discussion with
Fresenburg, an older man who volunteered in 1939, takes us back to the beginnings of the war. Fresenburg had joined up because he believed in the
defense of the nation, regardless of who started the war, but he has now seen
that this was all trickery and that he — who had served in the First World
War — should have known better. Graeber, though, began to wonder about
the situation as soon as Germany had ceased to win victories, but was still
able to put things out of his mind. While well aware of the inhumanities
perpetrated by Nazis, he is still able to distance himself from guilt. He is
quite genuinely not like Steinbrenner, and this is not the pharisaical attitude
demonstrated in *Der Funke Leben* by Neubauer, who compares himself favorably to those who actually carry out the atrocities. Fresenburg agrees that
the SS are to be blamed, but points out to Graeber that it is the SS for
whom they are now fighting. When Graeber goes on leave for the first time
in two years, Fresenburg commends him to Pohlmann, a former teacher — if
he is still alive. At this stage Graeber cannot understand why there should be
any doubt, and he travels home, expecting Germany to be unchanged.

Before reaching their homes the soldiers are given a lecture by a Nazi
political officer in which they are instructed not only to give no details of
where they are fighting, but always to confirm that Russia is practically defeated and that they are well supplied, although we have seen the contrary.
They are then given a food parcel to take home as proof of how well they are
being treated. The propaganda machine is still functioning, but it becomes
clear that things in Germany are not well when those with leave passes for
the Rhineland are told that leave is barred and that they must go elsewhere
— to the bafflement of a soldier whose family is in Cologne. The soldiers are
unaware of the extent and effect of the allied bombing.

Graeber arrives in his hometown of Werden, again based on Osnabrück,
but soon finds that his family house has been bombed. When he says in desperation to an air-raid warden that he has just come from the front line, he is
told "Meinen Sie, das hier ist keine Front?" (88, Do you think this isn't the
front?). The warden proves, in fact, to be crazy: his sporadic appearances

later on — as he hovers around the bombed area — have the effect of a Shakespearean fool, and his ostensibly insane comments have an ironic effect. In his attempts to locate his parents, Graeber meets up with a soldier called Böttcher who is trying to find his wife, and who directs him to the emergency barracks where he can stay. Böttcher is a nicely drawn figure with a predilection for large women, a comic pendant to Graeber, whose search for his parents is fruitless; they were presumably killed in the air raids. Later on Graeber even searches the local cemetery — one of the busiest places in the town, he notes — and he learns that only the concentration camps have proper crematoria. At an early stage, however his search leads him to try to find a doctor who had treated his mother. The doctor is no longer there, and even the mention of his name leads to hostility, but he meets the doctor's daughter Elisabeth Kruse, with whom he had been at school, and discovers that her father is in a concentration camp, denounced by Frau Lieser, the woman who is now in charge of the house. The crime is unspecified, perhaps the so-called defeatism for which Elfriede, Remarque's sister, was executed. Elisabeth, now a lodger in what was her own home, has refused to move because she does not want to give up, something that Graeber initially does not understand. His learning process will be focused upon the need to take a stand, however futile it might seem. An air raid also soon shows Graeber, who had been under fire in a cellar in Russia, that the situation here is more or less the same.

Graeber's next chance meeting, however, is with a Nazi *Kreisleiter* (local official) in the SA, who invites him back to the opulent villa he has acquired. Alfons Binding, whom Graeber had also known at school, is an ambiguous, but interesting and extremely important creation. It is not difficult to portray the Nazi as a monstrous figure,[27] and several of these are encountered in the novel. But Binding incorporates most clearly of all the low-level banality of evil[28] as an even more ordinary version of the commandant Neubauer in *Der Funke Leben*. Binding has done comfortably for himself, using his position in the party to provide himself with women and with looted food and alcohol in large quantities. Neubauer is a petit-bourgeois who has made deliberate attempts to increase his social status by what are clearly evil acts that he reconstructs in his mind to place in an acceptable light when it becomes necessary to do so. Binding is at once simpler and psychologically more complex, allowing the reader a greater understanding, though not a pardoning, of his crimes. His often petty inhumanity is patent — he has had a teacher he disliked sent to a concentration camp, an interesting turn of the revenge taken upon Kantorek in *Im Westen nichts Neues* — but he is not shown to be immediately and recognizably monstrous in the way that some of his SS acquaintances clearly are. He listens to their tales of murder and torture with approval and pleasure, but he also shows (and Graeber notices this) the same kind of admiration for Graeber's medal ribbons. His desire to be liked is the controlling factor, and he also helps Graeber, something that the latter also notes. Equally importantly, though, Graeber accepts his help, not only in the ultimately unsuccessful quest for his parents, but with his gifts of lodging, food, and drink. Graeber (and the reader) comes into contact through Binding with more clearly evil Nazis, but the association with Binding himself (for all Graeber protests at various points that he never liked him) is above all else an indication of a readiness to use the regime, to go along with it when expedient. How easy, Graeber comments later, is this kind of corruption.

The beginning of the love relationship with Elisabeth coincides with Graeber's learning process in political terms as they arrange to meet again to dine out and try to forget the war for a brief time. This is set off by the sexual adventures of Böttcher, the sustained comic foil, who has a brief liaison with an ample landlady, and when he eventually locates his wife, is appalled to find that she has lost a great amount of weight — an ironic context being provided for the more serious conditions of the time. Before his rendezvous with Elisabeth, Graeber borrows an NCO's uniform so that he can take her to a restaurant for officers, and he is also given tips on how to behave there. The scene is a light one, but from it we learn that Graeber really has been an NCO but had been demoted. The set-piece meal in the Germania restaurant (there was a large hotel of that name in Osnabrück) shows the pair trying to find a brief snatch of happiness, but that the whole thing is, in a sense, spurious, is interesting, and this will be pointed out later in the novel when the Germania has been bombed, and they eat instead at a homely restaurant as the sole guests. For now, however, the two enjoy the luxury, and when Elisabeth worries about the payment, Graeber comments that he has two years pay, which only needs to last for the two weeks leave. In another echo of the First World War novel, too, Graeber fails to salute a major in the reserve, but this time the major, seeing the borrowed uniform, rounds on him for not being at the front. The incident, like others in *Im Westen nichts Neues* is reworked completely, although like Bäumer, Graeber resolves to wear civilian clothes the next day.

A further visit to Binding permits Graeber to hear from a drunken SS officer at a concentration camp about a range of atrocities that he has committed (these were left out of the censored version of the novel). After the SS man has left to pursue his sadistic hobbies, Binding voices the view that the camp inmates are traitors anyway, apart, of course, from the teacher that he wanted out of the way, that worse things happen to better people in the bombing, and that neither he nor Graeber is responsible. To Graeber's comment that responsibility is a complicated matter, Binding again puts the standard view: one is only responsible for one's own actions, and then not if one is obeying orders. Binding is entirely comfortable with this, and he even takes at face value the notion that "Wenn wir eine Stadt bombadieren, ist das eine strategische Notwendigkeit; wenn die andern es tun, ist es ein gemeines

Verbrechen" (179, If we bomb a town it is a strategic necessity; if the other side does it, it is a wicked crime). Binding has an antecedent in Mücken-haupt in *Der Weg zurück;* the difference, though, is in the nature of the deeds for which Binding is rejecting responsibility. He lacks, however, the overt self-delusion of Neubauer or the cynicism of some of the more hard-line Nazis, like Weber, in *Der Funke Leben.*

Later, Graeber sees the SS man on a lonely street and considers how easy it would be to stab him. He does not do so, and is anyway prevented from action by the appearance of others in the street, but that he should think of doing so strikes him as significant. He suddenly realizes that it is part of the despair he has felt at the front, and now he needs to understand things more fully. This is the turning point in his awareness, and he decided to seek out Pohlmann, the teacher to whom Fresenburg had sent him, in search of an answer. His encounter with Pohlmann, a former teacher of religion and history, at the end of the thirteenth chapter, once more roughly in the middle of the novel, which has twenty-six chapters, is central in all respects, voicing the main theme of the work, the question of *Mitschuld,* shared guilt. Remarque himself played the role of Pohlmann in the Douglas Sirk film, and Pohlmann is the catalyst for Graeber, not giving him the answer, but guiding him towards a way of thinking.[29] Pohlmann's teaching subjects are significant, and he has, we assume, been dismissed from his post for disagreeing with the government line either on religion, of which the Nazis had, in a sense, their own, or on history, which they largely rewrote. Graeber is a soldier fighting for that regime, whether or not he had any part in its rise to power. Furthermore, in the course of his two-week leave he regularly uses the Nazi Binding, among others, to assist in his personal affairs. Remarque shows us through Graeber's thoughts and also his actions the difficulty of avoiding guilt when living in the Nazi state, especially as a soldier, as he becomes aware of the possibility and the extent of his *Mitschuld.* Postwar writers such as Hans Helmut Kirst in the popular *08/15* (*Gunner Asch*) series distanced their positive characters more completely from Nazis and avoided the issue altogether, while others, like Alfred Andersch in the autobiographical *Die Kirschen der Freiheit* (The Cherries of Freedom), laid heavy emphasis (with hindsight) upon their own inner rejection of Nazi ideologies.[30] The confusion in Graeber, however, must have struck chords in Germany's postwar attempt to come to terms with its past.

The name of Fresenburg takes away Pohlmann's initial suspicions of Graeber, and the meeting between the two now becomes a classic example of the turning point in a novel of development. Just as in the medieval German romance of *Parzival,* where the young knight is sent to a hermit, confesses his sins, and asks for advice, so, too, Graeber asks simply for "the truth." His refining of the question encapsulates the problem of the work: "Ich möchte wissen, wieweit ich an den Verbrechen der letzten zehn Jahre beteiligt war," sagte er. "Und ich möchte wissen, was ich tun soll" (186, "I want to know how far I am responsible for the crimes of the last ten years," he said, "and I want to know what to do"). By crimes he does not mean just the war, but everything the Nazis have done (including the substance of *Der Funke Leben*), the lies, the slave labor, the camps, and the mass murder of civilians. Extra force is given to the question when Pohlmann agrees that the war is effectively lost, and that to continue fighting at this stage is not to defend Germany, but knowingly to prop up for a short while longer a corrupt and evil regime. It is his moral complicity in this for which Graeber seeks help. He now uses the word *Mitschuld,* "collective guilt, shared guilt."

> "Wieweit werde ich zum Mitschuldigen, wenn ich weiss, dass der Krieg nicht nur verloren ist, sondern auch, dass wir ihn verlieren müssen, damit Sklaverei und Mord, Konzentrationslager, SS und SD, Massenausrottung und Unmenschlichkeit aufhören — wenn ich das weiss und in zwei Wochen wieder hinausgehe, um weiter dafür zu kämpfen." (187)

> [To what extent do I share the guilt, given that I know not only that the war is lost, but that we have to lose it, so that slavery and murder, concentration camps, the SS and their security service, mass extermination and inhumanity can all be stopped — if I know all this, and have to go out and fight for them again in two weeks?]

Pohlmann gives no direct answer. Instead he allows Graeber to work out the possibilities: refusal to fight would have him executed, desertion would lead at best to a concentration camp, and to refuse to defend himself at the front would be suicide. Even to seek a post behind the lines would be a kind of desertion, and collective guilt is equally possible behind the lines. Pohlmann taught religion as well as history, but whether or not God is aware of the level of complicity is not helpful, and Graeber even dismisses the idea of original sin, the basic human sinfulness, as irrelevant when he is concerned with a personal guilt (in Catholic theological terms, original sin is wiped out only by the Redemption, but actual sin by some kind of penance). It is actual sin, rather than original sin for which Graeber is seeking a kind of absolution. But even the religion teacher admits that the Christian religion will offer no help when it can set "love thy neighbor" and "thou shalt not kill" against "render under Caesar . . ." To be sure, Pohlmann claims later to believe only "an Gott. Und an das Gute im Menschen" (265, in God. And in the goodness in mankind), but he has doubted a great deal, and this has left him with a belief that is unsupported by much positive proof. Later, too, even his reference to the way in which Christianity started with a few believers in the catacombs draws the response from Graeber that National Socialism also started with a few believers in a Munich beer hall.

Pohlmann can give Graeber no definitive answer because he himself is even more torn. When Graeber visits him again he says so expressly. Graeber was too young to experience the beginning of the Nazi movement, whereas Pohlmann's generation allowed evil to triumph because good men did nothing. The contrast with *Im Westen nichts Neues* is again interesting; in the First World War the teachers had betrayed the young men with their outdated and unreflective patriotism. Pohlmann, also a teacher (as some of the former soldiers had become in *Der Weg zurück*), blames himself for a sin of omission. The only answer that can be given to Graeber is that he should accept personal responsibility and cope with it on an individual basis in any way he can. The problem, specific as it may sound, is in any case a general existential one. Probably the most famous immediate postwar work of German literature is Wolfgang Borchert's drama of 1946, *Draussen vor der Tür* (*The Man Outside*), which Remarque would certainly have known, and in which a representative returning soldier after the war is faced with the fact that it is impossible (and not just in a war) not to incur some kind of guilt, whether or not you deserve it. At the climax of the play he asks: "Wer schütz uns davor, dass wir nicht Mörder werden? Wir werden jeden Tag ermordet, und jeden Tag begehen wir einen Mord. Wir gehen jeden Tag an einen Mord vorbei!" (Who protects us from becoming murderers? We are murdered every day, and every day we commit a murder. We walk past a murder every day!).

That expression of existential despair is apposite in the context of *Zeit zu leben und Zeit zu sterben*. After Beckmann, the soldier in Borchert's play, has called in vain for a response from his more optimistic self, the *Jasager*, or from "the old man who calls himself God," the play ends with the repeated cry: "Gibt keiner Antwort?" (Will nobody answer?) and a threefold question mark before the curtain falls. But the answer cannot come from outside, only from within, both for the fictitious stage character Beckmann, and for the audience.[31] In *Zeit zu leben und Zeit zu sterben* the principal protagonist is also a German soldier in the 1940s, and the answer is again that there is no answer except from within. Pohlmann asks Graeber: "Und Sie sind so ruhig. Weshalb schreien Sie nicht?" "Ich schreie," erwiderte Graeber. "Sie hören es nur nicht" (190, "And you're so calm. Why aren't you screaming?" "I am screaming," replied Graeber. "It's just that you can't hear it"). Remarque saw Germany as having been a fruitful field for the Nazis because of a national tendency towards the unconditional obedience that took away the need for any personal responsibility, and this is the heart of the problem explored in both of the Second World War novels.[32] The questions posed are difficult and bold ones in the context of the postwar German *Bewältigung der Vegangenheit*, then. But away from that context they can also be generalized: to be a soldier always means having to be sure of one's moral ground.

Graeber, like other of Remarque's figures, draws strength first of all from the powerful force of nature when he sees, on leaving Pohlmann, a lime tree in leaf, an encouraging symbol of pure existence without doubt and despair.[33] The discussion with Pohlmann is followed immediately, too, by the resolution of the love that has developed between Graeber and Elisabeth Kruse. A second meal planned at the deluxe Germania restaurant is curtailed by an air raid before they can even eat, and Graeber acquires instead a quantity of food from Binding, takes the food to Elisabeth, and they now celebrate their love. It is, incidentally, sometimes held as a criticism of Remarque that so much of his writing centers upon food: here the point is made overtly how in wartime any ideas of happiness are connected with eating. They were hungry times.

The development of the love between Elisabeth and Graeber runs parallel with his ongoing questioning, but where Pohlmann's views were focused upon the past, Elisabeth and Graeber can have a kind of future, and the chapter ends positively. When Graeber proposes marriage, Elisabeth is initially reluctant, as she is also reluctant to continue enjoying the *Beutegut*, the looted food and drink, but later she agrees, as Graeber explains as a nice casuistry that the time they have spent together, while apparently short, is the leave equivalent of two years at the front. Once again, however, the preparations for the wedding are effected with the help of Binding. Graeber uses provisions from him and indeed invokes his name when necessary.[34] A further apparently trivial incident, which picks up an earlier one, underlines the problems of Graeber's use of Binding, however. He had taken a bath at Binding's house and used perfumed bath oil. In civilian clothes, he has yet another brush with a major who assumes this time that he is a homosexual and refers to him as a *männliche Hure,* a male whore. Graeber reflects that this is perhaps indeed what he has become: "Ich bin verdammt rasch von meiner Tugendhöhe heruntergepurzelt" (246, I damned quickly tumbled down from my moral high ground). The association with Binding is questioned by Graeber throughout the work.

This scene is followed by an incident cut from the censored edition in which Graeber visits the family of the part-Jewish soldier Hirschland and finds that he has been reported dead. Steinbrenner, it turns out, has done this maliciously. Several more minor scenes echo and vary those from the First World War novels. Graeber bribes a quartermaster to get a new uniform (an echo of *Der Weg zurück*) and then visits a hospital in a scene that partly repeats the point made in *Im Westen nichts Neues* that war maims as much as it kills. Here too, though, there is small variation; the *Stadtkrankenhaus* contains the seriously wounded, of course, but one, who has lost both legs, loudly insists in spite of Graeber that the war will still be won — Hitler has promised. He is desperately convincing himself of victory, of course, so that he will not be a crippled beggar "wie die nach dem ersten Kriege" (22, like those after the first war).

The marriage to Elisabeth now takes place, again with small incidents that make their own points. Graeber manages to find some flowers, which the florist wraps in newspaper on which Graeber sees a photograph of the *Vorsitzender des Volksgerichtshofs* (the president of the "people's court," Roland Freisler, a "true sadist in legal robes"), together with a description of four people who have been executed for no longer believing in Germany's victory. The climate of fear is apparent in both of the Second World War novels and the allusion to Remarque's sister is once again clear.[35] In a second incident, Elisabeth and Graeber find themselves trapped by bureaucracy when they need a witness to their marriage; Graeber had wished to avoid using Binding, so as not to have a Nazi name on their certificate, but the service is in the event provided for them by an SS *Obersturmbannführer* in civilian clothes, whose signature will prove useful again in a later encounter with the SS. The copy of Hitler's *Mein Kampf,* always given to newly married couples, is passed on by Graeber to another soldier in a nice ironic exchange for a salami.

A few days after the marriage, Graeber experiences a bombing attack that threatens the factory in which Elisabeth works making uniforms; she says later that she does not want to make munitions. She is unhurt, but among the casualties is a five-year-old girl. The reminder that this war — whatever the underlying rights or wrongs — killed large numbers of the innocent leads to an indictment of war as such. Graeber ponders this point:

> Nach diesem Krieg würde entsetzlich viel zu vergeben und nicht zu vergeben sein. Ein einziges Leben würde dafür nicht ausreichen. Er hatte mehr tote Kinder gesehen als diese — er hatte sie überall gesehen, in Frankreich, in Holland, in Polen, in Afrika, in Russland, und alle hatten Mütter gehabt, die um sie weinten, nicht nur die deutschen — falls sie noch weinen konnten und nicht bereits von der SS liquidiert worden waren. Aber wozu dachte er das? Hatte er vor einer Stunde nicht selbst: Schweine! Schweine! zum Himmel geschrien, der die Flugzeuge enthielt. (290)

> [After this war there would be a terrifyingly large amount of things to forgive and not to forgive. One single lifetime would not be enough for it. He had seen more dead children than these — he had seen them everywhere, in France, Holland, Poland, Africa, Russia — and they had all had mothers to cry over them, not just the Germans, provided they could still cry and had not been wiped out by the SS. But why was he thinking that? Only an hour ago had he not shouted "You bastards, you bastards!" at the heavens, when they were full of planes?]

The bombs also destroy Binding's house and he is killed, having just had a hearty meal in the company of an attractive blonde. Although the housekeeper is disappointed that he died very much out of uniform, Graeber reassures her that it was not the worst way to go. She also tells Graeber that Binding admired him because he had made no demands and because he had fought in the war. The SA man Alfons Binding is a literary creation of considerable interest, and his fitting, but certainly not tragic death cannot, except in an ironic sense, even be seen as some kind of just retribution. He is a Nazi, but he is essentially weak and opportunistic, desperate for friendship on any terms, and hence a natural admirer of what he perceives as strength. The attraction held by dictators for this kind of personality is familiar, although in different circumstances he might have directed his admiration elsewhere. His role in the novel is polyvalent. He is the link between Graeber and the regime, and provides Graeber both with evidence to underpin a growing revulsion with the Nazi state, but also with an awareness of the inherent moral problems in taking his favors. Binding is not the embodiment of absolute evil; rather he is a picture of human weakness that was seduced by that evil. His petty revenge-taking, his willingness to bully and to accept looted goods, to use his position for his own creature comforts and sexual benefit show how inadequate ordinariness could be corrupted in what in some respects is a simple desire for friendship. None of this exonerates him in any way: Binding's acts are inexcusable, but he is more understandable, and hence less comfortable in the context of *Bewältigung der Vergangenheit,* than other Nazis. Faced with tales of burning prisoners alive, it is easy to say that one could never have done such a thing. But that one might have been tempted towards opportunism at some small level is far less easy to deny, and Graeber's relationship with him, while part of his educational process, is also opportunistic, despite the housekeeper's assurances while giving him supplies of food that survived the bombing, that he as a soldier has more right to it than "diese Nazis, die sich hier warme Posten halten" (these Nazis with soft jobs back here).[36]

Pohlmann is sheltering a Jewish refugee, Josef, and Graeber takes food for him too. This new episode is the first opportunity for Graeber to make a small practical stand against the regime, but it also gives him a chance to discuss with Josef the whole question of Binding and indeed the question of *Mitschuld.* Graeber describes Binding, in fact, as "ein harmloser und gutmütiger mensch" (315, a harmless, good-natured chap), even if he was a Nazi *Kreisleiter,* and explains that it is possible to be both "wenn man charakterlos oder ängstlich oder schwach ist und deshalb mitmacht (316, if you are lacking in character or timid or weak, and go along with things for that reason). Josef, whose family has all perished in the camps and who has himself been tortured, is skeptical of the "elastic conscience" of mankind and offers a different perspective. Even a tiny bit of evil in someone's nature is enough to spread a great deal of misery. The reader is left to weigh up the different views and set them against the objective picture provided by the novel.

Elisabeth's house is bombed, and the pair have to find somewhere to stay; they sleep first in the cloisters of the church, which gives an opportunity for comments on those medieval tortures carried out in the name of God that provided such excellent examples for the modern torturers in the camps. Before nightfall, however, the pair are able to eat a modest meal in a restaurant that survives. The soup and beer provided by Frau Witte contrasts with the "false pretenses" meal in the Germania, and Elisabeth notes that they are now living like human beings, rather than like princes. While Elisabeth is at work, Graeber accepts a letter for her summoning her to the Gestapo offices. Hearing from Josef that Pohlmann has also just been arrested, he is fearful that Elisabeth is being sought. He takes the letter himself to the Gestapo, but eventually is made simply to sign a lot of paperwork for the receipt of a cigar box containing the ashes of Elisabeth's father, who has clearly been killed in the camp. Since mass cremations were required in the camps, these are presumably a random handful of ashes, but Graeber is baffled by the combination of inhumanity and bureaucracy that makes the inhumanity that much worse. Graeber secretly buries the ashes in the cloister gardens of the church, next to the grave of some long-dead canon. He writes on the box that these are the ashes of a Catholic concentration-camp victim, but he is himself aware that what he is doing has symbolic significance: the ashes are certainly a mixture of Protestant, Jewish, and Catholic remains, and his improvised and secret grave is an equivalent to the tomb of the Unknown Soldier that he had seen in Paris.

Graeber's leave is over, though he and Elisabeth are able to spend a night together, defying an air raid, incidentally, as a kind of idyll, the unrealistic nature of which has been noted by some critics, in the homely Gasthaus kept by Frau Witte. Although not pointed up as such (the image is used in a different and ambiguous context elsewhere in the novel), the scene is an island of hope, and a new idea is voiced when Elisabeth expresses the quite specific hope that she may be pregnant.[37] Graeber's reaction is first of all to reject the idea: what kind of a world is this to bring a child into, and even if the war is over the ground will be poisoned (the image is interesting) for many years to come. Would they simply be providing a child for the next war? Elisabeth's counter argument is simple: this will be hers and Graeber's child: "Sollen nur die Barbaren welche haben? Wer soll dann die Welt in Ordnung bringen?" (357, Is it only the barbarians who are to have children? Who is going to put the world right?). This is the variation on the spark of life that is so strong in all of the novels. Here the spark of life is in the — possible — child, something that opens a future for Graeber that he had not envisaged, or indeed a future at all. It offers him "diesen armen und trostvollen Betrug der Unsterblichkeit" (359, this poor and comforting illusion of immortality).

Graeber returns to the front, finding that many of the new recruits are very young indeed, a further echo of *Im Westen nichts Neues* and part of the realities of the end of the Second World War. The soldiers are more critical than before, but Steinbrenner's malice seems greater than ever. Fresenburg, too, has been wounded, but assures Graeber that he will not give up — he and those who think like him have to fight on, although the notion of the enemy has changed. In the final chapter Graeber is ordered to guard a group of suspected Russian partisans, and when he treats them humanely, they suggest that he release them and come with them, since Germany has clearly been defeated, but he rejects the idea. Finally, however, the Russian army breaks through, and they have to retreat again. Steinbrenner wants to shoot the Russians, but Graeber will not allow him to do so, and when threatened, shoots Steinbrenner instead. This is Graeber's climax, the final personal protest against the regime, a small gesture of revolt in the large scale of things, but all that he is able to do. It is similar to, but not quite the same as Ravic's killing of Haake in *Arc de Triomphe,* Steiner's of Steinbrenner in *Liebe Deinen Nächsten,* or even of 509's shooting of Weber in *Der Funke Leben,* though these are all more personal acts of revenge.[38] Graeber was unable to kill the SS man at home, but here he can do so. He is still confused, however:

> Mörder, sagte er, und wusste nicht, wen er meinte. Er starrte auf Steinbrenner. Er fühlte nichts. Mörder, sagte er noch einmal, und meinte Steinbrenner und sich selbst und unzählige andere. (398)

> [Murderer, he said, and did not know whom he meant. He stared at Steinbrenner. He felt nothing, Murderer, he said again, and meant Steinbrenner and himself and countless others.]

Questioning the definition of murder is one of Remarque's most important themes, and the omission of this in the censored version weakened the ending considerably. It is an important and final ambiguity in a work that is ambiguous in a variety of respects, and thus correspondingly thought provoking.[39] As the partisans run, however, one turns and fires at Graeber, so that the work ends with his death. As he falls, a single tiny plant fills his entire vision, the power of nature that will survive his death. Graeber's death may be in expiation for his part in the initial shooting of the partisans, or indeed for the murder of Steinbrenner, since this is still murder; but he has reached a form of enlightenment to be able to do so, to resist the Nazis as an individual. Graeber received no definitive answer from Pohlmann on what he should do, and he acts therefore as an individual, not knowing for certain whether this is right or wrong. The reader will make the judgment, however, and although Graeber dies, there is the hope — it needs to be stressed that it is no more than that — that there will be a child who may then begin to set things right again.

At one level this is again a historical novel in that it looks back from the time of writing to a period ten years earlier, but it is a political work — Hans Wagener, comparing it with *Im Westen nichts Neues,* rightly notes how it marks the development of Remarque from a writer of the lost generation to a *homo politicus.* This is a political work, of course, in that it is anti-Nazi, but it is in favor not of a party but of humanity,[40] and it is addressed to, and addresses the problems of, postwar Germany, although the existence of the so-called censored version for so many years means that it was even less a reflection of the cold war than was *Der Funke Leben.*[41] But one of the major aspects of coming to terms with at times uncomfortable questions about the past was that of the extent of *Mitschuld*. As with so many of Remarque's novels, this novel removes or calls into doubt potential excuses (such as having known no other system; orders are orders), but offers the characters and the reader no clear — and certainly no comforting — answers.[42] Pohlmann and Fresenburg raise the question of how the Nazis were permitted to come to power, Graeber, that of how to react once he understands the nature of the regime for which he is fighting. At the end, Fresenburg is badly wounded, Pohlmann is in a camp where he will presumably suffer the fate of Elisabeth's father, and Graeber himself is dead. Graeber's death may serve as a cathartic expiation not only of the individual acts, but of the fact that he has in all kinds of small ways consciously shared in the collective guilt.

In this context the importance of the figure of Binding, the weak hero-worshipper, requires reiteration. Binding is a brave invention, although it is of course unlikely that the reader would wish to identify with him in any way, and empathy is clearly with the central figure, who is portrayed largely as a victim.[43] The only shot he fires in genuine anger is against another German, to kill a Nazi. But he has associated with Binding. The strength of the novel is in its ambiguity, and this is underlined finally by the various titles by which it, and the film based upon it, are known. The title *Zeit zu leben und Zeit zu sterben* is almost biblical, a close echo of the third chapter of Ecclesiastes, "a time to be born and a time to die." The fated inevitability of all things is there in the German title. The English title is, however, equally clear: this is a love story, and the human love between Graeber and Elisabeth is important in a loveless world. Finally, the French translation, also of the full and unamended text, is called *L'île d'espérance* (The Island of Hope). This could imply that Graeber and Elisabeth form an island of hope in a dark world, but as a citation from the book, at the end of the tenth chapter, the central character despairs that the islands of hope have all sunk into the monotony of death (135).

The function of the two novels, *Zeit zu leben und Zeit zu sterben* and *Der Funke Leben* is both memorial and admonitory, and confronting Germany with the ideas expressed in these two works was a bold act by any postwar German writer. Beyond the Second World War, the Nazis, and their specific national-historical problems for a German audience, however, either in the 1950s or well beyond that, there are other more general themes and questions kept open by both books. Nazi Germany may have established a historical model for a modern atrocity, but there were others at the time. There have been other wars, other atrocities, even other situations like the concentration camps in other countries in many different parts of the world, so that the admonitory aspect has never lost its validity. Whether changes can be made to human nature as exposed in the works — the sometimes enormous corruption brought about by a small amount of power, especially when not associated with responsibility — is an open question that is recurrent in Remarque's political novels. In an age that has produced emblematic, appalling, but hard-to-grasp statistics of the dead — six million murdered in the holocaust, tens of millions of soldiers and civilians killed in the Second World War — Remarque's two novels remind us, as his First World War novels had done, and are able to do so because they are novels, that those incomprehensible numbers were made up of individuals, all possessed of the spark of life, the force that can and will survive or be passed on.

Notes

[1] See for example A. J. P. Taylor, *From Sarajevo to Potsdam* (London: Thames and Hudson, 1966), 58. See Remarque's own comments on the "different war" in a review published in *Der Spiegel* in 1965, "Frontal durch Krieg und Frieden," in *Ein militanter Pazifist*, 134–37, and *Das unbekannte Werk*, vol. 4, 418–21.

[2] "Practical Education Work in Germany after the War" ("Praktische Erziehungsarbeit in Deutschland nach dem Krieg"), trans. Thomas Schneider in *Ein militanter Pazifist*, 66–83; *Das unbekannte Werk*, vol. 4, 387–403, 534–35 nn; *Herbstfahrt*, 226–42.

[3] See Sargeant, *Kitsch und Kunst* for an analysis of a range of such works, and also her paper "Memory, Distortion, and the War in German Popular Culture: the Case of Konsalik," in Kidd and Murdoch, *Memory and Memorials*, 195–206. As an example of a possible treatment of the war, see Walter Nutz, "Der Krieg als Abenteuer und Idylle: Landershefte und triviale Kriegsromane," in *Gegenwartsliteratur und Drittes Reich: Deutsche Autoren in der Auseinandersetzung mit der Vergangenheit*, ed. Hans Wagener (Stuttgart: Reclam, 1977), 265–83. Wagener's important collection contains a range of relevant pieces, most notably his own "Soldaten zwischen Gehorsam und Gewissen: Kriegsromane und -Tagebücher," 241–64.

[4] Texts cited are: *Der Funke Leben*, afterword — with quotations from the early hostile reviews — by Tilman Westphalen (Cologne: Kiepenheuer and Witsch, 1998) and *Zeit zu leben und Zeit zu sterben*, afterword by Tilman Westphalen (Cologne: Kiepenheuer and Witsch, 1998). The latter was first published in 1954 in a translation by Denver Lindley as *A Time to Love and a Time to Die* in *Collier's Weekly* as a serial, then in book form (New York: Harcourt, Brace, 1954). Note that the title has "love" rather than "live." *Spark of Life*, translated by James Stern (New York: Appleton-Century-Crofts, 1952) appeared just before the German text of *Der Funke Leben* (Cologne and Berlin: Kiepenheuer and Witsch, 1952) and was a bestseller in the United States in contrast to sales in Germany. Interestingly Remarque seems to have thought of the English title for the book earlier: "Titel für ein Buch: Spark of Life: Der Funke Leben," diary entry for 31 December 1941, in *Das unbekannte Werk*, vol. 5, 357. Unlike *Zeit zu leben und Zeit zu sterben*, filmed by Douglas Sirk for Universal and released in 1958, *Der Funke Leben* has

never been filmed, though a dramatization was mooted at one stage, and contemporary critics said of Remarque's direct and visual style in the work that it had been written with an eye to filming: Harald Keller, "Hollywood und anderswo — Remarque-Adaptation in Film und Fernsehen," in Schwindt und Westphalen, *Man kann alten Dreck nicht vergraben,* 119–36, see 119. Full bibliographies are in Claudia Glunz and Thomas Schneider, *Erich Maria Remarque: Werke der frühen fünfziger Jahre* (Osnabrück: Rasch, 1995). See Heinrich Placke, "Wie zuverlässig ist die KiWi-Taschenbuchausgabe der Remarque-Romane von 1998," *Jahrbuch* 13 (2003): 82–91 with reference to *Der Funke Leben.*

[5] The reference in a diary entry as early as 17 November 1944 to a proposed novel on the theme "Soldat der zurückkommt" (returning soldier) is not especially relevant to the chronology, and *Zeit zu leben und Zeit zu sterben* is a historical piece with a general message (*Das unbekannte Werk,* vol. 5, 388). A scene not unlike the death of Graeber is described in a letter of 5 March 1942 (*Das unbekannte Werk,* vol. 5, 362). However, Remarque clearly researched the novel over a long period. In a diary entry for 18 February 1952 (5, 468) he refers to the *nostra culpa* idea and the problem of collective guilt in general.

[6] See Sternburg, *"Als wäre alles,"* 362–63, on the original publication plans. Rejected — to Remarque's annoyance — by the Swiss publisher who had originally bought the rights for the German edition, it was eventually published by Kiepenheuer and Witsch, with whom Remarque stayed thereafter.

[7] The original version was published in Germany (Cologne and Berlin: Kiepenheuer and Witsch, 1954). On the cuts in the first German edition, see Glunz and Schneider, *Werke der frühen fünfziger Jahre,* 68, and Westphalen's afterword to the new edition. See also R. W. Last, "The 'Castration' of Erich Maria Remarque," *Quinquereme* 2 (1979), 10–22, and Thomas F. Schneider and Angelika Howind, "'Weiterschweigen heisst seine Schuld eingestehen': *Zeit zu leben und Zeit zu sterben*: Die Zensur eines Antikriegsromans in der BRD und ihre Revision," *Krieg und Literatur/War and Literature* 1 (1989): 79–142; Thomas F. Schneider, "'Und Befehl ist Befehl. Oder nicht?' Erich Maria Remarque: *Zeit zu leben und Zeit zu sterben* (1954)" in *Von Böll bis Buchheim: Deutsche Kriegsprosa nach 1945,* ed. Hans Wagener (Amsterdam and Atlanta, GA: Rodopi), 231–47; and also his "'Ein ekler leichenwurm': Motive und Rezeption der Schriften Erich Maria Remarques zur national-sozialistischen deutschen Vergangenheit," *Text+Kritik* 149 (2001): 42–54. There is an excellent brief summary of the far-reaching implications of the changes in Sternburg, *"Als wäre alles,"* 376–77.

[8] *Elfriede Scholz, geb. Remark: Im Namen des deutschen Volkes: Dokumente einer justitiellen Ermordung,* ed. Claudia Glunz and Thomas Schneider (Osnabrück: Rasch, 1997). Remarque's sister was guillotined; he did not know of her death until June 1946.

[9] Repgow, "Wir haben nicht auf Herrn Remarque gewartet," *Sonntagsblatt* (Hannover), Nr 42 (19 October 1952), 9. See on the reception and on Böll's review (the title of which he quotes): Thomas Schneider, "'Heißes Eisen in lauwarmer Hand': Zur Rezeption von E. M. Remarque's *Der Funke Leben,*" *Jahrbuch* 4 (1994): 29–44, and Claudia Glunz, "'Eine harte Sache': Zur Rezeption von Erich Maria Remarques *Der Funke Leben*" in *"Reue ist undeutsch": Erich Maria Remarques Der Funke Leben und das Konzentrationslager Buchenwald,* ed. Thomas F. Schneider and Tilman Westphalen (Bramsche: Rasch, 1992), 21–27.

[10] Thomas Mann, *Deutsche Hörer! Radiosendungen nach Deutschland aus den Jahren 1940–1945* (Frankfurt am Main: Fischer, 1987). The reference to the Goebbels-quotation was in a broadcast of May 1942 (64); the broadcast at the end of the war is on 149–51.

[11] Text published as "Der Funke Leben" (Thomas Schneider's translation), in: *Ein militanter Pazifist*, 94–95. The piece survives in English as "Spark of Life" in a typescript attached to the manuscript of the novel in the Library of Congress, and was presumably written in 1952 or 1953: see Schneider's notes, 150–51. It is cited also in Tilman Westphalen's own slightly different translation in his afterword to the text. There is a copy in the Osnabrück archive. Remarque noted in his diary in New York on 22 April 1948: "Buch von vorne angefangen, wieder mal. Vielleicht besser, in Europa zu arbeiten. Näher" (Started the book from the beginning, yet again. Maybe better to work in Europe. Closer) See also: *Das unbekannte Werk*, vol. 5, 397).

[12] See Schneider, *Remarque*, 101. On the literary use of Jewish suffering, see my essay "Transformations of the Holocaust: Auschwitz in Modern Lyric Poetry," *Comparative Literature Studies* 11 (1974): 123–50; the indictment of Sylvia Plath, for example, for having "no right" to use Auschwitz as an image is also discussed by Janet Malcolm, *The Silent Woman* (London: Macmillan, 1994), 64–65.

[13] Heather Valencia, "The KZ Experience: *Der Funke Leben* in the Light of Recent Works on the Holocaust in Literature," in Murdoch, Ward, Sargeant, *Remarque Against War*, 145–69. She argues that Remarque's novel shares the moral imperative of others in the genre of "the necessity of recording, of making people remember" (168). See on the genre Jan Strümpel, "Kammersymphonie des Todes: Erich Maria Remarques *Der Funke Leben*, Anna Seghers' *Das siebte Kreuz* und eine Gattung namens 'KZ-Roman,'" *Text+Kritik* 149 (2001): 55–64.

[14] See the introduction by Arthur Herzberg to an essay on the holocaust that first appeared in German in 1995: Wolfgang Benz, *The Holocaust*, trans. Jane Sydenham-Kwiet (London: Profile, 2000), vii–x. This edition has the subtitle "A German Historian Examines the Genocide." Of the many large-scale studies of the holocaust, see Martin Gilbert, *The Holocaust: The Jewish Tragedy* (London: Collins, 1986).

[15] Wagener, *Understanding*, 75, considers that the work "contains too many truisms" and that the overall effect is not convincing, a view hard to accept. Antkowiak, *Remarque*, 94–101, praises its sensitivity, however uncomfortable he may have been with its attacks on communism. Critical studies include: Heinrich Placke, "Naturrecht und menschliche Würde: Anmerkungen zum Sinnpotential des Romans *Der Funke Leben*," in Schneider and Westphalen, *Reue ist undeutsch*, 28–40; Thomas Schneider's "Mörder, die empfindlich sind," on the development of the novel in the same volume, 14–20; and Hubert Orlowski, "Stacheldrahtuniversum und Literatur: Zu Remarque und anderen," *Jahrbuch* 4 (1994): 5–28. There is a full discussion in Bernhard Nienaber, *Vom anachronistischen Helden zum larmoyanten Untertan*, 34–101. On the *Historikerstreit*, see *Reworking the Past: Hitler, the Holocaust, and the Historians' Debate*, ed. Peter Baldwin (Boston: Beacon, 1990), and the excellent brief summary by Stefan Berger, "Historians' Debate," in the *Encyclopaedia of German Literature*, ed. Matthias Konzett (Chicago and London: Fitzroy Dearborn, 2000), 1, 469–71.

[16] Primo Levi, *If This Is a Man* and *The Truce*, trans. Stuart Woolf (London: Abacus, 1987); the two connected works were first published in Italian in 1958 and 1963 re-

spectively. Wieslaw Kielar, *Anus Mundi: Five Years in Auschwitz,* trans. Susanne Flatauer (Harmondsworth: Penguin, 1982); first published in Polish in 1972, the English translation is of the 1979 German edition. Tadeusz Borowski, *This Way for the Gas, Ladies and Gentlemen,* selected and trans. Barbara Vedder (Harmondsworth: Penguin, 1976); these stories appeared in Polish in 1959, eight years after his suicide. He escaped the gas chambers in Auschwitz because he was not Jewish. Valencia, "KZ Experience" discusses this work. As a single illustration, these works confirm the use of the term "Mussulman" in the camps, for example. On the literature of the holocaust see Lawrence Langer, *The Holocaust and the Literary Imagination* (New Haven and London: Yale UP, 1976) and Susan Cernyak-Spatz, *German Holocaust Literature* (New York: Peter Lang, 1985). For other novels, see especially Bruno Apitz, *Nackt unter Wölfen* (Naked Among Wolves) (Cologne: Röerberg, 1958) and the paper linking it with Remarque under the heading "Buchenwald-Bücher" by Walfried Hartinger, "Bruno Apitz, *Nackt unter Wölfen:* Zur zeitgeschichtlichen Relevanz und langdauernden Wirkung des Romans," *Jahrbuch* 5 (1995): 5–18.

[17] See the *Reue ist undeutsch* volume for parallels. Gilbert, *Holocaust,* cites on 62 the song composed in Buchenwald by the Jewish librettist Fritz Beda with the ending "Whatever our fate/We still say 'yes' to life." Many other characters in Remarque's writings, including the play *Die letzte Station,* are portrayed as having had experiences in the camps, from Ravic in *Arc de Triomphe* to Clerfayt in *Der Himmel kennt keine Günstlinge.*

[18] This is noted by Gordon, *Heroism and Friendship,* 79, comparing the relationship with that of Ernst and Elisabeth in *Zeit zu leben und Zeit zu sterben.* A closer relationship may of course be imagined later, after the novel has ended.

[19] The (now rare) sixteen-page pamphlet is dated 24 April 1945: Victor Gollancz, *What Buchenwald Really Means* (London: Gollancz, 1945). The eminent Jewish publisher Sir Victor Gollancz (1893–1967), who founded the Left Book Club in the 1930s, was known for his anti-fascist views and also for his support for the starving in Germany after 1945. His essay has a great deal to do with national responsibility on all sides. It provoked a response by letter from the philosopher Ludwig Wittgenstein (texts and that of the pamphlet are available online in the 1995 *Wittgenstein Studies* from the University of Passau), and there were printed responses: Franz Burger, *Gollancz's Buchenwald Never Existed* (London: Hutchinson, 1945). There is much of relevance in the pamphlet, however, as also in Gollancz's letter to the London *News Chronicle* on 27 August 1945. See Ruth Dudley Edwards, *Victor Gollancz* (London: Gollancz, 1987). It has been pointed out that the earliest victims of the gas chambers were actually ethnic Germans, who had been certified as insane and were therefore classified — as were later on Jews, Gypsies, some Slavs, and others — as inferior beings (*Untermenschen*): Ernest Mandel, *The Meaning of the Second World War* (London: Verso, 1986), 91.

[20] Barker and Last, *Remarque,* 136–40, offer a detailed analysis of this figure, as does Valencia "KZ Experience," who stresses his sentimentality as well as his capacity for self-delusion.

[21] The black-and-white news footage of, say, the liberation of Belsen leaves an indelible visual impression, but black-and-white film also now inevitably betokens historicity. The timelessness of a novel, and the ability to suggest smells and sounds as well, can be effective. It is appropriate to mention, too, the paintings of human skeletons by Felix Nussbaum, born in Osnabrück not long after Remarque, and killed in Auschwitz in

1944: see the catalogue edited by Eva Berger and others, *Felix Nussbaum: Verfemte Kunst — Exilkunst-Widerstandskunst*, 3d ed. (Bramsche: Rassch, 1995), esp. "Die Ver dammten" (The Damned, 1944), 426–51.

[22] See Sternburg, *"Als wäre alles,"* 361, on the novel as dealing with contemporary issues (*Gegenwartsroman*). During the cold war, the authorities in the then German Democratic Republic made much of the holding of political positions by former Nazis. One case in point was Hans Globke (1898–73), who had been much involved with Hitler's race laws but who served nevertheless in the postwar West German government. The GDR issued in 1963 a *Steckbrief,* a wanted notice, with "then and now" photographs of him, and tried him *in absentia* for genocide. See Robert Wistrich, *Who's Who in Nazi Germany* (London: Weidenfeld and Nicolson, 1982), 93–94. On the other side of the coin, the return of totalitarian politicians under another banner is a well-documented phenomenon, especially after the collapse of communism. Antkowiak, *Remarque,* 100–101 is predictably concerned about the attacks in *Der Funke Leben* on communism, but his comments on Remarque's "unwillingness to align himself with the forces of progress in history" now have an irony all of their own.

[23] Sternburg, *"Als wäre alles,"* 362, sees this as the start of ongoing disillusionment with the new postwar world. But it is at least ambiguous: the allusion to Genesis and the return to human beings (*Menschen*) after all the lack of *Menschlichkeit* can only be positive.

[24] See on this aspect especially Nienaber, *Vom anachronistischen Helden zum larmoyanten Untertan,* and Placke, *Die Chiffren des Utopischen.* In the important diary entry of 18 February 1952 referred to already, which is concerned largely with the question of *Allgemeinschuld* (general guilt, even existential guilt), which also notes that there have been concentration camps in plenty of other countries, Remarque refers to communism not as a political system but as a religion, with all the dreadful fanatical power of all religions: *Das unbekannte Werk,* vol. 5, 468.

[25] See also Remarque's play, *Die letzte Station* (The Last Stopping Place, 1956; in English as *Full Circle,* 1973) and the film script written for G. W. Pabst's film *Der letzte Akt* (*The Last Act,* 1954; also filmed as *Ten Days to Die,* 1955), both set in April–May 1945. They were both first published in *Das unbekannte Werk,* vol. 3, 153–257 and 11–151 (see the notes for the somewhat convoluted textual details of both). Both develop the idea of responsibility and the question of hiding behind the concept of obeying orders. *Der letzte Akt* takes the problem into the highest circle of the Nazi leaders in the Hitler bunker at the end of the war; *Die letzte Station* is set in May 1945.

[26] Wagener, *Understanding,* places the opening in 1943, just after Stalingrad, but this seems unlikely. The German retreat took a long time. When Graeber returns to the front at the end of the book, we hear how young recruits are now being sent out, the sustained bombing of Germany points also to 1944, and there are references to the Nazis having one more year in power.

[27] Wagener's criticism of *Zeit zu leben und Zeit zu sterben* that the characters are stereotypes when he sets Steinbrenner against Graeber is not really tenable. Steinbrenner may be a stereotype (and stereotypes do exist), but the real balance is between Graeber and Binding, a far more important picture of a Nazi; Wagener, "Soldaten zwischen Gehorsam und Gewissen," 246–47.

[28] Wagener, *Understanding*, 74, applies Hannah Arendt's phrase (originally used of Adolf Eichmann) to Neubauer in *Der Funke Leben*, as have other critics, though it is even more appropriate for Binding. In the opening stage directions to *Die Letzte Station*, Remarque notes that the three SS figures are also not to be shown as obvious types: one of them might, he tells us, in other times have been a bank clerk, another is "gedankenlos, kräftig und grob" (thoughtless, strong, and coarse), and the third has grown up under the Nazis, knows nothing else, and in other times would have been an enthusiastic member of the *Wandervögel* youth movement; *Das unbekannte Werk*, vol. 3, 157–58. Frank Pierson's 2001 film *Conspiracy*, about the Wannsee Conference where Hitler's "final solution" was agreed, illustrates particularly well the aspect of banality. One might consider in this context Christopher R. Browning, *Ordinary Men: Reserve Police Battalion 101 and the Final Solution* (New York: Harper-Collins, 1992) and the controversial work by Daniel Jonah Goldhagen, *Hitler's Willing Executioners: Ordinary Germans and the Holocaust* (London: Little, Brown, and Company, 1996). An appropriate literary parallel might be Arnold Zweig's novel *Das Beil von Wandsbek* (Stockholm: Neuer Verlag, 1948), trans. Eric Sutton as *The Axe of Wandsbek* (London: Hutchinson, 1948) in which a butcher acts as an executioner to earn money.

[29] Most critics note the centrality of this scene. Remarque himself made some interesting comments on the film in "Das Auge ist ein starker Verführer" (surviving in English as "The Eye is a Strong Seducer," 1957), trans. by Thomas F. Schneider in *Ein militanter Pazifist*, 102–5; *Das unbekannte Werk*, vol. 4, 410–14; *Herbstfahrt*, 249–53. See Schneider, *Remarque*, 119, for the powerful still from the film with Remarque as Pohlmann and John Gavin as Graeber.

[30] Both writers are discussed in this context by Sargeant, *Kitsch und Kunst*, 141–70 and 103–40.

[31] Wolfgang Borchert, *Draussen vor der Tür* (1946), in *Das Gesamtwerk* (Hamburg: Rowohlt, 1949), 99–165, see 164–65. Beckmann goes to a series of people for answers, and each time is disappointed and left standing outside — hence the title. He is always thrust back upon himself, and even attempts suicide, though it is made clear to him that this, too, is no answer.

[32] See his piece "Seid wachsam! Zum Film *Der letzte Akt*." The article, written in 1956, appeared first in English translation in the London *Daily Express* on 20 April 1956. The German text from the typescript is in *Ein militanter Pazifist*, 96–101; *Das unbekannte Werk*, vol. 4, 404–9; *Herbstfahrt*, 243–48. See also Remarque's 1961 unpublished review of a book by a friend, Robert M. W. Kempner, *Über Eichmann und Komplicen*, on the ordinariness of those who simply accepted the way things were: *Ein militanter Pazifist*, 107–9, *Das unbekannte Werk*, vol. 4, 415–17 and notes 538–39. The lawyer Kempner attempted without success to reopen the case against the denouncer of Remarque's sister Elfriede.

[33] Wagener, *Understanding*, 80, draws attention to the tree. Some of the discussion with Pohlmann was cut in the censored version. See Remarque's own comments in his diary entry for 27 March 1954, *Das unbekannte Werk*, vol. 5, 495.

[34] Johannes Mario Simmel's comedy *Der Schulfreund* (*The School Friend*, 1959), filmed as *Mein Schulfreund*, plays not only with the idea of being able to speak the truth only when declared insane, but of using school acquaintanceship with a Nazi (this time Hermann Goering). In the last analysis, however the central figure realizes the truth of

the saying: "Wer mit dem Teufel essen will, der muss einen langen Löffel haben!: Aber das stimmt nicht! Einen *so* langen Löffel gibt es überhaupt nicht" (Whoever sups with the devil needs a long spoon. But that isn't true. There is no spoon *that* long!): *Der Schulfreund* (Reinbek bei Hamburg: Rowohlt, 1964), 126. See my "*Bewältigung der Vergangenheit* and Catch-22: Johannes Mario Simmel's *Schulfreund*," *Modern Languages* 69 (1988), 124–9. The idea of the SS having access to excellent food even as late as May 1945 is used at the start of *Der letzte Akt, Das unbekannte Werk,* vol. 3, 18.

[35] The description of Freisler (1893–1945) is from Wistrich, *Who's Who in Nazi Germany,* 80–81. Freisler was killed by an allied bomb in February 1945. In a diary entry for 22 March 1952 Remarque noted that nearly ten thousand people were executed for listening to overseas radio broadcasts: *Das unbekannte Werk,* vol. 5, 469. Pohlmann says to Graeber that he could be excuted for asking the sort of questions he is asking, however, Graber replies: "Man wird für nichts an der Front getötet" (18, you can be killed at the front for nothing).

[36] Antkowiak, Barker, and Last, and other critics do not mention Binding, and Wagener refers to him simply as "somewhat problematic," *Understanding,* 80. Sargeant, *Kitsch und Kunst,* 100, notes his ambiguity but considers that it is not carried through sufficiently well. She develops his role more in her paper "A Lost War," in Murdoch, Ward, Sargeant, *Remarque Against War,* 119–44.

[37] Last and Barker, *Remarque,* 133 (followed by Wagener, *Understanding,* 80) associate the scene with the poetic realism of the nineteenth century, specifically with Gottfried Keller's *Romeo und Julia auf dem Dorfe* (*A Village Romeo and Juliet*). Remarque is fond of this kind of set-piece idyll, though they are often interrupted by air raids. There may even be a connection between Elisabeth, who is first seen in the novel surrounded by light, 111, and the pregnancy of Elizabeth, the future mother of John the Baptist.

[38] There is a parallel incident in Alfred Andersch's *Sansibar, oder der letzte Grund* (1957; *Zanzibar*) when the Pastor, Helander, makes a single resistance by shooting a Nazi soldier before he is gunned down by others.

[39] Last, "Castration," 16–17, and Tims, *Remarque,* 175, both comment on the significance of the omitted passage.

[40] See Antkowiak, *Remarque,* 117, on the changes from Immermann as communist to social democrat in the censored version, and Sargeant, *Kitsch,* 82. The general question was dealt with more fully in *Der Funke Leben,* of course.

[41] Hans Wagener, "Erich Maria Remarque, *Im Westen nichts Neues — Zeit zu leben und Zeit zu sterben:* Ein Autor, zwei Weltkriege," *Jahrbuch* 10 (2000): 31–52. On the work as reflecting especially the problems within the new *Bundesrepublik* in the context of the cold war, see Bern(har)d Nienaber, "Der Blick zurück: Remarques Romane gegen die Adenauer-Restauration," in *Erich Maria Remarque 1898–1970,* ed. Tilman Westphalen (Bramsche: Rasch, 1988), 79–93; "Remarque gegen die Restauration: der Russlandkriegsroman *Zeit zu leben und Zeit zu sterben* (1954)," *Krieg und Literatur/ War and Literature* 1 (1989): 53–8 (with an interesting designation of the novel in his title); and *Vom anachronistischen Helden zum larmoyanten Untertan,* especially 102– 64. There is a great deal of important material in the last-named extensive and also stylistic analysis, although some of the parallels discerned with Adenauer's Germany are less convincing. He is of course, concerned with the version of the text that was available

in the period of which he is writing. The restitution of the original version at about the time the Berlin Wall fell is an interesting irony.

[42] See again Placke, *Chiffren des Utopischen,* on the nature of the discourse, with reference to the two Second World War novels and also *Der schwarze Obelisk.*

[43] See Nienaber, *Humanismusrezeption,* 117–24.

Title page of serialization of
Station am Horizont in *Sport im Bild*

English edition of
Der Himmel kennt keine Günstlinge

7: The Lap of the Gods: From *Station am Horizont* to *Der Himmel kennt keine Günstlinge*

REMARQUE'S OCCASIONAL DISMISSAL as a trivial writer presumably rests upon the fact that some of his novels have seemed insignificant in terms of content. For most of his works this criticism clearly does not apply: their subjects are the defining political themes of twentieth-century history — war, refugees, the struggle for survival in situations of hardship. On the human level, however, there are overarching themes that link all of his novels, whether their setting is expressly political or not. Probably the most significant is that used by Remarque as a title for his concentration camp novel: *Der Funke Leben,* the spark of life. That vital impulse is attested to by most of Remarque's characters, even in the earliest stages of his writing. The simple, but not simplistic, existentialist philosophy that we should cling to life because it is all we have in the face of the inevitability of death functions as a base line in virtually all of his novels, and as the death of Bäumer makes clear, the urge to cling to that spark of life overrides even the personality of the individual. The philosophy carries with it the permanent awareness of death and separation as the other aspect of the human condition, thrown into sharper relief by anything that brings death noticeably closer, be it war, illness, or exposure to dangers of some other sort. The popularity of existentialism in much of the twentieth century has been well documented — the awareness, that is, that one's individual and finite existence is all that one can be sure of — and it can be heightened in what Karl Jaspers called *Grenzsituationen* (situations on the edge). It is an isolating philosophy, even or especially for the closest of lovers. The response to death is a separate matter; existentialism might or might not have a transcendental or religious dimension, although more typically it is at least agnostic. The imperative that one has to nurture the spark of life can on occasion, but only on occasion, seem in Remarque's novels to be given some kind of transcendental support.

One possible reaction to the situation, however, is that summed up by the tag *carpe diem,* seize the moment, live life while one can. To follow that injunction — summed up in an even more worldly form as that to eat, drink, and be merry, for tomorrow we die — requires conditions where it is at least possible to eat, drink, and be merry, and it is not hard to picture circumstances where even the grasping of a small measure of happiness is quite impossible. Remarque's principal characters almost invariably manage to snatch some delight, even if this throws into relief the inevitability of death. The role of chance in Remarque's works is of concomitant importance: given that there are only rare hints of any transcendental moments, chance, *Zufall,* is all that can be perceived as the driving force of life. It is also associated more strongly with the pagan or classical tradition — with the gods — more than with Christianity, and shifts of focus occur in Remarque's writings between the two theogonies. The power of *Zufall* (or the ineffability of a divine plan) is underlined in the title of the principal subject of this final chapter, *Der Himmel kennt keine Günstlinge:* heaven has no favorites, anything, good or bad, can happen to anyone, and in any case death will happen to everyone, even if they seem to be loved by the gods. The philosophy of a life based upon personal decisions by the isolated individual might be summed up in the words of Oscar Wilde, who noted in 1891 in his essay "The Soul of Man Under Socialism" the shift from the older injunction to "know thyself" to that of "be thyself."[1] They are not, of course, mutually exclusive. Remarque uses these themes throughout his works, and *Der Himmel kennt keine Günstlinge* might serve as a summary of Remarque's work as a whole.

Der Himmel kennt keine Günstlinge is a novel with an extensive and involved ancestry, and it is perhaps partly because of that ancestry that this novel has been dismissed as trivial or merely popular. *Der Spiegel* referred to it, for example, in 1993 as a "hemmungslos mißglückter Kolportageroman . . . (draufgängerische Autorennfahrer liebt Schwindsüchtige)" (unrestrainedly failed trashy novel . . . [reckless racing driver loves consumptive girl]).[2] Such a judgment is misplaced. The novel may, it is true, be linked in thematic terms with several other earlier works of various sorts, and their examination may demonstrate a process in which Remarque worked towards a culmination in his combination of themes, but the novel itself is an independent and quite separate entity. The 1977 English paperback edition of Richard and Clara Winston's translation carries on its inappropriately kitschy cover, a heart-shaped wreath inscribed "In Loving Memory," the familiar rider to Remarque's name: "Author of *All Quiet on the Western Front,*" but despite the thematic and stylistic differences, and as important as it is to refute the idea of Remarque as a one-novel author, the reminder is appropriate in this case. The two works have closely and patently deliberate parallel endings showing the death of an individual observed by an outsider, and both assert the insistence upon life in the face of inevitable but random death.

Of the two full-scale novels that belong in this loose complex, the earliest, *Station am Horizont* (Stopping Place on the Horizon), is, on the surface, a novel about motor racing, which first (and in Remarque's lifetime only) appeared in serial form *Sport im Bild* in 1927–28, a magazine with a largely male readership, while the much later *Der Himmel kennt keine Günstlinge* was in its serialized publication, which also had a different main title, first subtitled "Geschichte einer Liebe," translatable as "a love story," but more accurately, "the story of a love." That serialization appeared in 1959 in the magazine *Kristall* in German, and in *Good Housekeeping* in English, both female-orientated publications. Nevertheless, the early novel is by no means only about fast cars, and the later one is a book about death just as much as about love.[3]

Various other writings are linked thematically with the two novels. A short story, *Das Rennen Vanderveldes* (Vandervelde's Race) matches an incident in *Station am Horizont* closely, and had appeared in *Sport im Bild* in 1924 and in the *Deutsche Motorsport-Zeitung* later in the same year. Remarque wrote other short pieces involving sports cars, and in his major novels the juxtaposition of motor racing with that of sickness as part of a love story is present in *Drei Kameraden*. Far closer to *Der Himmel kennt keine Günstlinge* is the 1947 film *The Other Love*, based on a brief prose piece with the same title that Remarque never published and which exists only in a typescript in English written some time between 1940 and 1946. All these works merit some independent attention, although the charge of triviality is easier to level at the earlier pieces, which were written either for a sport-orientated magazine or for Hollywood. They can, however, help address criticisms of the 1961 novel, including the question of whether or not it falls entirely outside Remarque's role as a chronicler of the twentieth century.[4] Remarque expressed in several places a desire to move away from historical themes to something completely different, but while *Der Himmel kennt keine Günstlinge* is set neither against a background of war, nor of political upheaval or oppression, the Second World War is never far away.[5] *Der Himmel kennt keine Günstlinge* is, incidentally, the only one of Remarque's novels to be set in a postwar world — the later 1940s — even though some critics seem to think that it belongs nevertheless to the time before the Second World War.[6] It is true that it was not well reviewed, especially in Europe, although recent American criticism in particular has taken the work seriously. But whether this is Remarque's weakest book, as critics (and once apparently Remarque) have claimed, is questionable.[7]

Station am Horizont

The earliest piece by Remarque to have any direct links with the novels, the 1924 short story *Das Rennen Vanderveldes,* can be summarized briefly. Vandervelde, a racing driver, is seen with a woman named Lilian Dunquerke (the name remains, although the spelling goes through a series of permutations over the years), and an observer expresses surprise that she has been with one man for such a long time, because she is "die unbekümmertste und schönste Abenteuerin des Kontinents" (48, the most free-spirited and most beautiful adventuress of the continent). The story explains how this liaison came about: Vandervelde had his dog with him in his car during a race, a fire had threatened to hurt the dog, and he had stopped just before the finish line to look after the animal, throwing away a race that was nearly his. This incident effectively wins the affections of Lilian. It is interesting that the narrator comments at the end that he does not know whether it was a genuine impulse on Vandervelde's part, or a clever trick.

Das Rennen Vanderveldes is not intended to be more than a brief entertainment, although the narrator's comment is nicely ambiguous. The incident is, however, reused with a variation in *Station am Horizont*. Although largely concerned with motor racing, *Station am Horizont* is closer to the only slightly earlier *Gam* in that it explores the relationship of the main character, Kai, another racing driver, with three different women, although there is less in the way of overt sexuality than in either *Gam* or the 1961 novel. Alfred Antkowiak, writing in 1965 in the former German Democratic Republic dismisses it fairly predictably, but in a memorably damning phrase, as the *Credo eines Snob* (creed of a snob). He justifies his criticism on the grounds that for the wealthy but shallow characters around whom the action revolves, motor racing is a substitute for depth, and that only occasionally do they condescend (he uses the verb *sich herablassen*) to chat about philosophy. More recently Sternburg has supported some aspects of Antkowiak's judgment of the novel as undemanding *Trivialliteratur,* while noting that Remarque had developed away from the manifestly overblown style of *Die Traumbude*.[8]

Station am Horizont was not published as a book until 1998, and there are (unusually) no translations. Remarque seems not to have been much interested in the text in later life, and it was implicitly rejected together with his other early works when he described *Im Westen nichts Neues* as his first novel. In *Station am Horizont* the rich landowner Kai (we do not learn his other name) is characterized by a kind of permanent restlessness, forever aware "daß Minuten und Sekunden seines Lebens ohne Wiederkehr versanken" (8, that minutes and seconds of his life were disappearing and would not come back), although it is never made clear why. The period in which the work is set is imprecise, but the single image of a racing car sounding like a shell places it after the First World War, and from Kai's age we might guess that his restlessness may derive from it, but there is no real indication of this, so that his attitude comes across simply as a Romantic malaise. His restlessness causes him at the start of the novel to drive off more or less on a whim, leaving behind him the security offered by the first of the women with whom he is juxtaposed, the young, dependable (and not fully drawn) Barbara. He discusses in several somewhat forced discussions with an elderly Italian noblewoman later on his permanent pursuit of something indefinable — the *Station am Horizont* — and she criticizes his attempts to envisage the future as a goal, offering instead a simpler *que sera, sera* philosophy, urging him to live for the moment.

Kai drives south in his sports car to the Riviera, where much of the novel is set, and enters the world of the wealthy, whose interests are principally the casino; this underlines the exotic and wealthy milieu, but also permits the author to develop the ideas of random chance that recur as an image in several of his later novels right down to *Der Himmel kennt keine Günstlinge*. Kai becomes involved, after a chance encounter with an old friend, Liéven, with testing a new type of racing car, initially only as an observer. More chance in the form of a minor motor accident also permits him to meet the second of the women in the novel, the American Maud Philby. When Liéven's driver Hollstein (variations of whose name will be used again) is injured, Kai takes over, so that yet again it is chance, *Zufall,* that makes him into a racing driver. The nature of motor racing itself as something that faces the driver with the chance of life or death is not yet fully developed, and Kai is an amateur, not a professional driver.

Racing brings him into contact with another driver, the American Murphy, who will be a rival for Maud Philby's affections. Although the novel centers upon Kai and his thoughts, the third-person narrator frequently indulges in a fairly simple psychological analysis of the relationship between the three: "Murphy verriet seine Enttäuschung nicht . . . Kai wollte nicht durch eine neue abwegige Antwort den Eindruck erwecken . . . Maud Philby hingegen begriff . . ." (50, Murphy did not reveal his disappointment . . . Kai did not want to create the impression, with another dismissive answer . . . Maud Philby, however, grasped . . .). The triangular relationship is the principal love interest of the story, and the conflict between the two men for the woman, in which she herself is by no means a passive object, is complemented by and directly linked with the competitive nature of the motor race. The relatively thin plot revolves around what is even described as a duel between Murphy and Kai both for the race and for Maud Philby. There are lengthy passages invoking the tension of the motor race itself, often a little technical, and clearly intended for the more specialized readers of *Sport im Bild,* and an incident in which Kai throws a race to save in this case two dogs reuses the Vandervelde story. This time, however, it is the introspective Kai who is unable to explain to himself why he indulged in what he knows to have been a grand gesture. A third woman now comes into his life, also taken, apparently, from the earlier short story, the adventuress Lilian Dunquerke. After a somewhat implausible scene that almost involves a real duel with Lilian's younger suitor, Kai embarks on an affair with Lilian, but this comes to an end, and at the last his interests settle upon Maud Philby, described as the middle way between the adventuress Lilian and the young Barbara, who is something of the conventional girl next door. Kai wins the race and relinquishes Barbara almost formally to the younger driver Hollstein, feeling that he is making a genuine sacrifice in doing so.

The novel is not an especially satisfactory one, although the general milieu, the motor racing details, and the tension not only in the races but in the narrowly averted duel were plainly what were demanded by readers of *Sport im Bild* towards the end of the 1920s. To refer to it, however, as expressing the creed of a snob, goes too far. The novel aims at more than that, and if it does not succeed, then it is because Remarque himself was on the one hand still being experimental in what he wanted to write, and on the other concerned to provide the kind of work for which he was being paid. In parallel with *Gam,* it sets up three women not just as personality types, but as markers for Kai's attempts at finding a path through life, and this is why the novel does not really work any more than on the superficial level. Barbara and Lilian are extremes, Maud too obviously the middle ground — though she is not without personality. Kai has to go through his experiences to learn this, so that the work is still an *Entwicklungsroman,* a novel of development. Whether, on the other hand, Kai has reached or ever will reach the *Station am Horizont,* the nebulous stopping point on the horizon at which he has been aiming, is unclear. The word *Station* is difficult to translate, but it does convey the sense of a stage, which will be followed perhaps by another one. As other characters in Remarque's novels will learn, he has to continue to move forward: "Zurückkommen war nicht Heimkehr — Kai wußte es jetzt" (214, going back was not the same as going home — Kai had learned that). But he is no longer entirely the Romantic superfluous man that he felt himself to be. As a literary character, too, Kai, still has a long way to go before he develops into the professional racing driver Clerfayt in *Der Himmel kennt keine Günstlinge,* and by the time of that novel, Lilian Dunquerke will have changed beyond recognition, and only a version of her name will survive.

The Other Love

The ninth edition of *Halliwell's Film Guide* describes the 1947 film *The Other Love* as a "fairly icky 'woman's picture' with uncomfortable performances" from the principals, David Niven, Barbara Stanwyck, and Richard Conte.[9] That pungently expressed judgment is not completely fair, although the film is overly sentimentalized and the acting is wooden. Of course, like many black-and-white films made soon after the Second World War, *The Other Love* causes problems of reception for audiences accustomed both to more realistic cinematic techniques, for example, a scene in a speedboat is glaringly artificial and occasionally the music continues after Stanwyck has stopped playing the piano, and to different modes of speech, like Niven's clipped tones, perhaps. It does, however, contain a number of elements that recall details from *Station am Horizont* and, more frequently, anticipate *Der Himmel kennt keine Günstlinge,* although it remains very much a Hollywood film of its time. The poster and the opening credits of the film itself gave Remarque full billing — "Erich Maria Remarque's *THE OTHER LOVE*," and claimed that the screenplay by Ladislas Fodor and Harry Brown was adapted from a short story called "Beyond." Thomas Schneider has made clear in a detailed discussion of later legal arguments about Remarque's copyright and royalties for the film, that the short story never actually existed, but has also retranslated and published as *Die andere Liebe* the English "treatment" or film synopsis from Remarque's archive. There are considerable differences between this and the final screenplay for *The Other Love*.

In a diary entry in 1940 Remarque referred to a story involving a sanatorium and the "sports car of Kai" — the central character of the early novel — and originally it seems to have been intended as a film vehicle for Marlene Dietrich. By the time *The Other Love* was made, Remarque was attempting to distance himself from it, claiming that the story was Fodor's and no longer his. If indeed the prose treatment was the intended basis for the film, then that is certainly true. However, as Schneider rightly points out, both treatment and film may nevertheless be situated in the line of development that runs from *Das Rennen Vanderveldes* to *Der Himmel kennt keine Günstlinge,* most notably in the handling of the theme of death, which is now introduced. The film *The Other Love,* which was not shown in Germany until a television broadcast in July 1988, has, despite all the caveats on authorship, a somewhat different status from the films made of the major novels.[10]

In the prose treatment, the amateur racing driver Kai of the early novel has become a professional, Key Stanton (the surname would be reassigned in the film). He is visiting his co-driver, who is being treated for tuberculosis in a Swiss sanatorium, when he encounters another patient, Lillian Dunquerque, both parts of whose name have acquired a new spelling, and her companion, a Russian called Vladimir Orloff (one of the recurrent names used by Remarque), his car nearly causing an accident with their sleigh. The treatment refers to the "mysteriöse und morbide Charme dieser Krankheit" (133, the mysterious and morbid charm of this disease), and it is one of the recurrent themes of the whole complex, found also in the émigré novels, that the patients look well, but are deceptively close to death. The racing driver allows his colleague to drive his car, and when Lillian reproves him because it could be dangerous, he insists that it is actually therapeutic, and then voices the cliché that it is better to live for a month like a god than twenty years like a petit-bourgeois. This thought prompts Lillian to leave the sanatorium to set off on what she thinks of as an adventure. Remarque notes — we may recall that this not a finished literary piece — that Orloff assumes Lillian to be in love with Stanton. In any event, she leaves with him and immerses herself in what she sees as life, "eine tobende Existenz" (141, a wild existence), but realizes eventually that the philosophy he has offered her is too simple. She observes other people, wondering that they remain apparently unaware of the permanent *memento mori* that stands behind everyone. At a casino Lillian is reminded of Orloff, and Remarque calls for "eine spannungs-geladene Eifersuchtsszene" (143, a tension-filled jealousy scene), reminding us that this is still conceived as a cinematic love story. Sorry for Stanton, who does not really understand how ill she is, she agrees to his plans for the future; Stanton is killed in a crash while racing, and Lillian now returns to the sanatorium. Remarque notes how "die Nähe des Todes dort oben gibt dem Leben Kraft, Größe und Schönheit; gibt ihm Heroismus, Tragik und Sieg" (147, the proximity of death up in the mountains gives life strength, great-ness, and beauty, gives it heroism, tragedy, and victory). Lillian is reconciled to her fate and understands that she loves Orloff, and her repeated last words are "Ich bin glücklich" (I am happy). Lillian, who is clearly the central fig-ure, grasps that Stanton's view that a short but exciting life is better than a longer dull one is too facile, and her search for life with him was not the an-swer. Her final resignation recalls Bäumer's "Ich bin sehr ruhig" (I am very calm) at the end of *Im Westen nichts Neues*. The love story element is strong here, but the last line shows us Orloff speaking in vain to Lillian, who has died. It is as if Remarque was still trying to write a more or less straightfor-ward love story, but a more serious point was coming through nevertheless. The sketch, however is significantly closer to *Der Himmel kennt keine Günst-linge* than it is to the film *The Other Love,* which as a different medium and for a different audience plays up precisely and predictably that love story element, and in doing so loses a number of more serious points.

The love triangle in the film is between the principal female character, now a celebrated concert pianist, a new role not found in any of Remarque's written versions, called Karen Duncan (Stanwyck) — the name is perhaps an anglicized Dunkerque —, the sanatorium doctor, Anthony Stanton (Niven), and the racing driver Paul Clermont (Conte). Karen Duncan is attracted to the doctor, but is herself unaware of how ill she actually is. The arrival of Clermont involves once more the near-accident, but a major difference is that he does not know that she is from the sanatorium or indeed that she is ill. Again he suggests that she go away with him, and she is spurred into do-ing so when she discovers that a friend who was about to leave the sanato-rium has died. This turns her against Stanton, whom she accuses of lying to the patients, and she is herself now determined to seize hold of life, impa-tient at the doctor's regime. One of the flaws of the film is that her thought processes at this point and others have to be expressed without dialogue in close-up shots. She leaves with Clermont, who is little more than a playboy, into a world of parties, casinos, yachts, and dance music. There is a deliber-ate contrast with the latter and the music that we have heard her play several times; at one point Karen Duncan listens to a recording of herself and tries to play the piano, but cannot. In frustration she smashes the record, and the scene cuts immediately to a dance band playing in the village hotel where she will meet Clermont. She conceals her illness, and the extended casino scenes are an obvious image of gambling with death. The doctor comes to find her and reveals to Clermont how ill she is, but apparently relinquishing her to him. The shallow playboy now realizes that he is genuinely in love with her and plans to take her somewhere where the climate will help her. That night, however, she slips away and returns to the sanatorium, using a ring to persuade someone to help her. Clermont follows her and refuses to believe that she is dying until Stanton shows him her room, in which she is lying in an oxygen tent. Clermont leaves, taking with him an antique pillbox once given to her by the doctor and which she, the doctor admits, will no longer need. The balance of these two possessions, the ring and the pillbox, has the feel of Remarque's writing, as have other similar motifs, such as that of the white orchids sent to her by mistake and intended for a woman who has died, an incident used in a different way in *Der Himmel kennt keine Günstlinge*. Many other smaller details point to that novel or hark back to the sanatorium scenes at the end of *Drei Kameraden,* such as the death of apparently improving patients, the freedom of the ride in a car, sneaking out of the sanatorium to a ball, even a Russian count.

The ending of the film is more fully in the tradition of Hollywood sentimentality, however, than that of Remarque's writing, and the conventions are already clear in the love interest provided by the handsome doctor rather than by a vaguely drawn Russian. Karen Duncan now admits that her life really lay with the doctor. They marry at once, but since this is Hollywood in the late 1940s, and sex and death were discouraged on screen, she does not die until, we presume, after the credits. The relationship with Clermont is never visibly sexual, and of course, he survives.[11] The motor racing element this time is pushed into the background, although sometimes the dialogue alludes to it, and it remains a story about love and death, cast however within a genre with rigid conventions, and thus without many visible manifestations of either. The overall effect is somewhat awkward, as if a plot with serious points, such as the deceptive nature of disease and the need for a single human being to come to terms with things alone, has been forced into the straightjacket of the love triangle that the title implies. There is an irony in the billing of the film as based on a presumably nonexistent story called "Beyond," a story of which we have, therefore, only a title. Presumably it would have been called *Jenseits,* which can mean "on the other side," "not in this world."

Der Himmel kennt keine Günstlinge

The history of the genesis of *Der Himmel kennt keine Günstlinge* provided by Werner Fuld is instructive in illustrating an attitude towards the contextualization of the novel. At the end of the 1950s the magazine *Kristall,* published by the Axel Springer House in Hamburg, was losing circulation and wanted a serialized novel from a prominent writer. Fuld cites Johannes Mario Simmel as having turned down the commission and having recommended Remarque, who then reportedly demanded and received a large fee. The novel was produced in a relatively short time and marketed as a "new Remarque," and the author was cited in the publicity as having claimed that it would be "eines meiner Hauptwerke" (one of my major works), an interesting contrast with the diary comment in which he seems to have said the opposite. Fuld considers that the novel was initially poorly received because it was assumed that it had been written to be filmed, something that was critically suspect at the time. But he considers, too, that Remarque simply went back to old material, most notably the prose text "*The Other Love*," and cobbled something together in a short time. "Aus diesen Restbeständen und Altlasten schmiedete der Routinier Remarque 1959 seinen Roman . . . zusammen" (from these remnants and leftovers the hack Remarque put his novel together in 1959). Fuld concludes that Remarque himself, had he lived to see the ongoing success of the novel, would have been amused.[12] A proper comparison of the various earlier stages with the final version, and an analysis of that novel itself, however, make it clear that *Der Himmel kennt keine Günstlinge* in fact is a new novel, albeit one in which some of the themes have something of an ancestry. It is, in fact, perfectly possible to see it as having taken not a short time to produce, but a long time, more than thirty years, with the commission from *Kristall* serving as a final catalyst. It is even possible to turn Werner Fuld's irony back on itself. He considers the critics right to have dismissed the book, but feels that they did so for the wrong reason, not having recognized it as recycled material. The real irony, though, is that the critics genuinely were wrong. The novel deserved success in literary terms.

After the shorter and slightly different magazine serialization of *Geborgtes Leben* (Borrowed Life) in *Kristall* in 1959 (which also appeared in book form in translation in Russian), the final version of the novel first appeared as a book in German in 1961 with a new main title, and with the descriptive subtitle "Geschichte einer Liebe" replaced by the simple designation "a novel": *Der Himmel kennt keine Günstlinge. Ein Roman.* Following the 1977 film adaptation with the title *Bobby Deerfield* (it kept the title *Heaven Has No Favorites* in Australia),[13] the English translation of the novel was reprinted with that new title over Remarque's name. The cover of the Fawcett paperback edition, with a picture of Al Pacino as Bobby Deerfield, describes it as "A Love Story," taking us back to the serialization. The new name may just be an acoustic echo of Clerfayt, and it joins the long list of those by which the racing driver, who is by no means always the same character, is known, from Kai, without a surname, who had a different role in another early short story, to Key Stanton, to Paul Clermont, and finally to Clerfayt, this time without a forename, and who had a different role in *Gam*.[14] The blurb on the new paperback describes the novel as "a tremendous tale of bittersweet love and haunting passions," linking it (a trifle tenuously) with Erich Segal's *Love Story,* which had enjoyed great popular success as a film in 1970. All this is just a byway of Remarque bibliography, but the change of title to focus upon the principal male protagonist begs the important question of where the central emphasis of the work lies. The German title indicates that heaven favors neither Lillian nor Clerfayt. If there is a greater emphasis on one or the other of the main characters, then it is arguably on Lillian, but in fact they are interdependent.

The title *Der Himmel kennt keine Günstlinge* might equally easily be a biblical or a classical allusion. The serialization title, *Geborgtes Leben,* literally "borrowed life" but perhaps more freely "borrowed time," indicates a wider theme than that simply of a love story, while the final title is broader still in its implications. And it is indeed a new work, even if it draws on motifs used before. The retention of roles or names can in this case be misleading because the characters are almost never really comparable. Clerfayt resembles Vandervelde, Kai, Stanton, or Clermont only in that he is a racing driver, although in this case a professional one approaching the end of his career; still clearly well-off, he is less of a playboy, and he has acquired the burden of a past, something that none of his precursors had. Lillian Dunkerque, thus her final spelling, is a long way from the adventuress who does not really appear in the *Vandervelde* story, and who has a relationship with Kai in *Station am Horizont;* the Lillian of the treatment is somewhat shadowy, but certainly the new central figure has little in common with the concert pianist in *The Other Love* except her desire to seize life. The final version also pushes the idea of a love story into the background, just as the word *Liebe* has disappeared from the subtitle. There is certainly no real conflict, and Boris Wolkow, clearly the descendant of Vladimir Orloff, is hardly prominent. The story juxtaposes the fates of Clerfayt and Lillian as isolated individuals to provide an exploration of the themes of life, death, separation, and chance, the themes that had preoccupied Remarque almost from the start. Individual elements in the story, too, echo not just the obviously related works, but *Drei Kameraden* and *Arc de Triomphe* in particular, and, indeed *Im Westen nichts Neues,* as well as pointing to the next novel that Remarque wrote, *Die Nacht von Lissabon.*

Clerfayt has a past located within recognizable history: he is in his early forties at the time of the action, which is identified as being a few years after the end of Second World War. Like other characters in the novels, he has been, we learn, a prisoner of the Nazis, a refugee, and has suffered; when the couple arrive in Paris, Lillian finds out about Clerfayt's background:

"Wo wohntest du, als du hier warst im Krieg?"

"Nach der Rue Cambon, nachdem ich aus dem Gefangenenlager zurückgekommen war. Es war ein gutes Versteck; niemand erwartete, dass man dort unterkriechen würde. Mein Bruder wohnte damals an der Place Vendôme auf der deutschen Seite. Wir sind Elsässer. Mein Bruder hat einen deutschen, ich einen französischen Vater." (176)

["Where did you live when you were here during the war?"

"[In the Ritz], facing the Rue Cambon, after I got out of the camp. It was a good hiding place; nobody expected you to creep in there. My brother was living on the German side, facing the Place Vendôme. We are from Alsace. My brother has a German father, I have a French one."]

It is interesting that Remarque makes his principal male character into a Frenchman who is at the same time a kind of German outsider, and who is associated with Germany by coming from the disputed border territory of Alsace, and having a German half-brother, who plays no part in the story, although we are told that there was no love lost between them, and he would not have helped Clerfayt.

There are regular references to the war(s), either in ironic allusions to "unserem großartigen Jahrhundert" (57, this marvelous century of ours), or more specifically but slightly obliquely, as when Clerfayt explains why he is a racing driver. It is not, he says, out of some kind of romanticism — and in this Remarque seems deliberately to be distancing Clerfayt from the earlier racing drivers — even though death remains always a possibility. He does it purely and simply for a living: "Ich fahre nicht aus Romantik. Ich fahre für Geld, und weil ich nichts anderes kann — nicht aus Abenteuerlust. Abenteuer habe ich in unserer verdammten Zeit genug gehabt, ohne es zu wollen" (69, I don't race because of some romantic dream. I drive for money and because I can't do anything else — not for adventures. I've had enough adventures in this damned age without asking for them). There is an echo of the denial in some versions of the Motto in *Im Westen nichts Neues* that war could be an adventure. Clerfayt does not seek adventure any more.

The Second World War is never far away, without being dominant. The opening scene contains a nice irony, when Clerfayt encounters a Swiss garage hand called Göring, who tells him that he is not related to the family of Hermann Goering; the irony is picked up and developed later when it becomes clear that the new wave of German tourists tip him well because of his name, so that he certainly won't be changing it. Other allusions to the war and Nazi period, and thus to Clerfayt's past are more indicative. The smell of the crematorium close to the sanatorium reminds him of other crematoria: "Es war nur die Erinnerung an Öfen, die Tag und Nacht gebrannt hatten — Öfen, nicht weit von dem Lager, in dem er gefangengehalten worden war. Öfen, die er vergessen wollte" (45, It was just the memory of the ovens that had burned day and night, not far from the camp in which he had been a prisoner. Ovens that he wanted to forget). References to imprisonment also recur, Clerfayt's past contrasting with Lillian's views of the sanatorium as a prison. He tells Lillian that after the war he felt that he was thirty-six and eighty, and clearly he has spent some time in a conscious effort to forget the war. A telling and again brief exchange occurs when Lillian asks, apparently quite trivially, about Clerfayt's ability to operate a hotel switchboard:

> "Natürlich. Ich habe das im Kriege gelernt."
> Sie lehnte sich mit den Ellbogen auf den Tisch. "Du hast viel im Kriege gelernt, wie?"
> "Das meiste. Es ist ja fast immer Krieg." (161)

> ["Of course. I learned how to do that during the war."
> She leaned with her elbows on the table. "You learned a lot in the war, didn't you?"
> "Most things. After all, there's almost always a war on."]

In *Station am Horizont,* Kai's restlessness might or might not have come from the First World War. It is, however, clear where Clerfayt's attitude has come from, and he is neither an amateur like Kai nor a playboy like Paul Clermont. He is a professional, as he has told us, but he is also nearing the end of his career. He is aware of the proximity of death for anyone in his job, and he has none of the facile "don't be frightened of speed" found in the figure of Clermont in *The Other Love.*

Clerfayt's story is one strand in the novel, and Lillian's runs parallel with it for much of the time, but despite the closeness of the pair — the relationship is a sexual one — their fates are in the last analysis separate. Even the fact that Lillian ultimately seems to return to the sanatorium to be with Wolkow does not make this a love story, still less the love triangle seen in the film. Hollywood may have been the appropriate milieu for a concert pianist torn between a dashing racing driver and a handsome doctor, but Lillian Dunkerque in the novel is different. She is twenty-four, and even when we encounter her in the Swiss sanatorium we are made privy to her thoughts and to the reason that she is ill in terms that once again cannot but recall Bäumer in *Im Westen nichts Neues,* although this time the novel is ostensibly a third-person narrative:

> Ich bin vierundzwanzig Jahre alt, dachte sie . . . Vier Jahre bin ich hier oben. Davor war fast sechs Jahre lang Krieg. Was kenne ich vom Leben? Zerstörung, die Flucht aus Belgien, Tränen, Angst, den Tod meiner Eltern, Hunger, und dann die Krankheit durch den Hunger und die Flucht. (25)

> [I'm twenty-four-years-old, she thought . . . I've been up here for four years. Before that there were nearly six years of war. What do I know of

life? Destruction, escaping from Belgium, crying, fear, the death of my parents, hunger, and then the illness caused by hunger and flight.]

Happiness, she concludes, meant a room that was not under fire. Both main characters demonstrate the psychological and physical effects of the war as victims.[15] The desire on the part of both of them to seize happiness and to maintain the spark of life, rather than give way to death, is what links them, however different they may be in other respects.

The broad outlines of the story match those of the film "treatment" (rather than of the film) of *The Other Love*. Lillian encounters Clerfayt in the sanatorium, called Bella Vista in the novel, although he is aware of her illness and in fact has come to visit Hollmann, his co-driver. Some of the incidents already encountered are reused: the motif of the orchids, intended in the film for a woman who is already dead and delivered to Karen by mistake, is intensified here as Clerfayt buys them for Lillian from an unscrupulous florist, unaware that they have already been used on a coffin. The initial meeting, with his car frightening the horses, is as in the treatment, which already contained the Russian companion who disappeared from the film entirely. Lillian decides to go with Clerfayt, however, as a completely rational decision, wishing only to escape from what she sees as a prison, and to see something at least of the life of which she feels she knows nothing. She has a past, it is true, and we hear of her constant flight from danger later on, but it is not the past of a fulfilled life, as was presumably the case with the pianist Karen Duncan and certainly not that of an adventuress. Lillian resists the attempts of Wolkow and of the doctor (here so far removed from the suave good looks of David Niven as to be referred to only by his nickname of "the Dalai Lama") to retain her, and as she leaves the narrator comments that her fellow patients watch her go "wie die Japaner im Kriege ihre Selbstmordflieger angesehen haben mochten" (107, As the Japanese during the war might well have looked at their kamikaze pilots) And at the end of that sixth chapter, as they drive away, Clerfayt's comments are quite unlike those of the shallow Clermont in *The Other Love*. The patients watching them leave, says Clerfayt, are like the spectators at a bullfight, to which Lillian responds: "Aber was sind wir? Die Stiere oder die Matadore?" "Immer die Stiere. Aber wir glauben, wir wären die Matadore" (109, But which are we, the bulls or the bullfighters? We're always the bulls. But we think we are the bullfighters). They leave, then, with the awareness both of being victims and of living with an illusion. While they are traveling, ostensibly in pursuit of life, both of them change, each learning from the different experiences of the other.[16] Lillian escapes from what she sees as the prison of the sanatorium into what she sees as life, and thus the balance is set up between them. Clerfayt faces death as part of his profession, and Lillian knows that death in the form of her disease is just behind her all the time. Their actual journey from the sanatorium is, however, ironically linked more than once with a journey into death, rather than towards life. There are references to crossing the Styx, and to the travel by train through the Gotthard tunnel in what looks like a literary descent into the infernal regions, as Lillian sees the cars on the transporter as "Kabinen auf dem Weg zum Hades" (114, cabins traveling to Hades), rather than towards life, even though Lillian is supposedly going away from what she thinks of as the infernal regions, an ironic reversal of the usual geography of Hell. She will eventually discover that it is impossible to get away from Hades, but the way in which she frames her thoughts at this point is significantly ambiguous. She will not, she thinks, ever be able to return: "sie konnte nicht zurück, so wenig man zweimal den Styx überqueren konnte" (115, she could not go back, any more than you could cross the Styx twice). But of course she has already crossed it once when she went to the sanatorium, so that it is her present would-be journey into life which is in fact an impossibility. The emphasis on Hades is strong and is maintained: the roar of the train is *acherontisch* (Acheronian), and later, when she falls ill on a visit to Venice, the gondolier summoned to take her to hospital looks to her like the ferryman across the Styx.

What joins the two main characters is the metaphor of life as a race potentially beset by dangers. The twentieth-century symbol of the motor race — fast, dangerous, competitive, but circular, autotelic, and essentially pointless — is possible as a reading in any of the works in which such races figure. The unevenness of that parallel is pointed out, however, shortly after the trip through the Gotthard tunnel, in the thoughts of Clerfayt about the relationship between the two of them. The passage is a striking one in a literary sense. Lillian's face

> war vom Schein der Geschwindigkeitsmesser, der Uhren, und der Geräte zum Messen der Zeit und der Schnelligkeit beleuchtet, und es schien, im Kontrast dazu, für einen Herzschlag völlig zeitlos und unberührt davon zu sein — zeitlos, spürte Clerfayt plötzlich, wie der Tod, mit dem es ein Rennen startete, gegen das alle Automobilrennen Kinderei waren. (116)

> [was lit up with the glow of the speedometer, of the clocks and other instruments for the measurement of time and speed, and for a single heartbeat her face seemed — in contrast with those instruments — completely timeless and untouched by time, timeless as death, Clerfayt suddenly felt, against which that face was setting off in a race compared to which all motor races were mere games.]

This is not so much borrowed time as the image of a character who is for the moment outside time. It has been claimed that the life which Lillian now seizes, using a trust fund administered by an elderly uncle who disapproves of her actions and who by implication has never himself really experienced life, is trivial in that is consists largely of buying expensive dresses and eating well. The first is done deliberately by Lillian and the Balenciaga dresses become allies, take on a life, so to speak, of their own. They are precisely objects of fashion, and therefore serve as images of transitoriness, something of which Lillian is well aware when she says, in the final lines of chapter 8, that she will only need them for a summer. That motif, too, was hinted at briefly in *Drei Kameraden,* where it is given a twist at the end, when Pat is seen making alterations to clothes that have "become to large" as she loses weight. Food, too, is an image for living — hardly a difficult one to decipher — in many of Remarque's novels.

The life that Lillian now embraces in Paris and elsewhere has been seen both as a trivialized *carpe diem* and as a *Lebenslüge* (living a lie),[17] but it contains more than the simple philosophy of enjoying life while you can, and the reactions of the two main characters diverge at this point. To cite once again (somewhat unfairly) the blurb on the paperback edition of *Bobby Deerfield,* it is said of Lillian that "she knows that without risk life is not sweet." Versions of this opinion are found in more serious criticism, too, but it is not the case. There is no element of risk in her case, since hope is never really held out to her as it is to Karen Duncan in *The Other Love,* or far more significantly, to Pat Hollmann in the early parts of *Drei Kameraden.* She knows that her life is — as in the earlier title — borrowed, and this is underscored when, on her trip to Venice she is helped by a young man who is in fact a gigolo, and who tells her that "dein Gigolo ist der Tod. Der Unterschied ist nur, dass er dir treu bleibt. Dafür aber betrügst du ihn, wo du kannst" (211–12, Your gigolo is death. The only difference is that he is faithful to you. But you try to cheat on him whenever you can). Her absolute certainty of death — a heightened version of the human condition — is clearest when her relationship with Clerfayt comes to a head. Clerfayt is offered a post as a car salesman and wishes to take this secure (in all senses of the word) position so that he can marry Lillian. Her initial reaction, however, is that of a renewed fear of imprisonment, this time of the prison of mediocrity. Clerfayt may have changed so that he can — for the sake of Lillian — contemplate a different way of life, but although she realizes that he has changed, Lillian's own learning process still has a way to go. The situation is a reversal of that in the relationship between Ravic and Joan Madou in *Arc de Triomphe,* although Ravic's reasons for rejecting the idea of a "hübsche, kleine Bürgerlichkeit" (189, a lovely little bourgeois life) are not quite the same as Lillian's. There is a resonance, too, in *Die Nacht von Lissabon* and the marriage of Schwarz and Helen.

After Clerfayt's proposal the two argue, and Clerfayt voices what she has not yet acknowledged to herself: "Du willst zurück! Das ist es. Du willst zurück! (281, You want to go back! That's it. You want to go back!) Although Boris Wolkow has been invoked, there is no love triangle, nor is Clerfayt jealous of Wolkow, because he is aware that something else is calling her back. In a clear difference from the film of *The Other Love*, where the doctor marries Karen even though it will presumably only be for a short time and claims that that is enough, Lillian realizes that if she, in her state of health, were to marry Clerfayt, this would simply be an episode in his life, but it would be the whole of her life, and his love would be a prison because he would ensure that she is "zu Tode gepflegt" (282, cared for to death). But just as he, when they first left the sanatorium, saw her as someone outside time, she now sees that time is precisely what she does not have enough of. They have had a love, but it cannot be revived or prolonged, and she experiences a moment of realization: life for her has been a flight from death, and that flight has to continue. The real happiness has been achieved. She is not physically out of danger; she has simply realized that she must go, and even now she is not fully clear where, although Clerfayt has told her. She agrees to marry him, knowing that she cannot do so, and this stark divergence from the sentimentalized ending ("we shall always be together") of *The Other Love* is striking. For Clerfayt, it might even be argued that his decision to retire from racing, which he knew he would have to do anyway, has almost reinterpreted itself in Goethean terms, as he begs for the beautiful moment to stay. But time cannot be stopped, as he already knows.

But there is a further twist. Clerfayt, the healthy one, is mortally injured in an accident in what is supposed to be his last race. The irony of the situation — his death from a hemorrhage — does not escape Lillian, and there are further ironies when an unpleasant sister appears and accuses her of gold-digging when she discovers that Clerfayt had left his house to her. Boris appears and although it may seem as if she has realized — in terms of the love triangle — that she wishes to return to him, his function is merely to conduct her back to the sanatorium. On the way there they see Hollmann, now cured, driving away to take Clerfayt's place on the racing team. Lillian, though, has returned to face death on her own terms. Time stopped for her while she was on her adventure outside the sanatorium, but it was a temporary flight. Clerfayt also died when he wanted to stop time, but the deaths are independent of one another. Both characters die alone, and it is notable that even Boris Wolkow is away from Lillian when she dies. It is Boris whom Remarque allows to think (but not to know) that she was happy — as far as that is possible.

The question of whether or not Lillian or Clerfayt is happy is a recurrent theme, culminating in the last, ambiguous comment, and happiness itself is always elusive even as a concept; Lillian confesses once to Clerfayt that although she is happy, she has no idea what the word really means. Clerfayt agrees that he has often been happy in different ways, and when pressed about his happiest moment, he answers "Allein" (alone). The motif recurs at various points throughout the novel: "Ich bin in diesem Augenblick glücklich," sagte er. "Ganz gleich ob wir wissen, was das ist, oder nicht" (176–77,

"At this moment I am happy," he said. "Regardless of whether we know what that means or not"). What is notable, however, is that the two principal characters achieve happiness separately. Lillian herself first does so in an incident to which several critics have drawn attention, even referring to it as an epiphany, when she visits the Sainte-Chapelle in Paris, where she and her mother had hidden from pursuers during the war. The light in the church (there is good imagery of X-rays here) turns the past horrors not into admonitory memories but into a wholeness of experience. It is interesting that the radiation of the X-rays on which she has been dependent is also burned up by the radiance of the sun,[18] which represents life. But of course it is only temporary. Happiness, — the small, sharp happiness — lies only in the decision to make your own decision.

For a modern German-language author to set a work, at least partly, in a Swiss sanatorium cannot escape inviting comparison with Thomas Mann and *Der Zauberberg* (*The Magic Mountain*, 1924), and it is hardly possible that Remarque would have been unaware that such a link would be made, or even that critics would probably make unfavorable comparisons, which indeed they did.[19] Equally, Remarque was hardly trying — nor would he — to write another *Zauberberg*. The basic metaphors are there, but there are also basic differences. Mann's massive novel remains in the sanatorium for the most part: here the point is the attempted escape, to try and find answers elsewhere. Nor is it in any way a seductive *Venusberg*, even in the film *The Other Love*. The affirmation of life as a resistance to death, which Mann's central character Hans Castorp discovers, for example, in the much-discussed and lengthy chapter in which he is lost in the snow, and learns — the idea is partly set in italics in the novel — that although it must be acknowledged, death must not rule in one's thoughts:

> Ich will dem Tode Treue halten in meinem Herzen, doch mich hell erinnern, daß Treue zum Tode und Gewesenen nur Bosheit und finstere Wollust und Menschenfeindschaft ist, bestimmt sie unser Denken und Regieren. *Der Mensch soll um der Güte und Liebe willen dem Tode keine Herrschaft einräumen über seine Gedanken.*

> [I will keep faith with death in my heart, yet well remember that faith with death and the dead is evil, is hostile to mankind, so soon as we give it power over thought and action. For the sake of goodness and love, man shall let death have no sovereignty over his thoughts.]

It is there in Remarque too. Like Castorp, Lillian also has to keep faith with death, since death keeps faith with her at all times, however hard she tries to stray, and she does keep faith with death at the end. But it must not dominate.[20]

There is a familiar literary antecedent to *Der Himmel kennt keine Günstlinge,* but the most important parallel is not Thomas Mann's massive work, nor even his equally famous short story *Der Tod in Venedig* (*Death in Venice,*

1911), though with that, too, there are some connections. Venice has been used more than once in literature as a setting for death and decay, and Lillian goes to Venice as part of her ongoing vain flight, because there are no mountains and no cars there — the two representatives of death by sickness and by danger. But she comes close to death, and the gondolier is like the ferryman of the Styx. The strongest literary parallel, however, is found in a far older story, well-known from Virgil, Ovid, and Boethius, but frequently reworked, and with plenty of examples even in modern German literature. The references in the work to the Styx and to the routes to Hades may sometimes be ambiguous in the novel, and there is an irony in Lillian's comment that you can only cross the Styx once, but they all provide a clue to the fact that behind the story lies the myth of Orpheus and Eurydice. Indeed, the absolute separateness of the pair is probably most clearly expressed in modern literature in Rilke's poem *Orpheus. Eurydike. Hermes* (Orpheus. Eurydice. Hermes, written in 1904 and in the 1907 *Neue Gedichte*), which Remarque would certainly have known.[21] The link with the myth is made explicit in the novel, and is not present in the earlier related works, in a discussion between Clerfayt and another character at roughly the midpoint. Clerfayt had found Lillian, he says, at the gates of Hades, to which his friend Levalli says:

> "Vor den Toren des Hades. Ich will Sie nicht weiter fragen. Es ist genug, um die Phantasie blühen zu lassen. In dem grauen Zwielicht der Hoffnungslosigkeit, dem nur Orpheus entrann. Aber er selbst musste den Preis zahlen: dopplete Einsamkeit — so paradox das auch klingt — weil er eine Frau aus dem Hades zurückholen wollte. Sind Sie bereit zu zahlen, Clerfayt?" (182)

> [At the gates of Hades. I won't ask for any other details. That's enough to engage the imagination. In the grey twilight of hopelessness, from which only Orpheus managed to escape. But even he had to pay the price. Double solitude, however paradoxical that sounds, because he wanted to bring a woman back from Hades. Are you prepared to pay the price, Clerfayt?]

The myth is the key to the novel, even though the parallels are not always exact. Eurydice had been killed by a snakebite, and Orpheus charms the gods to let him bring Eurydice back from Hades; he is allowed to do so provided he does not look back at her. He does so, she returns to Hades, and after a time Orpheus is himself torn to pieces by the Maenads. Clerfayt attempts to take Lillian away from the prison of death, the sanatorium, but it is impossible to bring her back into life, just as Orpheus could never really bring back Eurydice, however much his art may have made him look for a while like a favorite of the gods. It is not the infringement of a prohibition to look back at Lillian that causes the catastrophe for Clerfayt, but the attempt to keep her permanently. As soon as he attempts to marry her, to embrace with her an ongoing domesticity, to chain her with love on his terms — the reason why Orpheus could not stop himself looking back, he has openly defied the inevitable. He is punished by death, and she necessarily returns — as she was bound to anyway — to the sanatorium. Orpheus's fate in the myth is determined by a clear rule laid down by the gods, and so is Clerfayt's.

There is a further apparent difference from the myth that is in fact not a true difference: Lillian and Clerfayt are not and in reality never become a couple, and even their first meeting in the (here ironically elevated) infernal regions was by chance. In the myth, Orpheus and Eurydice have been together, it is true, but the sting of the serpent had also separated them irrevocably, turning them for the purpose of the particular myth into two isolated individuals. The myth is about death, not love, and certainly it is not a love story in the sense of other literary pairs, Hero and Leander, Tristan and Isolde, Romeo and Juliet, in which their shared death is an integral part of the story. Nor is it a love story in the same way at the relationship between Robby Lohkamp and Pat in *Drei Kameraden,* where there is — at least for a time — a genuine hope provided by Professor Jaffé.[22] This time there is not even the *sanfter Betrug,* the gentle deception provided by love and found with variations in *Der Schwarze Obelisk,* from which the term is taken, and *Zeit zu leben und Zeit zu sterben,* where there is a similar formulation, but which does show a close relationship. More comparable, perhaps, are Bodmer and Isabelle in *Der schwarze Obelisk,* where it is made clear that death is individual and where Isabelle was always unreal. In *Arc de Triomphe,* too, Ravic defines jealousy as beginning with the fact that one of any pair has to die first, and Schwarz has to come to terms with it in *Die Nacht von Lissabon.* However, *Der Himmel kennt keine Günstlinge* goes further than all of these and makes the point of ultimate separation that much clearer. It is not a love story, and Clerfayt is perhaps a victim of his own image of Lillian. In the classical myth, too, it is Orpheus who is blamed, and it is his obsession with an impossible love that lies behind the tale. With Orpheus and Eurydice, their relationship is already over when the myth begins, and what the myth encapsulates is the impossibility of reversing death in spite of the human desire to make the attempt. The myth presents a situation, rather than recommending any answers or attitudes beyond acceptance: it points out a human reluctance to accept reality, and that particular reality is a preoccupation of Remarque's in many of the novels. The relationship between Clerfayt and Lillian realizes this aspect of the myth especially well; whatever illusions they may have, and however Lillian may interpret her visit to the living world, it was always doomed. Remarque uses the Orpheus myth as an affirmation of life — in the human urge to keep hold of it — but also to underline the inevitability and irrevocability of isolation and of death. The spark of life will force you to try to flee from death while you can, but it is always there, and the message that has to be learned in the end is that it cannot be outrun. Just as Hans Castorp discovered in Mann's *Zauberberg,* we must keep faith with death, but not let it dominate our thoughts. Keeping faith with it means, however, accepting its randomness and that it can be caused by anything — risk, disease. However, we may return to the point that war is probably the most common cause — as it is in the last analysis for both of the deaths in the novel — and as Clerfayt had pointed out: "Es ist ja meistens Krieg" (There is mostly a war). But in a war and outside, between comrades in arms or between lovers, death is a matter for the individual, and this is the ultimate message of the novel. From Fritz in *Die Traumbude* to Bäumer, Georg Rahe, Pat, Ernst, the solitariness of death is a regular motif. The lines already cited from *Der schwarze Obelisk* might stand as a motto over all: "Jeder hat seinen eigenen Tod und muss ihn allein sterben, und niemand kann ihm dabei helfen" (89, Everyone has his own death and has to die that death alone, and no one can help him).

Remarque has with *Der Himmel kennt keine Günstlinge* combined themes used in several earlier works, but has created a new novel: the basic existentialism of the work, the way in which humans cling to life and to their own existence in the face of the awareness of their mortality, does not pretend to offer any answers, or even to offer a working philosophy. Its aim is to show the way humanity works under the pressure of that special knowledge. In terms of style and structure, too, the 1961 novel cannot really be compared, except on the most superficial level, either with *Station am Horizont* or with *The Other Love.* The former centers upon a romantic, almost a nineteenth-century figure (in spite of his racing car), and *The Other Love* is, in the film version, a sentimental love story centering upon the marriage of Stanton and Karen Duncan and ending with a brief union at least, within the confines of the film. Even *Drei Kameraden,* for all the similarities in individual motifs in the sanatorium scenes at the end, is a developed love story. Only the prose treatment looks like a genuine earlier stage of the 1961 novel, with Remarque moving away from a conventional love story to a pair of parallel stories, converging and then diverging again to express two facts: that the time of one's death is in the lap of the gods, and that it is the life of the individual that matters. The differences between Clerfayt and Lillian, and their own gradual processes of learning and losing are balanced with the classical myth on the one hand, and the recurrent question of happiness — which is never really resolved — on the other. However much Remarque may have wished to move away from the "dark themes," the wars of the twentieth century were just too powerful to escape. The pasts of the two main characters have reinforced their own existentialist views of life and death. It would be unfortunate if the accusation of snobbery, which was not even entirely justified with *Station am Horizont,* were to transfer itself to *Der Himmel kennt keine Günstlinge,* where there is little that would support such an accusation. Even the expensive Paris fashions have a part in the work that is not to do with luxury for its own sake, but is symbolic. Far more difficult to answer, however, is the question of whether this is a German novel. Clerfayt is strongly linked with Germany, one might even say is "almost" German, from the permanently disputed territory of Alsace, with a German half-brother, but one who has been captured by and fled from the Nazis; Lillian is more truly international, half Belgian and half Russian, we are told. In earlier incarnations, this might have been part of her exoticism, but here it is part of her reason for flight from the Nazis. The surface geography of the work, too, is Switzerland, France, and Italy, by way of the Gotthard tunnel, although the symbolic (and ironic) geography places the work between the world of the living and the regions of the dead, earth and Hades, by way of the Styx. In fact the work is, like many of the novels, both German and universal. The characters have been affected by a German regime and by a more German war than that which affected Bäumer; but the real theme is that of the human condition, of separate and isolated individuals at the mercy of chance, in their pursuit of life and of happiness, which at the last they may or may not have achieved. There is a complexity here and a hesitation about the notion of happiness that is again different from the simple equation of love and happiness in the scene between Pat and Robby after her major hemorrhage in chapter 16 of *Drei Kameraden,* where Pat's "Ich bin ja glücklich" — I am happy — is not qualified, and is accepted and understood by Robby. Since they still have hope, it does not need to be qualified — yet.

Nor, indeed, does Remarque permit the reader to claim happiness for the characters. The new third-person narrator at the end of *Im Westen nichts Neues* could only speculate upon whether Bäumer was content not to have to face the uncertain future, and the ending of *Der Himmel kennt keine Günstlinge* is remarkably similar.[23] This time there has been a third-person narrator present throughout the work, but a distancing is achieved at this point when that narrator attributes the thoughts on the death of Lillian Dunkerque to another character, Wolkow. The subjunctives are as noticeable as they were in Bäumer's case: "Er glaubte auch, dass sie glücklich gewesen sei, soweit man einen Menschen jemals glücklich nennen könne" (318, He also believed that she had been happy, insofar as one might ever call a human being happy). In an earlier incident, Lillian, walking at night in Paris, finds a woman on the pavement. She assumes at first that she is drunk, but then realizes she is dead. She is struck by the infinite emptiness in the woman's face, but unlike the commentators at the end of Remarque's two novels, she makes no attempt to read her emotions. Having been persuaded to leave and call the police anonymously, the next day she looks for information in the newspapers: "Sie fand nichts. Es war zu unbedeutend für eine Zeitungsnotiz, dass ein Mensch gestorben war" (270, She found nothing. It was too unimportant to be mentioned in the papers that a human being had died). Bäumer's death is also not reported because it is equally not news-worthy, offering *nichts Neues*. This otherwise unconnected minor incident, placed, however, in significant position at the end of a chapter with an ironic summary points to the isolation of Lillian's own death, something that mat-ters only to the person whose death it is. Death throws into relief the events of their life, but no one knows about this unknown woman's. We do know about Bäumer's and indeed about Lillian's lives.

Call no man happy until he is dead. The classical tag alluded to in the last lines of the novel is found in Herodotus, and a variation comes at the end — significantly — of Sophocles' *Oedipus Rex*. The two instances differ somewhat in their contexts. Herodotus attributes to the philosopher Solon — who is telling King Croesus just how chancy life can be — the words (in Aubrey de Selincourt's translation): "until he is dead, keep the word 'happy' in reserve. Till then he is not happy, but only lucky." This could be applied to the figure of Clerfayt. The ending of *Oedipus the King,* on the other hand is more clearly fixed to the notion of *memento mori* (remember we shall die). The Chorus, summarizing the fall of Oedipus, who has been envied but has suffered massive misfortune, declares that:

> . . . mortal man must always look to his ending.
> And none can be called happy until that day when he carries
> His happiness down to the grave in peace.[24]

Taking this as a general precept, since that individual always has an individual understanding of happiness, the outsider can never know for sure precisely what that individual has taken to the grave. We are shown the lives and deaths of Bäumer, Clerfayt, and Lillian in detail, being privy much of the time even to their thoughts on that subject, but our views on their happiness must always remain, in the last analysis, speculative.

Remarque's novels have the spark of life as their commonest theme, but they are also dominated by death, and the death of the individual is often the close of the novel as such. Bäumer, Georg Rahe, Pat Hollmann, Graeber, and both Clerfayt and Lillian all die at the end of the respective novels. Sometimes we may be given a hint of what comes after: a generation of oth-ers like Bäumer did escape the shells, Graeber's spirit may live on in the po-tentiality of the child. But often the ending is — so to speak — an end in itself. That in *Der Himmel kennt keine Günstlinge* is more closed, in fact, even than the myth on which it depends. When the link with the Orpheus myth is voiced in mid-novel, the reader sensitive to the allusion will know how it has to end, because it has already ended before the tale begins: Eury-dice is dead and has to stay dead. Orpheus lives on in some versions of the legend, and that is presented within Remarque's novel as a worse fate, the suffering of the double solitude; for this reason, perhaps, Clerfayt is killed just after he looks back.

In a concluding essay to a collection of studies, appropriately enough about endings in the classical world, Deborah Roberts draws a distinction between end and aftermath in literature, and talks about the reader's role and responsibility in constructing the ending beyond the ending. She comments that in some texts neither the reader nor the author/narrator is in complete control, and this is the case here. The reader has only the information that the author has given to determine whether or not the life presented was happy, for example; but the narrator/author (and Remarque is aware of this) has no absolute control over the reader, especially as regards the value of human life, which is the theme of every one of Remarque's works. The reader can form his or her judgments about the life concerned, and will do so. At the conclusion of her stimulating essay, Roberts talks about Tom Stoppard's play *Arcadia,* and her final statement is relevant to Remarque. Stoppard reminds us in the play of yet another classical tag: *et in Arcadia ego* (I [Death] am there even in Arcadia). But in Stoppard's play the characters defy death overtly in the only way possible for mortals: by mockery, "reminding us that life, although transient, is necessarily more vivid than death. Death is always the aftermath, but death is only the aftermath."[25] Remarque's novels often cannot go past their endings as far as the central character is concerned, because the ending is so often that of the character, and we have usually been given no hint of any transcendental speculation. They become, therefore, novels of review, in which the reader looks back over the life of that character and may draw parallels and generalizations from it. The message might be specific, such as basic pacifist or anti-Nazi points, but it might be as general as that of mortality itself, that death is always there, but that it is only death, and life is an imperative while we still have it. This is what Lillian Dunkerque and perhaps Clerfayt too learn in their *Bildungsroman.* Her death is not more heroic than that of Clerfayt, but it is more of a fulfillment because she is able to come to accept it, and know to some extent how long she has left for the vivid process that comes before death. There is a difference between knowing a universal truth and really believing it, and Lillian is no different from the rest of humanity, just more focused upon its common fate and her own, so that perhaps, after all, she is favored by heaven or the gods. The title may be as ironic as *Im Westen nichts Neues.* For all that, neither is really the single main character. Lillian's learning process is more completely drawn, but even before his own death Clerfayt knew that Lillian would have to go back. Orpheus knows only longing and love, Clerfayt becomes aware of the inevitability of death. Lillian, however, just like Eurydice, knows death already.

* * *

Remarque's novels frequently have a brief epilogue — most famously in the words of that third-person narrator at the end of *Im Westen nichts Neues,* but present too in a slightly different form at the end of, say, *Die Nacht von Lissabon,* where a final page or so contextualizes the whole of the work, and it may be appropriate to do the same thing here by way of a conclusion. Remarque's principal themes can be summed up fairly readily. Above all is the awareness of the human insistence on maintaining the spark of life under all circumstances; and of living that life well, since it may be — the frequent debates in churches and with the clergy leave other possibilities open, if never affirmed — all we have. Nature is the mirror of life, and life is really the only thing of which we can be certain. Beyond that we are ruled by chance. With this goes yet another potentially enormous theme, that of love, both *agape* and *eros.* The love of one's neighbor — and the all too frequent absence of that love — is the theme of several novels and even the title of one. The love between a man and a woman is both a revitalizing force and intrinsically difficult because it is, in the last analysis, always condemned by the seemingly innocent proviso in the marriage service: "till death us do part." Death is something that is individual, the eternal night where we have to sleep alone. Remarque, too, may be the author, but the voices that are immediate in the novels are either those of a first-person narrator or there is a clear focus on one central character: the individuals speak.

To life and love we may add politics. Remarque is a chronicler of the twentieth century and the far-reaching politics of what his characters occasionally call the worst century of all, which included two world wars that are never far away in the works. In this context, too, he is a German novelist as well as an international one, though the reception of his novels will of course have changed depending upon when and where they have been read. The history of the twentieth century in general and in Germany in particular is marked by periods of social chaos even outside wars — the 1920s are a case in point — but the two world wars have distorted normal values beyond recognition, even redefining such apparently basic concepts as murder. Politics impact upon everyone, and in the twentieth century everyone, like it or not, is a *zoon politikon.* This does not mean that Remarque's novels offer overt political polemics, although some critics seem to have wanted them to do so. But another of his key themes is that of the observer, not the completely detached outsider, but often the impotent, occasionally enraged observer, unable to do more than watch and record. But the novelist's trade is to record and memorialize, and thereby perhaps direct the mind of the reader. The novels *as novels* capture the interest in the lives of the people portrayed, and make the pacifist, or the anti-fascist, or the anti-extremist, or the tolerance point while engaging the reader's thoughts, emotions and, yes, sentiments. Remarque has always been a popular novelist, and that, too is part of the point. His novels are secular, vitalist, existential — any of those words can be applied — even if the door of the, or at least *a,* generalized church is left ajar in some of them. But it is no accident, even with Remarque's location in a western Christian tradition, that two of his works have biblical quotations or echoes as titles: "love thy neighbor" is the secular part of the new law, the only part Remarque really was able to comment on. And the echo of Ecclesiastes, the gentle cynic, in "a time to live (or love) and a time to die" is also of great relevance in the overall philosophy of the works.

And to move from the Bible to the classical tradition — the title *Der Himmel kennt keine Günstlinge* seems to bridge the two great sources of influence — are we to call no man happy until he is dead? Those words might serve as an epitaph for Remarque, who also enjoyed great fortune and great misfortune in his life — fame and relative wealth as a novelist, beautiful women and a playboy existence, but driven for most of his life into exile from his own country by one of the worst regimes known to history, which even murdered his own sister. The endings of *Im Westen nichts Neues* and *Der Himmel kennt keine Günstlinge* share the feature that the final judgment comes from an outside observer, and that outside observer within the novel may or may not be accurate. The real observer is always the reader, whose task it is to make a judgment based upon the evidence of what has been given.

Notes

[1] It is hardly possible to offer a discussion of existentialism in the twentieth century, or earlier, given the important influence — and also relevance to Remarque's novels — of Kierkegaard's *The Concept of Dread*, 2d ed., trans. Walter Lowrie (Princeton: Princeton UP, 1957); see however the admirable brief summary by Günter Schulte, *Schnellkurs Philosophie* (Cologne: DuMont, 2001), 138–48. Schulte draws attention to the literary connections, through Sartre and Camus in particular, and cites the comment by Oscar Wilde on 139.

[2] "Ein Weltbürger aus Osnabrück," *Der Spiegel* 8/1993 (February 22), 198–207, cited 202.

[3] Sternburg, *"Als wäre alles,"* 407, stresses the point.

[4] Texts are as follows, in chronological order of writing: "Das Rennen Vanderveldes" is cited from: *Herbstfahrt*, 46–52, also in *Das unbekannte Werk*, vol. 4, 155–61); originally in *Sport im Bild* 30 (1924), no. 12, 684 and 712. *Station am Horizont*, ed. Thomas F. Schneider and Tilman Westphalen (Cologne: Kiepenheuer and Witsch, 2000), also in *Das unbekannte Werk*, vol. 1, 363–553; originally in *Sport im Bild* 33 (1927) nos. 24–26, and 34 (1928) nos. 1–4. "Die andere Liebe," is Thomas F. Schneider's translation of an unpublished piece written during or just after the Second World War that survives in Remarque's papers as "The Other Love," in *Herbstfahrt*, 132–47. *Der Himmel kennt keine Günstlinge*, ed. with an afterword by Tilman Westphalen (Cologne: Kiepenheuer and Witsch, 1998); originally published as *Geborgtes Leben* in *Kristall* (Hamburg) 14 (1959), nos. 15–26. The first edition in book form was actually a Russian version of *Geborgtes Leben* (*Zhizn' vzaymi: Istoriya odnoi lyubvi*), published by the Foreign Literature Publishing House in Moscow in 1960, using the magazine version title and subtitle, the year before the German book was first published in 1961. See the afterword by

Schneider to the KiWi edition of *Station am Horizont,* 217–25, and his notes in *Herbstfahrt,* especially 279–82. *Das unbekannte Werk,* vol. 4, contains a number of small pieces from the 1920s concerned with sports cars and motor racing from various magazines, including "Das Planetenauto," 1924, 184–91; "Das Glück der stählernen Pferde," 1925, 219–21; "Avus und Avusfieber," 1925, 222–23; "Das unheilvolle Automobilrennen," 1926, 241–47; "Kleiner Auto-Roman," 1926, 270–72 — the last also in *Herbstfahrt,* 55–57. *Heaven Has No Favo(u)rites,* trans. Richard and Clara Winston, copublished in English (New York: Harcourt, Brace, and World, 1961; and London: Hutchinson, 1961); the British paperback referred to was published in London by Star Books (W. H. Allen), in 1977; the paperback edition as *Bobby Deerfield* (Greenwich, CT: Fawcett Crest, n.d [1977]). The film, *Bobby Deerfield,* does not follow the novel closely; Sternburg, *"Als wäre alles,"* 410–11 notes this and also speculates on the curious renaming.

[5] Remarque's diary entry for 10 January 1954 (*Das unbekannte Werk,* vol. 5, 488) expresses the desire to move away from historical "dark" themes to something completely different. Attention is drawn to the passage by Werner Fuld, "Ein Treffen mit alten Bekannten: Zur Vorgeschichte des Romans *Der Himmel kennt keine Günstlinge,*" *Text + Kritik* 149 (2001): 65–68. See also his comments in the interview with Friedrich Luft, "Das Profil," *Ein militanter Pazifist,* 125.

[6] See Gordon, *Heroism and Friendship,* 141. Taylor, *Biography,* 235, considers that with minor changes it could have been set in the thirties, and notes (not especially relevantly) that the "Remarque's experiences which serve as the basis for the story all antedate 1939." The novel in its 1961 publication does carry a prefatory apology from Remarque for any inaccuracies in his descriptions of motor racing, but this need not mean that he was recycling out-of-date material. Nor, of course, are the actual details of racing of primary importance in the story: novelists always run the risk of obsessive responses from the aficionado.

[7] See Remarque's letter to Reinhold Neven Du Mont on 27 May 1968 (*Das unbekannte Werk,* vol. 5, 227–28). Owen, *Bio-Bibliography,* 310, describes a review by Reich-Ranicki that criticized the work on the grounds of style and sentimentality as "probably the most damning lines ever written about Remarque": Marcel Reich-Ranicki: "Knalleffekte in Todesnähe: Erich Maria Remarque, von *Im Westen nichts Neues* zu *Der Himmel kennt keine Günstlinge,*" *Die Zeit* (6 October 1961). See Reich-Ranicki's *Deutsche Literatur in West und Ost* (Munich: Piper, 1966), 256. Other reviews are noted by Owen, 309–12, with comments also on the *Geborgtes Leben* serialization, 309. See also Firda, *Thematic Analysis,* 227, and 291–92, who rightly attacks Reich-Ranicki's facile judgments, notes more positive reviews in the United States, and offers a positive view himself.

[8] See Antkowiak, *Remarque,* 9; Sternburg, *"Als wäre alles,"* 142–47. Thomas Schneider titles his afterword to the recent KiWi edition "Nur das Credo eines Snobs?" 217–25.

[9] John Walker, ed. (London: Harper-Collins, 1993), 901.

[10] See Schneider's detailed notes, *Herbstfahrt,* 279–82, citing notes and letters from Remarque on the film. Schneider refers to another story — also now lost — apparently called "Fate." The details of Remarque's financial dealings with Enterprise Productions, who also filmed *Arch of Triumph,* which appeared in the following year with an even stronger cast, are complex. Earlier studies did not always have access to these details: Barker and Last, *Remarque,* 26. However, see Hans Wagener, "Erich Maria Remarque,"

in *Deutsche Exilliteratur seit 1933: I. Kalifornien,* edited by J. M. Spalek and J. Strelka (Bern and Munich: Francke, 1976), 591–605, especially 601–2. *The Other Love* was directed by André de Toth for Enterprise Productions, with a score by Miklos Rozsa and the use of various familiar classical piano pieces. See Taylor, *Biography,* 235–37, on *The Other Love.* He notes that Stanwyck received bad reviews for her inability to express emotions.

[11] In *Der Himmel kennt keine Günstlinge* the relationship between the two characters is sexual, but Lillian takes care never to wake up with Clerfayt, as this would make the illness too obvious. The concealment, at least of the extent of the disease, continues.

[12] "Ein Treffen," 68. Fuld's view of the novel as recycling is expressed even more clearly by Antkowiak in his very negative comments on the work, *Remarque,* 142–43. Even Barker and Last, *Remarque,* 95, who treat the novel rather awkwardly as a kind of adjunct to *Drei Kameraden,* seem to endorse Antkowiak, and consider the work "superficial."

[13] *Bobby Deerfield* was directed by Sydney Pollack for Columbia/Warner Brothers in 1977 with a screenplay adapted from the novel by Alvin Sargent, on which see Owen, *Bio-Bibliography,* 308. This film and *The Other Love* are discussed by Firda, *Thematic Analysis,* 241–46, with reference to contemporary reviews, and see Taylor, *Biography,* 237–39, on *Bobby Deerfield.* The latter film, made well after Remarque's death, need not concern us, although Taylor, who is thoroughly critical of it, notes neatly that the skeleton of Remarque's novel is present, "but the characters are imposters."

[14] Firda, *All Quiet,* 28, seems to imply that the racing drivers are all the same character and certainly all "stock romantic heroes," though his treatment of *Der Himmel kennt keine Günstlinge* in *Thematic Analysis* is good overall. There is a quite unconnected Robert Hirsch in the fragmentary version of the last novel, *Das gelobte Land.*

[15] Antkowiak, *Remarque,* 142, is dismissive of this point, claiming (wrongly) that the reader discovers that the work is set after the war only in a "flüchtige, vorbeihuschende Passage" (fleeting, transitory passage). He claims that other references to the war are slight, and that the novel "hängt . . . im luftleeren Raum" (is in a temporal vacuum). This is not the case. Barker and Last point out, *Remarque,* 94, that both Lillian and Pat Hollmann in *Drei Kameraden* have contracted tuberculosis as a result of malnutrition brought about by the privations during the war(s), and are thus also both victims of the war.

[16] This point is well noted by Wagener, *Understanding,* 95–96, though few other critics have taken the novel as seriously. Although he is correct in noting that their romantic involvement is not the point of the novel, he is, however, perhaps less accurate when he determines that Lillian is the center of attention: the story balances the fates of each. As an aside, the tagline of the film *Bobby Deerfield* also focused on the male character, "he had to meet her — to find himself!"

[17] Antkowiak, *Remarque,* 143. Again Pat Hollmann in *Drei Kameraden* voices the idea that she wanted to live frivolously for a while, as does Helen in *Die Nacht von Lissabon.*

[18] Firda, *Thematic Analysis,* 235; Wagener, *Understanding,* 96. How religious an experience this is, is debatable. There is no other religious element in the work, and she herself notes the irony that the rays illuminate a prison as well — remembering the prison motif of the sanatorium (text, 276).

[19] Barker and Last, *Remarque*, 93; Wagener, *Understanding*, 94, both draw attention to the critics' (inevitable) comments.

[20] See the chapter "*Schnee*" in Thomas Mann, *Der Zauberberg* (1924; Frankfurt am Main: Fischer, 1960), 686. The translation by Helen Lowe-Porter cited here is that first published in 1928, *The Magic Mountain* (Harmondsworth: Penguin, 1960), 496–97. See on this passage Arnold Bauer, *Thomas Mann*, trans. Alexander and Elizabeth Henderson (New York: Ungar, 1971), 46–47. Paul Bäumer's experience *in extremis* in the shell-hole after killing Duval in *Im Westen nichts Neues* has been seen as having been influenced possibly directly by the *Schnee* chapter: Hartung, "Wahrheitsgehalt," 13.

[21] Virgil's fourth *Georgic* has the story with references to not being allowed to cross the Styx twice, and it is there in Ovid's *Metamorphoses*. Later, Boethius's *Consolation of Philosophy* was also well-known and much translated. Modern German interpretations of the story of Orpheus other than Rilke's include most notably Max Frisch in *Homo Faber* (1957, same title in English), which even contains the snakebite motif, and where the main character's typewriter is a called a Hermes Baby, Hermes being the god who leads Orpheus out of Hades. See also Herbert Marcuse, *Eros and Civilisation* (London: Sphere, 1969) for further insight.

[22] Gordon, *Heroism and Friendship*, 78–79, makes the point that the couple are not lovers in the same way as Robby and Pat, or Ernst and Elisabeth in *Zeit zu leben und Zeit zu sterben*.

[23] Taylor, *Remarque*, 234, and Wagener, *Understanding*, 98.

[24] Herodotus, *The Histories*, trans. Aubrey de Selincourt (Harmondsworth: Penguin, 1954), 25 [= I.32]; Sophocles, *The Theban Plays*, trans. E. F. Watling (Harmondsworth: Penguin, 1947), 68 [= final lines of *Oedipus the King*]. The idea is also voiced earlier by the chorus in the play. The tag was used for the title of the translation of André Maurois's memoirs, a translation provided by Remarque's own translator, Denver Lindley, in 1943.

[25] Deborah H. Roberts, "Afterword: Ending and Aftermath: Ancient and Modern," *Classical Closure*, ed. Deborah H. Roberts, Francis M. Dunn, and Don Fowler, Princeton: Princeton UP, 1997), 251–73; the last page is cited.

Select Bibliography

I. Primary Texts

REMARQUE'S NOVELS ARE listed chronologically, giving (where appropriate) the first book edition; the first book edition in German where this is different; the German book edition used in this study; English translation(s) when not the first edition of the novel; and any other relevant edition, which may contain valuable notes, for example. Details of pre-publication serializations, of films, and of other translations may be found in the notes to the relevant chapters. A second section lists collections of other writings by Remarque that have been used in this study. Further information can be had from the various bibliographies noted in the Secondary Literature. Primary works by writers other than Remarque cited in the text are not listed.

1: Remarque's Novels

Die Traumbude. Dresden: Verlag der Schönheit, 1920 (=Bücherei der Schönheit). Also in *Das unbekannte Werk*, vol. 1, edited by Thomas F. Schneider and Tilman Westphalen, 19–173. Cologne: Kiepenheuer and Witsch, 1998.

Gam. In *Das unbekannte Werk*, vol. 1, edited by Thomas F. Schneider and Tilman Westphalen, 175–361. Cologne: Kiepenheuer and Witsch, 1998.

Station am Horizont. Edited by Thomas F. Schneider and Tilman Westphalen. Cologne: Kiepenheuer and Witsch, 2000. Also in *Das unbekannte Werk*, vol. 1, edited by Thomas F. Schneider and Tilman Westphalen, 363–553. Cologne: Kiepenheuer and Witsch, 1998.

Im Westen nichts Neues. Berlin: Propyläen, 1929. Also edited and with an afterword by Tilman Westphalen. Cologne: Kiepenheuer and Witsch, 1998. Also ed. Brian Murdoch. London: Methuen, 1984. Reprint, with corrections, London: Routledge, 1988. In English: *All Quiet on the Western Front*. Translated by A. W. Wheen. London: G. .P. Putnam's Sons, 1929, and with some differences, Boston: Little, Brown, and Company, 1929. Also translated by Brian Murdoch. London: Cape, 1994. See also: Thomas F. Schneider, *Erich Maria Remarque: Im Westen nichts Neues: Text, Edition, Entstehung, Distribution und Rezeption, 1928–1930*. Habilitationsschrift: University of Osnabrück, 2000. Reprint with CD, Tübingen: Niemeyer, 2004.

Der Weg zurück. Berlin: Propyläen, 1931. Also edited and with an afterword by Tilman Westphalen. Cologne: Kiepenheuer and Witsch, 1998. In English: *The Road Back*. Translated by A. W. Wheen. London: G. .P. Putnam's Sons, 1931.

Drei Kameraden. Danish translation by Sonja Heise under the title *Kammerater*. Copenhagen: Gyldendal, 1936. In German: *Drei Kameraden*. Amsterdam: Querido, 1938. Edited and with an afterword by Tilman Westphalen. Cologne: Kiepenheuer and Witsch, 1998. In English: *Three Comrades*. Translated by A. W. Wheen. Boston: Little, Brown, and Company, 1937.

Liebe Deinen Nächsten. In English: translated by Denver Lindley under the title *Flotsam*. Boston: Little, Brown, and Company, 1941. In German: *Liebe Deinen Nächsten*. Stockholm: Fischer, 1941. Also edited and with an afterword by Tilman Westphalen. Cologne: Kiepenheuer and Witsch, 1998.

Arc de Triomphe. In English: translated by Walter Sorell and Denver Lindley under the title *Arch of Triumph*. New York: Appleton-Century-Crofts, 1945. In German: *Arc de Triomphe*. Zurich: Micha, 1946. Also edited and with an afterword by Tilman Westphalen. Cologne: Kiepenheuer and Witsch, 1998.

Der Funke Leben. In English: translated by James Stern under the title *Spark of Life*. New York: Appleton-Century-Crofts, 1952. In German: *Der Funke Leben*. Cologne and Berlin: Kiepenheuer and Witsch, 1952. Also edited and with an afterword by Tilman Westphalen. Cologne: Kiepenheuer and Witsch, 1998.

Zeit zu leben und Zeit zu sterben. In English: translated by Denver Lindley under the title *A Time to Love and a Time to Die*. New York: Harcourt, Brace, 1954. In German: *Zeit zu leben und Zeit zu sterben*. Cologne: Kiepenheuer and Witsch, 1954. Uncensored German version, Cologne: Kiepenheuer and Witsch, 1989; edited and with an afterword by Tilman Westphalen. Cologne: Kiepenheuer and Witsch, 1998.

Der schwarze Obelisk. Cologne: Kiepenheuer and Witsch, 1956. Also edited and with an afterword by Tilman Westphalen. Cologne: Kiepenheuer and Witsch, 1998. In English: *The Black Obelisk*. Translated by Denver Lindley. New York: Harcourt, Brace, 1957. See also Peter Junk. *Isabelle: Szenen nach Erich Maria Remarques Der schwarze Obelisk*. Osnabrück: Universität Osnabrück, 1994.

Der Himmel kennt keine Günstlinge. First published under the title *Geborgtes Leben* in *Kristall* (Hamburg) 14 (1959) nos. 15–26.; In Russian: *Zhizn' vzaymi: Istoriya odnoi lyubvi*. Moscow: Foreign Literature Publishing House, 1960. In German: *Der Himmel kennt keine Günstlinge*. Cologne: Kiepenheuer and Witsch, 1961. Also edited and with an afterword by Tilman Westphalen. Cologne: Kiepenheuer and Witsch, 1998. In English: *Heaven Has No Favorites*. Translated by Richard and Clara Winston. New York: Harcourt, Brace, and World; *Heaven Has No Favourites*, London: Hutchinson, 1961. Also translated as *Bobby Deerfield*. Greenwich, CT: Fawcett Crest, n.d [1977].

Die Nacht von Lissabon. Cologne: Kiepenheuer and Witsch, 1962. Also edited and with an afterword by Tilman Westphalen. Cologne: Kiepenheuer and Witsch, 1998. In English: *The Night in Lisbon.* Translated by Ralph Manheim. New York: Harcourt, Brace, 1961 (predated by the German serialization).

Schatten im Paradies. Munich: Droemer Knaur, 1971. Edited and with an afterword by Tilman Westphalen. Cologne: Kiepenheuer and Witsch, 1998. In English: *Shadows in Paradise.* Translated by Ralph Manheim. New York: Harcourt, Brace, 1972.

Das gelobte Land. In *Das unbekannte Werk,* vol. 2, edited by Thomas F. Schneider and Tilman Westphalen. Cologne: Kiepenheuer and Witsch, 1998.

2: Other Writings by Remarque

Der Feind. In English: translated by A. W. Wheen under the title *The Enemy* (and other stories). First published in *Collier's* magazine, 1930–1931. In German: *Der Feind: Erzählungen.* Retranslation by Barbara von Bechtolsheim. Cologne: Kiepenheuer and Witsch, 1993.

Herbstfahrt eines Phantasten. Edited by Thomas F. Schneider. Cologne: Kiepenheuer and Witsch, 2001. See also *Das unbekannte Werk* for short stories and articles.

Der letzte Akt (1954). In *Das unbekannte Werk,* vol. 3, edited by Thomas F. Schneider and Tilman Westphalen, 11–51. Cologne: Kiepenheuer and Witsch, 1998.

Die letzte Station (1956). In *Das unbekannte Werk,* vol. 3, edited by Thomas F. Schneider and Tilman Westphalen, 153–257. Cologne: Kiepenheuer and Witsch, 1998. English adaptation: *Full Circle.* Adapted by Peter Stone. New York: Harcourt, Brace, Jovanovich, 1974.

Ein militanter Pazifist: Texte und Interviews, 1929–1966. Edited by Thomas F. Schneider. Cologne: Kiepenheuer and Witsch, 1994.

"Sag mir, daß du mich liebst" . . . Zeugnisse einer Leidenschaft. [Letters to Marlene Dietrich.] Edited by Werner Fuld and Thomas F. Schneider. Cologne: Kiepenheuer and Witsch, 2001. See also *Das unbekannte Werk.*

Das unbekannte Werk. Vols. 3 [diaries and letters] and 4 [short prose and poems]. Edited by Thomas F. Schneider and Tilman Westphalen. Cologne: Kiepenheuer and Witsch, 1998.

II. Secondary Literature

This bibliography lists works directly concerned with Remarque and his writings, and accordingly does not include most general literary or historical studies or reference works, and only the more significant and useful studies are listed (not all, however, have been cited in the notes). For details of the numerous minor publications — such as reviews — see in particular the works by Claude R. Owen, Richard Arthur Firda, and Harley U. Taylor in section 1 below, as well as the Osnabrück series of bibliographies. Although a few reviews and short notices are included, the study notes on *All Quiet on the Western Front,* for example, are not. There is an excellent current bibliography in the *Erich Maria Remarque Jahrbuch/Yearbook* (here as *Jahrbuch*). Section 2 lists studies centered upon the individual novels.

1: Biographies, General Studies, Studies of More Than One Novel, and Collections of Essays

Amgwerd, Fabienne. "Form und Funktion des Komischen bei Remarque." *Jahrbuch* 15 (2005): 7–35.

Antkowiak, Alfred. *Erich Maria Remarque: Leben und Werke.* East Berlin: Volk und Wissen, 1965; West Berlin: Das europäische Buch, 1983.

Barker, Christine, and Rex Last. *Erich Maria Remarque.* London: Wolff, 1979.

Baron, Ulrich, and Hans-Harald Müller. "Weltkriege und Kriegsromane." *LiLi: Zeitschrift für Literaturwissenschaft und Linguistik* 19 (1989): 14–38.

Baumer, Franz. *E. M. Remarque.* Berlin: Colloquium, 1970. 3d ed., Berlin: Morgenbuch, 1994.

Beller, Hans. "Schreiben im Schatten des Paradieses: Erich Maria Remarque und der Film: Eine Collage." *Jahrbuch* 9 (1999): 39–61.

Bergonzi, Bernard. *Heroes' Twilight: A Study of the Literature of the Great War.* 2d ed. London: Macmillan, 1980.

Bornebusch, Herbert. *Gegen-Erinnerung: Eine formsemantische Analyse des demokratischen Kriegsromans der Weimarer Republik.* Frankfurt am Main: Peter Lang, 1985.

Bostock, J. K. *Some Well-known German War Novels, 1914–30.* Oxford: Blackwell, 1931.

Eksteins, Modris. *Rites of Spring: The Great War and the Birth of the Modern Age.* London: Transworld, 1990.

Firda, Richard Arthur. *Erich Maria Remarque: A Thematic Analysis of His Novels.* New York, etc.: Peter Lang, 1988.

Fussell, Paul. *The Great War and Modern Memory.* London: Oxford UP, 1977.

Gilbert, Julie Goldsmith. *Opposite Attraction: The Lives of Erich Maria Remarque and Paulette Goddard.* New York: Pantheon, 1995; German trans. Düsseldorf: List, 1997.

Glunz, Claudia, and Thomas Schneider. *Erich Maria Remarque: Werke der frühen fünfziger Jahre.* Osnabrück: Rasch, 1995.

————, eds. *Elfriede Scholz, geb. Remark: Im Namen des deutschen Volkes: Dokumente einer justitiellen Ermordung.* Osnabrück: Rasch, 1997.

Gollbach, Michael. *Die Wiederkehr des Weltkrieges in der Literatur: Zu den Frontromanen der späten zwanziger Jahre.* Kronberg im Taunus: Athenaeum, 1978.

Gordon, Haim. *Heroism and Friendship in the Novels of Erich Maria Remarque.* New York, etc.: Peter Lang, 2003.

Gruber, Helmut. "'Neue Sachlichkeit' and the World War." *German Life and Letters* NS 20 (1966–67): 138–49.

Hartung, Günter. "Gegenschriften zu *Im Westen nichts Neues* und *Der Weg zurück.*" In *Erich Maria Remarque: Leben, Werk, und weltweite Wirkung,* edited by Thomas F. Schneider, 109–50. Osnabrück: Rasch, 1998.

Keller, Harald. "Hollywood und anderswo — Remarque-Adaptation in Film und Fernsehen." In *Man kann alten Dreck nicht vergraben: Er fängt immer wieder an zu stinken: Materialien zu einen Erich Maria Remarque-Projekt,* edited by Lothar Schwindt and Tilman Westphalen, 119–36. Osnabrück: Universität/Fachbereich SLM, 1984.

Kerker, Armin. "Zwischen Innerlichkeit und Nacktkultur: Der unbekannte Remarque." *Die Horen* 19/Heft 3 (1974): 3–23.

Krause, Martina. "'. . . in den Fluten des radiumhaltigen Kleinstadtwassers': Erich Maria Remarque und Osnabrück." *Jahrbuch* 7 (1997): 27–72.

Linder, Anne P. *Princes of the Trenches: Narrating the German Experience of the First World War.* Columbia, SC: Camden House, 1996.

Löffler, Sigrid. *Wer sagt uns, was wir lesen sollen? Die Bücherflut, die Kritik und der literarische Kanon.* London: Institute of Germanic Studies, 2002.

Midgley, David. *Writing Weimar: Critical Realism in Weimar Literature 1918–1933.* Oxford: Oxford UP, 2000.

Müller, Hans-Harald. *Der Krieg und die Schriftsteller: Der Kriegsroman der Weimarer Republik.* Stuttgart: Metzler, 1986.

————. "Politics and the War Novel." In *German Writers and Politics, 1918–39,* edited by Richard Dove and Stephen Lamb, 103–20. London: Macmillan, 1992.

Murdoch, Brian. "Innocent Killing: Erich Maria Remarque and the Weimar Anti-War Novels." In *German Novelists of the Weimar Republic: Intersections of Literature and Politics,* edited by Karl Leydecker, 207–39. Rochester, NY: Camden House, 2006.

Murdoch, Brian, Mark Ward, and Maggie Sargeant, eds. *Remarque Against War.* Glasgow: Scottish Papers in Germanic Studies, 1998.

Nienaber, Bernhard. "Der Blick zurück: Remarques Romane gegen die Adenauer-Restauration." In *Erich Maria Remarque, 1898–1970,* edited by Tilman Westphalen, 79–93. Bramsche: Rasch, 1988.

———. *Vom anachronistischen Helden zum larmoyanten Untertan: Eine Untersuchung zur Entwicklung der Humanismuskonzeption in Erich Maria Remarques Romanen der Adenauer-Restauration.* Würzburg: Königshausen und Neumann, 1997.

Nienaber, Bern(har)d. "Remarque gegen die Restauration: der Russlandkriegsroman *Zeit zu leben und Zeit zu sterben* (1954)." *Krieg und Literature/War and Literature* 1 (1989): 53–58.

Owen, Claude R. *Erich Maria Remarque: A Critical Bio-Bibliography.* Amsterdam: Rodopi, 1984.

Parfitt, George. *Fiction of the First World War.* London: Faber, 1988.

Parvanova, Mariana. ". . . *das Symbol der Ewigkeit ist der Kreis": Eine Untersuchung der Motive in den Romanen von Erich Maria Remarque.* Berlin: Tenea, 2003.

Pfeiler, William K. *War and the German Mind.* 1941; reprint, New York: AMS, 1966.

Placke, Heinrich. "Wie zuverlässig ist die KiWi-Taschenbuchausgabe der Remarque-Romane von 1998." *Jahrbuch* 13 (2003): 82–91.

———. *Die Chiffren des Utopischen: Zum literarischen Gehalt der politischen 50er-Jahre Romane Remarques.* Göttingen: Vandenhoek und Ruprecht, 2004.

Sargeant, Maggie. *Kitsch und Kunst: Presentations of a Lost War.* Bern: Peter Lang, 2005.

Schneider, Thomas F. "'Ein ekler Leichenwurm': Motive und Rezeption der Schriften Erich Maria Remarques zur national-sozialistischen deutschen Vergangenheit." *Text+Kritik* 149 (2001): 42–54.

———. *Erich Maria Remarque: Der Nachlaß in der Fales Library — New York University: Ein Verzeichnis,* 2d ed. Osnabrück: Universität Osnabrück, 1991; and the volume of *Nachträge.* Osnabrück: Universität Osnabrück, 1991.

———. *Erich Maria Remarque: Ein Chronist des 20. Jahrhunderts: Eine Biographie in Bildern und Dokumenten.* Bramsche: Rasch, 1991.

———, ed. *Erich Maria Remarque: Leben, Werk, und weltweite Wirkung.* Osnabrück: Rasch, 1998.

———. *Der Weg zurück* [Exhibition Catalogue] Osnabrück: Universität Osnabrück, 1989.

Schneider, Thomas F., and Hans Wagener, eds. *Von Richthofen bis Remarque: Deutschsprachige Prosa zum I. Weltkrieg.* Amsterdam and New York: Rodopi, 2003.

Schneider, Thomas F., and Donald Weiss, eds. *Erich Maria Remarque: "Die Traumbude," "Station am Horizont," Die unselbständigen Publikationen (1916–1998).* Osnabrück: Rasch, 1995.

Schreckenberger, Helga. "'Durchkommen ist alles': Physischer und psychischer Existenzkampf in Erich Maria Remarque's Exil-Romanen." *Text + Kritik* 149 (2001): 30–41.

———. "Erich Maria Remarque im amerikanischen Exil." In *Erich Maria Remarque: Leben, Werk, und weltweite Wirkung,* edited by Thomas F. Schneider, 251–66. Osnabrück: Rasch, 1998.

Schwarz, Wilhelm J. *War and the Mind of Germany I.* Bern and Frankfurt am Main: Peter Lang, 1975.

Schwindt, Lothar, and Tilman Westphalen, eds. *Man kann alten Dreck nicht vergraben; Er fängt immer wieder an zu stinken: Materialien zu einen Erich Maria Remarque-Projekt.* Osnabrück: Universität/Fachbereich SLM, 1984 [typescript].

Sternburg, Wilhelm von. *"Als wäre alles das letzte Mal": Erich Maria Remarque: Eine Biographie.* Cologne: Kiepenheuer and Witsch, 2000.

———. "Pazifist und Einzelgänger," *Frankfurter Rundschau,* 6 June 1998.

Stickelberger-Eder, Margrit. *Aufbruch 1914: Kriegsromane der späten Weimarer Republik.* Zurich and Munich: Artemis, 1983.

Taylor, Harley U. *Erich Maria Remarque: A Literary and Film Biography.* New York: Peter Lang, 1988.

Text+Kritik 149 (January 2001): *Erich Maria Remarque.*

Thornton, Thomas. *A Time to Live: The Life and Writings of Erich Maria Remarque.* New York: Fales Library, 1998.

Tims, Hilton. *Erich Maria Remarque: The Last Romantic.* London: Constable, 2003.

Travers, M. P. A. *German Novels of the First World War.* Stuttgart: Heinz, 1982.

Wagener, Hans. "Erich Maria Remarque." In *Deutsche Exilliteratur seit 1933. 1. Kalifornien,* edited by J. M. Spalek and J. Strelka, 591–605. Bern and Munich: Francke, 1976.

———. "Erich Maria Remarque, *Im Westen nichts Neues — Zeit zu leben und Zeit zu sterben:* Ein Autor, zwei Weltkriege." *Jahrbuch* 10 (2000): 31–52.

———. "Remarque in Amerika — zwischen Erfolg und Exilbewusstsein." *Jahrbuch* 9 (1999): 18–38.

———. *Understanding Erich Maria Remarque.* Columbia, SC: U of South Carolina P, 1991.

Westphalen, Tilman, ed. *Erich Maria Remarque: Bibliographie.* Osnabrück: Universität Osnabrück, 1988.

———, ed. *Erich Maria Remarque 1898–1970.* Bramsche: Rasch, 1988.

Wohl, Robert. *The Generation of 1914.* London: Weidenfeld and Nicolson, 1980.

Woods, Roger. "The Conservative Revolution and the First World War: Literature as Evidence in Historical Explanation." *Modern Language Review* 85 (1990): 77–91.

Ziemann, Benjamin. "Die Erinnerung an den Ersten Weltkrieg in den Milieukulturen der Weimarer Republik." In Vol. 1 of *Kriegserlebnis und Legendenbildung,* edited by Thomas F. Schneider, 249–70. Osnabrück: Rasch, 1998.

2: Studies of Individual Novels

Die Traumbude

Firda, Richard Arthur. "Young Remarque's *Traumbude.*" *Monatshefte* 71 (1979): 49–55.

Oerke, Petra. "'Geliebter Fritz': Entstehung und biographischer Hintergrund von Remarques erstem Roman *Die Traumbude.*" In *Erich Maria Remarque: Leben, Werk, und weltweite Wirkung,* edited by Thomas F. Schneider, 41–55. Osnabrück: Rasch, 1998.

Im Westen nichts Neues

Arnold, Heinz Ludwig. "Erich Maria Remarque und Ernst Jünger." *Jahrbuch* 10 (1999): 5–17.

Bance, Alan F. "*Im Westen nichts Neues:* A Bestseller in Context." *Modern Language Review* 72 (1977): 359–73.

Bekes, Peter. *Erich Maria Remarque: Im Westen nichts Neues.* Munich: Oldenbourg, 1998.

Campbell, Ian. "Remarking Remarque: The Arthur Wheen Papers." *National Library of Australia News* 8, no. 7 (April, 1998): 3–7.

Chambers, John Whiteclay. "*All Quiet on the Western Front* (1930): The Antiwar Film and the Image of the First World War." *Historical Journal of Film, Radio, and Television* 14 (1994): 377–411.

De Leeuw, Howard M. "Remarque's Use of Simile in *Im Westen nichts Neues.*" *Jahrbuch* 4 (1994): 45–64.

Firda, Richard Arthur. *All Quiet on the Western Front: Literary Analysis and Cultural Context.* New York: Twayne, 1993.

Gruhn, Klaus. "'Wehrkraftzersetzend': Schüler des Gymnasium Laurentianum Warendorf lernen 1944 *Im Westen nichts Neues* kennen." *Jahrbuch* 15 (2005): 93–100.

Hartung, Günter. "Zum Wahrheitsgehalt des Romans *Im Westen nichts Neues.*" *Jahrbuch* 1 (1991): 5–17.

Hermand, Jost. "Versuch, den Erfolg von Erich Maria Remarques *Im Westen nichts Neues* zu verstehen." In *Weimar am Pazifik: Festschrift für Werner Vordtriede,* edited by Dieter Borchmeyer and Till Heimeran, 71–78. Tübingen: Niemeyer, 1985.

Horn, Peter. "Der 'unbeschreibliche' Krieg und sein fragmentierter Erzähler: Zu Remarques Kriegsroman *Im Westen nichts Neues.*" *Heinrich Mann Jahrbuch* 4/1986 (1987): 85–108.

Howind, Angelika. "Ein Antikriegsroman als Bestseller: Die Vermarktung von *Im Westen nichts Neues* 1928 bis 1930." In *Erich Maria Remarque, 1898–1970,* edited by Tilman Westphalen, 55–64. Bramsche: Rasch, 1988.

Kelly, Andrew. "*All Quiet on the Western Front:* 'Brutal Cutting, Stupid Censors, and Bigoted Politicos.'" *Historical Journal of Film, Radio, and Television* 9 (1989): 135–50.

———. *Filming "All Quiet on the Western Front."* London and New York: I. B. Tauris, 1998.

Klein, Holger M. "Dazwischen Niemandsland: *Im Westen nichts Neues* and *Her Privates We.*" In *Grossbritannien und Deutschland: Festschrift für John W. P. Bourke,* edited by Ortwin Kuhn, 488–512. Munich: Goldmann, 1974.

———. "Grundhaltung und Feindbilder bei Remarque, Céline, und Hemingway." *Krieg und Literatur/War and Literature* 1 (1989): 7–22.

Kloiber, Harald. "Struktur, Stil, und Motivik in Remarques *Im Westen nichts Neues.*" *Jahrbuch* 4 (1994): 5–78.

Kuxdorf, Manfred. "Mynona versus Remarque, Tucholsky, Mann, and Others: Not So Quiet on the Literary Front." In *The First World War in German Narrative Prose: Essays in Honour of George Wallis Field,* edited by Charles N. Genno and Heinz Wetzel, 71–91. Toronto, Buffalo, and London: U. Toronto P, 1980,

Liedloff, Helmut. "Two War Novels," *Revue de Littérature Comparée* 42 (1968): 390–406.

Littlejohns, Richard. "'Der Krieg hat uns für alles verdorben': The Real Theme of *Im Westen nichts Neues.*" *Modern Languages* 70 (1989): 89–94.

Mitchell, George J. "Making All Quiet on the Western Front." *American Cinematographer* 66 (1985): 34–43.

Murdoch, Brian. "All Quiet on the Trojan Front: Remarque's Soldiers and Homer's Heroes in a Parody of *Im Westen nichts Neues.*" *German Life and Letters* 43 (1989), 49–62.

———. "'Hinter die Kulissen des Krieges sehen': Evadne Price, Adrienne Thomas — and E. M. Remarque." *Forum for Modern Language Studies* 28 (1992): 56–74.

———. "Narrative Strategies in Remarque's *Im Westen nichts Neues.*" *New German Studies* 17 (1992–93), 175–202.

———. "Paul Bäumer's Diary." In *Remarque Against War,* edited by Brian Murdoch, Mark Ward, and Maggie Sargeant, 1–23. Glasgow: Scottish Papers in Germanic Studies, 1998.

———. *Remarque: Im Westen nichts Neues.* Glasgow: Glasgow University French and German Publications, 1991; 2d rev. ed. 1995.

———. "Translating the Western Front: Λ. W. Wheen and E. M. Remarque." *Antiquarian Book Monthly Review* 18 (1991): 452–60.

———. "'We Germans . . .?' Remarques englischer Roman *All Quiet on the Western Front.*" *Jahrbuch* 6 (1996): 11–34.

Neumann, Robert. "Die Meute hinter Remarque." *Die Literatur* 32 (1929–30): 199–200.

Norrie, Kathleen, and Malcolm Read. "Pacifism, Politics, and Art: Milestone's *All Quiet on the Western Front* and Pabst's *Westfront 1918."* In *Remarque Against War,* edited by Brian Murdoch, Mark Ward, and Maggie Sargeant, 62–84. Glasgow: Scottish Papers in Germanic Studies, 1998.

Owen, Claude R. *"All Quiet on the Western Front:* Sixty Years Later." *Krieg und Literatur/War and Literature* 1 (1989): 41–48.

Poppe, Reiner. *Erich Maria Remarque; Im Westen nichts Neues.* Hollfeld: Beyer, 1998.

Rowley, Brian. "Journalism into Fiction: *Im Westen Nichts Neues.*" In *The First World War in Fiction,* edited by Holger Klein, 101–11. London: Macmillan, 1976.

Rüter, Hubert. *Erich Maria Remarque: "Im Westen nichts Neues": Ein Bestseller der Kriegsliteratur im Kontext.* Paderborn: Schöningh, 1980.

Schneider, Thomas F. *Erich Maria Remarque Im Westen nichts Neues: Bibliographie der Drucke.* Bramsche: Rasch, 1992.

———. *Erich Maria Remarque: Im Westen nichts Neues: Das Manuskript.* Bramsche: Rasch, 1996.

———. "'Es ist ein Buch ohne Tendenz': *Im Westen nichts Neues:* Auto- und Textsystem im Rahmen eines Konstitutions- und Wirkungsmodells für Literatur," *Krieg und Literatur/War and Literature* 1 (1989): 23–40.

———. "'Krieg ist Krieg schließlich': Erich Maria Remarque: *Im Westen nichts Neues* (1928)." In *Von Richthofen bis Remarque: Deutschsprachige Prosa zum I. Weltkrieg,* edited by Thomas F. Schneider and Hans Wagener, 217–32. Amsterdam and New York: Rodopi, 2003.

———. "'Die Meute hinter Remarque': Zur Diskussion um *Im Westen nichts Neues* 1928–1930," *Jahrbuch zur Literatur der Weimarer Republik* 1 (1995): 143–70.

Schräder, Bärbel, ed. *Der Fall Remarque: "Im Westen nichts Neues" — eine Dokumentation.* Leipzig: Reclam, 1992.

Schumaker, Richard. "Remarque's Abyss of Time: *Im Westen nichts Neues.*" *Focus on Robert Graves and His Contemporaries* 1, no. 11 (Winter 1990): 124–35.

Ulbrich, David J. "A Male-Conscious Critique of Erich Maria Remarque's *All Quiet on the Western Front.*" *Journal of Men's Studies* 3 (1995): 229–40.

Der Weg zurück

Devine, Kathleen. "The Way Back: Alun Lewis and Remarque," *Anglia* 103 (1985): 320–35.

Fotheringham, John. "Looking Back at the Revolution." In *Remarque Against War,* edited by Brian Murdoch, Mark Ward, and Maggie Sargeant, 98–118. Glasgow: Scottish Papers in Germanic Studies, 1998.

Murdoch, Brian. "Vorwärts auf dem Weg zurück." *Text+Kritik* 149 (2001): 19–29.

Ward, Mark. "The Structure of *Der Weg zurück.*" In *Remarque Against War,* edited by Brian Murdoch, Mark Ward, and Maggie Sargeant, 85–97. Glasgow: Scottish Papers in Germanic Studies, 1998.

Drei Kameraden

Christoffersen, Rikke. "Three Comrades — One Perspective: Conceptualizing Remarque's *Drei Kameraden* with the Two Early War Novels." *Jahrbuch* 15 (2005): 36–62.

Jeglin, Reiner, and Irmgard Pickerodt. "'Weiche Kerle in harter Schale': Zu *Drei Kameraden.*" In *Erich Maria Remarque: Leben, Werk, und weltweite Wirkung,* edited by Thomas F. Schneider, 216–34. Osnabrück: Rasch, 1998.

Schneider, Thomas F. "Von *Pat* zu *Drei Kameraden:* Zur Entstehung des ersten Romans der Exil-Zeit Remarques." *Jahrbuch* 2 (1992): 67–78.

Liebe Deinen Nächsten

Kamla, Thomas A. *Confrontation with Exile: Studies in the German Novel.* Frankfurt am Main: Peter Lang, 1975.

Der Funke Leben

Glunz, Claudia. "'Eine harte Sache': Zur Rezeption von Erich Maria Remarques *Der Funke Leben.*" In *"Reue ist undeutsch": Erich Maria Remarques "Der Funke Leben" und das Konzentrationslager Buchenwald,* edited by Thomas F. Schneider and Tilman Westphalen, 21–27. Bramsche: Rasch, 1992.

Hartinger, Walfried. "Bruno Apitz, *Nackt unter Wölfen:* Zur zeitgeschichtlichen Relevanz und langdauernden Wirkung des Romans." *Jahrbuch* 5 (1995): 5–18.

Orlowski, Hubert. "Stacheldrahtuniversum und Literatur: Zu Remarque und anderen." *Jahrbuch* 4 (1994): 5–28.

Placke, Heinrich. "Naturrecht und menschliche Würde: Anmerkungen zum Sinnpotential des Romans *Der Funke Leben*." In *"Reue ist undeutsch": Erich Maria Remarques "Der Funke Leben" und das Konzentrationslager Buchenwald*, edited by Thomas F. Schneider and Tilman Westphalen, 28–40. Bramsche: Rasch, 1992.

Schneider, Thomas. "'Heißes Eisen in lauwarmer Hand': Zur Rezeption von E. M. Remarque's *Der Funke Leben*." *Jahrbuch* 4 (1994): 29–44.

Schneider, Thomas F., and Tilman Westphalen, eds. *"Reue ist undeutsch": Erich Maria Remarques "Der Funke Leben" und das Konzentrationslager Buchenwald*. Bramsche: Rasch, 1992: see also Schneider's "Mörder, die empfindlich sind," 14–20.

Strümpel, Jan. "Kammersymphonie des Todes: Erich Maria Remarques *Der Funke Leben*, Anna Seghers' *Das siebte Kreuz* und eine Gattung namens 'KZ-Roman.'" *Text+Kritik* 149 (2001): 55–64.

Valencia, Heather. "The KZ Experience: *Der Funke Leben* in the Light of Recent Works on the Holocaust in Literature." In *Remarque Against War*, edited by Brian Murdoch, Mark Ward, and Maggie Sargeant, 145–69. Glasgow: Scottish Papers in Germanic Studies, 1998.

Zeit zu leben und Zeit zu sterben

Last, R. W. "The 'Castration' of Erich Maria Remarque." *Quinquereme* 2 (1979): 10–22.

Nutz, Walter. "Der Krieg als Abenteuer und Idylle: Landershefte und triviale Kriegsromane." In *Gegenwartsliteratur und Drittes Reich: Deutsche Autoren in der Auseinandersetzung mit der Vergangenheit*, ed. Hans Wagener. Stuttgart: Reclam, 1977, 265–83.

Sargeant, Maggie. "A Lost War." In *Remarque Against War*, edited by Brian Murdoch, Mark Ward, and Maggie Sargeant, 119–44. Glasgow: Scottish Papers in Germanic Studies, 1998.

Schneider, Thomas F. "'Und Befehl ist Befehl. Oder nicht?' Erich Maria Remarque: *Zeit zu leben und Zeit zu sterben* (1954)." In *Von Böll bis Buchheim: Deutsche Kriegsprosa nach 1945*, edited by Hans Wagener, 231–47. Amsterdam and Atlanta, GA: Rodopi.

Schneider, Thomas F., and Angelika Howind. "'Weiterschweigen heisst seine Schuld eingestehen': *Zeit zu leben und Zeit zu sterben*: Die Zensur eines Antikriegsromans in der BRD und ihre Revision." *Krieg und Literatur/War and Literature* 1 (1989): 79–142.

Wagener, Hans. "Soldaten zwischen Gehorsam und Gewissen: Kriegsromane und -Tagebücher." In *Gegenwartsliteratur und Drittes Reich: Deutsche Autoren in der Auseinandersetzung mit der Vergangenheit*, edited by Hans Wagener, 241–64. Stuttgart: Reclam, 1977.

Der schwarze Obelisk

Woesthoff, Frank. "Zur Verfilmung der Isabelle-Szenen für die Inszenierung der Probebühne *Der schwarze Obelisk.*" In *Man kann alten Dreck nicht vergraben: Er fängt immer wieder an zu stinken: Materialien zu einen Erich Maria Remarque-Projekt,* edited by Lothar Schwindt and Tilman Westphalen, 26–32. Osnabrück: Universität/Fachbereich SLM, 1984.

Der Himmel kennt keine Günstlinge

Fuld, Werner. "Ein Treffen mit alten Bekannten: Zur Vorgeschichte des Romans *Der Himmel kennt keine Günstlinge.*" *Text+Kritik* 149 (2001): 65–68.

Reich-Ranicki, Marcel. "Knalleffekte in Todesnähe: Erich Maria Remarque, von *Im Westen nichts Neues* zu *Der Himmel kennt keine Günstlinge.*" *Die Zeit,* 6 October 1961.

Schatten im Paradies/Das gelobte Land

Küster, Marc Wilhelm. "Die Manuskriptlage zu Remarques *Schatten im Paradies.*" *Jahrbuch* 5 (1995): 88–108.

Wagener, Hans. "Erich Maria Remarque: Shadows in Paradise." In *Exile: The Writer's Experience,* edited by John M. Spalek and Robert F. Bell, 247–57. Chapel Hill: U. North Carolina P, 1982.

Index

Note: Remarque's works are indicated as such and listed individually under their German titles only; films are listed under their (usually English) original titles. Modern critics are included only when referred to in the body of the text, and locations only when significant to the novels.

Erich Maria Remarque is a writer of high importance and great popularity who has rightly been described as a "chronicler of the twentieth century." He is both a German writer and a genuinely international one. Although he spent much of his life in exile from Germany, most of his novels reflect its twentieth-century history: the two world wars and the successive Weimar and Nazi regimes, and especially their effects on the individual. His portrayals of the lives of refugees from Nazi Germany are especially vivid and show them as individuals, "just people." His themes are universal, dealing with human relationships, with love in particular, and with the provisional nature of life. Often seen as a one-novel writer due to the immense success and canonical status of *All Quiet on the Western Front,* Remarque's wrote many other novels that are major works and have nearly all been filmed and remain popular. His refugee novels, his two novels of the Second World War (one set in a concentration camp), and what might look like — but is not — a simple but tragic love story, *Heaven Has No Favorites* all merit serious attention. Nor should it be ignored that his works are above all else immensely readable: not a negligible criterion. This new study of Remarque's novels treats them as a chronicle of the century, but also looks at each one as a work that goes beyond the reflection of historical events.

BRIAN MURDOCK is Emeritus Professor of German in the School of Languages, Cultures, and Religions at the University of Stirling, Scotland.

Murdoch has consolidated his and others' research in this useful treatment of Remarque's life and work. Those new to Remarque will find this an excellent introduction to the author's entire literary corpus.

CHOICE

This book champions Remarque's novels as representing a solid track record of first-class literature. Murdoch successfully strives to overcome the stigma of critics who have relegated Remarque as a trivial writer. . . .

GERMAN STUDIES REVIEW

This book offers a concise survey of Remarque's novels that underscores the values of his novels that have been previously overlooked. As an introductory survey, it will be an important contribution to the teaching of Remarque's works.

H-NET REVIEWS

Murdoch has . performed a great service in registering exactly what Remarque published, in what order and when, and how various films relate to the writings — tasks made all the more difficult because Remarque enjoyed playing the mystery-man.

MLR

Murdoch aims to present Remarque as a German writer who was also prominent internationally and, beyond this, a writer whose significance goes far beyond his best-known work, *Im Westen nichts Neues*. At the same time he attempts to show that he was no mere writer of escapist literature.

MONATSHEFTE

CPSIA information can be obtained at www.ICGtesting.com
Printed in the USA
LVOW032204090112

263050LV00022B/198/P